CONGRESSIONAL POLICIES, PRACTICES AND PROCEDURES

A CLOSER LOOK AT FARM BILLS

Congressional Policies, Practices and Procedures

Additional books and e-books in this series can be found on Nova's website under the Series tab.

CONGRESSIONAL POLICIES, PRACTICES AND PROCEDURES

A CLOSER LOOK AT FARM BILLS

ARTURO BURNS
EDITOR

snova
New York

Library of Congress Cataloging-in-Publication Data

ISBN: 978-1-53614-893-0

Published by Nova Science Publishers, Inc. † New York

CONTENTS

Preface		**vii**
Chapter 1	Farm Bills: Major Legislative Actions, 1965-2018 *Jim Monke*	**1**
Chapter 2	The House and Senate 2018 Farm Bills (H.R. 2): A Side-by-Side Comparison with Current Law *Mark A. McMinimy*	**11**
Index		**285**

PREFACE

Congress has been active in establishing federal policy for the agricultural sector on an ongoing basis since the 1930s. Over the years, as economic conditions and technology have evolved, Congress has regularly revisited agricultural policy through periodic farm legislation. Across these decades, the breadth of policy areas addressed through such farm bills has expanded beyond providing support for a limited number of agricultural commodities to include establishing programs and policies that address a broad spectrum of related areas, such as agricultural conservation, credit, rural development, domestic nutrition assistance, trade and international food aid, organic agriculture, forestry, and support for beginning and veteran farmers and ranchers, among others. On June 21, 2018, the House voted to approve H.R. 2, the Agriculture and Nutrition Act of 2018, an omnibus farm bill that would establish farm and food policy for the next five years. The Senate passed its version of H.R. 2, the Agriculture Improvement Act of 2018, on June 28, 2018.

Chapter 1 - The farm bill provides an opportunity for Congress to address agricultural and food issues comprehensively about every five years. Over time, farm bills have tended to become more complicated and politically sensitive. As a result, the timeline for reauthorization has become less certain, and in general recent farm bills have taken longer to enact than in previous decades. Recent farm bills, beginning with the 2008 farm bill (P.L. 110-246), have been subject to various developments that have delayed enactment, such as insufficient votes to pass the House floor, presidential vetoes, or short-term extensions.

In 2018, a farm bill reauthorization was reported from the House Agriculture Committee on April 18 (H.R. 2). An initial floor vote on passage on May 18 failed in the House 198-213, but floor procedures allowed that vote to be reconsidered (H.Res. 905). The House passed H.R. 2 in a second vote of 213-211 on June 21, 2018. In the Senate, the Agriculture Committee reported its bill (S. 3042) on June 13 by a vote of 20-1. The

Senate passed its bill as an amendment to H.R. 2 by a vote of 86-11 on June 28, 2018. Conference proceedings officially began on September 5, 2018.

By comparison, the 2014 farm bill took more than 21 months from introduction to enactment and spanned the 112th and 113th Congresses. The House rejected a bill in 2013 and then passed separate farm and nutrition assistance components before procedurally recombining them for conference with the Senate. Somewhat similarly, the 2008 farm bill took more than a year to enact and was complicated by revenue provisions from another committee of jurisdiction, temporary extensions, and vetoes.

Expiration of a farm bill on a September 30 fiscal year matters for programs with fiscal year authorizations. These programs include certain nutrition, conservation, and trade programs; various agricultural programs excluding the Title I commodity programs; and many authorizations for discretionary appropriations. Although the Supplemental Nutrition Assistance Program is authorized by fiscal year, it can continue to operate with an appropriation. The 2002 farm bill was the most recent to be enacted before the fiscal year expiration date for such programs.

Expiration a few months later at the end of a calendar year matters mostly for the farm commodity programs. In the event that the current farm law would expire with replacement legislation or an extension, the first commodity to be affected would be dairy, whose crop year begins on January 1, 2019.

Most farm bills have been introduced in the first session of a two-year Congress (the odd-numbered year). Of three farm bills that were introduced in the second session—like the 2018 farm bill proposals—the 1970 and 1990 farm bills were enacted during a lame duck Congress in late November of the same year, and the 2014 farm bill was the first farm bill to start in one Congress (2012), remain unfinished, and require reintroduction in a subsequent Congress.

This chapter examines the major legislative milestones for the last 11 farm bills covering 53 years and illustrates trends that may provide useful background and context as the current farm bill debate proceeds.

Chapter 2 - Congress sets national food and agriculture policy through periodic omnibus farm bills that address a broad range of farm and food programs and policies. The 115th Congress has the opportunity to establish the future direction of farm and food policy, because many of the provisions in the current farm bill (the Agricultural Act of 2014, P.L. 113-79) expire in 2018.

On June 21, 2018, the House voted 213-211 to approve H.R. 2, the Agriculture and Nutrition Act of 2018, an omnibus farm bill that would authorize farm and food policy for FY2019-FY2023. The Senate passed its version of H.R. 2, the Agriculture Improvement Act of 2018, also a five-year bill, on June 28, 2018, on a vote of 86-11.

In terms of cost, the Congressional Budget Office (CBO) score of July 24, 2018, of the programs in both bills with mandatory spending—such as nutrition programs, commodity support programs, major conservation programs, and crop insurance—over a

10-year budget window (FY2019-FY2028) amounts to $867 billion in the Senate-passed bill and $865 billion in the House-passed bill. These cost projections compare with CBO's baseline scenario of an extension of existing 2014 farm bill programs with no changes of $867 billion. In both the House and Senate versions of H.R. 2, most existing programs would be extended through FY2023. Overall, the bills provide a relatively large measure of continuity with the existing framework of farm and food programs even as they would modify numerous programs, alter the amount and type of program funding that certain programs receive, and exercise discretion not to reauthorize some others.

Both bills would extend commodity support programs largely along existing lines while modifying them in different ways. For instance, the House bill could raise the effective reference price for crops enrolled in the Price Loss Coverage program (PLC) under certain market conditions. It would also amend payment limits and the adjusted gross income (AGI) limit for eligibility for farm program payments and increase the number of producer exemptions from payment and income limits. In contrast, the Senate bill would leave payment limits unchanged while lowering the AGI limit for payment eligibility. The Senate would also leave PLC unchanged while adopting changes to the Agricultural Risk Coverage program (ARC) that could enhance its appeal as a program option. Both bills would amend disaster assistance programs but under different approaches. Both bills would also rename the dairy program and expand coverage choices for milk producers, and both bills extend the sugar program with no changes.

The House and Senate bills would reauthorize the Supplemental Nutrition Assistance Program (SNAP) for five years, and both bills include polices intended to improve error and fraud detection. Among their differences, the House bill includes multiple changes to who is eligible for SNAP and the calculation of benefits, which are not included in the Senate bill. The House bill includes major changes to work requirements, while the Senate bill would make changes that are minor by comparison.

Within the conservation title, the two bills would raise the acreage limit on enrollment in the Conservation Reserve Program (CRP), with the House bill setting a higher limit than the Senate does. Among other differences, the House bill would repeal the Conservation Stewardship Program (CSP), whereas the Senate bill would extend CSP but lower the limit on acreage enrollment. The House bill also increases funding for the Environmental Quality Incentives Program (EQIP), while the Senate bill reduces funding for EQIP. Within the credit title, both bills increase the maximum loan amounts for the U.S. Department of Agriculture's guaranteed farm ownership loans and guaranteed farm operating loans. The Senate bill would also raise the limits for direct farm ownership loans and direct farm operating loans, whereas the House bill would not. The miscellaneous title of both bills establishes an animal disease preparedness program and a vaccine bank, although they diverge over funding.

The Senate bill includes a number of provisions that are intended to facilitate the possible commercial cultivation of industrial hemp, while the House bill would amend certain regulatory requirements that apply to industrial hemp. For rural communities, the House bill would authorize the Secretary of Agriculture to reprioritize certain loan and grant programs and take other actions to respond to specific health emergencies, and it would require the Secretary to promulgate minimum acceptable standards for broadband service. The Senate bill would establish priorities for awarding loans and grains for rural broadband projects and add a new program on substance abuse education and prevention. Both bills extend most bioenergy programs, but the House bill places them within the title on rural development and infrastructure, while the Senate bill maintains a separate energy title. Moreover, while the House bill would provide discretionary funding for these programs but no mandatory funding, the Senate bill would provide both mandatory and discretionary funding.

In: A Closer Look at Farm Bills
Editor: Arturo Burns
ISBN: 978-1-53614-893-0

Chapter 1

Farm Bills: Major Legislative Actions, 1965-2018*

Jim Monke

Summary

The farm bill provides an opportunity for Congress to address agricultural and food issues comprehensively about every five years. Over time, farm bills have tended to become more complicated and politically sensitive. As a result, the timeline for reauthorization has become less certain, and in general recent farm bills have taken longer to enact than in previous decades. Recent farm bills, beginning with the 2008 farm bill (P.L. 110-246), have been subject to various developments that have delayed enactment, such as insufficient votes to pass the House floor, presidential vetoes, or short-term extensions.

In 2018, a farm bill reauthorization was reported from the House Agriculture Committee on April 18 (H.R. 2). An initial floor vote on passage on May 18 failed in the House 198-213, but floor procedures allowed that vote to be reconsidered (H.Res. 905). The House passed H.R. 2 in a second vote of 213-211 on June 21, 2018. In the Senate, the Agriculture Committee reported its bill (S. 3042) on June 13 by a vote of 20-1. The Senate passed its bill as an amendment to H.R. 2 by a vote of 86-11 on June 28, 2018. Conference proceedings officially began on September 5, 2018.

By comparison, the 2014 farm bill took more than 21 months from introduction to enactment and spanned the 112th and 113th Congresses. The House rejected a bill in 2013 and then passed separate farm and nutrition assistance components before procedurally recombining them for conference with the Senate. Somewhat similarly, the 2008 farm bill took more than a year to enact and was complicated by revenue provisions from another committee of jurisdiction, temporary extensions, and vetoes.

---

* This is an edited, reformatted and augmented version of Congressional Research Service, Publication No. R45210, Updated September 21, 2018.

Expiration of a farm bill on a September 30 fiscal year matters for programs with fiscal year authorizations. These programs include certain nutrition, conservation, and trade programs; various agricultural programs excluding the Title I commodity programs; and many authorizations for discretionary appropriations. Although the Supplemental Nutrition Assistance Program is authorized by fiscal year, it can continue to operate with an appropriation. The 2002 farm bill was the most recent to be enacted before the fiscal year expiration date for such programs.

Expiration a few months later at the end of a calendar year matters mostly for the farm commodity programs. In the event that the current farm law would expire with replacement legislation or an extension, the first commodity to be affected would be dairy, whose crop year begins on January 1, 2019.

Most farm bills have been introduced in the first session of a two-year Congress (the odd-numbered year). Of three farm bills that were introduced in the second session—like the 2018 farm bill proposals—the 1970 and 1990 farm bills were enacted during a lame duck Congress in late November of the same year, and the 2014 farm bill was the first farm bill to start in one Congress (2012), remain unfinished, and require reintroduction in a subsequent Congress.

This chapter examines the major legislative milestones for the last 11 farm bills covering 53 years and illustrates trends that may provide useful background and context as the current farm bill debate proceeds.

The farm bill provides an opportunity for Congress to address agricultural and food issues comprehensively about every five years.[1] Over time, farm bills have tended to become more complicated and politically sensitive. This has made the timeline for reauthorization less certain. Recent farm bills have been subject to developments that have delayed enactment, such as insufficient votes to pass the House floor, presidential vetoes, and short-term extensions.

For example, the 1973 farm bill was enacted less than three months after being introduced. In contrast, the 2014 farm bill took more than 21 months from introduction to enactment, spanning the 112th and 113th Congresses.[2] The House rejected a bill in 2013 and then passed separate farm and nutrition assistance components—the first time a chamber-passed farm bill reauthorization did not include a nutrition title since nutrition became part of the farm bill in 1973. The House later procedurally recombined them for conference with the Senate.

Both the 2002 and 2008 farm bills had expired for about three months (from October through December in 2007 and 2012) before extensions were enacted. In each case, the fiscal year began under a continuing resolution for appropriations. The extensions of the 2002 farm bill were for relatively short periods totaling about five months during final House-Senate negotiations. However, the extension of the 2008 farm bill in 2013 was for a full year, since the 112th Congress had ended and it was necessary to reintroduce farm bill legislation in the 113th Congress.

---

[1] See CRS In Focus IF10187, Farm Bill Primer: What Is the Farm Bill?

[2] These dates span only the official introduction of a bill marked up by committee until the President signed the bill. They do not include background hearings before committee markup, which would extend the timeline.

In 2018, a farm bill reauthorization was reported from the House Agriculture Committee on April 18 (H.R. 2). An initial floor vote on passage on May 18 failed in the House 198-213, but procedures allowed that vote to be reconsidered (H.Res. 905). The House passed H.R. 2 in a second vote of 213-211 on June 21, 2018. In the Senate, the Agriculture Committee reported its bill (S. 3042) on June 13 by a vote of 20-1. The Senate passed its bill as an amendment to H.R. 2 by a vote of 86-11 on June 28, 2018. This is the first time since at least 1965 that both chambers completed floor action before the end of June. Conference proceedings officially began September 5, 2018.

This chapter examines the major legislative milestones for the last 11 farm bills over 53 years, a period representing modern farm bills with growing complexity. It discusses trends that may provide historical perspective as the current farm bill debate proceeds. *Table 1* contains a history of major legislative action on farm bills since 1965. *Figure 1* shows the dates on a timeline for each farm bill from introduction to enactment.

TIMELINES FOR ENACTMENT, EXTENSION, AND VETOES

Different parts of a farm bill are authorized for different periods of time. Fiscal years, calendar years, and crop years can be important to different programs. Programs authorized by the 2014 farm bill (the Agricultural Act of 2014, P.L. 113-79) generally expire either at the end of FY2018 (September 30, 2018) or with the 2018 crop year, which varies among crops and, for dairy, is the end of the calendar year 2018.

Timeline Relative to Fiscal Years

Expiration at the end of a fiscal year (September 30) matters for programs with fiscal year authorizations. These programs include certain nutrition, conservation, and trade programs; various agricultural programs, excluding the Title I commodity programs; and many authorizations for discretionary appropriations. Although the Supplemental Nutrition Assistance Program is authorized by fiscal year, it can continue to operate with an appropriation.

Enacting farm bills after the end of the final fiscal year for which programs have been authorized has been a common occurrence. In the past 41 years covering the eight farm bills since 1976— when the federal government began using a fiscal year

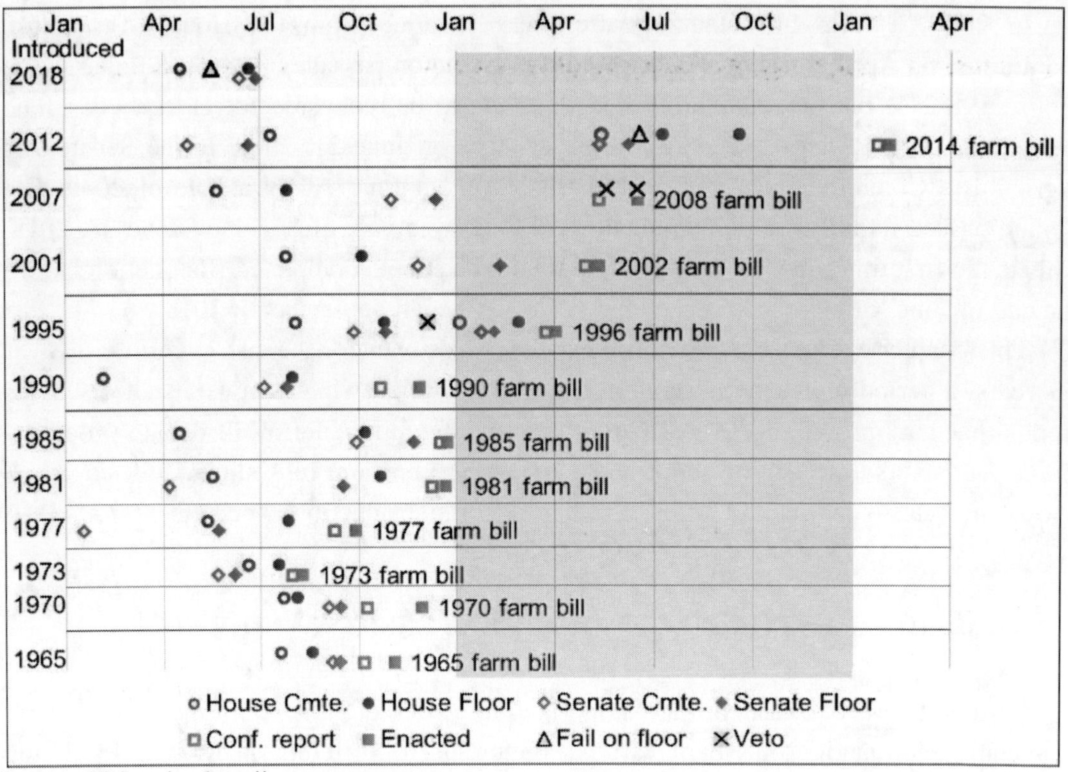

Source: CRS, using http://www.congress.gov.

Figure 1. Major Legislative Actions on Farm Bills, 2018-1965.

that began on October 1[3]—only the 1977 and 2002 farm bills were enacted before the September 30 expiration date for programs that would have been affected by the fiscal year.[4]

The 1981, 1985, and 1990 farm bills were enacted within three months after the final fiscal year for which programs were authorized had ended. The 1996 farm bill was enacted in April 1996 following the September 30, 1995, expiration of some of the authorizations in the 1990 farm bill.[5] The 2008 and 2014 farm bills were enacted well after their original September 30 expirations and following the enactment of extensions.

---

[3] The federal government changed the timing of the fiscal year in 1976, when a "transition quarter" was used to change the fiscal year from July 1-June 30, to October 1-September 30. See Office of Management and Budget, *Historical Tables: Budget of the U.S. Government*, annual issues.

[4] Before the 1973 farm bill, which was the first to incorporate reauthorization of the food stamp program that had a fiscal year expiration, the focus of the farm bill was the farm commodity programs that operated by crop years.

[5] While the 1996 farm bill was not pressured by the expiration of farm commodity programs in the 1990 farm bill—since budget reconciliation in 1993 had extended them through the 1996 and 1997 crop years (see footnote 8)—some of the original FY1995 expiration dates for food stamps, certain conservation programs, and various authorizations of appropriations continued unchanged and were not extended by the reconciliation act.

Timeline Relative to Calendar Years

Expiration at the end of a calendar year matters mostly for the farm commodity programs—which are traditionally Title I of recent farm bills—and particularly the dairy program, because it would be the first to revert to "permanent law" on January 1.[6] The farm commodity programs are tied to a crop year—that is, the year in which a crop is harvested. If the suspension of permanent law were to expire, thereby reactivating commodity programs authorized by permanent law for the 2019 crop year, the first commodity to be affected by would be dairy, whose crop year begins on January 1, 2019.

All farm bills since 1965—except those in 2014 and 2008—have been enacted before December 31 in the year of their expirations.[7] For the 2014 farm bill, the previous 2008 farm bill was extended for one year in 2013, but that extension expired for five weeks before the 2014 bill was enacted in February 2014. For the 2008 farm bill, several short-term extensions of the 2002 farm bill from December 2007 to May 2008 prevented permanent law from becoming effective.

Timeline Relative to the Two-Year Congressional Term

Since 1965, eight out of 11 enacted farm bills were introduced in the first session of a two-year Congress (the odd-numbered year). The other three farm bills (1970, 1990, and 2014) were introduced in the second session of a two-year Congress (the even-numbered year)—like the current 2018 farm bill proposals.[8] Of these three, the 1970 and 1990 farm bills were enacted after an election during a lame duck Congress in late November of the same year. The 2014 farm bill, which was introduced in 2012, was the first farm bill to start in one Congress, remain unfinished, and require reintroduction in a subsequent Congress.

---

[6] *Permanent law* refers to non-expiring farm commodity programs that are generally from the 1938 and 1949 farm bills. The temporary suspension of permanent law is included as a section in all recent farm bills. If the suspension of permanent law were to expire at the end of a crop year, the permanent law provisions would take effect unless a new farm bill, or an extension of the most recent bill, continues the suspension. For more details about permanent law and its consequences, see the heading on permanent law in CRS Report R42442, *Expiration and Extension of the 2008 Farm Bill*.

[7] The 1965 farm bill was extended for one year, but that extension occurred more than a year before expiration and before the reauthorization process had begun in 1970. The 1996 and 2002 farm bills may appear to have been delayed by being reintroduced (1996) or going through the new year into May (2002), but their predecessors did not require extensions. The 1990 farm bill's original expiration date of the end of the 1995 crop year had less of an effect on the 1996 farm bill's timeline because budget reconciliation in 1993 had extended the farm commodity programs through at least 1996 and, in some cases, the 1997 crops. The 2002 farm bill was enacted before the 1996 farm bill expired on September 30, 2002, and before the 2002 crop year ended. In fact, the 2002 farm bill superseded the last year of the 1996 farm bill by beginning with the 2002 crop year.

[8] Technically, the bill that became the 2014 farm bill (H.R. 2642) was introduced in 2013 (the first session of the 113th Congress), but many consider it a reintroduction of the bills started in 2012 (the second session of the 112th Congress).

House or Senate Action First

The House and Senate have taken turns in initiating action on a farm bill. Since 1965, the Senate was first to mark up farm bills in 1973, 1977, 1981, 2012, and 2013. The House was first to mark up bills in 1965, 1970, 1985, 1990, 1995 (and 1996), 2001, 2007, and 2018.

Short-Term Extensions

Extensions of a prior farm bill while its successor is being written have been atypical, though the past two reauthorizations have involved extensions. Only the 2002 and 2008 farm bills have required extensions in 2007-2008 and 2013, respectively, as their successors were being written.[9]

When the 2002 farm bill expired, portions of it were extended six times for less than a year total beginning in December 2007. The first of those extensions continued authority for many expiring programs for about three months.[10] Because final agreement was pending, five more extensions— ranging from a week to a month—were needed. With a few exceptions, these extensions continued all 2002 farm bill provisions that were in effect on September 30, 2007. Dairy and sugar programs were included, as were price support loan programs for wool and mohair. But the direct, counter-cyclical, and marketing loan programs for the 2008 crop year for all other supported commodities (i.e., the primary supported commodities such as feed grains, oilseeds, wheat, rice, cotton, and peanuts) were specifically *not* extended.[11] Moreover, the first extension in December 2007 did not address permanent law, but the second and subsequent extensions in 2008 did extend the 2002 farm bill's suspension of permanent law.[12]

When the 2008 farm bill expired on September 30, 2012, the continuing resolution providing appropriations (P.L. 112-175, §§101, 111) continued discretionary programs,

---

[9] See also footnote 8.

[10] "Except as otherwise provided in this Act ... authorities provided under the Farm Security and Rural Investment Act of 2002 ... (and for mandatory programs at such funding levels), as in effect on September 30, 2007, shall continue, and the Secretary of Agriculture shall carry out the authorities, until March 15, 2008." P.L. 110-161, §751.

[11] Other programs that were *not* included in the extensions were peanut storage payments, agricultural management assistance, community food projects, the rural broadband program, value-added market development grants, federal procurement of biobased products, the biodiesel fuel education program, and the renewable energy systems program.

[12] Permanent law refers to nonexpiring provisions in Agriculture Adjustment Act of 1938 and the Agriculture Act of 1949 that are temporarily suspended by each modern farm bill. The commodity support provisions of permanent law are inconsistent with today's farming, marketing, and trade agreements and potentially costly to the federal government. See CRS Report RL34154, *Possible Expiration (or Extension) of the 2002 Farm Bill*.

the Supplemental Nutrition Assistance Program (SNAP), and certain related nutrition programs. Certain other mandatory programs—such as the Market Assistance Program and the Conservation Reserve Program—ceased to operate insofar as new activity.[13] On January 2, 2013, the entire 2008 farm bill, as it existed on September 30, 2012, was extended for the 2013 fiscal year and the 2013 crop year (P.L. 112-240). This avoided reverting to permanent law for the farm commodity programs, which was imminent for the dairy programs.

The situation from October to December 2013 somewhat repeated the end of 2012. Most of the discretionary parts of the farm bill expired again on October 1, 2013. Some programs ceased new operations, while others were able to continue under appropriations. For SNAP and the discretionary programs, farm bill expiration coupled with the two-week lapse during October 2013 of FY2014 appropriations (the "government shutdown") did create difficulties in operating some farm bill programs. From January 1, 2014, until enactment of the 2014 farm bill on February 7, 2014, the dairy program had technically reverted to permanent law, though federal officials did not implement it, since a conference agreement was imminent.

Presidential Vetoes

Presidential vetoes of farm bills are not common. Since 1965, only the 2008 farm bill has been vetoed as stand-alone measure; it was vetoed twice. A 1995 farm bill was vetoed as part of a larger budget reconciliation package.[14]

President George W. Bush vetoed the 2008 farm bill (H.R. 2419). When Congress overrode the veto to enact P.L. 110-234, it accidentally enrolled the law without Title III (the trade title). Congress immediately reintroduced the same bill with the trade title (H.R. 6124). President Bush vetoed this version as well, and Congress again overrode the veto to enact P.L. 110-246, a complete 2008 farm bill that included the trade title. The overrides in 2008 were the only time that a farm bill was enacted as a result of a veto override.

President Clinton vetoed a 1995 budget reconciliation package that included the first version of what became the 1996 farm bill, but the veto was not due to the farm bill itself but rather the controversial nature of the reconciliation bill in which the farm bill was embedded.

---

[13] See CRS Report R42442, Expiration and Extension of the 2008 Farm Bill.

[14] Prior to 1965, the first veto of a farm bill was in 1956, when President Eisenhower vetoed H.R. 12, the first version of the Agricultural Act of 1956.

IMPLICATIONS FOR CONGRESS

As farm bill reauthorization has tended to become more complex and engender greater political sensitivity, the process of enacting a new farm bill prior to the expiration of the existing law has become more difficult. As stakeholders in the farm bill have become more diverse, more people are affected by the legislative uncertainty around this process. This lack of certainty may translate into questions about the availability of future program benefits, some of which may affect agricultural production decisions or market uncertainty for agricultural commodities.

Table 1. Major Legislative Actions on Farm Bills, 2018-1965

					Conference Report Approval			
	House Cmte.	**House Passage**	**Senate Cmte.**	**Senate Passage**	**Conf. Report**	**House Passage**	**Senate Passage**	**Public Law**
2018 farm bill *(115th Congress)* **Agriculture and Nutrition Act of 2018** Would cover 2019-2023 crops or until 9/30/2023	4/18/2018 H.R. 2 Vote of 26-20 5/3/2018 H.Rept. 115-661	5/18/2018 H.R. 2 Initial vote failed by 198-213 Reconsider under H.Res. 905 6/21/2018 Passed by vote of 213-211	6/13/2018 S. 3042 Vote of 20-1	6/28/2018 H.R. 2 Vote of 86-11	-----	-----	-----	-----
Agricultural Act of 2014 *(113th Congress)* Covers 2014-2018 crops or until 9/30/2018	5/15/2013 H.R. 1947 Vote of 36-10 5/29/2013 H.Rept. 113-92	6/20/2013 H.R. 1947 Failed by 195-234 7/11/2013 H.R. 2642 Farm part vote of 216-208 9/19/2013 H.R. 3102 Nutrition part vote of 217-210 9/28/2013 H.Res. 361 combines House bills	5/14/2013 S. 954 Vote of 15-5 9/4/2013 S.Rept. 113-88	6/10/2013 S. 954 Vote of 66-27	1/27/2014 H.Rept. 113-333	1/29/2014 H.R. 2642 Vote of 251-166	2/4/2014 H.R. 2642 Vote of 68-32	2/7/2014 P.L. 113-79
Agriculture Reform, Food, and Jobs Act *(112th Congress)*	7/11/2012 H.R. 6083 Vote of 35-11 9/13/2012 H.Rept. 112-669	—	4/26/2012 S. 3240 Vote of 16-5 8/28/2012 S.Rept. 112-203	6/21/2012 S. 3240 Vote of 64-35	—	—	—	—
Early extension:		Extended five conservation programs of the 2008 farm bill through FY2014 (AMA, CSP, EQIP, FPP, and WHIP).						11/18/2011 P.L. 112-55
Extension:		One-year extension of the 2008 farm bill until 9/30/2013 and for the 2013 crop year (dairy price support extended until 12/31/2013, and MILC extended until 9/30/2013). Did not provide funding for programs without mandatory baseline.						1/2/2013 P.L. 112-240 Title VII

	House Cmte.	House Passage	Senate Cmte.	Senate Passage	Conference Report Approval: Conf. Report	Conference Report Approval: House Passage	Conference Report Approval: Senate Passage	Public Law
2008 farm bill	5/22/2007	7/27/2007	11/2/2007	12/14/2007	5/13/2008	5/14/2008	5/15/2008	5/21/2008
Food, Conservation, and Energy Act of 2008 Covers 2008-2012 crops or until 9/30/2012	H.R. 2419 Introduced 7/23/2007 H.Rept. 110-256	H.R. 2419 Vote of 231-191	S. 2302 S.Rept. 110-220	Amdt. to H.R. 2419 Vote of 79-14	H.Rept. 110-627	H.R. 2419 Vote of 318-106	H.R. 2419 Vote of 81-15	Enrolling error omits Title III Vetoed
						5/21/2008 Passed over veto 316-108	5/22/2008 Passed over veto 82-13	5/22/2008 P.L. 110-234
					Re-passed as new bill w/Title III	5/22/2008 H.R. 6124 Vote of 306-110	6/5/2008 H.R. 6124 Vote of 77-15	6/18/2008 Vetoed
						6/18/2008 Passed over veto 317-109	6/18/2008 Passed over veto 80-14	6/18/2008 P.L. 110-246
Early extensions:		Extended the early-expiring MILC program of the 2002 farm bill for two years from 9/2005 through 8/2007 and two conservation programs (EQIP and Conservation Security Program) until FY2010.						2/8/2006 P.L. 109-171
Extensions:		Extended parts of the 2002 farm bill until 3/15/2008 but did not extend the direct and counter-cyclical farm commodity programs. See Division A, §751.						12/26/2007 P.L. 110-161
		Continued extension until 4/18/2008 and added extension of suspension of permanent law.						3/14/2008 P.L. 110-196
		Continued extension until 4/25/2008.						4/18/2008 P.L. 110-200
		Continued extension until 5/2/2008.						4/25/2008 P.L. 110-205
		Continued extension until 5/16/2008.						5/2/2008 P.L. 110-208
		Continued extension until 5/23/2008.						5/18/2008 P.L. 110-231
2002 farm bill	7/26/2001	10/5/2001	11/27/2001	2/13/2002	5/1/2002	5/2/2002	5/8/2002	5/13/2002
Farm Security and Rural Investment Act Covers 2002-2007 crops or until 9/30/2007	H.R. 2646 8/2/2001 H.Rept. 107-191	H.R. 2646 Vote of 291-120	S. 1731 12/7/2001 S.Rept. 107-117	Amdt. to H.R. 2646 Vote of 58-40	H.Rept. 107-424	H.R. 2646 Vote of 280-141	H.R. 2646 Vote of 64-35	P.L. 107-171
1996 farm bill	1/5/1996	2/29/1996	1/26/1996	2/7/1996	3/25/1996	3/29/1996	3/28/1996	4/4/1996
Federal Agriculture Improvement and Reform Act of 1996 Covers 1996-2002 crops or until 9/30/2002	H.R. 2854 introduced Vote of 29-17 2/9/1996 H.Rept. 104-462	H.R. 2854 Vote of 270-155	S. 1541 introduced	S. 1541 Vote of 64-32 3/12/1996 Amdt. to H.R. 2854 Voice vote	H.Rept. 104-494	H.R. 2854 Vote of 318-89	H.R. 2854 Vote of 74-26	P.L. 104-127
Balanced Budget Act of 1995	10/26/1995 H.R. 2491 includes H.R. 2195	10/26/1995 H.R. 2491 Vote of 227-203	10/28/1995 S. 1357 includes Senate bill	10/28/1995 Amdt. to H.R. 2491 Vote of 52-47	11/16/1995 H.Rept. 104-347	11/20/1995 H.R. 2491 Vote of 235-192	11/17/1995 H.R. 2491 Vote of 52-47	12/6/1995 Vetoed
Freedom to Farm Act	8/4/1995 H.R. 2195 introduced 9/20/1995 fails cmte.	—	9/28/1995 unnumbered bill	—	—	—	—	—
Extension:		More than a year before expiration, extended the dairy program of the 1990 farm bill until 1996 and extended programs for wheat, feed grains, cotton, rice, peanuts, wool, and mohair until 1997 and honey until 1998.						8/10/1993 P.L. 103-66

Table 1. (Continued)

	House Cmte.	House Passage	Senate Cmte.	Senate Passage	Conference Report Approval Conf. Report	House Passage	Senate Passage	Public Law
1990 farm bill **Food, Agriculture, Conservation, and Trade Act of 1990** Covers 1991-1995 crops or until 9/30/1995	2/5/1990 H.R. 3950 introduced 7/3/1990 H.Rept. 101-569	8/1/1990 H.R. 3950 Vote of 327-91	7/6/1990 S. 2830 S.Rept. 101-357	7/27/1990 S. 2830 Vote of 70-21	10/22/1990 H.Rept. 101-916	10/23/1990 S. 2830 Vote of 318-102	10/25/1990 S. 2830 Vote of 60-36	11/28/1990 P.L. 101-624
1985 farm bill **Food Security Act of 1985** Covers 1986-1990 crops or until 9/30/1990	4/17/1985 H.R. 2100 introduced 9/13/1985 H.Rept. 99-271	10/8/1985 H.R. 2100 Vote of 282-141	9/30/1985 S. 1714 S.Rept. 99-145	11/23/1985 H.R. 2100 Vote of 61-28	12/17/1985 H.Rept. 99-447	12/18/1985 H.R. 2100 Vote of 325-96	12/18/1985 H.R. 2100 Vote of 55-38	12/23/1985 P.L. 99-198
1981 farm bill **Agriculture and Food Act of 1981** Covers 1982-1985 crops or until 9/30/1985	5/18/1981 H.R. 3603 introduced 5/19/1981 H.Rept. 97-106	10/22/1981 S. 884 Vote of 192-160	4/7/1981 S. 884 introduced 5/27/1981 S.Rept. 97-126	9/18/1981 S. 884 Vote of 49-32	12/9/1981 H.Rept. 97-377 12/10/1981 S.Rept. 97-290	12/16/1981 S. 884 Vote of 205-203	12/10/1981 S. 884 Vote of 67-32	12/22/1981 P.L. 97-98
1977 farm bill **Food and Agriculture Act of 1977**	5/13/1977 H.R. 7171 introduced 5/16/1977 H.Rept. 95-348	7/28/1977 Amdt. to S. 275 Vote of 294-114	1/18/1977 S. 275 introduced 5/16/1977 S.Rept. 95-180	5/24/1977 S. 275 Vote of 69-18	9/9/1977 S.Rept. 95-418	9/16/1977 S. 275 Vote of 283-107	9/9/1977 S. 275 Vote of 63-8	9/29/1977 P.L. 95-113
Covers 1978-1981 crops or until 9/30/1981								
1973 farm bill **Agriculture and Consumer Protection Act** Covers 1974-1977 crops or until 6/30/1977	6/20/1973 H.R. 8860 introduced 6/27/1973 H.Rept. 93-337	7/19/1973 Amdt. to S. 1888 Vote of 226-182	5/23/1973 S. 1888 introduced S.Rept. 93-173	6/8/1973 S. 1888 Vote of 78-9	7/31/1973 H.Rept. 93-427	8/3/1973 S. 1888 Vote of 252-151	7/31/1973 S. 1888 Vote of 85-7	8/10/1973 P.L. 93-86
1970 farm bill **Agricultural Act of 1970** Covers 1971-1973 crops	7/23/1970 H.R. 18546 H.Rept. 91-1329	8/5/1970 H.R. 18546 Vote of 212-171	9/4/1970 Amdt. to H.R. 18546 S.Rept. 91-1154	9/15/1970 Amdt. to H.R. 18546 Vote of 65-7	10/9/1970 H.Rept. 91-1594	10/13/1970 H.R. 18546 Vote of 191-145	11/19/1970 H.R. 18546 Vote of 48-35	11/30/1970 P.L. 91-524
Extension:		More than a year before expiration, extended the 1965 farm bill for one-year until 12/31/1970.						10/11/1968 P.L. 90-559
1965 farm bill **Food and Agricultural Act** Covers 1966-1969 crops	7/20/1965 H.R. 9811 H.Rept. 89-631	8/19/1965 H.R. 9811 Vote of 221-172	9/7/1965 Amdt. to H.R. 9811 S.Rept. 89-687	9/14/1965 Amdt. to H.R. 9811 Vote of 72-22	10/6/1965 H.Rept. 89-1123	10/8/1965 H.R. 9811 Vote of 219-150	10/12/1965 H.R. 9811 Voice vote	11/4/1965 P.L. 89-321

Source: CRS, using http://www.congress.gov. Includes only major legislative actions. Excludes subsequent revisions, such as in budget reconciliation, except for extensions as noted.

In: A Closer Look at Farm Bills
Editor: Arturo Burns
ISBN: 978-1-53614-893-0

Chapter 2

THE HOUSE AND SENATE 2018 FARM BILLS (H.R. 2): A SIDE-BY-SIDE COMPARISON WITH CURRENT LAW*

Mark A. McMinimy

Congress sets national food and agriculture policy through periodic omnibus farm bills that address a broad range of farm and food programs and policies. The 115th Congress has the opportunity to establish the future direction of farm and food policy, because many of the provisions in the current farm bill (the Agricultural Act of 2014, P.L. 113-79) expire in 2018.

On June 21, 2018, the House voted 213-211 to approve H.R. 2, the Agriculture and Nutrition Act of 2018, an omnibus farm bill that would authorize farm and food policy for FY2019-FY2023. The Senate passed its version of H.R. 2, the Agriculture Improvement Act of 2018, also a five-year bill, on June 28, 2018, on a vote of 86-11.

In terms of cost, the Congressional Budget Office (CBO) score of July 24, 2018, of the programs in both bills with mandatory spending—such as nutrition programs, commodity support programs, major conservation programs, and crop insurance—over a 10-year budget window (FY2019-FY2028) amounts to $867 billion in the Senate-passed bill and $865 billion in the House-passed bill. These cost projections compare with CBO's baseline scenario of an extension of existing 2014 farm bill programs with no changes of $867 billion. In both the House and Senate versions of H.R. 2, most existing programs would be extended through FY2023. Overall, the bills provide a relatively large measure of continuity with the existing framework of farm and food programs even as

* This is an edited, reformatted and augmented version of Congressional Research Service, Publication No. R45275, dated July 27, 2018.

they would modify numerous programs, alter the amount and type of program funding that certain programs receive, and exercise discretion not to reauthorize some others.

Both bills would extend commodity support programs largely along existing lines while modifying them in different ways. For instance, the House bill could raise the effective reference price for crops enrolled in the Price Loss Coverage program (PLC) under certain market conditions. It would also amend payment limits and the adjusted gross income (AGI) limit for eligibility for farm program payments and increase the number of producer exemptions from payment and income limits. In contrast, the Senate bill would leave payment limits unchanged while lowering the AGI limit for payment eligibility. The Senate would also leave PLC unchanged while adopting changes to the Agricultural Risk Coverage program (ARC) that could enhance its appeal as a program option. Both bills would amend disaster assistance programs but under different approaches. Both bills would also rename the dairy program and expand coverage choices for milk producers, and both bills extend the sugar program with no changes.

The House and Senate bills would reauthorize the Supplemental Nutrition Assistance Program (SNAP) for five years, and both bills include polices intended to improve error and fraud detection. Among their differences, the House bill includes multiple changes to who is eligible for SNAP and the calculation of benefits, which are not included in the Senate bill. The House bill includes major changes to work requirements, while the Senate bill would make changes that are minor by comparison.

Within the conservation title, the two bills would raise the acreage limit on enrollment in the Conservation Reserve Program (CRP), with the House bill setting a higher limit than the Senate does. Among other differences, the House bill would repeal the Conservation Stewardship Program (CSP), whereas the Senate bill would extend CSP but lower the limit on acreage enrollment. The House bill also increases funding for the Environmental Quality Incentives Program (EQIP), while the Senate bill reduces funding for EQIP. Within the credit title, both bills increase the maximum loan amounts for the U.S. Department of Agriculture's guaranteed farm ownership loans and guaranteed farm operating loans. The Senate bill would also raise the limits for direct farm ownership loans and direct farm operating loans, whereas the House bill would not. The miscellaneous title of both bills establishes an animal disease preparedness program and a vaccine bank, although they diverge over funding.

The Senate bill includes a number of provisions that are intended to facilitate the possible commercial cultivation of industrial hemp, while the House bill would amend certain regulatory requirements that apply to industrial hemp. For rural communities, the House bill would authorize the Secretary of Agriculture to reprioritize certain loan and grant programs and take other actions to respond to specific health emergencies, and it would require the Secretary to promulgate minimum acceptable standards for broadband service. The Senate bill would establish priorities for awarding loans and grains for rural broadband projects and add a new program on substance abuse education and prevention. Both bills extend most bioenergy programs, but the House bill places them within the title on rural development and infrastructure, while the Senate bill maintains a separate energy title. Moreover, while the House bill would provide discretionary funding for these programs but no mandatory funding, the Senate bill would provide both mandatory and discretionary funding.

INTRODUCTION

Congress has been active in establishing federal policy for the agricultural sector on an ongoing basis since the 1930s. Over the years, as economic conditions and technology have evolved, Congress has regularly revisited agricultural policy through periodic farm legislation. Across these decades, the breadth of policy areas addressed through such farm bills has expanded beyond providing support for a limited number of agricultural commodities to include establishing programs and policies that address a broad spectrum of related areas, such as agricultural conservation, credit, rural development, domestic nutrition assistance, trade and international food aid, organic agriculture, forestry, and support for beginning and veteran farmers and ranchers, among others.

On June 21, 2018, the House voted 213-211 to approve H.R. 2, the Agriculture and Nutrition Act of 2018, an omnibus farm bill that would establish farm and food policy for the next five years, covering FY2019-FY2023. The vote to approve H.R. 2 followed a failed vote of 198-213 on the same bill on May 18, 2018. The final passage vote on June 21 followed a vote of 233-191 approving a motion to reconsider, which was made after the unsuccessful vote on final passage of May 18. The Senate passed its version of H.R. 2, the Agriculture Improvement Act of 2018, on June 28, 2018, on a vote of 86-11.

Both the House- and Senate-passed versions of H.R. 2 continue the tradition of multi-year farm bills that would establish policy for farm programs and nutrition assistance. To this end, H.R. 2 addresses agriculture and food policy across 11 titles in the House bill and 12 titles in the Senate bill. These titles cover commodity support programs, agricultural conservation, trade and international food aid, domestic nutrition assistance, credit, rural infrastructure and economic development, research and extension, forestry, horticulture, and a variety of other policies and initiatives. The disparity in the number of titles between the two bills reflects the provision of a separate title for energy programs in the Senate bill, whereas the House bill would eliminate what had been a separate energy title in the 2014 farm bill and place these agricultural energy programs within the title on rural infrastructure and economic development.

The Congressional Budget Office (CBO) issued its scores of H.R. 2 as passed by the House and the Senate on July 24, 2018. CBO projected that spending on mandatory programs in the Senate bill would total $867 billion over the 10-year period FY2019-

FY2028 and $865 billion in the House bill. These totals compare with CBO's estimate of the cost of extending the current 2014 farm bill for 10 years of $867 billion. According to CBO, the estimated costs across titles and individual programs frequently differ between the House-passed bill and the Senate-passed bill as well, reflecting the program priorities and policy preferences of each chamber. The Budget Impact section of this chapter includes a breakdown of these differences in the two bills.

Both versions of H.R. 2 would supersede the current slate of farm programs and policies authorized by the 2014 farm bill, P.L. 113-79, many of which are to expire in 2018 unless Congress acts to reauthorize or extend them. Certain programs, such as crop insurance, are permanently authorized and would continue to operate in the absence of new farm legislation or an extension of the current farm bill. The Supplemental Nutrition Assistance Program (SNAP) could continue to operate as long as funding is appropriated. But if the current farm law were to expire, many other programs—such as revenue support programs for producers of major agricultural commodities—including corn, wheat, milk, sugar, and others—would be governed by so-called permanent laws, which date from the late 1930s and 1940s and do not expire.

These permanent laws, including the Agricultural Adjustment Act of 1938 (P.L. 75-430) and Agricultural Act of 1949 (P.L. 81-439), rely on supply controls to buttress price support regimes that would raise market prices of these basic farm commodities above existing levels. A change in farm policy along these lines could restrict production and prove to be broadly disruptive for farmers, farm input suppliers, agricultural exporters, food manufacturers, and consumers. Many other programs, such as conservation programs and rural development programs, would cease to function. In the past, when Congress has faced the prospect of expiring farm legislation without enacting successor legislation, it has acted to extend the existing policies, as it did when the 2002 and 2008 acts expired.

A change in the current policy environment from the situation that prevailed when the 2014 farm bill was being debated and enacted is the reduced profitability of the U.S. farm economy. The U.S. Department of Agriculture (USDA) forecasts that for 2017 and 2018, net cash farm income—a measure of the profitability of farming—will be about one-third below the high levels reached in 2012 and 2013, when Congress was considering the 2014 farm bill. The decline in net cash farm income over this period reflects declining prices for many commodities. More recently, trade disputes involving major U.S. agricultural export markets—including China, Canada, Mexico, and the EU—has led to imposition of tariffs by these trading partners on a range of U.S. farm product exports. Agricultural exports provide critical support to U.S. commodity prices and farm profitability. The tariffs have coincided with a further decline in prices for some U.S. agricultural products while fostering uncertainty about the near-term prospects for U.S. agricultural exports and, by extension, farm income.

This chapter provides a title-by-title summary of the policies and provisions in the House- and Senate-passed versions of H.R. 2 and compares them with current law. Following an analysis of the budgetary implications of both bills, summaries of some of the changes that the House and Senate bills would make in each of their 11 and 12 titles, respectively, are provided. These summaries are followed by title-specific side-by-side comparison tables that briefly describe the provisions in the House- and Senate-passed versions of H.R. 2 and compare them with the current law or relevant existing policy.

BUDGETARY IMPACT[1]

A farm bill authorizes funding in two ways. It authorizes and pays for **mandatory** outlays with multiyear budget estimates when the law is enacted. It also sets the parameters for **discretionary** programs and authorizes them to receive future appropriations but does not provide funding. Mandatory programs often dominate farm bill policy and the debate over the farm bill budget.

Baseline

The budgetary impact of mandatory spending proposals is measured relative to an assumption that certain programs continue beyond the end of the farm bill. The benchmark is the CBO **baseline**—a projection at a particular point in time of future federal spending on mandatory programs under current law. The baseline provides funding for reauthorization, reallocation to other programs, or offsets for deficit reduction.[2]

In April 2018, CBO released a baseline for farm bill programs with mandatory spending that will be used for the rest of the legislative year.[3] It projects that, if current law were extended, farm bill programs would cost $867 billion over the next 10 years, FY2019-2028, 77% of which is in the nutrition title for the Supplemental Nutrition Assistance Program (SNAP). The remaining $203 billion baseline is for agricultural programs, mostly in crop insurance, farm commodity programs, and conservation. Other titles of the farm bill contribute about 1% of the baseline (Table 1, Figure 1), some of which are funded primarily with discretionary spending.

---

[1] This section was written by Jim Monke, Specialist in Agricultural Policy.

[2] See CRS In Focus IF10783, *Farm Bill Primer: Budget Issues*.

[3] CBO, "Baseline Projections for Selected Programs," April 2018, https://www.cbo.gov/about/products/baseline-projections-selected-programs, and in the table notes in CBO, "Cost Estimates for H.R. 2 as passed by the House of Representatives and as passed by the Senate," https://www.cbo.gov/publication/54284, July 24, 2018.

Scores

When a new bill is proposed that would affect mandatory spending, the **score** (cost impact) is measured in relation to the baseline. Changes that increase spending relative to the baseline have a *positive* score; those that decrease spending relative to the baseline have a *negative* score. Budget enforcement uses these baselines and scores and may follow "PayGo" and other budget rules (that in part may require no increase to the federal deficit).[4]

Relative to the baseline, CBO released its scores of H.R. 2 as passed by the House and as passed by the Senate (Table 1).[5]

- The 10-year score of House-passed H.R. 2 is a net reduction of $1.8 billion from the federal budget (-0.21% below the $867 billion baseline). This is the result of a decrease in projected outlays of $1.3 billion and $0.5 billion of new revenue from fees that would be paid by contractors in the SNAP program. On a shorter-time-period basis, the five-year score shows a net increase of $2.2 billion over the $426 billion baseline that is more than offset by net reductions in the second five years of the budget window.[6]
- The 10-year score of the Senate-passed amendment to H.R. 2 is budget neutral ($0, +0%), with an overall increase in outlays of $68 million (+0.01%) that is offset by a $68 million increase in revenue from fees for an oilheat program. As in the House bill, the five-year score shows a net increase ($1.6 billion) that is offset by net reductions in the second five years of the budget window.

The overall relatively small scores (measured in percentage changes) of the bills are the net result of sometimes relatively larger increases and reductions across individual titles (Table 1, Figure 2).

- In the House bill, the 10-year score of outlays shows increases for the commodities, trade, research, and miscellaneous titles. These increases are more than offset by net reductions in the nutrition, conservation, energy (rural infrastructure), and crop insurance titles, as well as a revenue provision in the nutrition title.

---

[4] See CRS Report 98-560, *Baselines and Scorekeeping in the Federal Budget Process*.

[5] CBO, "Cost Estimates for H.R. 2 as passed by the House of Representatives and as passed by the Senate," https://www.cbo.gov/publication/54284, July 24, 2018.

[6] Although the farm bill is generally considered a five-year authorization that would cover FY2019-FY2023, budget rules require it to be scored over a 10-year budget window.

- In the Senate bill, the 10-year score shows increases for the trade, energy, horticulture, research, and miscellaneous titles. These increases are offset by net reductions in the rural development and commodities titles, along with a revenue provision in the miscellaneous title.

Some of the overall scores within an individual title are the net result of increases in individual provisions, which are offset by reductions in other provisions within a title.

- In the House bill, the nutrition and conservation titles have numerous provisions with relatively large cumulative increases that are offset by provisions with relatively large decreases in their scores (Table 3, Figure 3).
- In the Senate bill, while none of the titles' cumulative increases and decreases are as large in magnitude as the changes to nutrition and conservation programs in the House bill, the section-by-section scores of the Senate bill nonetheless show both increases and decreases from the baseline. Titles such as rural development, horticulture, and research have larger scores in the Senate bill than in the House bill (Table 3, Figure 4).

For several of a subset of programs in the 2014 farm bill that received mandatory funding but do not have a baseline beyond the end of FY2018,[7] both the House and Senate bills would provide continuing funding and, in some cases, permanent baseline.

- In the House bill, certain trade title programs would receive $470 million and permanent baseline. A food insecurity program in the nutrition title would receive $472 million in mandatory funding and permanent baseline. Other affected programs that receive mandatory funding, but not permanent baseline, include organic research and beginning farmer programs in the research title ($250 million), two organic programs in the horticulture title ($10 million), and outreach for socially disadvantaged farmers and the wool and cotton trust funds in the miscellaneous title ($150 million). In the conservation title, small watershed rehabilitation, wetlands mitigation, voluntary public access, and grassroots source water protection programs receive over $500 million of mandatory funding.
- In the Senate bill, organic research would receive $450 million in mandatory funds and permanent baseline. The beginning farmer program would be combined with other outreach programs to receive $466 million and permanent

[7] See CRS In Focus IF10780, *Farm Bill Primer: Programs Without Baseline Beyond FY2018.*

baseline. Trade title programs would receive $515 million and permanent baseline. Farmers market and value-added promotion programs are combined to receive $558 million and permanent baseline. A food insecurity program in the nutrition title would receive $401 million in mandatory funding and permanent baseline. Other affected programs that receive mandatory funding, but not permanent baseline, include an agricultural research foundation ($200 million); various bioenergy programs ($375 million); three other horticulture programs ($68 million); and Pima cotton, wool, and citrus programs in the miscellaneous title ($336 million).

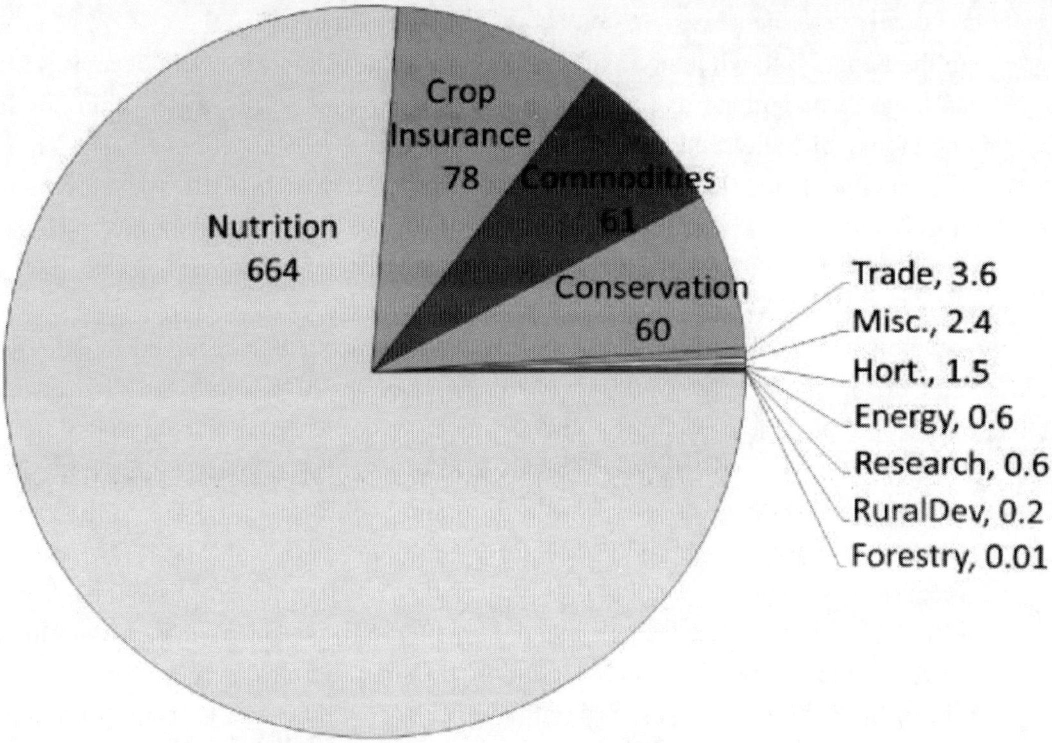

Source: CRS, using CBO Baseline by Title (unpublished; April 2018), based on the CBO Baseline (https://www.cbo.gov/about/products/baseline-projections-selected-programs; April 2018).

Figure 1. CBO Baseline under Current Law, by Title; (10-year projected outlays, FY2019-FY2028, billions of dollars).

Table 1. Budget for a 2018 Farm Bill: Baseline and Scores, by Title (outlays in millions of dollars, 5- and 10-year totals)

	Five years (FY2019-FY2023)			10 years (FY2019-FY2028)		
Farm Bill Titles	**CBO Baseline**	**CBO Score House-passed**	**CBO Score Senate-passed**	**CBO Baseline**	**CBO Score House-passed**	**CBO Score Senate-passed**
Commodities	31,340	+198	-23	61,151	+284	-408
Conservation	28,715	+656	+290	59,754	-795	+0
Trade	1,809	+235	+258	3,624	+470	+515
Nutrition	325,922	+862	+224	663,828	-1,426	+94
Credit	-2,205	+0	+0	-4,558	+0	+0
Rural Dev.[a]	98	+0	-832	168	+0	-2,340
Research	329	+168	+426	604	+250	+685
Forestry	5	+0	+5	10	+0	+5
Energy[a]	362	-267	+311	612	-517	+375
Horticulture	772	+10	+323	1,547	+10	+626
Crop Insurance	38,057	-70	-1	78,037	-161	-2
Miscellaneous	1,259	+553	+594	2,423	+566	+517
Subtotal	426,462	+2,344	+1,573	867,200	-1,320	+68
Increase in Revenue	-	+115	+33	-	+465	+68
Total	426,462	+2,229	+1,540	867,200	-1,785	0

Source: CRS, using the CBO Baseline by Title (unpublished; April 2018), based on the CBO Baseline (https://www.cbo.gov/about/products/baseline-projections-selected-programs; April 2018), CBO Cost Estimate of H.R. 2 (https://www.cbo.gov/publication/53819; May 2, 2018), and the CBO Cost Estimate of S. 3042 (https://www.cbo.gov/publication/54092; June 21, 2018).

Note: Scores reflect the most recently published estimates by CBO of the committee-reported bills. Floor amendments may have made relatively minor changes to specific titles.

[a] The House bill combined rural development and energy into a Rural Infrastructure and Economic Development title. This table retains the separate titles consistent with the 2014 farm bill, the CBO baseline, and the Senate bill.

TITLE-BY-TITLE SUMMARY

Commodities[8]

Title I commodity programs of both the House- and Senate-passed farm bills authorize support programs for dairy, sugar, and covered commodities—including major grain, oilseed, and pulse crops—as well as agricultural disaster assistance. Major field-crop programs include the Price Loss Coverage (PLC) and Agricultural Risk Coverage (ARC) programs and the Marketing Assistance Loan (MAL) program (see Table 4). The

[8] This section was written by Randy Schnepf (farm commodity support) and Mark McMinimy (sugar), Specialists in Agricultural Policy; Joel Greene (dairy) and Sahar Angadjivand (farm commodity support), Analysts in Agricultural Policy; and Megan Stubbs (disaster assistance), Specialist in Agricultural Conservation and Natural Resources Policy.

Table 2. CBO Score of House-Passed H.R. 2, by Section (Projected change in outlays relative to April 2018 baseline, FY2019-FY2028, millions of dollars)

Provision	FY2019-28	Provision	FY2019-28
Title I—Commodity Programs		Food Insecurity Nutrition Incentive	472
Agriculture Risk Coverage—Individual	-143	Emergency Food Assistance	499
Agriculture Risk Coverage—County	-111	National Gateway	601
Dairy Program	-20	Nutrition Education	632
Economic Adjustment Assistance for Textiles	23	Transitional Benefits	895
Implementation	25	Retailer-Funded Incentives Pilot	1,204
Payment Limitations	40	Child Support Agency Cooperation	3,494
Supplemental Agriculture Disaster Assistance	62	Earned Income Deduction	4,640
Price Loss Coverage	408	Workforce Solutions: Administration	7,300
Subtotal, Title I	284	**Subtotal, Title IV**	-1,426
Title II—Conservation		**Title V—Credit**	0
Repeal Conservation Stewardship Program	-12,618	**Title VI—Rural Develop., Energy**	
Conservation Reserve Program	-23	Rural Energy for America Program	-435
Grassroots Source Water Protection	5	Biorefinery Assistance	-82
Wetlands Mitigation Banking	10	**Subtotal, Title VI**	-517
Voluntary Public Access and Habitat Protection	50	**Title VII—Research**	
Feral Swine Eradication and Control Pilot	100	Beginning Farmers and Ranchers	100
Small Watershed Rehabilitation Program	459	Organic Research Extension Initiative	150
Regional Conservation Partnership Program	1,308	**Subtotal, Title VII**	**250**
Agricultural Conservation Easement Program	2,221	**Title VIII—Forestry**	**0**
Environmental Quality Incentives Program	7,693	**Title IX—Horticulture**	
Subtotal, Title II	**-795**	National Organic Program Technology	5
Title III—Trade		Organic Production Data Initiative	5
International Development Program	470	**Subtotal, Title IX**	**10**
Subtotal, Title III	**470**	**Title X—Crop Insurance**	
Title IV—Nutrition		Education and Risk Mgt. Assistance	-125
Workforce Solutions: Benefits	-14,100	Increase Cat. Coverage Fee to $500	-72
Update to Categorical Eligibility	-3,965	Research and Development Priorities	-45
Standard Utility Allowances Energy Receipt	-2,930	Program Administration	-18
Duplicative Enrollment Database	-588	Whole Farm to Beginning Farmers	9
State Performance Indicators	-432	Treatment of Forage and Grazing	90
Disqualification of Certain Convicted Felons	-23	**Subtotal, Title X**	**-161**
Mobile Technologies	12	**Title XI—Miscellaneous**	
SNAP Benefit Transfer Transaction Data Report	30	Noninsured Assistance Program	-37
Interactions	35	Outreach to Socially Disadvantaged	50
Simplified Homeless Housing Costs	76	Textile Trust Fund	103
Adjustment to Recovered Funds Retained	102	National Animal Disease Preparedness	450
Basic Allowance for Housing	116	**Subtotal, Title XI**	**566**
Implementation Funds	150	**Total Changes in Direct Spending**	**-1,320**
Prohibited Fees	153	Increases in Revenue	465
Adjustment to Asset Limitations	201	**Net Effect on the Deficit**	**-1,785**

Source: CRS, sorted within titles using the CBO cost estimate for H.R. 2 as passed by the House, July 24, 2018.

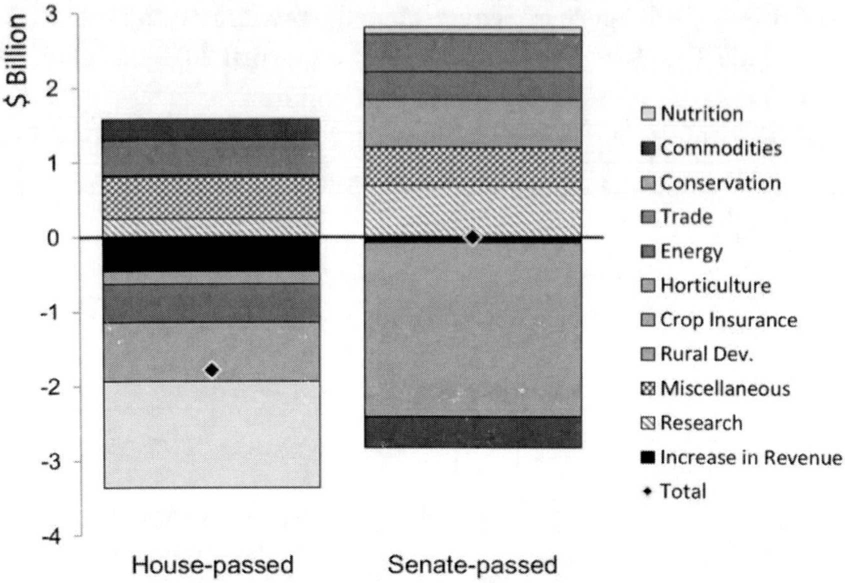

Source: CRS, using the CBO Cost Estimates for H.R. 2 as passed by the House of Representatives and as passed by the Senate (https://www.cbo.gov/publication/54284, July 24, 2018).

Figure 2. CBO Scores, by Title, of House and Senate Farm Bills (Projected change in 10-year outlays relative to baseline, FY2019-FY2028).

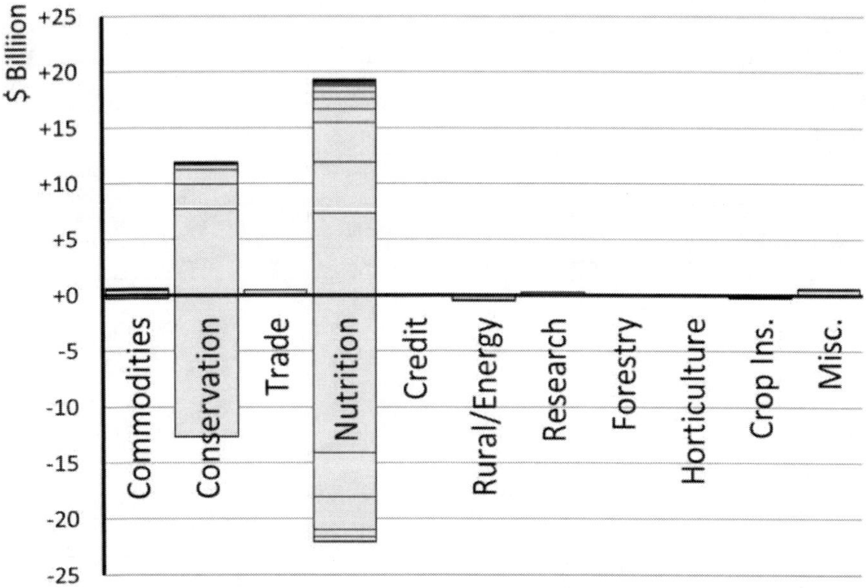

Source: CRS, sorted within titles using the CBO Cost Estimate for H.R. 2 as passed by the House, July 24, 2018.

Figure 3. CBO Score of House-passed H.R. 2 by Section and Title vs. Baseline.

Table 3. CBO Score of Senate-Passed Amendment to H.R. 2, by Section (Projected change in outlays relative to April 2018 baseline, FY2019-FY2028, millions of dollars)

Provision	FY2019-28	Provision	FY2019-28
Title I—Commodity Programs		**Title VII—Research and Extension**	
Economic Adjustment Assistance for Cotton	-328	Biomass Research and Development	15
Adjusted Gross Income Limitation of $700,000	-263	Urban, Indoor, and Other Emerging Ag.	20
Actively Engaged in Farming Requirement	-211	Foundation for Food and Ag. Research	200
Dairy Product Donation Program	-53	Organic Research Extension Initiative	450
Producer Election (ARC Default Choice)	-9	**Subtotal, Title VII**	685
Cat. Coverage $5.00 with 40 Percent Cap	-3	**Title VIII—Forestry**	5
Supplemental Agricultural Disaster Assistance	11	**Title IX—Energy**	
Loss of Peach and Blueberry Crops Due to Cold	18	Carbon Utilization Education Program	10
Additional Assistance for Volcanic Activity	30	Biobased Market Program	15
Milk Donation Program	53	Bioenergy for Advanced Biofuels	75
Repayment of Dairy Risk Coverage Premiums	78	Biomass Crop Assistance Program	125
Dairy Risk Coverage	97	Biorefinery Assistance	150
Agriculture Risk Coverage (ARC)	172	**Subtotal, Title IX**	375
Subtotal, Title I	-408	**Title X—Horticulture**	
Title II—Conservation		Organic Production Data Initiative	5
Environmental Quality Incentives Program	-1,481	Organic Certification/Trade Tracking	5
Conservation Stewardship Program	-1,000	National Organic Certification	58
Conservation Reserve Program	0	Local Agriculture Market Program	558
Regional Conservation Partnership Program	874	**Subtotal, Title X**	626
Agricultural Conservation Easement Program	1,607	**Title XI—Crop Insurance**	
Subtotal, Title II	0	Enterprise Units Across County Lines	-27
Title III—Trade		Crop Productionon Native Sod	-7
Trade Promotion, Development, and Assistance	515	Funding for Information Technology	2
Subtotal, Title III	515	Submission of Policies and Materials	8
Title IV—Nutrition		Whole Farm Revenue Agent Incentives	10
Interstate Data Matching	-588	Pasture, Rangeland, Forage for Indians	12
Quality Control	-420	**Subtotal, Title XI**	-2
Assistance for Community Food Projects	-40	**Title XII—Miscellaneous**	
Income Verification	10	Merchandise Processing Fee	-371
Harvesting Health Pilot Projects	20	Direct Operation Microloans	5
Improvements to Electronic Benefit Transfer	28	Cattle Tick Inspection in Livestock	7
Food Distribution Program Reservations	37	Administrative Units	7
Definition of Certification Period	205	Wool Research and Promotion	10
Emergency Food Assistance Programs	206	National Oil heat Research Alliance	68
Work Requirements for SNAP	235	Pima Agriculture Cotton Trust Fund	80
Food Insecurity Nutrition Incentive	401	Wool Apparel Manufacturers Trust Fund	121
Subtotal, Title IV	94	Emergency Citrus Trust Fund	125
Title V—Credit	0	Farming Opportunities Outreach	466
Title VI—Rural Development		**Subtotal, Title XII**	517
Cushion of Credit: Deposits, Interest Rate	-2,350	**Total Changes in Direct Spending**	68
Mandatory Funding for Rural Electric Program	10	Increases in Revenue: Title XII—Oilheat	68
Subtotal, Title VI	-2,340	**Net Effect on the Deficit**	0

Source: CRS, sorted within titles using the CBO Cost Estimate for H.R. 2 as passed by the Senate, July 24, 2018.

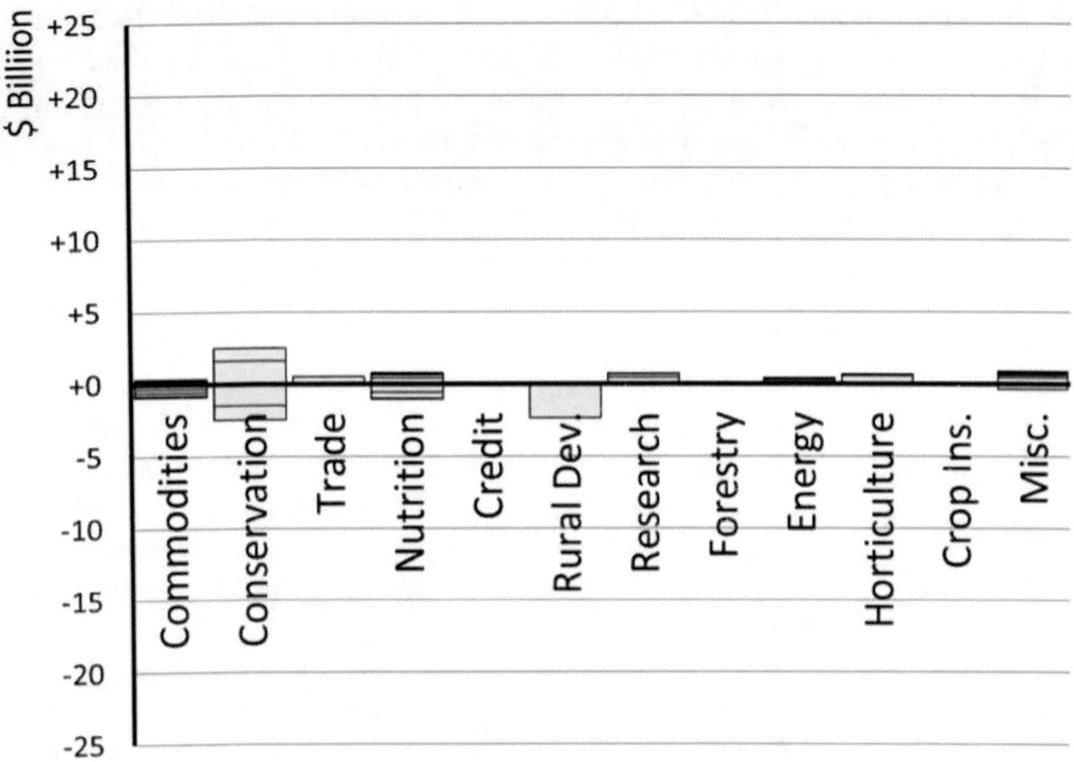

Source: CRS, sorted within titles using the CBO cost estimate for H.R. 2 as passed by the Senate, July 24, 2018.

Figure 4. CBO Score of Senate Amendment to H.R. 2 by Section and Title vs. Baseline.

dairy program involves protecting a portion of the margin between milk and feed prices. The sugar program provides a combination of price support, border protection, and producer production allotments. Four disaster assistance programs that focus primarily on livestock and tree crops were permanently authorized in the 2014 farm bill. These disaster assistance programs provide federal assistance to help farmers recover financially from natural disasters, including drought and floods. Title I also includes several administrative provisions that suspend permanent farm law from 1938 and 1949; assign payment limits for individuals, joint ventures or partnerships, and corporations; specify the adjusted gross income (AGI) threshold for program payment eligibility; and identify other details regarding payment attribution and eligibility.

Both bills extend authority for most current commodity programs but with some modifications to programs for covered commodities and dairy as well as agricultural disaster assistance. The Senate bill eliminates the transition assistance for producers of upland cotton. Under both bills, the sugar program is extended but is otherwise unchanged.

In general, program changes affecting covered commodities under the House farm bill make PLC a more attractive option for producers than ARC. In particular, the House farm bill includes an escalator provision that would raise a covered commodity's effective reference price (used in the PLC payment formula) by as much as 115% of the statutory PLC reference price based on 85% of the five-year Olympic average[9] of farm prices. In addition, producers participating in PLC that experienced at least 20 consecutive weeks of severe drought during 2008-2012 would be allowed to update their program yields (used in the PLC payment formula). Producers enrolled in the county-level ARC program (or the stacked income protection plan for cotton) would be ineligible for crop insurance coverage under an area yield and loss basis or the supplemental coverage option. Furthermore, the individual, farm-level ARC program is eliminated.

In contrast, the Senate farm bill leaves the PLC program unchanged but proposes changes to ARC that make it a more attractive option: ARC would use a trend-adjusted yield and would increase the yield floor (available to producers under certain conditions) to 75% of the transitional county yield (up from 70%) when calculating the benchmark county revenue guarantee. In addition, ARC would become the default option when a producer fails to choose between ARC and PLC at signup. The Senate farm bill also specifies that the county in which a farm is located be used for the benchmark and actual ARC revenue calculations, and it instructs USDA to use a single data source for county yield estimates to avoid the disparity in ARC payments that some neighboring counties experienced in recent years. The Senate farm bill would also require USDA to publish ARC and PLC payment rates within 30 days after the end of the crop marketing year and would obligate USDA to review and report on the establishment, calculation, reallocation, adjustment, and reduction of base acres.

With respect to payment limits and the AGI limit, the Senate farm bill would leave payment limits unchanged but tighten the AGI limit to $700,000 (down from $900,000 under current law). In contrast, the House farm bill proposes to expand the list of producer exemptions from payment and income limits under certain conditions. First, MAL program benefits would be exempted from inclusion under both payment limits and the AGI limit. Second, payment limits would be affected by the House farm bill's treatment of eligible payment entities. Under current law, partnerships and joint ventures are treated as collections of individuals, each with their own payment limits, whereas a corporation is treated as a single individual subject to a single payment limit. The House bill would alter the treatment of certain corporations by defining *qualified pass-through entity* (QTPE) as including partnerships, joint ventures, limited liability corporations, and S corporations.[10] This would allow each separate owner of a QTPE (meeting all program eligibility criteria) to have an individual payment limit. Also, the House bill would redefine *family farm* to include first cousins, nieces, and nephews, thus increasing the

---

[9] The Olympic average excludes the high- and low-price years from calculation of the average.

[10] S corporations meet the requirements of subchapter S of the Internal Revenue Code.

potential pool of individuals eligible for individual payment limits on family farming operations.

Both the House and the Senate bills amend the permanent agricultural disaster assistance programs, but there is no overlap between the amendments. The House bill amends the limits on payments received under select disaster assistance programs and waives the AGI requirement if more than 75% of the producer's income comes from farming, ranching, or silviculture. The House bill also expands payments for livestock losses caused by disease, whereas the Senate bill expands payments for losses of unweaned livestock that occur before vaccination. The Senate bill also expands the definition of an eligible producer to include Indian tribes or tribal organizations and increases replanting and rehabilitation payment rates for beginning and veteran orchardists.

Both the House and the Senate bills would rename the current dairy Margin Protection Program (MPP)—Dairy Risk Management Program (DRMP) under the House bill and Dairy Risk Coverage (DRC) by the Senate. Like MPP, both the DRMP and DRC would pay participating dairy producers the difference (when positive) between a producer-selected margin and the national milk margin (calculated as the all-milk price minus an average feed cost ration). Both bills would lower the catastrophic margin protection level. Under current law, for a $100 administrative fee, participating dairy producers automatically receive payments on 90% of their first 5 million pounds or less of milk production when the milk margin falls below $5.00 per hundredweight (cwt.). Under both DRMP and DRC, the catastrophic margin is lowered to $4.00/cwt.

Both bills would also expand coverage choices for milk producers. Under current law, premiums paid by producers vary with coverage levels selected across two production tiers: Tier I is the first 5 million pounds of milk production; Tier II is milk production above 5 million pounds. Currently, dairy producers select a percent coverage ranging from 25% to 90% of the farm's historical milk production. Both DRMP and DRC propose extending the percent coverage range to 5% to 90% of a farm's milk production history.

Both DRMP and DRC would reinstate premiums for the $4.50/cwt. and $5.00/cwt. margins and add margin levels of $8.50/cwt. and $9.00/cwt. under Tier I. DRMP would substantially reduce premiums for the other Tier I margins ranging from $5.50/cwt. to $8.00/cwt., while premiums for Tier II would be left unchanged. In contrast, DRC would slightly raise premiums for the other Tier I margins ranging from $5.50/cwt. to $7.50/cwt., while the $8.00/cwt. margin would be lowered slightly. DRC would raise the premiums for all Tier II margins. DRC would partially offset higher premiums by providing premium discounts for small- and medium-sized participating dairy operations: Discounts of 50% are available on Tier I and Tier II premiums for milk production history of 2 million pounds or less, and premium discounts of 25% are available on milk production history over 2 million pounds but not greater than 10 million pounds. Finally,

DRC requires USDA to repay any calendar-year positive net premiums (i.e., premiums paid minus both margin-payments received and MPP program costs) to dairy operations that participated in MPP during 2015-2017.

Under DRC, as under current law, dairy producers would make annual elections of a margin coverage level and a percentage of milk production to cover. Under DRMP, dairy producers would make a single one-time election, which would last the duration of the farm bill.

Both the House and the Senate bills would extend through FY2023 the Dairy Forward Pricing Program, the Dairy Indemnity Program, and the Dairy Promotion and Research Program. The House bill would eliminate the provision prohibiting dairy producers from participating in both the DRMP and the Livestock Gross Margin-Dairy insurance program, although dual coverage cannot be on the same milk production. The Senate bill would retain the current law prohibition on joint participation in both margin programs. Both bills would amend the formula for the Class I skim milk price used for calculating the Class I price under Federal Milk Marketing Orders.

Finally, the House bill, but not the Senate bill, would require USDA to conduct studies on whether the feed cost ration is representative of actual feed costs used in the margin calculation and on the cost of corn silage versus the feed cost of corn. The bill also directs USDA to report alfalfa hay prices in the top five milk-producing states.

Conservation[11]

USDA administers a number of agricultural conservation programs that assist private landowners with natural resource concerns. These can be broadly grouped into working lands programs, land retirement and easement programs, watershed programs, emergency programs, technical assistance, and other programs. Both the House and the Senate bills amend portions of programs in all of these categories (see Table 5). However, the general focus is on the larger working lands, land retirement, and easement programs. The House and the Senate bills reauthorize all current conservation programs with the exception of the largest—the Conservation Stewardship Program (CSP)—which the House bill would repeal. The House bill would increase funding for conservation by $656 million in the short term (in the first five years) but overall reduce funding by nearly $800 million in the long term (over 10-years). The Senate bill would increase funding for conservation programs by $185 million over the first five years of authorization but would be budget neutral over 10 years. Generally, the House bill would eventually shift funding out of the

---

[11] This section was written by Megan Stubbs, Specialist in Agricultural Conservation and Natural Resources Policy.

conservation title, while the Senate bill would reallocate funding within the title among the larger programs.

Working Lands Programs

In general, working lands programs provide technical and financial assistance to help farmers improve land management practices. The two largest working lands programs—Environmental Quality Incentives Program (EQIP) and CSP—account for more than half of all conservation program funding.[12] Overall funding for both programs is reduced under the House and Senate bills, compared with current law, but in different ways and to different degrees.

The House bill repeals CSP, whereas the Senate bill reauthorizes CSP and reduces program enrollment. CSP provides financial and technical assistance to producers to maintain and improve existing conservation systems and to adopt additional conservation activities in a comprehensive manner on a producer's entire operation. Currently more than 70 million acres is enrolled in CSP. The House bill provides a more limited version of the CSP stewardship contract within EQIP with the proviso that no more than 50% of EQIP funding may be used for these contracts. Repealing CSP is the primary driver behind the projected decline in spending under the conservation title of the House bill, since CSP contracts would all expire by FY2023. The House bill provides an overall increase in annual funding for EQIP, providing for annual incremental increases through FY2023 to $3 billion from $1.75 billion in FY2018. This increase in funding for EQIP would be less than the savings that would result from repealing CSP. The Senate bill reduces EQIP funding from the current level of $1.75 billion in FY2018 to $1.5 billion in FY2019 while providing for annual incremental increases to $1.6 billion in FY2023. The Senate bill also reduces CSP enrollment to 8.8 million acres annually, down from the current 10 million acres annually. The Senate bill amends CSP in a number of ways that are aimed at achieving increased environmental benefits.

The House bill makes fewer changes to EQIP, when compared to the Senate bill, among which the House adds a stewardship contract, removes the allocation requirement that 60% of payments relate to livestock production, and expands options for irrigation and drainage entities. The Senate bill contains a number of amendments that focus on water quality and quantity-related practices and wildlife habitat improvement. The Senate bill also retains and reduces the allocation for livestock-related practices to 50% and increases the allocation for wildlife-related practices from 5% to 10%. Both bills amend Conservation Innovation Grants, a subprogram under EQIP. The House bill limits funding for program, while the Senate bill adds to the types of projects that may be carried out under the program.

---

[12] EQIP and CSP combined received approximately $2.6 billion in FY2017. Total mandatory spending in FY2017 was approximately $5.3 billion.

Land Retirement and Easement Programs

Land retirement and easement programs provide federal payments to private agricultural landowners for accepting permanent or long-term land-use restrictions. Both bills reauthorize and amend the Conservation Reserve Program (CRP), the largest land retirement program. CRP provides annual rental payments to producers to replace crops on highly erodible and environmentally sensitive land with long-term resource-conserving plantings. Both bills would increase CRP enrollment from the current limit of 24 million acres in FY2018, with the House bill providing for annual incremental increases to a maximum of 29 million acres in FY2023, whereas the Senate bill would allow enrollment to increase to 25 million through FY2023. In order to offset this increased enrollment level, both bills would reduce payments to participants. The House bill would limit annual rental payments to 80% of the rental rate (less for reenrollment), allow for a one-time early termination of select CRP contracts without penalty in FY2019, reduce incentives for continuous contracts, and limit cost-share assistance. The Senate bill would limit annual rental payments to 88.5% of the rental rate, delete the early termination provision, codify the existing continuous contract initiatives, create an easement program, and expand the transition option for new and limited resource producers. Both bills make a number of other changes that would further expand grazing and commercial uses on CRP acres but through different approaches.

Both bills also reauthorize and amend the Agricultural Conservation Easement Program (ACEP). ACEP provides financial and technical assistance through two types of easements: (1) agricultural land easements that limit nonagricultural uses on productive farm or grasslands and (2) wetland reserve easements that protect and restore wetlands. In both bills, most of the changes to ACEP focus on the agricultural land easements in which USDA enters into partnership agreements with eligible entities to purchase agricultural land easements from willing landowners. Both bills would provide additional flexibilities to ACEP-eligible entities, including amendments to the nonfederal cost share requirements, consideration of geographical differences, terms and conditions of easements, and certification criteria of eligible entities. Differences between the two bills center on planning requirements, eligible land criteria, eligible activities, AGI requirements, and total funding for the program. The House bill would increase overall funding to $500 million annually through FY2023 from $250 million in FY2018, whereas the Senate bill would increase funding incrementally to $450 million by FY2023.

Other Conservation Programs

The 2014 farm bill created the Regional Conservation Partnership Program (RCPP), which enrolls land through existing conservation programs in partnership with eligible partners. Under RCPP, partners define the scope and location of the project, provide 50% or more of the project cost, and work with eligible landowners to enroll in existing conservation programs. Both the House and Senate bills amend RCPP and increase annual funding—to $250 million and $200 million, respectively—from the current level of $100 million annually. Both bills also expand the set of conservation programs covered under the program and include the ability to renew partnership agreements. The Senate bill includes a number of other amendments that provide additional funding and flexibilities to partners.

Both bills include amendments to conservation programs and provisions with authorities both inside and outside of omnibus farm bill legislation, including various watershed and emergency conservation programs. Both bills also require reports related to natural resources but do not overlap in the specific reports required. Similarly, both bills create new conservation programs that do not overlap.

Trade[13]

The trade title—Title III under both House and Senate bills—addresses statutes concerning U.S. international food aid and agricultural export programs (see Table 6). Under the farm bill authority, U.S. international food assistance is distributed through three main programs: (1) Food for Peace (emergency and nonemergency food aid), (2) Food for Progress (agricultural development programs), and (3) the McGovern-Dole International Food for Education and Child Nutrition program (school lunch and feeding programs). The largest of these, the Food for Peace (FFP) program, receives about $1.5 billion in annual appropriations. Traditionally, these three programs have relied on donated U.S. agricultural commodities as the basis for their activities. However, recent farm bills have increasingly added flexibility to purchase food in local markets or to directly transfer cash or vouchers to needy recipients. FFP is administered by the U.S. Agency for International Development, while the other two programs are administered by the Foreign Agricultural Service of USDA.

Both the House and Senate farm bills would reauthorize all of the international food aid programs along with certain operational details such as prepositioning and micronutrient fortification. The House bill would specifically require that food vouchers, cash transfers, and local and regional procurement of non-U.S. foods avoid market disruption in the recipient country. Both bills would amend FFP to remove a minimum monetization requirement of 15% of FFP funds and to raise the minimum requirement used for nonemergency programs to $365 million (up from $350 million) or not more than 30% of FFP funding. Also, both House and Senate bills would extend authority for several other related international programs including the Farmer-to-Farmer program,

---

[13] This section was written by Randy Schnepf, Specialist in Agricultural Policy, and Jenny Hopkinson, Analyst in Agricultural Policy.

Bill Emerson Humanitarian Trust, and Global Crop Diversity Trust, as well as two associated fellowship programs: Cochran Fellowships and Borlaug Fellowships.

Current U.S. export promotion programs include the Market Access Program (MAP), the Foreign Market Development Program (FMDP), the Emerging Markets Program (EMP), and Technical Assistance for Specialty Crops (TASC). These programs are administered by the Foreign Agricultural Service.

Both the House and Senate farm bills would reauthorize these four programs. Under the House bill, all four export programs—MAP, FMDP, EMP, and TASC—are combined into a single program named the International Market Development Program (IMDP) while maintaining existing activities and eligibility requirements. IMDP would be authorized to receive $255 million in annual mandatory Commodity Credit Corporation (CCC) funds for FY2019-FY2023. The House bill further creates the Biotechnology and Agricultural Trade Program in Title III to assist with the removal of non-tariff and other trade barriers to U.S. agricultural products produced with biotechnology and other agricultural technologies.

The Senate bill would maintain the separate export promotion programs but adds to them the Priority Trade Fund, which gives the Secretary of Agriculture $6 million annually to further promote U.S. agricultural exports or to expand and maintain markets. The Senate bill would also allow for MAP and FMDP money to be spent on projects in Cuba (but subject to restrictions specified in a National Security Presidential Memorandum of June 16, 2017[14]) and would require the Secretary to include tribal agricultural and food products on trade missions. The Senate bill would authorize $260 million in annual mandatory CCC funds for these trade programs for FY2019-FY2023.

Both the House and Senate farm bills would require that no less than $200 million be spent on promotional activities for both generic and branded U.S. agricultural products, no less than $35 million on promotional activities for generic commodities, no more than $9 million for technical assistance to specialty crop groups looking to export their crops, and no more than $10 million on promoting U.S. agricultural goods to emerging markets. These funding levels reflect current authorization levels across MAP, FMDP, TASC, and EMP. Finally, both the House and Senate farm bills would reauthorize direct credits or export credit guarantees for the promotion of agricultural exports to emerging markets of not less than $1 billion in each fiscal year through 2023.

---

[14] "Strengthening the Policy of the United States Toward Cuba," *Federal Register*, vol. 82, no. 202, October 20, 2017, pp. 48875-48878.

Nutrition[15]

The Nutrition titles of House- and Senate-passed farm bills differ in their approach to eligibility and benefit calculation rules but include some similar policies in other topic areas (see Both bills would reauthorize SNAP and related programs for five years through the end of FY2023.

When CBO's 10-year estimates of the policies are totaled, the Nutrition titles of the Senate- and House-passed bills are about $1 billion apart. This difference obscures larger differences in terms of the scale and scope of policies proposed.

- For the House-passed bill, CBO estimates that the Nutrition title would reduce spending by approximately $1.4 billion over 10 years (FY2019-FY2028) but would also increase revenues by $465 million. This overall estimate includes (1) over $22.0 billion in savings (primarily from changes that would restrict eligibility and benefit amounts); (2) approximately $20.6 billion in increased spending (some from policies estimated to increase benefit amounts, most from funds for related grants and costs associated with administering SNAP); and (3) $465 million in revenues (from a policy that would collect fees from states).
- For the Senate-passed bill, CBO estimates that the Nutrition title would increase spending by $94 million over 10 years (FY2019-2028). The Senate bill's overall estimate includes (1) over $1 billion in savings (primarily from changes to integrity policies) and (2) over $1.1 billion in increased spending (from one eligibility change and increased funding for related grants and costs associated with administering SNAP).

SNAP Eligibility and Benefit Calculation

The House-passed bill includes multiple policies that would affect who is eligible for SNAP and how their benefits are calculated. Some of the most prominent are limits to categorical eligibility, changes to work-related rules (subjecting a greater share of the caseload to a 20-hour work requirement and requiring states to offer employment and training opportunities), and limits to how utilities may be calculated in benefit calculation (these are described in greater detail below). The proposal would increase asset limits and change how vehicles and savings accounts are counted. It also amends the way certain income is counted or excluded and requires households' cooperation with child support enforcement. On the other hand, the Senate-passed bill would largely maintain current law in these areas, though it would increase certification periods for certain households and make some changes to existing work-related rules, including additional employment and training pilot programs.

---

[15] This section was written by Randy Alison Aussenberg, Specialist in Nutrition Assistance Policy.

SNAP Fraud, Errors, and Related State Administration

Both bills propose policies intended to improve detection of errors and fraud. Often, the bills' policies are similar, but they are never identical. Both bills would establish or expand a data system to identify concurrent enrollment in multiple states, make changes to the Quality Control system, and increase USDA's oversight of state performance. The House bill repeals funding for performance bonuses, while the Senate bill reduces funding and limits them to application timeliness. The House bill alone would also allow states to contract out eligibility determination functions.

Electronic Benefit Transfer (EBT) and Retailers

Both bills propose a number of policies for SNAP's EBT system and benefit redemption. Few of the policies are in both bills. They both place new limits on the fees the processors may charge. Both bills would increase USDA oversight authority for the system, but only the House bill would establish a "national gateway" for routing transactions. The House bill alone would make multivitamins and dietary supplements eligible for purchase with SNAP benefits.

Other SNAP-Related Grants

In addition to making changes to SNAP Employment and Training, both bills make changes to, and in some cases increase, existing grant programs' funding, with the House bill providing greater increases. Both bills would expand SNAP bonus incentives for fruit and vegetable purchases and authorize the addition of milk for certain incentive pilot programs (one with mandatory funding in the House bill, one with discretionary funding in the Senate bill). Both bills reauthorize the Food Insecurity Nutrition Incentive (FINI) grant program, renaming it Gus Schumacher FINI and providing for evaluation, training, and technical assistance. The House bill increases FINI funding by $472 million over 10 years; the Senate bill increases funding by $401 million over two years. On nutrition education, the House bill moves SNAP's nutrition education component from SNAP state agencies to land-grant universities and increases program funding. The Senate bill makes some policy changes but does not change funding. The Senate bill also creates a new grant program that would receive $4 million in mandatory funding each year to fund produce prescription programs serving low-income individuals with diet-related diseases.

Food Distribution Programs

Both bills would expand certification periods for the Commodity Supplemental Food Program in similar but not identical ways. Both bills increase mandatory funding for the Emergency Food Assistance Program (TEFAP) foods, the House (+$45 million per year) to a greater extent than the Senate bill does (+$8 million in FY2019, +$20 million each year FY2020-FY2023). Both bills authorize new aspects of TEFAP, taking similar but not identical approaches, seeking to include new donated foods and reduce food waste.

Both bills would make changes to the Food Distribution Program on Indian Reservations. The House changes are minor compared to the Senate's changes, which would increase federal funding for administrative costs and create a demonstration project for tribes to purchase their own commodities.

Other Nutrition Programs and Policies

Both bills reauthorize the Senior Farmers' Market Nutrition Program and its funding. The House bill alone would amend the Fresh Fruit and Vegetable Program to include all forms of these foods (e.g., canned, dried, frozen). The House bill alone would require USDA to review its regulations on National School Lunch Program and School Breakfast Program nutrition standards, both the updated standards for meals and the standards for foods served outside the meal programs.

More Details on Selected House Eligibility and Benefit Calculation Changes

The House bill proposes a number of changes to the determination of households' financial and nonfinancial eligibility for SNAP benefits. Three of these policies were debated throughout House consideration of the bill and are described below. CBO published its *cost* estimates for the House-passed changes but did not publish its *participation* estimates for the House-passed changes. The text below includes the CBO participation estimates based on the House-*reported* bill. This text is in italics.

1) **Broad-based categorical eligibility.** The bill proposes to place additional limits on households that are eligible for SNAP based on their receipt of Temporary Assistance for Needy Families benefits. CBO estimates that the House-passed changes would reduce SNAP spending by approximately $4 billion over the 10-year window. *Regarding participation, CBO estimated, for the House-reported bill that, in an average year, about 400,000 households would lose SNAP eligibility. As SNAP recipients are also eligible for free school meals, CBO estimated that in an average year, 265,000 children would lose access to free meals, though many would still be eligible for reduced-price meals.*
2) **Work-related requirements.** The bill proposes to replace SNAP's general work requirements and time limit for able-bodied adults without dependents with a work requirement for all states. Beginning in FY2021, the proposal would require a minimum of 20 hours of work per week for nonexempt able-bodied adults. Unlike the current law time limit, which applies to 18- to 49-year-olds who do not have children, the proposed requirement would apply to 18- to 59-year-olds and would not exempt parents or caretakers of children age six or older. The proposal continues to give states authority to exempt a portion of the caseload and to request geographic waivers based on labor-market measures, with some amendments to current law. Unlike the current law time limit, the

proposal requires states to offer employment or training opportunities to those individuals subject to the requirements. The bill increases SNAP Employment and Training funding for the states, increasing mandatory funding in a formula grant for states from $110 million in current law to $270 million in FY2020 and to $1 billion in FY2021 and each year thereafter. CBO estimates that the House-passed work-related changes would reduce spending on SNAP benefits by approximately $14.1 billion over 10 years and would increase spending on program administration by approximately $7.3 billion—a net reduction of $6.8 billion. *CBO estimated for the House-reported bill that, in FY2028, in an average month, approximately 1.2 million recipients would no longer receive benefits, with each recipient losing an average annual SNAP benefit amount of $1,816.*

3) **Low Income Home Energy Assistance Program (LIHEAP) and benefit calculation.** Under current law, an eligible household's receipt of a LIHEAP payment over $20 has the potential to increase monthly benefit amounts, because this payment allows the household to have their benefits calculated using a standard utility allowance. Under this bill, for households without elderly or disabled members, LIHEAP would no longer confer this advantage regardless of the amount provided. *CBO estimated that the House-reported provision would reduce 560,000 households' SNAP benefits by an average of $84 per month.*

Credit[16]

Both the House- and Senate-passed farm bills would reauthorize and make several changes to provisions in the Consolidated Farm and Rural Development Act that governs the USDA farm loan programs. They would also modify the Farm Credit Act that governs the Farm Credit System and reauthorize the State Agricultural Loan Mediation Program (see Table 8).

For the USDA farm loan programs, the House and Senate bills would add specific conditions that the Secretary may use to reduce the requirement for three years of farming experience in order for beginning farmers to qualify for loans (e.g., coursework, military service, mentoring). Both bills raise the maximum loan size for guaranteed farm ownership loans and guaranteed farm operating loans from a statutory base of $700,000 in FY1996 ($1.4 million in FY2018 after adjusting for inflation) to a higher base of $1.75

[16] This section was written by Jim Monke, Specialist in Agricultural Policy, with assistance for the FCS Insurance Corporation from Raj Gnanarajah, Analyst in Financial Economics, and David H. Carpenter, Legislative Attorney.

million per borrower, which inflation adjusts to an effective maximum guaranteed loan amount of about $3.5 million in FY2019. The House bill would make this change permanently going forward. The Senate bill would change it for FY2019-FY2023. For direct loans, the Senate bill would increase the farm ownership loan limit to $600,000 and the farm operating loan limit to $400,000, both from $300,000 currently. For beginning and socially disadvantaged farmers, the Senate bill would exempt them from guarantee fees and raise the guarantee percentage to 95%.

For the State Agricultural Loan Mediation Program, both the House and Senate bill reauthorize the program to FY2023 so that it may continue to provide matching grants for mediation of credit and certain other agricultural disputes. The Senate bill also expands the range of issues covered by the program.

For the government-chartered, cooperative Farm Credit System (FCS), both bills would eliminate a host of obsolete references to outdated names and transition periods from the 1980s and 1990s. Both bills add clarification that FCS entities may share privileged information with the Farm Credit Administration (FCA) for regulatory purposes without altering the privileged status elsewhere. Both bills expand FCA's jurisdiction to hold accountable "institution-affiliated parties" (including agents and independent contractors) and makes the scope retroactive for a six-year period. The Senate bill adds the category of socially disadvantaged farmers to the reporting requirement for young, beginning, and small farms. The House bill would delete the compensation limit for FCS bank boards of directors.

For the Federal Agricultural Mortgage Corporation (FarmerMac), the House bill increases the acreage exception from 1,000 acres to 2,000 acres for the dollar limit to remain a qualified loan, subject to a study by FCA. The House bill also directs FCA to study the risks and capitalization of loans in the FCS and FarmerMac portfolios.

For the Farm Credit System Insurance Corporation (FCSIC), which insures repayment of certain FCS debt obligations, the Senate bill would provide greater statutory guidance regarding the powers and duties of the FCSIC when acting as a conservator or receiver of a troubled FCS institution and the rights and duties of parties affected by an FCS institution being placed into a conservatorship or receivership. The new conservatorship/receivership authorities would be largely modeled after the existing conservatorship/receivership statutory regime that is applicable to depository institutions insured by the Federal Deposit Insurance Corporation.

Rural Development[17]

Programs and policies that address rural development are addressed in both the House and Senate bills (see Table 9). In the House bill, the Rural Infrastructure and Economic Development title amends the Rural Development Act of 1972 (P.L. 92-419) to propose a new Subtitle A, Improving Health Outcomes in Rural Communities. The four sections of the proposed subtitle would permit the Secretary of Agriculture, after consultation with public health figures, to announce a temporary reprioritization of certain rural development loans and grants to assist rural communities in responding to a specific rural health emergency. The announced emergency would expire either when the Secretary has determined that the emergency has ended or 360 days after the announcement, whichever date is earlier. While the emergency is in effect, 10% of the funds available for the Distance Learning and Telemedicine Program would be made available to identify and treat individuals affected by the emergency. Under the Community Facilities program, priority would be given to entities providing prevention, treatment, and recovery services to those affected by the emergency. The subtitle would also reauthorize the Farm and Ranch Stress Assistance Network and authorize a new loan and grant program to help establish group health plans offered by agricultural associations.

Subtitle B of the House bill makes changes to the Enhancing Broadband Telecommunications Services in the Rural Areas Program. Provisions under this subtitle would establish minimum acceptable standards of broadband service of 25 megabits per second downstream transmission capacity and 3 megabits per second upstream transmission capacity and direct that projections of broadband service be developed five, 10, 15, 20, and 30 years into the future. Other provisions would require broadband infrastructure loan guarantees, provide incentives to reach more isolated rural areas by establishing a residential density measure for loan guarantee applicants, permit the Rural Utility Service to obligate but not disburse broadband funding support, and give priority to applicants who would provide broadband service to areas not predominantly for business. Other provisions would authorize loans for middle-mile broadband infrastructure, modify build-out requirements for loan applicants from three to five years, reduce reporting requirements for borrowers, and establish a task force in the Federal Communications Commission for reviewing the connectivity and technology needs of precision agriculture.

Subtitle C of the bill concerns provisions for rural communities, business development, and rural infrastructure. Its provisions would prioritize project applications that support implementation of strategic plans on a multi-jurisdictional basis and reserve a portion of funds for such projects, raise the maximum loan amount for water and waste

[17] This section was written by Tadlock Cowan, Analyst in Natural Resources and Rural Development.

water projects, increase funding for water and waste water technical assistance, and reauthorize a range of rural development programs authorized under the Consolidated Farm and Rural Development Act.

Three provisions in Subtitle C would change the population eligibility criteria in defining *rural* and *rural area*. Under current law, water and waste disposal loan and grants are limited to communities of 10,000 or fewer. A new provision would exclude loan guarantees from that 10,000-head threshold. A second provision would exclude incarcerated individuals in determining whether an area is rural. A third provision would similarly exclude the first 1,500 military personnel living in on-base housing in determining whether an area is rural.

Subtitle D of the House bill reauthorizes programs under the Rural Electrification Act of 1936 (P.L. 74-605), including expanding 911 access in rural areas and extending the rural economic development loan and grant program. Subtitle E amends and reauthorizes all of the agricultural energy programs in the 2014 farm bill that were previously in a separate title, extending most through FY2023. The House bill also modifies the type of funding available for these programs. In prior farm bills, many of these programs were provided with mandatory funding, whereas the House bill authorizes only discretionary funding.

Subtitle F reauthorizes the Value-Added Grants program and increases its discretionary funding authorization. The regional development commissions established in the 2008 farm bill are also reauthorized, and the current definition of *rural area* for the Rural Housing Service's programs is retained until the 2030 decennial census. Subtitle G repeals several unfunded programs, including the Rural Telephone Bank, the Rural Collaborative Investment Program, and the Delta Region Agricultural Development Grants Program. Subtitle H makes technical corrections to certain provisions of the Consolidated Farm and Rural Development Act (P.L. 92-419) and the Rural Electrification Act.

Similar to the House bill, the Rural Development title in the Senate bill makes significant changes to the Access to Broadband Telecommunications Services in Rural Areas. The bill establishes priorities for awarding loans and grants for broadband projects in rural communities. Unserved rural communities with no residential broadband and applications that offer the maximum level of broadband service to the greatest proportion of rural households in the proposed service area would get top priority. Within those priority categories, the highest priority would go to rural communities with a population of 10,000 or fewer, those experiencing outmigration that have adopted a strategic community investment plan, communities with high percentages of low-income residents, and those rural communities more isolated from population centers. Other broadband-related provisions would limit grant support to 50% of development costs and 75% of costs where the proposed project would occur in one of the priority communities. A new provision would also permit the Secretary to use up to 5% of appropriated broadband funds for technical training and assistance in developing broadband projects and preparing applications.

The Senate bill makes changes to the Rural Economic Development Loan and Grant Program by amending its source of funding, the "cushion-of-credit" account. The bill would terminate further deposits into the cushion-of-credit accounts in FY2019 and modify the interest rate structure that borrowers receive on their cushion-of-credit accounts. The provision also provides new mandatory and discretionary spending authorization of $5 million each in FY2022 and FY2023.

The Senate bill also amends the Consolidated Farm and Rural Development Act to establish a new grant program for the purpose of providing technical assistance and training to support funding applications for programs carried out under the Rural Business-Cooperative Service. The grants could be used to assist communities in identifying and planning for business and economic development needs, to prepare applications for financial assistance for small and emerging businesses, and to prepare reports and surveys necessary to request financial assistance for businesses in rural communities.

In reauthorizing the Distance Learning and Telemedicine Program and the Community Facilities Program, the Senate bill reserves 20% of the appropriation for each program to finance assistance for substance abuse disorder prevention and treatment services. In further addressing substance abuse disorder treatment and prevention, the Senate bill would amend rural health and safety education programs to add a new grant program on substance abuse and disorder education and prevention.

Research[18]

USDA is authorized under four major laws to conduct agricultural research at the federal level and to provide support for cooperative research, extension, and postsecondary agricultural education programs in the states through formula funds and competitive grants to land-grant universities (see Table 10). The House bill reauthorizes funding for these activities through FY2023, subject to annual appropriations.

With respect to the land-grant entities, the House bill authorizes a new scholarship program for the 1890 land-grant institutions. A provision in the bill would also prohibit any further entities from being designated as eligible to receive formula funding under the Hatch Act (24 Stat. 440), Smith-Lever Act (P.L. 63-95), and McIntire-Stennis Act (P.L. 87-788). Permissible indirect cost recovery for federal funding of agricultural research and extension would increase to 30% from 22% of funding.

[18] This section was written by Tadlock Cowan, Analyst in Natural Resources and Rural Development.

Under the House bill, several new research areas in the High Priority Research and Extension program are designated as high priorities: macadamia tree health, national turfgrass research, fertilizer management, cattle fever ticks, and laying hen and turkey research. The bill also reauthorizes the Organic Agriculture Research and Extension Initiative and increases mandatory funding levels to $30 million annually for FY2019-FY2023. The Specialty Crop Research Initiative (SCRI) would be reauthorized through FY2023 and continues to include carve-out funding for the Emergency Citrus Disease Research and Extension Program. SCRI also expands program eligibility to include "size-controlling rootstock systems for perennial crops" and "emerging and invasive species," among other production practices and technologies.

The Senate bill would provide new programs for the 1890 land-grant institutions and 1994 tribal colleges of agriculture, authorize new support for urban and indoor agricultural production, authorize new funding for industrial hemp research and development, and authorize an initiative supporting advanced agricultural research. Other provisions reauthorize and extend national genetic resources programs, the Organic Agriculture and Extension Initiative, and SCRI. The research title also makes changes to the Foundation for Food and Agriculture Research and reauthorizes several programs relating to agricultural biosecurity.

The Senate bill would create a new scholarship program for students attending 1890 universities. Authorized grants are for young African American students who commit to pursuing a career in the food and agricultural sciences. Another provision of the bill would also establish at least three Centers of Excellence, each to be led by an 1890 institution. The centers would concentrate research and extension activities in one or more defined areas, including nutrition, wellness and health, farming systems and rural prosperity, global food security and defense, natural resources, energy and the environment, and emerging technologies. A similar program, New Beginnings for Tribal Students, would offer competitive grants to 1994 tribal agriculture colleges to support recruiting, tuition, experiential learning, student services, counseling, and academic advising to increase the retention and graduation rates of tribal students at 1994 land-grant colleges. Another provision would also make 1994 tribal colleges that offer an associate's degree or a baccalaureate eligible to participate in McIntire-Stennis forestry research support.

Several provisions in the Senate bill authorize research and development funding for industrial hemp production. Under the Critical Agricultural Materials Act, hemp would be included as an industrial product eligible for support. Amending and expanding a provision in the 2014 farm bill (Section 7606, P.L. 113-79), the Senate bill would direct the Secretary to conduct a study of hemp production pilot programs to determine the economic viability of domestic production and sale of hemp. A new provision would also create a "Hemp Production" subtitle under the Agricultural Marketing Act of 1946, expanding the existing statutory definition of *hemp* and expanding eligibility to other producers and groups, including tribes and territories. States or Indian tribes wanting primary regulatory authority over hemp production would be required to implement a plan with specific requirements to further monitor and regulate their production of hemp.

Two provisions of the research title in the Senate bill would create new programs supporting advanced agricultural research and urban, indoor, and emerging agricultural production systems. The Agriculture Advanced Research and Development Authority (AGARDA) would be established as a component of the Office of the Chief Scientist to examine the applicability for advanced research and development in food and agriculture through a pilot program that targets long-term and high-risk research. Focal areas include acceleration of novel, early stage innovative agricultural research; prototype testing; and licensing and product approval under the Plant Protection Act and the Animal Health Protection Act, among other innovative research tools that might be used in the discovery, development, or manufacture of a food or agricultural product.

The Secretary would develop and make publicly available a strategic plan setting forth the agenda that AGARDA would follow and provide for consultation with other federal research agencies; the National Academies of Sciences, Engineering, and Medicine; and others. There are provisions to expedite contract and grant awards and the appointments of highly qualified scientists and research program managers without regard to certain statutes governing appointments in the competitive federal service.

To support the agenda of the AGARDA, the Senate bill would establish in the U.S. Treasury the Agriculture Advanced Research Development Fund, to be administered by the Chief Scientist. The fund would have an authorized appropriation of $10 million each year FY2019-FY2023. The program would terminate in FY2023.

The Senate bill would also authorize a new Urban, Indoor, and Emerging Agricultural Production, Research, Education, and Extension Initiative. The provision authorizes the Secretary to make competitive grants to facilitate development of urban and indoor agricultural production systems and emerging harvesting, packaging, and distribution systems and new markets. The grants could also support methods of remediating contaminated urban sites (e.g., brownfields); determining best practices in pest management; exploring new technologies to minimize energy, lighting systems, water, and other inputs for increased food production; and studying new crop varieties and agricultural products to connect to new markets. The provision provides mandatory and discretionary spending of $4 million and $10 million, respectively, for each year FY2019- FY2023. In addition, there is authorization of $14 million for a study of urban and indoor agriculture production under the 2017 Census of Agriculture, including data on community gardens, rooftop gardens, urban farms, and hydroponic and aquaponic farm facilities.

Forestry[19]

The Agriculture Committees have jurisdiction over forestry issues generally as well as over some National Forest System (NFS) lands managed by the USDA Forest Service (FS).[20] Previous farm bills have primarily addressed forestry research and programs to provide financial and technical assistance to nonfederal forest landowners, although more recent farm bills have also sometimes included provisions addressing management of federal forest land. The forestry title in both the House- and Senate-passed farm bills would establish, reauthorize, modify, and repeal several research and assistance programs (see Table 11). Both bills also contain several provisions that would address management of the NFS and the public lands managed by the Bureau of Land Management (BLM) in the Department of the Interior. While both bills include some similar provisions, there is also considerable variation between the House and Senate forestry titles.

Forestry assistance and research programs are primarily authorized under three main laws: the Cooperative Forestry Assistance Act,[21] the Forest and Rangeland Renewable Resources Research Act,[22] and the Healthy Forests Restoration Act.[23] Many forestry programs are permanently authorized to receive such sums as necessary in annual discretionary appropriations and thus do not require reauthorization in the farm bill. Some programs, however, are not permanently authorized and are set to expire in FY2018. The House bill would reauthorize, through FY2023, four assistance and research programs with authorizations expiring at the end of FY2018: Healthy Forest Reserve Program (HFRP), Rural Revitalization Technology program, National Forest Foundation (NFF), and Statewide Forest Resource Assessments. The Senate bill would reauthorize two of the same programs (HFRP and NFF)—but does not address the other two — and would reauthorize an additional program not addressed in the House bill (Rapid Insect and Disease Assessments). The House bill would amend two other programs by replacing their permanent authority to receive annual appropriations with an authorization limit and a FY2023 expiration (Forest Legacy and Community Forest and Open Space Conservation). The Senate bill does not address either of those same programs but would amend a different permanently authorized program with a sunset date of FY2023, although the authorization limit would remain the same as current law (Semiarid Agroforestry Research Center). The Senate bill would also repeal two programs (Biomass Commercial Utilization Program and the Biomass Energy Demonstration Project). Both the House and Senate bills would establish some new

---

19 This section was written by Katie Hoover, Specialist in Natural Resource Policy.

20 The Agriculture Committees have jurisdiction over any national forest not reserved from the public domain. The House Committee on Natural Resources and the Senate Committee on Energy and Natural Resources have jurisdiction over public lands generally, including national forests reserved from the public domain.

21 P.L. 95-313, 16 U.S.C. §§2101-2114.

22 P.L. 95-307, 16 U.S.C. §§1641 *et seq.*

23 P.L. 108-148, 16 U.S.C. §§6501-6591c. For more information on these programs, see CRS Report R45219, *Forest Service Assistance Programs*.

assistance programs—generally by providing explicit statutory authorization and congressional direction for current programs that are operating under existing, but broad, authorizations. For example, both bills would establish a Landscape Scale Restoration program to provide financial assistance for large restoration projects that cross landownership boundaries, although the specifics of each proposal differ.

The forestry title would also address issues related to the accumulation of biomass in many forests and the associated increased risk for uncharacteristic wildfires on both federal and nonfederal land. For example, both bills would provide various types of assistance for large hazardous fuel reduction projects that cross landownership boundaries. The Senate bill would authorize up to $20 million in annual appropriations to provide financial assistance to fund such projects. The House bill would encourage the Secretary of Agriculture to allocate existing funding and use existing authorities to provide assistance to encourage cross-boundary projects. Both the House and Senate bills would also establish, reauthorize, modify, and repeal research and assistance programs to promote wood innovation for energy use and building construction and to facilitate the removal of forest biomass, although the specifics of each proposal also differs.

The House and Senate bills would also change how FS and BLM comply with the requirements under the National Environmental Policy Act (NEPA)[24] and the consultation requirements under the Endangered Species Act[25] for specified management activities. For example, the House bill would establish 10 categorical exclusions (CEs) that would not be subject to the requirements to prepare an environmental assessment or environmental impact statement under NEPA. Six of the 10 apply to both FS and BLM actions, while four apply to just FS actions. The Senate bill would establish one CE for projects involving sage grouse mule deer habitat that is applicable to both FS and BLM. The House bill includes other related provisions, such as limiting the analysis requirements for specific projects and providing for expedited ESA consultations.

The forestry title also contains several provisions specific to the management of NFS lands. Both bills would address the authority provided in the 2014 farm bill to designate insect and disease treatment areas on NFS lands and procedures intended to expedite the environmental analysis for specified priority projects within those areas.[26] The House bill would expand the authorities in several ways, such as by adding hazardous fuels reduction as a priority project category and authorizing larger projects. The Senate bill would require FS to apply specific procedures when implementing the CE. In addition, both bills would also reauthorize the Collaborative Forest Landscape Restoration Program to receive appropriations through FY2023. The Senate bill would raise the

---

[24] P.L. 91-109, 42 U.S.C. §§4321-4347. For more information on NEPA, see CRS Report RL33152, *The National Environmental Policy Act (NEPA): Background and Implementation*.

[25] P.L. 93-205, 16 U.S.C. §1531 *et seq*. For more information, see CRS Report RL31654, *The Endangered Species Act: A Primer*.

[26] For more information on the forestry provisions in the 2014 farm bill, see CRS Report R43431, *Forestry Provisions in the 2014 Farm Bill (P.L. 113-79)*.

authorized level, while the House bill would modify the terms of the program. In addition to other NFS management provisions, both bills would also authorize the conveyance of NFS land through lease, sale, or exchange. While both bills include conveyance provisions for specific parcels, the Senate bill would also reauthorize and establish other disposal authorities.[27] The Senate bill would establish two watershed protection programs on NFS lands and would authorize the Secretary to accept cash or in-kind donations from specified nonfederal partners to implement projects associated with one of those programs. The Senate bill would also designate wilderness areas on NFS lands in Virginia and Tennessee.

The bills would address miscellaneous federal and tribal forest management issues. For example, both bills would expand the availability of Good Neighbor Agreements (GNA) to include federally recognized Indian tribes and county governments. The Senate bill would make any revenue generated from GNA projects exempt from any revenue-sharing laws. The House bill, in contrast, does not include that provision and would remove a similar exemption to revenue derived from Stewardship Contracts. The House bill would also direct the Secretary of Agriculture to exempt unprocessed dead and dying trees on NFS lands in California from the export prohibition for 10 years and would amend provisions of the Secure Rural Schools and Community Self-Determination Act of 2000,[28] a program that authorizes payments to counties containing NFS lands and certain BLM lands, among other provisions.

Energy[29]

Both the House and Senate bills (included within Title VI in the House bill and designated as Title IX in the Senate bill) modify the energy title. Both bills extend most of the energy title programs through FY2023. One of the key differences between the bills is that the House bill provides no mandatory funding, while the Senate bill retains mandatory funding (see Table 12).

The House bill addresses energy programs in three key ways—it reauthorizes many of the programs, it changes the placement of the programs within the farm bill, and it modifies the type of funding available for the programs. The House bill extends most of these programs through FY2023. In prior farm bills, the energy programs were included in a separate title (e.g., Title IX of the 2014 farm bill). But the House-passed bill includes

[27] For more information on FS land disposal, see CRS Report RL34273, *Federal Land Ownership: Acquisition and Disposal Authorities*.

[28] P.L. 106-393, 16 U.S.C. §§7101-7153. For more information, see Reauthorizing the Secure Rural Schools and Community Self-Determination Act of 2000.

[29] This section was written by Kelsi Bracmort, Specialist in Natural Resources and Energy Policy.

these programs within the title on Rural Development and Economic Development (i.e., Subtitle E of Title VI). In prior farm bills, many of these programs were provided with mandatory funding. For instance, the 2014 farm bill authorized a total of $694 million in mandatory funding and a total of $765 million in discretionary funding. In contrast, the House bill provides discretionary funding, but not mandatory funding, for the energy title programs.

The Senate bill maintains a separate energy title (Title IX), amends certain programs, and establishes a new biogas research initiative and a new carbon utilization education program. The bill modifies the definitions for biobased product, biorefinery, and renewable energy systems. It extends most of the programs through FY2023. Additionally, it provides mandatory funding for seven programs—the Biobased Markets Program, the Biorefinery Assistance Program, the Bioenergy Program for Advanced Biofuels, the Rural Energy for America Program, the Biomass Research and Development Initiative, the Biomass Crop Assistance Program, and the newly established carbon utilization education program—amounting to approximately $640 million over five years.

The two bills have similarities as well as differences. For instance, unlike the House bill, the Senate Agriculture Committee bill repeals the Repowering Assistance Program. Similar to the House bill, the Senate bill modifies the Biobased Markets Program to restrict federal agencies from placing certain limitations on the procurement of bio-based products. Additionally, unlike the House bill, the Senate bill expands the focus of the Biomass Research and Development Initiative to include carbon dioxide utilization and sequestration. The Senate bill would also establish a biogas research and adoption of biogas systems initiative and directs the Secretary of Agriculture to form an Interagency Biogas Opportunities Task Force and to partner with the National Renewable Laboratory to conduct a biogas study, among other things. The Senate bill also establishes a Carbon Utilization Education Program that provides competitive funding for eligible entities to provide education about the benefits of carbon utilization and sequestration.

Horticulture[30]

The House and Senate farm bills reauthorize many of the existing farm bill provisions supporting farming operations in the specialty crop, certified organic agriculture, and local foods sectors. These provisions (Title IX in the House bill and Title X in the Senate bill) cover several programs and provisions benefitting these sectors, including block grants to states, support for farmers markets, data and information collection, education on food safety and biotechnology, and organic certification, among

[30] This section was written by Renée Johnson, Specialist in Agricultural Policy.

other market development and promotion provisions (see Table 13). The Senate bill includes a number of provisions regarding industrial hemp within the bill's Horticulture title but also includes hemp-specific provision in the Research, Crop Insurance, and Miscellaneous titles of the bill. The House bill does not include comparable hemp provisions, but it would amend certain regulatory requirements under some federal statutes that are not contained in the Senate bill.

The House and Senate bills make changes both to farmers markets and local foods promotion programs but in fundamentally different ways. The House bill eliminates mandatory CCC funding for the Farmers Market Promotion Program (FMPP) and Local Food Promotion Program (LFPP) while reauthorizing discretionary appropriations for these programs of $30 million annually for FY2019-FY2023.[31] The Senate bill combines and expands the existing FMPP and LFPP, along with the Value-Added Agricultural Product Market Development Grants program, to create a new "Local Agriculture Market Program" with expanded mission and mandatory funding of $60 million for FY2019 and each year thereafter, plus authorized appropriations. The Senate bill also includes several provisions from S. 3005 (Urban Agriculture Act of 2018) supporting urban agriculture development (including new programs and funding in the Miscellaneous, Research, Conservation, and Crop Insurance titles).

The two bills differ in addressing funding for USDA's National Organic Program (NOP) and related programs. Both bills address concerns about organic import integrity by including provisions that strengthen the tracking, data collection, and investigation of organic product imports, including certain provisions in H.R. 3871 (Organic Farmer and Consumer Protection Act of 2017). Both bills also amend the eligibility and consultation requirements of the National Organic Standards Board, among other changes. Both bills reauthorize NOP appropriations above current levels while reauthorizing current funding for the Organic Production and Market Data Initiatives and for technology upgrades to improve tracking and verification of organic imports. The Senate bill also reauthorizes current mandatory funding for the National Organic Certification Cost Share Program, which the House bill does not reauthorize (although the program remains authorized).

The Senate bill includes a number of provisions from the introduced versions of the Hemp Farming Act of 2018 (S. 2667; H.R. 5485) that are intended to facilitate the possible commercial cultivation of hemp in the United States. Chief among these provisions is one that would amend the Controlled Substances Act (21 U.S.C. 802(16)) to exclude from the statutory definition of *marijuana* industrial hemp, as defined in the 2014 farm bill (P.L. 113-79, §7606), as containing no more than a 0.3% concentration of delta-9 tetrahydrocannabinol—marijuana's primary psychoactive chemical. The Senate farm

[31] The House bill takes a similar approach in Title VI with funding for the Value-Added Producer Grant (VAPG) program, which broadly benefits specialty crop and local food producers. The 2014 farm bill provided $63 million in mandatory funding for VAPG to remain available until expended. The House bill amends authorizations for discretionary appropriation, providing $50 million in annual appropriations (FY2019-FY2023) with no additional mandatory funding.

bill also creates a new hemp program under the Agricultural Marketing Act of 1946 (7 U.S.C. §1621 *et seq.*) expanding the existing statutory definition of hemp and also expanding eligibility to other producers and groups, including tribes and territories. States or Indian tribes that seek primary regulatory authority over hemp production would be required to implement a "plan" to further monitor and regulate hemp production. Other provisions in the bill's Crop Insurance title would make hemp producers eligible to participate in federal crop insurance programs, while provisions in the Research title of the bill would make hemp production eligible for certain USDA research and development programs.

The House bill includes several exemptions from certain regulatory requirements, amending existing provisions in the Federal Insecticide, Fungicide, and Rodenticide Act (FIFRA, 7 U.S.C. 136 *et seq.*), the Clean Water Act (33 U.S.C. §1251 *et seq.*), the Plant Protection Act (7 U.S.C. 7701 *et seq.*), and the Occupational Safety and Health Act (OSHA, 29 U.S.C. 651 *et seq.*). The House bill amends FIFRA to clarify federal and state roles in the regulation of pesticides to exempt certain pesticide discharges from point source discharge permitting requirements and to expressly state that the Environmental Protection Agency is not required to consult with other federal agencies regarding pesticide registrations and their potential impact on endangered species. It would also enact into law the House-passed H.R. 1029, the Pesticide Registration Improvement Enhancement Act of 2017, which would amend FIFRA to extend the authority to collect pesticide fees, among other purposes.[32] Finally, the House bill amends the Plant Protection Act regarding the use of methyl bromide in response to an emergency event and also amends the Occupational Health and Safety Administration to exempt agricultural retailers from process safety management requirements. These provisions are not included in the Senate bill.

Provisions affecting the specialty crop and certified organic sectors are not limited to the Horticulture title but are contained within several other titles. Among these are programs in the Research, Nutrition, and Trade titles, among others. Related programs outside the Horticulture title include the Specialty Crop Research Initiative, the Organic Agriculture Research and Extension Initiative, the Fresh Fruit and Vegetable Program, and Section 32 purchases for fruits and vegetables under the Nutrition title, among other farm bill programs.

[32] The Senate version of H.R. 2 does not include a similar provision. On June 28, 2018, the Senate passed an amendment to H.R. 1029.

Crop Insurance[33]

Crop insurance is designed to cover economic losses from a variety of natural causes as well as certain adverse market developments. The federal crop insurance program makes available subsidized crop insurance to producers who purchase policies to protect against losses in yield, crop revenue, margin, whole farm revenue, and other losses.

The House- and Senate-passed versions of the Crop Insurance title of H.R. 2 (Title X in the House bill and Title XI in the Senate bill) largely modify different provisions of the Federal Crop Insurance Act, the underlying statute that permanently authorizes the federal crop insurance program (see Table 14). Section 508(d) of the act (7 U.S.C. §1508(d))—which authorizes the Federal Crop Insurance Corporation (FCIC) to provide performance-based premium discounts to producers with "good insurance or production experience relative to other producers" of the same crop in the same area—is modified by both the House- and Senate-passed versions but in different ways.

The House-passed farm bill repeals Section 508(d) in its entirety, effectively removing authority for performance-based discounts for producers. In contrast, the Senate-passed farm bill expands FCIC's authority to offer discounts for practices that can be demonstrated to reduce risk relative to other practices. For the 2020 reinsurance year, under the Senate-passed farm bill, FCIC would have to specifically consider providing discounts for precision irrigation or fertilization, crop rotations, and cover crops.

House-Passed Farm Bill

The Crop Insurance title of the House-passed farm bill makes several modifications to the existing federal crop insurance program. According to CBO, it would decrease authorized spending for crop insurance relative to baseline levels by $70 million during the FY2019-FY2023 period by eliminating the crop insurance education and information program for targeted states carried out by the Risk Management Agency and the Agricultural Management Assistance program.

Additional savings would be achieved by increasing the administrative fee for catastrophic risk protection from $300 per crop per county to $500 and from provisions that would eliminate several past research and development (R&D) priorities, discontinue R&D partnerships, and reduce CCC funding for R&D contracting from $12.5 million to no more than $8 million annually.

Among other adjustments, the House farm bill expands coverage for forage and grazing by allowing separate crop insurance policies to be purchased for crops that can be both grazed and mechanically harvested on the same acres during the same growing season. Such separate policies can be independently indemnified for each intended use.

---

[33] This section was written by Isabel Rosa, Analyst in Agricultural Policy.

Also, *beginning farmer or rancher* is redefined as an individual having actively operated and managed a farm or ranch for less than 10 years, thus making these individuals eligible for federal subsidy benefits available for the purposes of research, development, and implementation of whole-farm insurance plans.

Crops for which the producer has elected ARC or that are enrolled in stacked income protection would be ineligible for coverage based on an area yield and loss basis or for the supplemental coverage option. The House farm bill also clarifies requirements for FCIC approval of reimbursement for the development of private submissions for modifying old plans of insurance or creating new ones.

Miscellaneous[34]

The Miscellaneous title of House-passed H.R. 2 contains seven subtitles: Livestock; Beginning, Socially Disadvantaged, and Veteran Producers; Textiles; United States Grain Standards Act; Noninsured Crop Disaster Assistance Program; Protect Interstate Commerce; and Other Matters. The Senate-passed H.R. 2, as amended, contains six subtitles: Livestock; Agriculture and Food Defense; Historically Underserved Producers; Department of Agriculture Reorganization Act of 1994, Amendments; Other Miscellaneous Provisions; and General Provisions. The provisions in the title—38 in the House bill and 82 in the Senate bill—cover a wide array of issues, with some overlapping provisions (see Table 15).

Both bills would establish an animal disease preparedness program and a vaccine bank that prioritizes the acquisition of foot-and-mouth disease vaccine. A key difference in the bills is funding. The House-passed bill would provide a combined $250 million in mandatory funding for the preparedness program and vaccine bank in FY2019, and $50 million for FY2020-2023. It also authorizes appropriations of $15 million for the National Animal Health Laboratory Network (NAHLN) each year FY2019-FY2023. The Senate-passed bill authorizes appropriations only for such sums as necessary for the preparedness and vaccine programs and authorizes appropriations of $30 million per year FY2019-FY2023 for the NAHLN.

The provisions in the House- and Senate-passed bills would expand USDA activities for beginning, socially disadvantaged, and veteran farmers and ranchers. Both the House and the Senate bills would prioritize youth agricultural employment and volunteer programs and promote the role of youth-serving organizations and school-based agricultural education programs. The House bill would create a Commission on Farm Transition to study issues affecting the transition of farm operations from established farmers and ranchers to the next generation. The Senate bill would establish a Tribal

[34] This section was written by Joel Greene, Analyst in Agricultural Policy.

Advisory Committee to advise USDA on tribal and Indian affairs. The House-passed bill provides $43 million (FY2019-FY2023) for the Outreach and Assistance to Socially Disadvantaged Producers program, and the Senate-passed bill provides $216 million (FY2019-FY2023) for the Farming Opportunities and Outreach Training program.

Both the House-passed and Senate-passed bills amend parts of current law to account for USDA reorganizational changes that created the Under Secretary for Trade and Foreign Agricultural Affairs, the Under Secretary for Farm Production and Conservation, and the Assistant to the Secretary for Rural Development. However, the Senate bill requires USDA to re-establish the position of Under Secretary of Agriculture for Rural Development that USDA abolished and replaced with an Assistant to the Secretary for Rural Development in its May 2017 reorganization. The Senate bill would also prohibit USDA from closing Natural Resource Conservation Service field offices without notifying the House and Senate agricultural committees.

Both bills would amend parts of NAP. The House bill would amend NAP crop eligibility to include crops that may be covered by crop insurance but only under whole farm policies. It would raise the service fees and reauthorize buy-up coverage through crop year 2023. The Senate bill would add data collection and coordination requirements, raise the service fee, and delete the sunset provision for buy-up coverage.

The House-passed bill would repeal the trust funds for the Pima Agriculture Cotton and Agriculture Wool Apparel Manufacturers. It would also repeal the Wool Research and Promotion grant funding program. In place of these funds, the House-passed bill would establish the Textile Trust Fund to reduce injury for domestic users of imported pima cotton and wool fabric in the event that tariffs on those products exceed the tariffs on certain finished imported pima cotton and wool apparel. Instead of establishing a new Textile Trust Fund, the Senate-passed bill would reauthorize the existing Pima and Wool trust funds and reauthorize the Wool Research and Promotion grant funding.

Both bills include animal welfare provisions on importing dogs and on the slaughter of dogs and cats for human consumption. The House bill would extend provisions banning animal fighting to U.S. territories. Both bills would establish a Century Farms Program under the Secretary that recognizes farms in continuous operation for at least 100 years and add South Carolina to the Virginia/Carolina region of the Peanut Standards Board.

The Protect Interstate Commerce provisions in the House-passed bill would prohibit a state or local government from setting standards or conditions on agricultural commodities produced in another state if the commodities are produced or manufactured in accordance with federal or state laws and regulations. The bill provides that producers, consumers, trade associations, governments, and other agents may bring an action against the standard or condition in the appropriate court. The Senate-passed bill does not include these provisions.

PROVISIONS OF THE HOUSE- AND SENATE-PASSED BILLS (H.R. 2) BY TITLE, COMPARED WITH CURRENT LAW

Table 4. Commodities

Current Law/Policy	House-Passed Bill (H.R. 2)	Senate-Passed Bill (H.R. 2)
Commodity Program Terms		
Actual crop revenue. The amount determined by the Secretary under the Agriculture Risk Coverage (ARC) program for each covered commodity for a crop year. **(7 U.S.C. 9011(1))**	Same as current law. **(§1111(1))**.	Continues current law.
ARC. Coverage provided under the ARC program. **(7 U.S.C. 9011(2))**	Same as current law. **(§1111(2))**.	Continues current law.
ARC guarantee. The amount determined by the Secretary under the ARC program for each covered commodity for a crop year. **(7 U.S.C. 9011(3))**	Same as current law. **(§1111(3))**.	Continues current law.
Base acres. For purposes of calculating farm program payments, base acres are the number of historical program acres of a specific covered commodity on a farm as established under the 2008 farm bill, as in effect on September 30, 2013 (except upland cotton), subject to adjustments (see 7 U.S.C. 90112 below). **(7 U.S.C. 9011(4))**	Individual crop-specific base acres are retained, as in effect as under the 2014 farm bill subject to any reallocation, adjustment, or reduction as described in Section 1112. **(§1111(4))**	Continues current law.
County coverage. Type of coverage under the ARC program to be obtained by the producer at the county level. **(7 U.S.C. 9011(5))**	No comparable definition.	Continues current law.
Covered commodities. Wheat, oats, and barley (including wheat, oats, and barley used for haying and grazing), corn, grain sorghum, long- grain rice, medium-grain rice, pulse crops, soybeans, other oilseeds, and peanuts. Effective beginning with the 2018 crop year, the term *covered commodity* includes seed cotton. **(7 U.S.C. 9011(6))**	Wheat, oats, and barley (including wheat, oats, and barley used for haying and grazing), corn, grain sorghum, long-grain rice, medium-grain rice, pulse crops, soybeans, other oilseeds, seed cotton, and peanuts. **(§1111(5))**	Continues current law.
Effective price. The price calculated by the Secretary under the Price Loss Coverage (PLC) program for each covered commodity for a crop year to determine whether PLC payments are required to be provided for that crop year. **(7 U.S.C. 9011(7))**	Same as current law. **(§1111(6))**.	Continues current law.

Current Law/Policy	House-Passed Bill (H.R. 2)	Senate-Passed Bill (H.R. 2)
No comparable definition.	**Effective reference price.** The term *effective reference price*, with respect to a covered commodity for a crop year, means the lesser of the following: (A) 115% of the reference price for such covered commodity; or (B) the greater of (i) the reference price for such covered commodity or (ii) 85% of the average of the marketing year average price of the covered commodity for the most recent five crop years, excluding each of the crop years with the highest and lowest marketing year average price. **(§1111(7))**	No comparable definition.
Extra long staple (ELS) cotton. Cotton that (A) is produced from pure strain varieties of the Barbadense species or any hybrid of the species or other similar types of ELS cotton, designated by the Secretary, having characteristics needed for various end uses for which U.S. upland cotton is not suitable, and grown in irrigated or other designated U.S. cotton- growing regions; and (B) is ginned on a roller-type gin or other authorized gin for experimental purposes. **(7 U.S.C. 9011(8))**	Same as current law. **(§1111(8))**.	Continues current law.
Generic base acres. The amount of cotton base acres in effect under the 2008 farm bill, as adjusted pursuant to Section 1101 of such act, as of September 30, 2013 **(7 U.S.C. 9011(9))**, subject to any adjustment or reduction. **(7 U.S.C. 9012(d))**.	No comparable provision. Generic base acres are indirectly retained via retention of base acres as under prior law by Section 1111(4). Base acres are discussed further in Section 1112.	Continues current law.
Individual coverage. Type of coverage selected by a producer under the ARC program at the farm (not county) level. **(7 U.S.C. 9011(10))**	No comparable definition.	Continues current law.
No comparable definition. Instead, the full text "national average market price received by producers during the 12-month marketing year" for a covered commodity is used in the PLC and ARC programs.	**Marketing year average price (MYAP).** The national average market price received by producer during the 12-month marketing year for a covered commodity. **(§1111(9))**	No comparable definition.
Medium-grain rice. Includes short grain rice and temperate japonica rice. **(7 U.S.C. 9011(11))**	Same as current law. **(§1111(10))**	Continues current law.
Other oilseed. A crop of sunflower seed, rapeseed, canola, safflower, flaxseed, mustard seed, crambe, sesame seed, or, if designated by the Secretary, another oilseed. **(7 U.S.C. 9011(12))**	Same as current law. **(§1111(11))**	Continues current law.

Table 4. (Continued)

Current Law/Policy	House-Passed Bill (H.R. 2)	Senate-Passed Bill (H.R. 2)
Payment acres. The number of acres for a farm, as determined under 7 U.S.C. 9014, that are eligible for payments under the PLC or ARC programs. **(7 U.S.C. 9011(13))**	Same as current law. **(§1111(12))**	Continues current law.
Payment yield. For a covered commodity, the yield used to make counter-cyclical payments under the 2008 farm bill as in effect on September 30, 2013, or the yield established under the PLC program. **(7 U.S.C.9011(14))**	For a covered commodity, the yield used to make PLC payments under the 2014 farm bill or the yield established in Section 1113. **(§1111(13))**	Continues current law.
Price Loss Coverage (PLC). Coverage provided under the PLC program. **(7 U.S.C. 9011(15))**	Same as current law. **(§1111(14))**	Continues current law.
Producer. Generally, an owner, operator, landlord, tenant, or sharecropper that shares in the risk of producing a crop and is entitled to share in the crop available for marketing from the farm or would have shared had the crop been produced. For a grower of hybrid seed, the existence of a hybrid seed contract and other program rules shall not adversely affect the ability to receive a payment. **(7 U.S.C. 9011(16))**	Same as current law. **(§1111(15))**	Continues current law.
Pulse crop. Dry peas, lentils, small chickpeas, and large chickpeas. **(7 U.S.C. 9011(17))**	Same as current law. **(§1111(16))**	Continues current law.
Reference prices: With respect to a covered commodity for a crop year: • For wheat, $5.50 per bushel (bu.). • For corn, $3.70 per bu. • For grain sorghum, $3.95 per bu. • For barley, $4.95 per bu. • For oats, $2.40 per bu. • For long-grain rice, $14.00 per hundredweight (cwt). • For medium-grain rice, $14.00 per cwt. • For soybeans, $8.40 per bu. • For other oilseeds, $20.15 per cwt. • For peanuts, $535.00 per ton. • For dry peas, $11.00 per cwt. • For lentils, $19.97 per cwt. • For small chickpeas, $19.04 per cwt. • For large chickpeas, $21.54 per cwt. • For seed cotton, $0.367 per lb. **(7 U.S.C. 9011(18))**	Same as current law (Section 1111(17)) but with the following addition: **Reference price for temperate japonica rice.** To reflect price premiums, the reference price for temperate japonica rice equals $14.00 per cwt., as adjusted by the formula for calculating the effective reference price (Section 1111(17)) multiplied by the ratio of the simple average of the MYAP of medium-grain rice from crop years 2012-2016 divided by the simple average of the MYAP of all rice from crop years 2012-2016. **(§1116(g))**	Continues current law.

Current Law/Policy	House-Passed Bill (H.R. 2)	Senate-Passed Bill (H.R. 2)
Secretary. The Secretary of Agriculture. **(7 U.S.C. 9011(19))**	Same as current law. **(§1111(18))**	Continues current law.
Seed cotton. Unginned upland cotton that includes both lint and seed. **(7 U.S.C. 9011(20))**	Same as current law. **(§1111(19))**	Continues current law.
State. Each of the U.S. states, the District of Columbia, the Commonwealth of Puerto Rico, and any other U.S. territory or possession. **(7 U.S.C. 9011(21))**	Same as current law. **(§1111(20))**	Continues current law.
Temperate japonica rice. Rice that is grown in high altitudes or temperate regions of high latitudes with cooler climate conditions in the Western United States, as determined by the Secretary, for the purpose of the reallocation of base acres, the establishment of a reference price and an effective price, and the determination of the actual crop revenue and ARC guarantee. **(7 U.S.C. 9011(22))**	Same as current law. **(§1111(21))**	Continues current law.
Transitional yield. Defined in Section 502(b) of the Federal Crop Insurance Act **(7 U.S.C. 502(b)(11))** as the maximum average production per acre or equivalent measure that is assigned to acreage for a crop year by the Federal Crop Insurance Corporation (FCIC) whenever the producer fails to certify that acceptable documentation of production and acreage for the crop year is in the possession of the producer or present the acceptable documentation. **(7 U.S.C. 9011(23))**	Same as current law. **(§1111(22))**	Continues current law.
United States. When used in a geographical sense, all of the states. **(7 U.S.C. 9011(24))**	Same as current law. **(§1111(23))**	Continues current law.
United States premium factor. The percentage by which the difference in the U.S. loan schedule premiums for Strict Middling 1 1/8- inch upland cotton and for Middling 1 3/32-inch upland cotton exceeds the difference in the applicable premiums for comparable international qualities. **(7 U.S.C. 9011(25)).**	Same as current law. **(§1111(24))**	Continues current law.
PLC and ARC Programs		
Base Acres		
One-time reallocation of base acres among covered commodities. Crop-specific base acres were subject to a producer's one-time choice to retain base acres or undertake a reallocation of total farm base acres among covered	No comparable provision. Base acres (subject to the 2014-farm-bill's one-time reallocation choice) are included through the retention of crop-specific base acres under prior law. **(§1114(a))**	Continues current law.

Table 4. (Continued)

Current Law/Policy	House-Passed Bill (H.R. 2)	Senate-Passed Bill (H.R. 2)
commodities based on average shares of planted base by commodity during the 2009-2012 period. Generic base acres are retained and may not be reallocated. **(7 U.S.C. 9012(a))**		
Seed cotton base acres. Not later than May 10, 2018, the Secretary shall require the owner of a farm to allocate all generic base acres based on whether the farm has a recent history of covered commodities (including seed cotton) being planted or prevented from being planted during the 2009-2016 crop years. If a farm has no such recent history, then the farm owner allocates the farm's generic base to unassigned crop base for which no ARC or PLC payments may be made. If a farm has such a recent history, then the farm owner allocates the farm's generic base among seed cotton and other covered commodities as (A) to seed cotton base acres in a quantity equal to the greater of 80% of generic base acres or the average of seed cotton acres planted or prevented from being planted on the farm during the 2009-2012 crop years (not to exceed the farm's total generic base acres) or (B) to commodity-specific base acres in proportion to each crop's share of planted (or prevented from being planted) acreage during 2009 to 2012. Following the base allocation under either (A) or (B), any residual generic base acres shall be allocated to unassigned crop base for which no ARC or PLC payments may be made. If a farm owner fails to make an election for generic base, then the farm owner shall be deemed to have elected to allocate all generic base acres in accordance with formulation (A) above. **(7 U.S.C. 9014(b)(4))**	No comparable provision. Seed cotton base acres are included indirectly through the retention of crop-specific base acres under prior law. **(§1114(a))**	Continues current law.
Adjustments to base. Base acres are increased/decreased when land leaves/enters conservation programs **(7 U.S.C. 9012(b))**.	The same as current law. **(§1112(a))**	Continues current law.
Prevention of excess base acres. Base is reduced if the sum of the base acres for the farm (including any new oilseed acreage and generic base acres) plus any acreage in the Conservation Reserve Program (CRP) or the Wetlands Reserve	The same as current law. **(§1112(b))**	Continues current law with technical correction to add specificity on originating authority of CRP and wetland reserve easements under the

Current Law/Policy	House-Passed Bill (H.R. 2)	Senate-Passed Bill (H.R. 2)
Program (WRP) (or any other federal conservation program that makes payments in exchange for not producing a crop) exceeds the actual cropland acreage on the farm. An exception shall be made in the case of certain double-cropped acreage as determined by the Secretary. The owner of the farm shall be given an opportunity to select the base acres that will be reduced. **(7 U.S.C. 9012(c))**		Agricultural Conservation Easement Program. **(§1709(a))**
Reduction of base acres. The farm owner may reduce, at any time, base acres for any covered commodity. Such reduction shall be permanent. Base is reduced proportionately when acreage has been subdivided and developed for multiple residential units or other nonfarming uses. **(7 U.S.C. 9012(d))**	Reduction of base acres is the same as current law **(§1112(c)(1-2))** but with two additional provisions under Section 1112(c)(3) and Section 1112(c)(4).	Continues current law.
No comparable provision.	**Treatment of unplanted base.** If no base acres are planted to a covered commodity during the period January 1, 2009, to December 31, 2017, then all the base acres on that farm are allocated to unassigned crop base for which no payment shall be made. **(§1112(c)(3))**	No comparable provision.
No comparable provision.	**Reconstitution of farm to expand base.** The Secretary shall ensure that a farm may not be reconstituted after the date of enactment of this section to alter the treatment of base acres. **(§1112(c)(4))**	No comparable provision.
Payment Yields		
Payment yields. For making PLC program payments, all covered commodities must use a program yield to derive a per-acre payment rate. In this regard, the Secretary shall establish a program yield for each farm for any designated oilseed for which a payment yield was not established under Section 1102 of the 2008 farm bill **(7 U.S.C. 9013(a))**; for designated oilseeds, such a payment yield on a farm equals the product of the average yield per planted acre for the 1998-2001 crop years (excluding years in which acreage planted was zero) and the ratio of the national average yield for the 1981-1985 crops and the national average yield for the 1998-2001 crops. If the yield per planted acre for a designated oilseed for any of the 1998-2001 crop years was less	To make PLC payments, this provision continues the Secretary's authority to establish payment yields for each farm for any designated oilseed that does not have a payment yield under the 014 farm bill. The payment yield is calculated as 90% of the most recent five-year-average yield (excluding any year in which the yield was zero). Provides that this subsection only applies to oilseeds designated after the date of enactment of the Agriculture and Nutrition Act of 2018. **(§1113(a))**	Continues current law

Table 4. (Continued)

Current Law/Policy	House-Passed Bill (H.R. 2)	Senate-Passed Bill (H.R. 2)
than 75% of the county yield for that designated oilseed, the Secretary shall assign a yield "plug" for that crop year equal to 75% of the county yield. **(7 U.S.C. 9013(b))** For other covered commodities, see the discussion under 7 U.S.C. 9013 (c)-(e).		
Absence of payment yield. In the case of a covered commodity on a farm for which base acres have been established or that is planted on generic base acres, if no payment yield has been established, the Secretary shall establish an appropriate payment yield by taking into consideration the farm program payment yields applicable to that covered commodity for similarly situated farms. The use of such data in an appeal, by the Secretary or by the producer, shall not be subject to any other provision of law. **(7 U.S.C. 9013(c))**	Authorizes the Secretary to establish a payment yield if no payment yield is otherwise established for a covered commodity using the program payment yields of similarly situated farms. **(§1113(b))**	Continues current law
Updating payment yields. The owner of a farm was given a one- time opportunity to update, on a covered commodity-by-covered- commodity basis, the payment yield used in calculating PLC payments for each covered commodity for which the PLC election was made. The election shall be made at a time and manner to be in effect beginning with the 2014 crop year as determined by the Secretary. The PLC payment yield update was equal to 90% of the average of the yield per planted acre for the covered commodity for the 2008-2012 crop years, excluding any crop year in which the acreage planted to the covered commodity was zero. If the yield for any of the 2008-2012 crop years was less than 75% of the average county yield, a "plug" yield was used for that crop year equal to 75% of the county average for 2008 to 2012. **(7 U.S.C. 9013(d))**	**Yield update for drought-affected counties.** Provides a one-time opportunity for a farm owner to update yields where the farm is located in a county that experienced 20 or more consecutive weeks of exceptional drought (rated D4 by the U.S. Drought Monitor) between January 1, 2008, and December 31, 2012. On a covered-commodity by covered-commodity basis, yields may be updated as 90% of average yield per planted acre for 2013-2017 crop years. If the farm-level yield is less than 75% of the average county yield for a covered commodity for any of the years (excluding any year in which the yield was zero), then the Secretary shall assign 75% of the 2013-2017 average county yield for the covered commodity for that crop year. The election must be made prior to the 2019 crop year. **(§1113(c))**	Continues current law
Payment yield for seed cotton. The payment yield for seed cotton for a farm shall be equal to 2.4 times the payment yield for upland cotton for the farm established under the 2008 farm bill, as in effect on September 30, 2013.	The average yield for seed cotton per planted acre equals 2.4 times the average yield for upland cotton per planted acre. At the discretion of the owner of a farm that meets the drought criteria described in this	Continues current law

Current Law/Policy	House-Passed Bill (H.R. 2)	Senate-Passed Bill (H.R. 2)
At the sole discretion of the owner of a farm with an established yield for upland cotton, the owner shall have a one- time opportunity to update the payment yield for upland cotton, as provided in 7 U.S.C. 9013(d), for the purpose of calculating the payment yield for seed cotton. **(7 U.S.C. 9013(e))**	section, the owner may update the payment yield for upland cotton, using the same method as described in this section. **(§1113(c))**	
Payment Acres		
Payment acres. With respect to PLC and county-level ARC payments, payment acres are 85% of the base acres of a covered commodity on a farm. For individual (farm-level) ARC, the payment acres equal 65% of the base acres for all of the covered commodities on the farm. Generic base is eligible for payments if a covered crop is planted on the farm. Specifically, for each crop year, generic base acres are attributed (i.e., temporarily designated as) base acres to a particular covered commodity base in proportion to that crop's share of total plantings of all covered commodities in that year. The amount of generic base attributed for a particular year cannot exceed the acreage planted to covered crops in that year (use of double- cropping for payment calculations is not allowed unless the practice is approved by the Secretary). **(7 U.S.C. 9014)**	Continues the establishment of payment acres for PLC and county-level ARC payments for each covered commodity on the farm at 85% of the base acres. **(§1114(a))** No reference is made to the individual farm-level ARC program or its associated payment acres.	Continues current law.
Exclusion from payment acres. Payment acres may not include any crop subsequently planted during the same crop year on the same land for which the first crop is eligible for PLC or ARC payments unless the crop was approved for double cropping as determined by the Secretary. **(7 U.S.C. 9014(c))**	No comparable provision.	Continues current law.
Minimal payment acres. A producer on a farm may not receive PLC payments or ARC payments if the sum of the base acres on the farm is 10 acres or less except for socially disadvantaged farmers/ranchers or limited resource farmers/ranchers. **(7 U.S.C. 9014(d))**	Same as current law. **(§1114(b))**	Continues current law.
Effect of planting fruits and vegetables on payment acres. Any crop may be planted without effect on base acres. However, payment acres on a farm are reduced in any crop year in which fruits, vegetables (other than mung beans and pulse crops), or wild rice (FVWR) have	Same as current law. **(§1114(c))**	Amends this section to specify that any plantings to FVWR, for which a reduction in payment acres is made under this subsection, shall not be used to reduce base acres, meaning that

Table 4. (Continued)

Current Law/Policy	House-Passed Bill (H.R. 2)	Senate-Passed Bill (H.R. 2)
been planted on base acres. The reduction to payment acres is one-for-one for each acre planted to these crops in excess of 15% of base acres for either the PLC or county coverage under the ARC program and in excess of 35% of base acres for ARC individual coverage. **(7 U.S.C. 9014(e)(1- 3))** No reduction to payment acres shall be made under this subsection, as determined by the Secretary, if FVWR are grown solely for conservation purposes and not harvested for use or sale or if a region has a history of double- cropping covered commodities with FVWR and the FVWR were so double-cropped on the base acres. **(7 U.S.C. 9014(e)(4))**		such plantings of FVWR shall be considered to be the same as the planting and production of a covered commodity for purposes of recalculating base acres. **(§1101)**
Unassigned crop base. Requires the Secretary to maintain information on generic base acres on a farm allocated as unassigned crop base under the formulation for seed cotton base acres. **(7 U.S.C. 9014(b)(4)(B,D); 7 U.S.C. 9014(f))**	Requires the Secretary to maintain information on unassigned crop base acres on a farm under the one-time reallocation of base acres under the 2014 farm bill and prevention of excess base acres. **(§1114(d))**	Continues current law.
Producer Election		
Producer election. For the 2014-2018 crop years, all producers involved in a single farm operation had to unanimously make a one- time, irrevocable election to obtain either (1) Price Loss Coverage program (PLC) or county-level ARC on a covered-commodity-by- covered-commodity basis or (2) ARC individual coverage applicable to all of the covered commodities on the farm. Failure to make a unanimous election for the 2014 crop year results in no program payments to the farm for the 2014 crop year, and the producers on the farm are deemed to have elected PLC for all covered commodities on the farm for the 2015-2018 crop years. If all the producers on a farm selected ARC county coverage for a covered commodity, the Secretary could not make PLC payments to the producers on the farm with respect to that covered commodity.	For the 2019-2023 crop years, all producers involved in a single farm operation must unanimously make a one-time, irrevocable election to obtain either PLC or county-level ARC on a covered-commodity-by-covered-commodity basis. **(§1115(a))** Failure to make a unanimous election for the 2019 crop year results in no program payments to the farm for the 2019 crop year, and producers on the farm are deemed to have elected PLC for all covered commodities on the farm for the 2020-2023 crop years. **(§1115(b))** Prohibits farm reconstitution to void or change an election made under this section. **(§1115(c))**	For the 2019-2023 crop years, all producers on a farm must unanimously make a one-time, irrevocable election to obtain either PLC or county-level ARC on a covered-commodity-by-covered- commodity basis. Failure to make a unanimous election for the 2019 crop year results in no program payments to the farm for the 2019 crop year, and producers on the farm are deemed to have elected county coverage for all covered commodities on the farm for the 2020 through 2023 crop years. Producers of seed cotton base were given a one-time election for their seed cotton base between PLC and county-level ARC in the 2018 crop year. That election extends through the 2023 crop year. **(§1102)**

Current Law/Policy	House-Passed Bill (H.R. 2)	Senate-Passed Bill (H.R. 2)
If all the producers on a farm selected individual coverage, payment calculations included the producer's share of all farms in the same state in which the producer has an interest and for which individual coverage was selected. Producers on a farm cannot reconstitute the farm to void or change a program election. **(7 U.S.C. 9015)**		
No comparable provision.	No comparable provision.	**Option to Change Producer Election.** Notwithstanding 7 U.S.C. 9015(a), amends current law to allow participating producers a one- time choice in crop year 2021 to change their election choice between ARC and PLC for crop years 2021-2023. **(§1106)**
Price Loss Coverage (PLC) Program		
PLC. Establishes the PLC program for crop years 2014-2018. PLC payments are made on a farm where the owners have unanimously elected to participate in PLC on a covered commodity- by-covered-commodity basis if the effective price is less than the reference price. **(7 U.S.C. 9016(a))**	Requires the Secretary to make PLC payments on a covered- commodity-by-covered-commodity basis where all of the producers on a farm have elected PLC for crop years 2019-2023 when the effective price for a crop year is less than the effective reference price. **(§1116(a))**	Extends the PLC program through 2023. **(§1103(1))**
PLC Effective Price		
Effective price. The higher of (1) the "national average market price received by producers during the 12-month marketing year" for the covered commodity, as determined by the Secretary, or (2) the national average loan rate for a marketing assistance loan. **(7 U.S.C. 9016(b))**	Same as current law. **(§1116(b))**	Continues current law.
Effective price for barley. The all-barley price. **(7 U.S.C. 9016(f))**	Same as current law. **(§1116(f))**	Continues current law.
Effective price for seed cotton. The MYAP for seed cotton, calculated as the quotient obtained by dividing (A) the sum obtained by adding (i) the product of the upland cotton lint MYAP and total U.S. upland cotton lint production, measured in pounds, and (ii) the product of the cottonseed MYAP and total U.S. cottonseed production, measured in pounds; by (B) the sum of total U.S. upland cotton lint production and total U.S. cottonseed production, both measured in pounds. **(7 U.S.C. 9016(h)).**	Same as current law.	Continues current law.

Table 4. (Continued)

Current Law/Policy	House-Passed Bill (H.R. 2)	Senate-Passed Bill (H.R. 2)
PLC Payment Rate and Payment Amount		
PLC payment rate. The difference between the reference price in statute and the MYAP or loan rate, if higher. **(7 U.S.C. 9016(c))**	Same as current law. **(§1116(c))**	Continues current law.
PLC payment amount. If PLC payments for a covered commodity are triggered for any of crop years 2014-2018, the payment amount equals the payment rate times payment acres times payment yield. **(7 U.S.C. 9016(d))**	If PLC payments for a covered commodity are triggered for any of crop years 2019-2023, the payment amount equals the payment rate times payment acres times payment yield. **(§1116(d))**	Continues current law.
Timing of PLC payment. Payments shall be made beginning October 1, or as soon as practicable thereafter, after the end of the applicable marketing year for the covered commodity. **(7 U.S.C. 9016(e))**	Same as current law. **(§1116(e))**	Not later than 30 days after the end of each applicable 12-month marketing year for each covered commodity, the Secretary shall publish the PLC payment rate. **(§1103(2))**
Agricultural Risk Coverage (ARC) Program		
ARC. Establishes the ARC program as either a county-level, commodity-specific ARC or an individual whole-farm ARC. Under the "producer election" (7 U.S.C. 9015), producers may select county-level ARC or PLC on a commodity-by-commodity basis for each farm or select individual farm- level ARC for all covered commodities on the farm. ARC payments for a crop year are triggered if the actual crop revenue is less than its ARC guarantee. Both the actual crop revenue and ARC guarantee are calculated differently based on the producer's election choice: either county- or farm-level ARC. **(7 U.S.C. 9017(a))**	Requires the Secretary to make ARC payments if all of the producers on a farm have elected ARC for crop years 2019-2023 if a covered commodity's crop-year actual crop revenue is less than its ARC guarantee. **(§1117(a))** (Refers only to the county-level ARC. Does not include the individual ARC coverage option.)	Extends the ARC program through 2023. Requires that payments are to be based on the physical location of the farm. **(§1104(1))**
Actual crop revenue. The actual crop revenue varies with the choice of county-level or farm-level ARC. County coverage for a crop year of a covered commodity: actual crop revenue per acre equals the actual average county yield per planted acre for a covered commodity times the higher of the MYAP, or the national average marketing assistance loan rate. **Individual (farm-level) coverage.** Actual crop revenue per acre is the producer's share of the aggregated revenue per acre for all covered	Defines actual crop revenue specific to county-level ARC for a crop year for a covered commodity as the product of the actual average county yield per planted acre for a covered commodity times the higher of the MYAP or the national average marketing assistance loan rate. **(§1117(b))** By omission, individual (farm-level) ARC expires at the end of the 2018 crop year.	Continues current law.

Current Law/Policy	House-Passed Bill (H.R. 2)	Senate-Passed Bill (H.R. 2)
commodities planted on all farms for which individual coverage has been selected. Actual crop revenue per acre equals the sum of covered commodity revenue (total production of each covered commodity on such farms times the higher of (i) the MYAP or (ii) the national average loan rate) divided by the total planted acres of all covered commodities on such farms. **(7 U.S.C. 9017(b))**		
ARC revenue guarantee. ARC guarantee per acre equals 86% times the benchmark revenue. The benchmark revenue varies with the choice of county-level or individual (farm-level) ARC. For county ARC coverage for a covered commodity for a crop year, benchmark revenue per acre equals the recent five-year average county yield (excluding the years with the highest and lowest yields, or "Olympic average") times the covered commodity's Olympic MYAP for the most recent five crop years. For individual ARC coverage for a crop year, benchmark revenue is based on the producer's share of all covered commodities planted on all farms for which individual coverage has been selected and in which the producer has an interest. Benchmark revenue is the summation of Olympic five-year average revenue for each covered commodity aggregated across all farms with individual coverage, adjusted to reflect current-year planted acreage shares by covered commodity. **(7 U.S.C. 9017(c))**	Same as current law. **(§1117(c))** By omission, individual (farm-level) ARC expires at the end of the 2018 crop year.	Continues ARC program as in current law, but with a trend-adjustment for both the average historical county yield (i.e., the 5-year Olympic MYAP) and the actual average county yield per planted acre for the county, crop, and year in question. The yield adjustment should not exceed the trend- adjusted yield factor used to increase yield history under the federal crop insurance endorsement for that crop and county. **(§1104(2)(E))**
Yield conditions in ARC actual revenue and revenue guarantee calculations. If, for the covered commodity for any of the five most recent crop years, the yield per planted acre or historical county yield per planted acre is less than 70% of the transitional yield, then 70% of the transitional yield shall be used for those years. **(7 U.S.C. 9017(c)(4))**	Same as current law. **(§1117(c)(3))**	If, for the covered commodity for any of the five most recent crop years, the yield per planted acre or historical county yield per planted acre is less than 75% of the transitional yield, then 75% of the transitional yield shall be used for those years. **(§1104(2)(C))**
Reference price in ARC revenue guarantee. The reference price is used if the MYAP for any of the five most recent crop years is lower than the reference price. **(7 U.S.C. 9017(c)(5))**	Same as current law. **(§1117(c)(4))**	

Table 4. (Continued)

Current Law/Policy	House-Passed Bill (H.R. 2)	Senate-Passed Bill (H.R. 2)
ARC payment rate. The payment rate for a covered commodity, in the case of either county coverage or individual coverage, is equal to the lesser of (1) the amount that the ARC guarantee exceeds the actual crop revenue for the crop year or (2) 10% of the benchmark revenue for the crop year. **(7 U.S.C. 9017(d))**	The payment rate for a covered commodity is equal to the lesser of (1) the amount that the ARC guarantee exceeds the actual crop revenue for the crop year or (2) 10% of the benchmark revenue for the crop year. **(§1117(d))**	Continues current law.
ARC payment amount. If ARC payments are required to be paid for any of the 2014-2018 crop years, then the payment amount equals the payment rate times the payment acres. **(7 U.S.C. 9017(e))**	If ARC payments are required to be paid for any of the 2019-2023 crop years, then the payment amount equals the payment rate times the payment acres. **(§1117(e))**	Extends ARC payments through crop year 2023. **(§1104(4))**
Timing of ARC payments. Payments shall be made beginning October 1, or as soon as practicable thereafter, after the end of the applicable marketing year for the covered commodity. **(7 U.S.C. 9017(f))**	Same as current law. **(§1117(f))**	Not later than 30 days after the end of each applicable 12-month marketing year for each covered commodity, the Secretary shall publish the ARC payment rate. **(§1104(3))**
Additional duties of the Secretary. In providing ARC, the Secretary shall use all available information and analysis, including data mining, to check for anomalies in the determination of ARC payments, calculating a separate actual crop revenue and ARC guarantee for irrigated and non- irrigated covered commodities, and, if necessary, assist with yield determinations as follows: For individual coverage, if the Secretary determines that the farm has planted acreage in a quantity that is insufficient to calculate a representative average yield for the farm, then the Secretary will assign an average yield for a farm on the basis of the yield history of representative farms in the state, region, or crop reporting district, as determined by the Secretary. For county coverage, if the Secretary cannot establish the actual or benchmark county yield for each planted acre for a crop year for a covered commodity in the county, or the yield is an unrepresentative average yield for the county, then the Secretary is to assign an actual or benchmark county yield for each planted acre for the crop year for the covered commodity on the basis of the yield history of representative farms	Sets forth additional duties of the Secretary, including using available information and analysis to check for anomalies in the determination of ARC payments; calculating a separate actual crop revenue and agriculture risk coverage guarantee for irrigated and nonirrigated covered commodities; assigning an actual or benchmark county yield for planted acres for a covered commodity for a crop year using first Risk Management Agency data, if sufficient, or, second, other sources of data as determined by the Secretary, or, third, the yield history of representative farms in the state, region, or crop reporting district; and making payments using the payment rate of the county of the physical location of the base acres of a farm. **(§1117(g))**	Continues additional duties of the Secretary as in current law with an additional specification regarding the determination of the actual or benchmark county yield under county coverage as follows. Effective for the 2019 through 2023 crop years, in the case of county coverage the Secretary shall: (A) assign an actual county yield for each planted acre for the crop year for the covered commodity by giving priority to (1) the use of actual county yields to the maximum extent practicable from a single source of data that provides the greatest national coverage of county-level data; (2) the use of a source of data that may be used to determine an average actual and benchmark county yield for the same county; and (3) for a county not included in any data source identified under (1) or (2), use other sources of county yield information or the yield history of representative farms in the state, region, or crop reporting district, as determined

Current Law/Policy	House-Passed Bill (H.R. 2)	Senate-Passed Bill (H.R. 2)
in the state, region, or crop reporting district, as determined by the Secretary. **(7 U.S.C. 9017(g))**		by the Secretary; and (B) for a farm with base acres that cross county boundaries, prorate the base acres based on the share in each county, and calculate the crop revenue in a similar prorated manner. **(§1104(5))**
No comparable provision.	No comparable provision.	**Separate ARC Yield Calculations for Irrigated and Non-Irrigated Acres.** USDA shall consider a one-time request to calculate separate yields for irrigated and non-irrigated acres in determining the ARC revenue guarantee and the actual revenue if, during the 2014 through 2018 crop years: (A) an average of not less than 5% of the planted and considered planted acreage of a covered commodity in the county was irrigated; and (B) an average of not less than 5% was non-irrigated. **(§1104(6))**
Producer Agreements		
Producer agreements. The Secretary may require producers agree to comply with certain provisions in exchange for receiving payments, issue rules to ensure compliance, and modify compliance requirements. Eligibility for PLC and ARC payments and marketing loans requires producers to comply with conservation and wetland protection, control noxious weeds, maintain sound agricultural practices, and use the farm's land attributable to base acres for agricultural or conserving use and not for nonagricultural commercial, industrial, or residential use as determined by the Secretary. **(7 U.S.C. 9018(a))**	Same as current law. **(§1118(a))**	Continues current law.
Termination of payments. A transfer of or change in the interest of the producers on a farm will result in the termination of payments unless the transferee or owner agrees to assume all compliance obligations. An exception to payment termination is made for producers who die or become incapacitated. **(7 U.S.C. 9018(b))**	Same as current law. **(§1118(b))**	Continues current law.

Table 4. (Continued)

Current Law/Policy	House-Passed Bill (H.R. 2)	Senate-Passed Bill (H.R. 2)
Annual acreage reports. Eligibility for PLC and ARC payments and marketing loans requires producers to submit annual acreage reports. **(7 U.S. Annual Crop Production reports. C. 9018(c))**	Same as current law. **(§1118(c))**	Continues current law.
Eligibility for ARC payments for individual (i.e., the whole-farm, farm-level) coverage (as opposed to the crop-specific, county-level ARC program) requires a producer to submit annual production reports for each covered commodity that is covered by the farm's ARC individual program—as produced on all farms in the same State. **[7 U.S.C. 9018(d)]**	No comparable provision.	Continues current law.
Effect of inaccurate reports. No penalties (with respect to benefits under PLC, ARC, or marketing loans) can be assessed against a producer for an inaccurate acreage or production report unless the Secretary determines that the producer knowingly and willfully falsified the report. **(7 U.S.C. 9018(e))**	Same as current law. **(§1118(d))**	Continues current law.
The Secretary shall provide adequate safeguards to protect the interests of tenants and sharecroppers and shall provide for the sharing of payments among producers on a farm. **(7 U.S.C. 9018(f-g))**	Same as in current law. **(§1118(e- f))**	Continues current law.
Transition Assistance for Producers of Upland Cotton		
Cotton Transition Assistance Payments. Transition payments are made available for upland cotton for the 2014 crop year (and or 2015 if STAX is not yet available – see Title XI). Payment equals program yield (divided by the national yield of 597 pounds per acre) times transition assistance rate times payment acres. Transition rate is based on cotton price decline between June 2013 and December 2013. Payment acres in 2014 equal 60% of 2013 cotton base acres and 36.5% in 2015. **(7.S.C. 9019)**	No provision.	Cotton Transition Assistance Payments are repealed. **(§1105)**
Nonrecourse Marketing Assistance Loan Program		
Nonrecourse marketing loans are available for any amount of loan of a loan commodity (see list below) produced in crop years 2014-2018. To receive a marketing assistance loan, a producer must comply with applicable	Authorizes nonrecourse loans for loan commodities for 2019-2023 crop years in the same manner as current law. Retains the requirement that producers must comply with applicable conservation and wetland protection requirements. **(§1201)**	Extends nonrecourse marketing assistance loans for all loan commodities (including peanuts) through crop year 2023. **(§1201(a))**

Current Law/Policy	House-Passed Bill (H.R. 2)	Senate-Passed Bill (H.R. 2)
conservation and wetland protection requirements during the term of the loan. **(7 U.S.C. 9031)**		
Peanuts nonrecourse marketing loans, authorized separately, may be obtained through a marketing cooperative or association approved by USDA. Storage to be provided on a nondiscriminatory basis and under any additional requirements. USDA shall pay storage, handling, and other associated costs incurred for peanuts placed under loan. Such costs must be repaid if the peanuts under loan are redeemed but not if forfeited. **(7 U.S.C. 9031(e))**	Same as current law. **(§1201(e))**	Continues current law.
Loan commodities and loan rates. For crop years 2014-2018, the loan rate for a nonrecourse marketing assistance loan for each loan commodity is as follows: • Wheat, $2.94 per bu. • Corn, $1.95 per bu. • Grain sorghum, $1.95 per bu. • Barley, $1.95 per bu. • Oats, $1.39 per bu. • ELS cotton, $0.7977 per lb. • Long-grain rice, $6.50 per cwt. • Medium-grain rice, $6.50 per cwt. • Soybeans, $5.00 per bu. • Other oilseeds, $10.09 per cwt. for sunflower seed, rapeseed, canola, safflower, flaxseed, mustard seed, crambe, sesame seed, or any other oilseeds designated by the Secretary. • Dry peas, $5.40 per cwt. • Lentils, $11.28 per cwt. • Small chickpeas, $7.43 per cwt. • Large chickpeas, $11.28 per cwt. • Graded wool, $1.15 per lb. • Nongraded wool, $0.40 per lb. • Mohair, $4.20 per lb. • Honey, $0.69 per lb. • Peanuts, $355 per ton. **(7 U.S.C. 90321)**	Continues the loan rates for commodities in current law for the 2019-2023 crop years, except (as described in Section 1202(a)(6))d for an adjustment to upland cotton and establishing a loan rate for seed cotton of $0.25 per lb. **(§1202)**	Extends the statutory loan rates for nonrecourse marketing assistance loans through crop year 2023. **(§1201(b))**
Upland cotton loan rate. The simple average of the adjusted prevailing world price for the two immediately preceding marketing years but in no case less than $0.45 per lb. or more than $0.52 per lb. (announced October 1 preceding the next domestic plantings). **(7 U.S.C. 9032(a)(6))**	The simple average of the adjusted prevailing world price for the two immediately preceding marketing years but in no case more than $0.52 per lb. nor less than $0.45 per lb. or an amount equal to 98% of the loan rate for the preceding year (announced October 1 preceding the next domestic plantings). **(§1202(a)(6))**	Continues current law.

Table 4. (Continued)

Current Law/Policy	House-Passed Bill (H.R. 2)	Senate-Passed Bill (H.R. 2)
Single county loan rate for other oilseeds is established in each county for each other kind of oilseed. **(7 U.S.C. 9032(b))**	Same as current law. **(§1202(b))**	Continues current law.
Seed cotton loan rate. Only for implementation of the PLC and ARC programs, the loan rate for seed cotton is deemed to be $0.25 per lb. This does not authorize a seed cotton nonrecourse marketing loan. **(7 U.S.C. 9032(c))**	Same as in current law. **(§1202(c))**	Continues current law.
Term of loans. Nine months after the day the loan is made. Extensions prohibited. **(7 U.S.C. 9033)**	Same as current law. **(§1203)**	Continues current law.
Repayment of loans. Loans may be repaid at the lesser of (1) the loan rate plus interest, (2) a rate based on average market prices during the preceding 30-day period, or (3) a rate determined by USDA that will minimize forfeitures, accumulation of stocks, storage costs, market impediments, and discrepancies in benefits across states and counties. Excludes upland cotton, rice, extra-long staple (ELS) cotton, confectionery, and each kind of sunflower seed (other than oil sunflower seed). **(7 U.S.C. 9034(a))**	Same as current law. **(§1204(a))**	Continues current law.
Special repayment rates. For upland cotton, long-grain rice, and medium-grain rice, repayment may be at the lesser of the loan rate plus interest or the prevailing world price for the commodity adjusted to U.S. quality and location. **(7 U.S.C. 9034(b))** ELS cotton repayment rate is the loan rate plus interest. **(7 U.S.C. 9034(c))** For confectionery and each kind of sunflower seed (other than oil sunflower seed), loans must be repaid at the lesser of the loan rate plus interest or the repayment rate for oil sunflower seed. **(7 U.S.C. 9034(f))**	Same as current law. **(§1204(b,c,f))**	Continues current law.
Prevailing world market price. The Secretary shall prescribe by regulation a formula to determine the prevailing world market price for each of upland cotton, long- grain rice, and medium-grain rice and a mechanism to announce periodically prevailing world market prices.	Same as current law. **(§1204(d,e))**	Continues current law for repayment of marketing assistance loans for each of upland cotton, long-grain rice, and medium-grain rice. Extends current law for adjustments to the prevailing world market price for upland cotton as used to determine the

Current Law/Policy	House-Passed Bill (H.R. 2)	Senate-Passed Bill (H.R. 2)
(7 U.S.C. 9034(d)) Provides explicit market conditions to USDA for adjustments to the prevailing world market price for quality and location (both rice and upland cotton) and additionally the potential for loan forfeitures (upland cotton). **(7 U.S.C. 9034(e))**		repayment rate of marketing assistance loans through crop year 2023. **(§1201(c)(1))**
Payment of cotton storage costs. For each of crop years 2014-2018, the Secretary shall make cotton storage payments available in the same manner and at the same rates as the Secretary provided storage payments for the 2006 crop of cotton, except that the rates shall be reduced by 10%. **(7 U.S.C. 9034(g))**	Extends current law for crop years 2019-2023. **(§1204(g))**	Same as House provision. **(§1201(c)(2))**
Repayment rate for peanuts. Loans may be repaid at the lesser of (1) the loan rate plus interest or (2) a rate determined by USDA that will minimize forfeitures, accumulation of stocks, storage costs, market impediments, and discrepancies in benefits across states and counties. **(7 U.S.C. 9034(h))**	Same as current law. **(§1204(h))**	Continues current law.
Authority to temporarily adjust repayment rates. USDA may temporarily, and on a short term basis only, adjust the repayment rates in the event of a severe disruption to marketing, transportation, or related infrastructure. **(7 U.S.C. 9034(i))**	Same as current law. **(§1204(i))**	Continues current law.
Loan deficiency payments (LDPs). For the crop years 2014-2018, USDA makes available LDPs to producers who agree to forego marketing loans. An LDP is computed by multiplying the payment rate (the amount that the loan rate exceeds the rate at which a marketing loan may be repaid) for the commodity times the quantity of the commodity produced. LDPs are available for unshorn pelts or hay and silage, even though they are not eligible for marketing loans. ELS cotton is not eligible. Payment rates determined using the rate in effect as of the date that producers request payment. (Producers do not need to lose beneficial interest.) **(7 U.S.C. 9035)**	Extends current law for crop years 2019-2023. **(§1205)**	Extends current law for loan deficiency payments through crop year 2023. **(§1201(d)(1))** Repeals loan deficiency payments for non-graded wool in the form of unshorn pelts. **(§1202)**

Table 4. (Continued)

Current Law/Policy	House-Passed Bill (H.R. 2)	Senate-Passed Bill (H.R. 2)
Payments in lieu of LDPs are available for grazed acreage of wheat, barley, oats, or triticale if a producer forgoes harvesting any crop from that acreage. Crop production on the grazed acreage is not eligible for crop insurance or noninsured crop assistance. **(7 U.S.C. 9036)**	Extends current law for crop years 2019-2023. **(§1206)**	Extends current law for payments in lieu of loan deficiency payments (and ineligibility for crop insurance or noninsured crop assistance) for grazed acreage through crop year 2023. **(§1201(d)(2))**
Special marketing loan provisions for upland cotton. Imposes a special import quota on upland cotton without an expiration date beginning on August 1, 2014, when price of U.S. cotton, delivered to a definable and significant international market, exceeds the prevailing world market price for four weeks. **(7 U.S.C. 9037(b))** Limited global import quota is imposed on upland cotton when U.S. prices average 130% of the previous three-year average of U.S. prices. **(7 U.S.C. 9037(b))**	Continues both provisions in the same manner as current law without an expiration date beginning on August 1, 2019. **(§1207(a,b))**	Continues current law.
Economic adjustment assistance to users of upland cotton provides assistance to domestic users of upland cotton for uses of all cotton regardless of origin to acquire, construct, install, modernize, develop, convert, or expand land, plant, buildings, equipment, facilities, or machinery. Rate is $0.03 per lb. effective beginning August 1, 2013. **(7 U.S.C. 9037(c)).**	Extends without an expiration date the economic adjustment assistance to users of upland cotton at the rate of $0.0315 per lb. **(§1207(c))**	Amends current law to extend the economic adjustment assistance to users of upland cotton at the rate of $0.03 per lb. through July 31, 2021. There are authorized to be appropriated such sums as are necessary to carry out this program. For subsequent years, the program is extended at the same payment rate but subject to funding availability through annual appropriations. **(§1203)**
Special competitive provisions for ELS cotton. Payments to domestic users and exporters are triggered whenever the world market price for the lowest priced ELS cotton is below the prevailing U.S. price for a competing growth of ELS cotton for a four-week period and the lowest priced competing growth of ELS cotton is less than 134% of the loan rate for ELS cotton. Effective through July 31, 2019. Payments equal the difference between the trigger prices (above) times the amount purchased by domestic users or exported by exporters in the week following the four-week trigger period. **(7 U.S.C. 9038)**	Continues the authorization through July 31, 2024, of the special competitive provisions for ELS cotton but adjusts the payment trigger to whenever the world market price for the lowest priced ELS cotton is below the prevailing U.S. price for a competing growth of ELS cotton for a four-week period and the lowest priced competing growth of ELS cotton is less than 113% of the loan rate for ELS cotton. This adjustment, in turn, alters the value of assistance available to domestic users of upland cotton. **(§1208)**	Extends current law for special competitiveness provisions for extra-long staple cotton through crop year 2023. **(§1201(d)(3))**

Current Law/Policy	House-Passed Bill (H.R. 2)	Senate-Passed Bill (H.R. 2)
Availability of recourse loan. For crop years 2014-2018, recourse loans for high-moisture feed grains and seed cotton are available for farms that normally harvest corn or sorghum in a high-moisture condition at rates set by the USDA. For recourse loans for seed cotton, repayment is at loan rate plus interest. **(7 U.S.C. 9039)**	Continues the authorization for recourse loans for certain crops for the 2019-2023 crop years in same manner as current law except for the addition of a provision providing for recourse loans for commodities that are contaminated but still merchantable. **(§1209)**	Extends current law for the availability of recourse loans for high-moisture feed grains and seed cotton through crop year 2023. **(§1201(d)(4))**
Adjustment of loans. Adjustments are authorized for any commodity (other than cotton) based on differences in grade, type, quality, location, and other factors. Allows county loan rates as low as 95% of the U.S. average if it does not increase outlays. Prohibits adjustments that would increase the national average loan rate. For cotton, loan rates may be adjusted for differences in quality factors (made after consultation with the U.S. cotton industry). For rice, loan rates may be adjusted for differences in grade and quality (including milling yields). **(7 U.S.C. 9040)**	Continues the authorization to adjust loan rates in the same manner as current law except for the inclusion of cost-saving option authority for the Secretary that requires the consideration of methods that minimize the potential for loan forfeitures. **(§1210)**	Continues current law.
Sugar Program		
Price support program. Requires USDA to the maximum extent practicable to operate the sugar nonrecourse loan program at no net cost by avoiding loan forfeitures to the CCC (i.e., no outlays recorded). **(7 U.S.C. 7272 (f))** Directs USDA to maintain market prices above loan rates by (1) limiting amount of sugar that processors of sugar beets and sugarcane sell into the U.S. market under marketing allotments (see Flexible Marketing Allotments below), (2) restricting imports tariff-rate quotas, and (3) operating the feedstock flexibility program for bioenergy producers (i.e., sugar-to- ethanol program) under specified conditions. **(7 U.S.C. 1359aa *et seq.*, 7 U.S.C. 8110)** Maintains sugar loan rates through the 2018 crop year at $0.1875 per lb. for raw cane sugar and $0.2409 per lb. for refined beet sugar. Continues other provisions found in prior law. **(7 U.S.C. 7272 (a, b, c, d, e, g, h, i))**	Same as current law except that all price-support-related provisions, including loan rates and flexible marketing allotments are extended through the 2023 crop year. **(§1301)** Extends the feedstock flexibility program (i.e., sugar-to- ethanol program) through 2023 crops. **(See §6409)**	Same as House bill **(§1301)**. For feedstock flexibility program **(See §9109)**.

Table 4. (Continued)

Current Law/Policy	House-Passed Bill (H.R. 2)	Senate-Passed Bill (H.R. 2)
Extends flexible marketing allotments for sugar, which limits amount of sugar food that processors can sell into the domestic market for human consumption each year, which is divided between sugarcane and sugar beet sectors, and then allocated to individual processors. Requires USDA each year to set the overall allotment quantity at not less than 85% of estimated U.S. human consumption. **(7 U.S.C. 1359aa-1359jj, 1359ll)**		
Dairy Programs		
No comparable provision.	**Review of data used in calculation of average feed cost.** No later than 60 days from enactment, USDA is to provide the House Committee on Agriculture and the Senate Committee on Agriculture, Nutrition, and Forestry a report that evaluates whether the average feed costs used to calculate dairy margins are representative of actual feed costs. **(§1401(a))**	No comparable provision.
No comparable provision.	**Corn silage report.** No later than one year from enactment, USDA is to provide the committees a detailed report on the cost for dairies to use corn silage as feed and the difference between the feed cost of corn silage and corn. **(§1401(b))**	No comparable provision.
No comparable provision.	**Collection of alfalfa hay data.** Not later than 120 days from enactment, the USDA National Agricultural Statistics Service is to revise monthly price survey reports to include the prices for high-quality alfalfa hay for the top five milk-producing states, by volume, in the month prior to the reported monthly price. **(§1401(c))**	No comparable provision.
Subtitle D—Dairy, Part I—Margin Protection Program for Dairy Producers. (Agricultural Act of 014 (P.L. 113-79))	Amends the heading to read "Part I—Dairy Risk Management Program for Dairy Producers." (DRMP) **(§ 1401(i)(1))**	Amends the heading to read "Part I—Dairy Risk Coverage." (DRC) **(§1401(a))**
Definitions. Section 1401 of the Agricultural Act of 2014 (P.L. 113-79) defines certain terms of the dairy MPP. **(7 U.S.C. 9051)**	Deletes paragraphs 5 and 6 of 7 U.S.C. 9051 and inserts new paragraphs that define the DRMP as the program required in Sections 1403 and 1406 of P.L. 113-79.	Similar to House bill. Replaces the term *margin protection program* where it appears and inserts *dairy risk coverage*. **(§1401(b))**

Current Law/Policy	House-Passed Bill (H.R. 2)	Senate-Passed Bill (H.R. 2)
	Deletes the term *margin protection* in paragraphs 7 and 8 of the section. **§1401(i)(2))**	Amends the section by adding *catastrophic coverage* defined as 40% of production history of participating dairy operations.
Calculation of actual dairy production margin. Calculates the margin for the MPP as the difference between the feed cost and all-milk price. **(7 U.S.C. 9052(b)(1))**	Amends the section by striking *margin protection* and inserting *dairy risk management.* **(§1401(i)(3))**	Amends the section by striking *margin protection* and inserting *dairy risk coverage.* **(§1401(c))**
Establishment of MPP for dairy producers. Requires USDA to establish and administer the MPP no later than September 1, 2014. **(7 U.S.C. 9053)**	The section heading is amended by deleting *Establishing Margin Protection* and inserting *Dairy Risk Management.* The September 1, 2014, date is struck and replaced with *The Secretary shall continue to administer a dairy risk management program. Margin protection payment* is replaced with *dairy risk management payment* where it appears. **(§1401(i)(4))**	The section heading is amended to *Dairy Risk Coverage Administration.* Requires USDA to administer the dairy risk coverage program beginning with 2019. The regulations in 7 C.F.R. 1430 (Margin Protection Program for Dairy Producers) in effect when the Agriculture Improvement Act of 2018 (Senate-passed H.R. 2) is enacted will remain in effect for the dairy risk coverage program beginning 2019. **(§ 1401(d))**
Participation of dairy operations in MPP. Describes eligibility, the registration process, and the annual administrative fee to participate in MPP. **(7 U.S.C. 9054)**	Strikes *Margin Protection* from section heading. Replaces *margin protection* with *dairy risk management* where it appears. **(§1401(i)(5))**	Similar to House bill. Replaces *margin protection* with *dairy risk coverage.* **(§1401(e))**
		Amends the section by adding a *catastrophic coverage* option that allows dairy producers select catastrophic coverage and receive a payment on 40% of production history when the margin is $5.00/cwt or less, instead of paying premiums to buy a selected margin level. Producers that select catastrophic coverage are required to pay $200 in administrative fees, the original $100 fee, plus an additional $100 fee. **(§ 1401(e))**
Treatment of multi-producer dairy operations. In dairy operations with more than one producer, all of the producers are treated as a single dairy operation for the purposes of participating in the dairy Margin Protection Program (MPP). **(7 U.S.C. 9054(b)(3))**	In multi-producer dairy operations, registration information may be excluded for producers with less than 5% ownership or who are entitled to less than 5% of income, revenue, profit, gain, loss, expenditure, deduction, or credit in a multi-producer operation. The dairy risk management payment to the multi-producer operation is reduced by the ownership share of	No comparable provision.

Table 4. (Continued)

Current Law/Policy	House-Passed Bill (H.R. 2)	Senate-Passed Bill (H.R. 2)
	the excluded owner(s) or the percentage of income, revenue, profit, gain, loss, expenditure, deduction, or credit of the excluded owner(s), whichever is greater. **(§1401(d))**	
Relation to livestock gross margin for dairy program. Dairy producers may participate in MPP or Livestock Gross Margin- Dairy (LGM-D) but not both programs. **(7 U.S.C. 9054(d))**	Amends the provision to allow dairy producers to participate in the renamed DRMP, and the LGM-D. The dual coverage cannot be on the same milk production. **(§1401(e))**	No comparable provision.
Production history. For MPP, the production history is equal to the highest annual milk marketings of dairy operations during any one of the three calendar years 2011, 2012, or 2013. In subsequent years, USDA shall adjust the production history to reflect any increase in the national average milk production. Also, describes adjustments to production history, elections for new dairy operations, and required information to establish production history in the MPP **(7 U.S.C. 9055)**	*Margin protection program* is replaced with *dairy risk management program* where it appears. **(§ 401(i)(6))** The DRMP uses the highest annual milk marketings during calendar years 2011, 2012, or 2013 for production history for participation through 2023. USDA is to adjust production history to reflect increases in national average milk production for calendar years ending before January 1, 2019. **(§ 1401(f)(1) and (2))**	Replaces *margin protection* with *dairy risk coverage.* **(§ 1401(f))**
No comparable provision.	**Limitation on changes to business structure.** Amends 7 U.S.C. 9055 by adding a subsection that limits changes to business structure of participating dairy operations. USDA may not make payments to dairy operations that reorganize for the sole purpose of qualifying as new dairy operations. **(§1401(f)(3))**	No comparable provision.
Margin protection payments. Participating dairy operations annually elect coverage level thresholds and the percentage of milk production history covered by margin payments. **(7 U.S.C. 9056)**	*Dairy Risk Management* replaces *Margin Protection* in the section heading. Strikes *margin protection* in each place it appears. Strikes *Margin Protection* from the heading of subsection (c). **(§1401(i)(7))**	Similar to House bill. Strikes *margin protection* in each place it appears and inserts *dairy risk coverage*. **(§1401(g))**
	Amends subsection (a) by deleting *annually* and inserting the following new subsection: **Deadline for election; duration.** Not later than 90 days after enactment of DRMP, participating dairies are to elect a coverage level threshold and a coverage percentage.	No comparable provision.

Current Law/Policy	House-Passed Bill (H.R. 2)	Senate-Passed Bill (H.R. 2)
	This election remains in effect for the duration of the DRMP. **(§1401(g)(1))**	
Participating dairy operations may elect a coverage level threshold from $4.00 to $8.00 in $0.50 increments. **(7 U.S.C. 9056(a)(1))**	Amends the section by adding $8.50 and $9.00 thresholds for the first 5 million pounds of milk production. **(§1401(g)(2))**	Amends the thresholds for the first 5 million pounds of milk production by removing the $4.00, $4.50, $5.00, and $5.50 threshold levels. Adds $5.00 threshold level for catastrophic coverage. Amends the coverage level thresholds for Tier I production to $5.50 to $9.00 as shown in the producer premium schedule. **(§1401(g)(3))**
Participating dairy operations may elect a coverage percentage, in 5% increments, from 25% to 90% of production history. **(7 U.S.C. 9056(a)(2))**	Amends the section by striking 25%. Dairy operations may elect a coverage percentage, in 5% increments, not to exceed 90% of production history. **(§1401(g)(3))**	Identical to the House bill on coverage percentage. Adds a coverage percentage of 40% for catastrophic coverage. **(§1401(g)(3))**
Premiums for MPP. Describes premium calculations, lists premiums for different coverage level thresholds and coverage percentages, and premium obligations. **(7 U.S.C. 9057(a))**	*Dairy Risk Management* replaces *Margin Protection* in the section heading. In subsection (a), *dairy risk management program* replaces *margin protection program*. Strikes subsection (e). **(§1401(i)(8))**	Strikes *margin protection* where is appears and inserts *dairy risk coverage*. **(§1401(h))**
Tier I Premiums for MPP. For the first 5 million pounds of milk production, producer premiums for coverage level thresholds per cwt. are $0 for $4.00, $4.50, and $5.00; $0.009 for $5.50, $0.016 for $6.00, $0.040 for $6.50, $0.063 for $7.00, $0.087 for $7.50, and $0.142 for $8.00. **(7 U.S.C. 9057(b)(2); as amended by the Bipartisan Budget Act (P.L. 115-123)).**	DRMP amends the producer coverage threshold premiums, per cwt., for the first 5 million pounds of milk production to $0 for $4.00, $0.002 for $4.50, $0.005 for $5.00, $0.008 for $5.50, $0.010 for $6.00, $0.017 for $6.50, $0.041 for $7.00, $0.057 for $7.50, $0.090 for $8.00, $0.120 for $8.50, and $0.170 for $9.00. **(§1401(h)(1))**	DRC amends the producer coverage threshold premiums, per cwt, for the first 5 million pounds of milk production to $0 for $4.00, $4.50, and $5.00, $0.020 for $5.50, $0.040 for $6.00, $0.070 for $6.50, $0.100 for $7.00, $0.120 for $7.50, $0.140 for $8.00, $0.160 for $8.50, and $0.180 for $9.00. **(§1401(h)(3))**
Tier II Premiums for MPP. For the first 5 million pounds of milk production, producer premiums for coverage level thresholds per cwt. are $0 for $4.00, $0.020 for $4.50, $0.040 for $5.00, $0.100 for $5.50, $0.155 for $6.00, $0.290 for $6.50, $0.830 for $7.00, $1.060 for $7.50, and $1.360 for $8.00. **(7 U.S.C. 9057(c)(2))**	No comparable provision.	DRC amends the producer coverage threshold premiums, per cwt, for the first 5 million pounds of milk production to $0 for $4.00, $4.50, and $5.00, $0.144 for $5.50, $0.240 for $6.00, $0.420 for $6.50, $1.080 for $7.00, $1.320 for $7.50, and $1.680 for $8.00. **(§1401(h)(4))**

Table 4. (Continued)

Current Law/Policy	House-Passed Bill (H.R. 2)	Senate-Passed Bill (H.R. 2)
No comparable provision.	No comparable provision.	**Small and Medium Farm Discount.** Tier I and Tier II premiums are discounted 50% for milk production history of 2 million pounds or less for participating dairies. The premiums are discounted 25% on milk production history over 2 million pounds and not greater than 10 million pounds. **(§1401(h)(6))**
No comparable provision.	No comparable provision.	**Repayment of Premiums.** Requires USDA to repay premiums to dairy operations that participated in MPP during 2015-2017. Dairy operations may receive a premium repayment if their amount of premiums paid exceeded the amount of margin payments, plus the MPP program costs, received for a calendar year. **(§1401(g))**
Time for payment of premiums. Requires USDA to provide more than one method for participating dairies to pay premiums to maximize payment flexibility and program integrity. **(7 U.S.C. 9057(d))**	In a technical correction, the subsection title is amended to **Method of Payment of Premiums. (§1401(h)(2))**	No comparable provision.
No comparable provision.	**Effective date.** The amendments establishing the DRMP take effect 60 days after the date of enactment. **(§1401(j))**	No comparable provision.
Duration. The margin protection program ends on December 31, 2018. **(7 U.S.C. 9059)**	Deletes *margin protection* and inserts *dairy risk management*. Amends the end date to December 31, 2023. **(§1401(k))**	Similar to House bill. Deletes *margin protection* and inserts *dairy risk coverage*. Amends the end date to December 31, 2023. **(§1401(j))**
Effect of failure to pay administrative fees or premiums. Dairy operations that participate in MPP are legally obligated to pay administrative fees and premiums. They may not receive MPP payments if payments are in arrears. **(7 U.S.C. 9058)**	Strikes *margin protection* where it appears and replaces it with *dairy risk management*. **(§1401(i)(9))**	Similar to House bill. Strikes *margin protection* where it appears and replaces it with *dairy risk coverage*. **(§1401(i))**
Administration and enforcement. The Secretary will promulgate regulations for (1) the MPP, (2) prohibiting reconstituting dairies to receive MPP payments, and (3) administrative appeals. **(7 U.S.C. 9060)**	Strikes *margin protection* where it appears and replaces it with *dairy risk management*. **(§1401(i)(10))**	Similar to House bill. Strikes *margin protection* where it appears and replaces it with *dairy risk coverage*. **(§1401(k))**

Current Law/Policy	House-Passed Bill (H.R. 2)	Senate-Passed Bill (H.R. 2)
Repeal, Amend, and Reauthorization of Other Dairy Programs		
Dairy Product Donation Program (DPDP). Requires USDA to purchase dairy products at prevailing market prices when the dairy margin (milk price-feed costs) is $4.00 per cwt. or lower for two-consecutive months. DPDP purchases end when certain conditions occur, such as three- consecutive months of purchases, or the margin moves higher than $4.00/cwt. Purchased dairy products are to be given to low- income populations utilizing the services of public and private nonprofit groups. DPDP is funded through the CCC. Expires December 31, 2018. **(7 U.S.C. 9071)**	Repeals DPDP. **(§1406)**	Amends DPDP by replacing it with the **Milk Donation Program**. No later than 180 days from enactment, USDA is required to establish and administer a milk donation program to (1) encourage the donation of fluid milk; (2) provide nutrition assistance to individuals in low- income groups; and (3) reduce food waste. **(§1413)** Under the program, dairy farmers, cooperatives, or processors, who account for milk under the federal milk marketing order system, may donate fluid milk to public or private nonprofit organizations that distribute donated milk and receive a reimbursement for costs associated with the donated milk.
		Participants are required to provide USDA donation and distribution plans that (1) describe how they will donate, process, transport, store, and distribute milk; (2) estimate how much milk will be donated and provide a plan for unanticipated donations; and (3) explain their reimbursement rate. The reimbursement rate may not exceed the value of the difference of Class I milk and the lower of Class III or Class IV milk in the federal milk marketing order pool for the applicable month. USDA is to review and approve the plans at least once a year, and USDA may verify the documentation for reimbursements by spot checks or audits. Donated milk is prohibited for resale and distributors who violate this will be barred from future participation in the program. The provision provides $8 million in CCC funding for FY2019, and $5 million for each year FY2020 through FY2023. Funds are available until expended.

Table 4. (Continued)

Current Law/Policy	House-Passed Bill (H.R. 2)	Senate-Passed Bill (H.R. 2)
Dairy Forward Pricing Program. Authorizes a dairy forward pricing program. Prices paid by milk handlers under forward contracts are deemed to satisfy the minimum price requirements of federal milk marketing orders. Forward contracts apply only to milk purchased for manufactured products (Classes II, III, and IV) and excludes milk purchased for fluid consumption (Class I). Expires on September 30, 2018. **(7 U.S.C. 8772)**	Extends program through FY2023. Allows for new contracts until September 30, 2023, but no contract can extend beyond September 30, 2026. **(§1403)**	Identical to the House bill. **(§1411(a))**
Dairy Indemnity Program. Authorizes payments to dairy farmers when a public regulatory agency directs removal of raw milk from the market because of contamination by pesticides, nuclear radiation or fallout, or toxic substances and other chemical residues. Expires September 30, 2018. **(7 U.S.C. 4551)**	Extends program through FY2023. **(§1404)**	Identical to the House bill. **(§1411(b))**
Dairy Promotion and Research Program. The Dairy Production Stabilization Act of 1983 authorized a generic dairy product promotion, research, and nutrition education program, funded by a mandatory $0.15 per cwt. assessment on milk produced/marketed in the 48 contiguous states. Importers in all 50 states, the District of Columbia, and Puerto Rico must also pay an assessment rate of $0.075 per cwt. on imported products. Expires September 30, 2018. **(7 U.S.C. 4504)**	Extends program through FY2023. **(§1405)**	Identical to the House bill. **(§1411(c))**
Federal Milk Marketing Orders		
Terms—milk and its products. Sets terms of classifying milk by its use and setting a minimum price for each classified use (Class I, II, III, and IV) that handlers pay producers or cooperatives. The prices are uniform to handlers subject to adjustments for (1) volume, market, and production differentials; (2) grade or quality of milk; and (3) location for delivery of milk to handlers. The section sets minimum dollar amounts of adjustments to Class I milk by marketing areas for a hundredweight of milk at 3.5% milkfat.	**Class I skim milk price.** Amends the section by striking the minimum adjustments to Class I milk, the table of marketing area adjustments, and the effective period. The amended Class I skim milk price per cwt. is to be calculated as the simple average of the USDA reported advanced Class III and Class IV skim milk pricing factors plus applicable differential adjustments as specified in regulation plus $0.74. **(§1402(a))** The amended pricing takes effect on the first day of the first month beginning more than 120 days after enactment. **(§1402(b)(1)**	Identical to the House bill. **(§1412)**

Current Law/Policy	House-Passed Bill (H.R. 2)	Senate-Passed Bill (H.R. 2)
The minimum adjustments went into effect on December 23, 1985, and are included in a table. **(7 U.S.C. 608c(5)(A))**	The amendment is not subject to (1) the notice and comment provisions of 5 U.S.C. 553, (2) the notice and hearing requirements of 7 U.S.C. 608c, (3) the order amendment requirements of 7 U.S.C. 608c(17), or (4) the referendum section of 7 U.S.C. 608c(19). **(§ 1402(b)(2)**	
Supplemental Agricultural Disaster Assistance Programs		
Definitions. Four terms are defined under the Supplemental Agricultural Disaster Assistance Program: *eligible producer on a farm, farm-raised fish, livestock*, and *Secretary*. *Eligible producer on a farm* is defined as an individual or entity that assumes the production and market risks associated with the agricultural production of crops or livestock. The terms *individual or entity* specifically refer to 1) a U.S. citizen, 2) a resident alien, 3) a partnership of U.S. citizens, or 4) a corporation, limited liability corporation, or other farm organization structure organized under State law. **(7 U.S.C. 9081(a))**	No comparable provision.	Adds *Indian tribe or tribal organization*, as defined in section 4 of the Indian Self-Determination and Education Assistance Act (15 U.S.C. 3504), to the list of *individual or entities* referenced in the definition of an *eligible producer on a farm*. **(§ 1501(a))**
The **Livestock Indemnity Program** compensates producers at a rate of 75% of market value for livestock mortality or livestock sold at a loss caused by adverse weather or reintroduced animal attacks. **(7 U.S.C. 9081(b))**	Expands payments to include losses from disease that is caused or transmitted by a vector and is not controlled by vaccination or other acceptable management practices. **(§1501(a))**	Specifies that USDA may disregard management practices, vaccination protocol, or lack of vaccination by the eligible producer when the loss from adverse weather was the death of unweaned livestock. **(§1501(b))**
Emergency Assistance for Livestock, Honey Bees, and Farm-Raised Fish Program (ELAP). See **Table 15 (7 U.S.C. 9081(d)(2))**	No comparable provision.	See **Table 15**. **(§12613)**
Total payments received under the **Livestock Forage Disaster Program (LFP)** and **ELAP** are limited to $125,000 for any crop year. **(7 U.S.C. 9081(f))**	Excludes ELAP from the $125,000 per crop year payment limit. LFP remains subject to a $125,000 per crop year payment limit. **(§1501(b)(1))**	No comparable provision.
No comparable provision.	Adds exclusion to the adjusted gross income limit (§1604) for participants under the Supplemental Agricultural Disaster Assistance Programs who receive more than 75% of their income from farming, ranching, or silviculture. **(§1501(b)(2))**	No comparable provision.
The **Tree Assistance Program (TAP)** provides payments to eligible orchardists and nursery growers to replant or rehabilitate trees, bushes and vines	No comparable provision.	Adds a new, increased payment rate for beginning and veteran producers of 75% of the cost of replanting and rehabilitation.

Table 5. (Continued)

Current Law/Policy	House-Passed Bill (H.R. 2)	Senate-Passed Bill (H.R. 2)
amaged by natural disasters. Eligible losses must exceed 15%, after adjustment for normal mortality. Payments cover 65% of the cost of replanting trees or nursery stock and 50% of the cost of rehabilitation (e.g., pruning and removal). **(7 U.S.C. 9081(e))**		**(§1501(c))**
No comparable provision.	No comparable provision.	**Peach and Blueberry Losses.** Provides $18 million in mandatory funding for peach and blueberry losses in CY2017 due to extreme cold. **(§1502)**
Noninsured Crop Disaster Assistance Program (NAP)		
See Table 15	**§§11501-11503**	**§§1601-1602**
Payment Limits		
Payment limitations. Establishes the maximum amount of payments per year to a person or legal entity from PLC and ARC payments, marketing loan gains, and LDPs for the sum of all covered commodities, except peanuts, at $125,000. Any benefits arising from forfeiture of crops held under marketing assistance loans is not subject to a payment limit. Peanuts has a separate payment limit of $125,000 for those same programs. **(7 U.S.C. 1308(a)-(d))**	Retains the payment limit of $125,000 per year for all covered commodities (with a separate limit for peanuts) to a person or legal entity but applies it only to the sum of PLC and ARC payments. **(§1603(a)(2))**	Continues current law.
Payments made to a legal entity are reduced proportionately by the ownership share of any person or legal entity that has otherwise exceeded the applicable payment limitation. **(7 U.S.C. 1308(e)(3)(B)(iii))**	Any benefits arising from marketing loan gains, LDPs, and forfeiture of crops held under marketing assistance loans are not subject to a payment limit. **(§1603(a)(3))** Amends the definition of *family member* (see below) **(§1603(a)(1)(B))** and adds *qualified pass through entity* as a payment recipient subject to specific treatment (see below). **(§1603(a)(1)(D))** All changes made to payment limits shall apply starting with the 2019 crop year. **(§1603(d))**	
Family member. A person to whom a member in the farming operation is related as lineal ancestor, lineal descendant, sibling, spouse, or otherwise by marriage. **(7 U.S.C. 1308(a)(2))**	Revises the definition of family member to include first cousins, nieces, and nephews. **(§1603(a)(1)(B))**	Continues current law.
No comparable provision.	**Defines a qualified pass- through entity (QPTE).** Based on the Internal Revenue Code definition (subchapter K, chapter 1),	No comparable provision.

Current Law/Policy	House-Passed Bill (H.R. 2)	Senate-Passed Bill (H.R. 2)
	QPTE includes partnerships, limited liability companies (LLCs), S corporations, and joint ventures. **(§1603(a)(1)(D))**	
Treatment of joint ventures and partnerships. Payment limit for joint ventures and general partnerships equals the payment limit for a person or legal entity of $125,000 times the number of eligible persons or legal entities that comprise the businesses ownership. **(7 U.S.C. 1308(e)(3)(B)(ii))**	**Treatment of QPTE.** The payment limit for joint ventures and partnerships is replaced with a broader payment limit for QPTEs that encompasses joint ventures, partnerships, limited liability companies, and S corporations. The payment limit equals the individual payment limit times the number of eligible persons or legal entities that comprise the QTPE. Thus, the payment passes through the QTPE and is attributed to its owners (either individuals or entities) depending on where taxable revenue is recognized. **(§1603(b))**	Continues current law.
Payment limit definitions. (7 U.S.C. 1308) No comparable definition.	No comparable provision.	Amends current law to add a definition for a "significant contribution of active personal management" as active personal management activities performed by a person with a direct or indirect ownership interest in the farming operation on a regular, continuous, and substantial basis to the farming operation, and that meet at least one of the following to be considered significant: (A) are performed for at least 25% of the total management hours required for the farming operation on an annual basis; or (B) are performed for at least 500 hours annually for the farming operation. **(§1704)**
Payments limited to active farmers. (7 U.S.C. 1308-1(b))	No comparable provision.	Amends current law to add specificity on the requirement for "actively engaged in farming (AEF)." (A) USDA shall consider not more than 1 person or legal entity per farming operation to be AEF using active personal management. (B) USDA may only consider a person or legal entity to be AEF using active personal management under subparagraph (A) if the person or legal entity—

Table 4. (Continued)

Current Law/Policy	House-Passed Bill (H.R. 2)	Senate-Passed Bill (H.R. 2)
		(i) together with other persons or legal entities in the farming operation qualifying as AEF under current law, does not collectively receive, directly or indirectly, an amount equal to more than the allowable payment limit; (ii) does not use the active management contribution allowed under this section to qualify as AEF in more than 1 farming operation; and (iii) manages a farming operation that does not substantially share equipment, labor, or management with persons or legal entities that, together with the person or legal entity, collectively receive, directly or indirectly, an amount equal to more than the allowable payment limit. **(§1705)**
Adjusted Gross Income (AGI) Limitation.		
AGI limitation. Prohibits farm commodity program benefits (including benefits under PLC, ARC, MAL, agricultural disaster assistance, or conservation programs) to an individual or entity if AGI exceeds $900,000. The AGI limit is calculated as the average AGI or comparable measure of the person or legal entity over the three taxable years prior to the most immediately complete taxable year. **(7 U.S.C. 1308-3a)**	Amends AGI limitation to no longer apply to any benefits under the MAL program **(§1604(a))**. Exempts QPTEs from the AGI limitation. **(§1604(b))** Provides authority to Secretary to waive AGI limitation, on case-by-case basis, to protect environmentally sensitive land of special significance. **(§1604 (b)(1)(B)** Applies the Section 1604 (a-b) changes starting with the 2018 crop, fiscal, or program year as appropriate. **(§1604(c))**	Amends current law to lower the AGI threshold to $700,000. **(§1706)**
Administrative Programs		
General administration. The Secretary may use the funds and facilities of the CCC to carry out this title **(7 U.S.C. 9091(a))**. Provides that a determination made by the Secretary under this title shall be final and conclusive **(7 U.S.C. 9091(b))**. Provides for an expedited implementation of this title: Not later than 90 days after February 7, 2014, USDA and the CCC shall promulgate such regulations as necessary **(7 U.S.C. 9091(c))**.	Continues these provisions as current law, noting that promulgation of implementing regulations shall occur not later than 90 days after enactment. **(§1601(a,b,c))**	Amends current law for expedited rulemaking to extend the authority to include title I of the 2018 farm bill, and the amendments made by this title. **(§1701)**

Current Law/Policy	House-Passed Bill (H.R. 2)	Senate-Passed Bill (H.R. 2)
Adjustment authority to comply with trade agreements. Provides the Secretary authority to adjust expenditures under this title to ensure that the United States remains in compliance with domestic support levels allowed under the World Trade Organization. **(7 U.S.C. 9091(d))**	Same as current law. **(§1601(d))**	Continues current law.
Suspension of permanent price support authority. Suspends the permanent price support authority of the Agricultural Adjustment Act of 1938 and the Agricultural Adjustment Act of 1949 for the 2014-2018 crop years (covered commodities, cotton, and sugar) and for milk through December 31, 2018. **(7 U.S.C. 9092)**	Extends the suspension of permanent price authority in the Agriculture Marketing Adjustment Act of 1938 and the Agricultural Act of 1949 for the 2019-2023 crop years for covered commodities, cotton, and sugar and for milk through December 31, 2023. **(§1602)**	Extends the suspension of permanent price authority in the Agriculture Marketing Adjustment Act of 1938 and the Agricultural Act of 1949 through December 31, 2023. **(§1702)**
Prevention of deceased individuals receiving payments under farm commodity programs. At least twice each year, the secretary shall reconcile Social Security numbers of all individuals who receive payments under this chapter, whether directly or indirectly, with the commissioner of Social Security to determine if the individuals are alive. The Secretary shall preclude the issuance of payments to, and on behalf of, deceased individuals that were not eligible for payments. **(7 U.S.C. 9003)**	Same as current law. **(§1605)**	Continues current law.
Assignment of payments. Provides the authority for a producer who receives a payment under this title to assign the payment to someone else after proper notice to the Secretary. **(7 U.S.C. 9003)**	Same as current law. **(§1606)**	Continues current law.
Tracking of benefits. Authorizes the Secretary to track the benefits provided to individuals getting payments under Titles I and II programs. **(7 U.S.C. 9003)**	Same as current law. **(§1607)**	Continues current law.
Signature authority. In carrying out a Title I or II program, if the Secretary approves a document, then the Secretary may not subsequently (or retroactively) determine that the document is inadequate or invalid due to the lack of authority of any person signing on behalf of another individual, entity, general partnership, or joint venture unless the person knowingly and willfully falsified the signature. **(7 U.S.C. 9003)**	Same as current law but with the addition of a QPTE to the list of potential represented groups. **(§1608)**	Continues current law.

Table 4. (Continued)

Current Law/Policy	House-Passed Bill (H.R. 2)	Senate-Passed Bill (H.R. 2)
Personal liability of producers for deficiencies. No producer shall be personally liable for any deficiency arising from the sale of the collateral securing any nonrecourse loan unless the loan was obtained through a fraudulent representation by the producer. However, USDA may require a producer to assume liability for a deficiency in the grade, quality, or quantity of a commodity stored on a farm or delivered by the producer; failure to properly care for and preserve a commodity; or failure or refusal to deliver a commodity in accordance with a program. **(7 U.S.C. 7284)**	Extends current law to include the provisions of this bill. **(§1609)**	Continues current law.
Implementation. Requires the Secretary to maintain base acres and payment yields for each covered commodity. **(7 U.S.C. 9097(a))** Requires the Secretary to continue to streamline administrative burdens and costs; to improve coordination, information sharing, and administrative work within USDA; and to use new technologies to enhance efficiency and effectiveness of program delivery. **(7 U.S.C. 9097(b))** The Secretary shall make $100 million available to implement this title. Additional funds are made available upon notification to House and Senate Agriculture Committees of significant progress by September 20, 2014 ($10 million) and full implementation by September 30, 2015 ($10 million). Also $3 million is available for state extension services to educate farmers and ranchers of their options under this title and $3 million to support qualified universities to develop and train producers on web-based decision aids. **(7 U.S.C. 9097(c))**. USDA shall use CCC funds to ensure that the MAL program and benefits are fully functional in any year that discretionary spending limits are enforced via sequestration or other means. **(7 U.S.C. 9097(d))**	Same as current law for all provisions except: • The Secretary is required to make $25 million available to implement this title **(§1610(c))**; and • USDA shall use CCC funds to ensure that PLC and ARC payments are fully made prior to enforcing in any year where discretionary spending limits are enforced via sequestration or other budgetary means. **(§1603(a)(4))**	Continues current implementation law with the following exceptions. Amends current law to update requirements of the acreage reporting and streamlining initiative to make available more detailed USDA data across agencies and accessible via a single Department- wide login. **(§1703(1))** Amends current law to require that any USDA payment obligations— that have not been disbursed or liquidated, and remain outstanding five years after the date on which the payment was obligated or made available—shall be de-obligated and revert to the Treasury. The Secretary may delay the date of de- obligation. **(§1703(2))**

Current Law/Policy	House-Passed Bill (H.R. 2)	Senate-Passed Bill (H.R. 2)
Exemption from certain reporting requirements for certain producers. Section 1244(m) of the Food Security Act of 1985, as amended by Section 766 of the Consolidated Appropriations Act of 2018 (P.L. 115-124), stipulates that select federal grant financial reporting requirements for producers (defined as producers and landowners eligible to participate in any USDA conservation program) should not apply to Natural Resources Conservation Service (NRCS) conservation programs. **(16 U.S.C. 3844(m))**	Expands the federal grant financial reporting requirement exemption for NRCS conservation programs to all USDA commodity and conservation programs administered by the Farm Service Agency and the NRCS. **(§1611)**	Similar to House bill. Retains the provision in the conservation title, but expands the exemption to all USDA commodity and conservation programs administered by the Farm Service Agency and the NRCS. **(§2305(d))**
Annual filing for ARC and PLC. In accordance with its authority to implement these programs (7 U.S.C. 1601), USDA is directed to issue regulations. Such regulations require that eligible producers of covered commodities with base acres must execute and submit an ARC or PLC program contract not later than June 1 of the applicable year for each of 2016 through 2018 fiscal year contracts. **(7 CFR §1412.41)**	**One-time filing for ARC and PLC.** Participating producers may file a one-time program contract with USDA to enroll in ARC or PLC through crop year 2023. Farmers must update their contract within one year if any changes are made to the farm operation. USDA shall provide a notice to each producer (filing a contract) that includes other USDA reporting requirements. **(§1612)**	
No comparable provision.	No comparable provision.	**Base acres review and report.** USDA shall review the establishment, calculation, reallocation, adjustment, and reduction of base acres specified under current law **(7 U.S.C. 9011 *et seq.*)**. Not later than 2 years after the date of enactment, USDA shall submit a report describing the results of the base acre review to the House and Senate Agriculture Committees. **(§1707)**
		Farm Service Agency (FSA) accountability. Not later than 1 year from enactment, USDA shall establish policies, procedures, and plans to improve accountability and integrity. Not later than 2 years after enactment, and annually thereafter through 2023, USDA shall submit a report to the House and Senate Agriculture Committees describing efforts: to improve FSA accountability; identified weaknesses; related data sampling and mining efforts;

Table 4. (Continued)

Current Law/Policy	House-Passed Bill (H.R. 2)	Senate-Passed Bill (H.R. 2)
		errors, waste, fraud, or abuse; and any plan of action or recommended legislative changes. **(§1708)**
		Use of CCC funds for Implementation of Title I. Provides $100 million of mandatory funds, to remain available until expended, from the CCC to implement Title I. **(§1710)**

Table 5. Conservation

Current Law/Policy	House-Passed Bill (H.R. 2)	Senate-Passed Bill (H.R. 2)
Conservation Programs and Provisions in title XII of the Food Security Act of 1985 (P.L. 99-198)		
Definitions		
Twenty seven terms are defined under the conservation title of the Food Security Act of 1985: *agricultural commodity, beginning farmer or rancher, conservation plan, conservation system, conservation district, cost sharing payment, converted wetland, farm, field, highly erodible cropland, highly erodible land, hydric soils, hydrophytic vegetation, Indian tribe, in-kind commodities, integrated pest management, livestock, nonindustrial private forest land, person and legal entity, rental payment, Secretary, shelterbelt, socially disadvantaged farmer or rancher, state, technical assistance, vegetative cover*, and *wetland*. Definitions apply to all conservation programs within the Food Security Act of 1985. **(16 U.S.C. 3801)**	No comparable provision.	Adds a definition of *acequia* as a political subdivision of a state organized for the purpose of managing operations of irrigation ditches and which cannot impose taxes or levies. Adds acequias to the list of land considered to be *nonindustrial private forest land.* **(§2504)**
Wetland Conservation		
Program ineligibility. The wetland conservation or "swampbuster" provision denies various USDA program benefits to producers who plant program crops on wetlands converted after December 23, 1985, or who convert wetlands, making agricultural commodity production possible, after November 28, 1990. For a producer to be found out of compliance, crop production does not actually have to occur; production only needs to be made	Requires the Secretary to consider all possible exemptions before denying program benefits to producers found to be out of compliance. **(§2101)**	Requires that a producer cannot be denied program benefits if an exemption applies to that producer. **(§2412)**

Current Law/Policy	House-Passed Bill (H.R. 2)	Senate-Passed Bill (H.R. 2)
possible through activities such as draining, dredging, filling, or leveling the wetland. Exemptions for compliance violators may be granted following a review. **(16 U.S.C. 3821 *et seq.*)**		
On-site inspection requirement. The Secretary is required to conduct an on-site visit before program benefits may be withheld for noncompliance. **(16 U.S.C. 3821(c))**	No comparable provision.	Requires that the on-site inspection be conducted in the presence of the affected person, as long as that person makes themselves available for the on-site visit. **(§2401)**
Minimal effect. The Secretary is required to exempt producers that are found in violation of the wetland conservation requirements if the action is determined to have a "minimal effect" on the functional hydrological and biological value of the wetland area, including wildlife. USDA has identified categorical minimal effect exemptions for activities that are routinely determined to have a minimal effect on wetland functions. **(16 U.S.C. 3822(d))**	Requires that categorical minimal effect exemptions be published no later than 180 days after the date of enactment. **(§2102(a))**	Similar to the House bill, but adds requirements for the categorical minimal effects exemptions to be (1) in compliance with applicable federal environmental laws (including the National Environmental Policy Act of 1969, NEPA); (2) in accordance with existing minimal effect determination and categorical minimal effect exemption regulations (as issued before the date of enactment); and (3) in consultation with select federal, state, and local agencies, and interested organizations. **(§2413(a))**
Wetland mitigation banking program. One option violators of wetland conservation have to mitigate the violation is through wetland mitigation banking. Wetland mitigation banking is a type of wetlands mitigation whereby a wetland is created, enhanced, or restored, and "credit" for those efforts is sold to others as compensation for the loss of impacted wetlands elsewhere. The 2014 farm bill created a permanent wetland mitigation banking program exclusively for farmers to comply with swampbuster. The program has a onetime authorization for $10 million in mandatory funding. **(16 U.S.C. 3822(k))**	Provides the wetland mitigation banking program with an additional $10 million in mandatory funding authority for FY2019 and authorizes the appropriation of $5 million for each of FY2019 through FY2023. **(§2102(b))**	Similar to House bill, but authorizes no additional mandatory funding. Authorizes the appropriation of $5 million for each of FY2019 through FY2023. **(§2413(b))**
Conservation Reserve Program (CRP)		
Authority. CRP is authorized through FY2018 to provide annual rental payments to producers to replace crops on highly erodible and environmentally sensitive land with long-term resource conserving plantings. **(16 U.S.C. 3831(a))**	Reauthorizes CRP through FY2023. **(§2201(a))**	Identical as House bill. **(§2101(1))**

Table 5. (Continued)

Current Law/Policy	House-Passed Bill (H.R. 2)	Senate-Passed Bill (H.R. 2)
Eligible land. Highly erodible land is considered eligible for enrollment in CRP if (1) untreated could substantially reduce the land's future agricultural production capability *or* (2) it cannot be farmed in accordance with a conservation plan; and has a cropping history or was considered to be planted for four of the six years preceding February 7, 2014 (except for land previously enrolled in CRP). **(16 U.S.C. 3831(b)(1))**	No comparable provision.	Amends the enrollment eligibility for highly erodible land to include both conditions (1) *and* (2) under current law. Extends the six-year cropping history to include land planted for four of the six years preceding enactment of the bill. **(§2101(2))**
Maximum enrollment. CRP is authorized to enroll up to 27.5 million acres in FY2014, 26 million acres in FY2015, 25 million acres in FY2016, and 24 million acres in both FY2017 and FY2018. **(16 U.S.C. 3831(d)(1))**	Increases enrollment limits to 25 million acres in FY2019, 26 million acres in FY2020, 27 million acres in FY2021, 28 million acres in FY2022, and 29 million acres in FY2023. **(§2201(b)(1))**	Increases enrollment limit to 25 million acres in FY2019 through FY2023. **(§2101(3)(A))**
Grasslands enrollment. CRP grassland enrollment is capped at 2 million acres between FY2014 and FY2018. **(16 U.S.C. 3831(d)(2)(A))**	Creates a minimum CRP grassland enrollment level of 3 million acres by the end of FY2023. Incrementally increases the enrollment of grassland acres to 1 million acres in FY2019, 1.5 million acres in FY2020, 2 million acres in FY2021, 2.5 million acres in FY2022, and 3 million acres in FY2023. If USDA cannot enroll grassland acres according to the defined schedule, the unenrolled acres may not be used to enroll other eligible land into the program. **(§2201(b)(2))**	Reauthorizes CRP grassland enrollment at 2 million acres through FY2023. Requires CRP grassland enrollment to prioritize expiring CRP land, land at risk of development, or land of ecological significance. **(§2101(3)(B))**
No comparable provision. CRP acres are enrolled based on the relative environmental benefits of the land offered.	**Minimum enrollment by state.** Requires a minimum enrollment rate per state based on historical enrollment. Enrollment rates must consider the average total number of acres enrolled in each state during FY2007 through FY2016, average number of acres enrolled in CRP during FY2007 through FY2016, and the acres available for enrollment for FY2019 through FY2023. Also requires that a general sign-up be held every year. **(§2201(b)(3))**	No comparable provision.
No comparable provision. There are two types of enrollment into CRP: general sign-up and continuous sign- up.	No comparable provision.	**Additional Enrollment Procedures.** Requires CRP grassland and continuous sign-up offers to be accepted on a

Current Law/Policy	House-Passed Bill (H.R. 2)	Senate-Passed Bill (H.R. 2)
A general sign-up is a specific period of time during which USDA accepts offers and competitively enrolls acres. Land offered under continuous sign-up may be enrolled at any time and is not subject to competitive bidding. CRP grassland offers are accepted on a continuous basis with periodic ranking periods. All sign-ups are subject to available acres within the authorized limits. **(7 C.F.R. 1410.30)**		continuous basis, subject to available acres within the authorized limits. Also requires USDA to enroll CRP land each fiscal year, subject to available acres within the authorized limits. **(§2101(3)(C))**
No comparable provision. See the description of the current State Acres for Wildlife Enhancement Initiative below.	No comparable provision.	**State Acres for Wildlife Enhancement (SAFE).** Requires offers in SAFE project areas to be given priority enrollment under continuous sign-up. At least 30% of total CRP continuous sign-up acres must be in a SAFE project area. **(§2101(3)(C))**
No comparable provision.	No comparable provision.	**Enrollment of water quality practices.** Requires offers that would have a positive impact on water quality and would be devoted to select water quality improving practices to be given priority enrollment under continuous sign-up. Not less than 40% of total CRP continuous sign- up acres must be enrolled under this priority. When establishing the water quality priority, USDA is required to consider watersheds impacted by sediment and nutrient loading, and where enrollment would reduce harmful algal blooms. A monthly and annual report is required. **(§2101(3)(C))**
Contract duration. CRP contracts are 10-15 years in duration. In the case of land devoted to hardwood trees, shelterbelts, windbreaks, or wildlife corridors, the landowner may specify the duration of the contract between 10 and 15 years. **(16 U.S.C. 3831(e))**	Amends the duration for CRP contracts by requiring select continuous enrollment contracts to enroll for 15-30 years. **(§2201(c))**	No comparable provision.
Reenrollment of expired land. All expiring CRP land is eligible for reenrollment in the program. **(16 U.S.C. 3831(h))**	Limits reenrollment for land devoted to hardwood trees to only one reenrollment. **(§2201(d))**	No comparable provision.
No comparable provision. The **State Acres for Wildlife Enhancement (SAFE) Initiative** is a CRP continuous sign-up initiative created by the George W. Bush Administration in 2008.	No comparable provision.	Establishes a format in which states and Indian Tribes may request "SAFE areas" under CRP.

Table 5. (Continued)

Current Law/Policy	House-Passed Bill (H.R. 2)	Senate-Passed Bill (H.R. 2)
SAFE project areas are proposed by conservation groups, nonprofit organizations, government agencies, biologists, farmers, and ranchers and must contain acres with wildlife species that may be threatened or endangered, suffering population decline, or provide value to the local community. Acres enrolled under the SAFE initiative receive a higher percentage of cost-share assistance, additional practice incentive payments, and a sign-up incentive payment.		Priority is given to SAFE area requests that 1) include habitat for species that are declining or in danger of declining; 2) would help prevent the listing of or remove a species as a threatened species or endangered species under the Endangered Species Act (16 U.S.C. 1531 *et seq.*); 3) is adjacent to other conservation land; or 4) provides economic or social value to the local community for outdoor recreation. Priority is also given for requests that offer to pay additional incentive payments for CRP contracts in SAFE areas. Regional balance must be maintained and, monthly and annual reports are required. **(§2101(4))**
No directly comparable provision. **Conservation Reserve Enhancement Program (CREP)** is a subprogram of CRP in which USDA enters into agreements with States to target select areas and resource concerns in exchange for continuous CRP sign-ups and higher payments for enrollment.	No comparable provision.	Adds a new provision establishing CREP as a permanent subprogram under CRP. Provisions are similar to the existing CREP. Allows USDA to enter into agreements with eligible entities to carry out CREP. Agreement requirements are defined and existing CREP agreements remain in force, but may be modified. Payments from an eligible partner may be in cash, in-kind, or through technical assistance. Includes additional requirements for select cost- share payments, incentive payments, and maintenance payments. Requires at least 20% of continuous contracts to be enrolled in CREP. Status reports are required 180 days after enactment. Dryland farming is allowed on CREP acres if the purpose of the CREP agreement is to address regional drought concerns. **(§2105(a))** and **(§12612)**
Farmable Wetlands Program (FWP). A subprogram under CRP authorized through FY2018 to enroll up to 750,000 acres of wetland and buffer acreage in CRP. USDA may, after a review,	Reauthorizes FWP through FY2023. Amends buffer acreage enrollment and reduces total enrollment to not more than 500,000 acres.	Reauthorizes FWP through FY2023. **(§2102)**

Current Law/Policy	House-Passed Bill (H.R. 2)	Senate-Passed Bill (H.R. 2)
increase the number of acres enrolled in FWP by 200,000 additional acres. **(16 U.S.C. 3831b(a)-(c))**	Deletes a provision allowing buffer acres and Conservation Reserve Enhancement Program (CREP) acres to be considered separate from the total enrollment cap. Deletes USDA's authority to increase acreage enrollment. **(§2202(a)-(c))**	
Owners and operators of FWP land must agree to (1) restore the hydrology of the wetland, (2) establish vegetative cover, (3) prohibit commercial use, and (4) carry out the other duties required of all CRP contracts. **(16 U.S.C. 3831b(e))**	Deletes the prohibition on commercial use. **(§2202(d))**	No comparable provision.
Under FWP, the Secretary is required to make rental payments and cost- share payments in accordance with CRP. Additional incentives are authorized to enroll filterstrips. **(16 U.S.C. 3831b(f))**	Reduces the annual rental rate and deletes the additional incentives for filterstrips. **(§2202(e))**	No comparable provision.
No comparable provision.	No comparable provision.	**CRP Easements.** Adds a new provision for select expiring land (see **§2106(a)(4)**) to be enrolled into a permanent easement under CRP. In exchange for a payment the landowner must maintain the land in accordance with an approved plan and the terms and conditions of the easement. Payments are based on the lowest of (1) the appraised fair market value of the land, (2) a corresponding geographical limitation, or (3) the landowner's offer. All payments are to be made in cash and may be received in a lump sum or ten annual payments. USDA may delegate the management, monitoring, and enforcement responsibilities of CRP easements to other federal, state, or local government agencies, or conservation organizations. There are no limits on the number of easements that may be entered into and enrollment is not restricted by the overall CRP enrollment limit. **(§2107)**
Duties of owners and operators. In exchange for payments under CRP, owners and operators agree to a number of requirements and restrictions on the land under contract.	Adds grazing as a management activity that may be undertaken to implement a conservation plan. Allows for a conservation plan to include permitted commercial uses.	No comparable provision.

Table 5. (Continued)

Current Law/Policy	House-Passed Bill (H.R. 2)	Senate-Passed Bill (H.R. 2)
These requirements are outlined in the CRP contract and conservation plan. **(16 U.S.C. 3832)**	Adds a requirement for hardwood and other trees, excluding windbreaks and shelterbelts, to carry out thinning and forest management practices. **(§2203)**	
Duties of the Secretary. In return for a CRP contract, landowners are compensated for a percentage of the cost (cost-share) of carrying out conservation measures within the contract and an annual rental rate. **(16 U.S.C. 3833(a))**	No comparable provision.	Amends cost-share payments to include the cost of fencing and water distribution practices. **(§2103(a))**
Specified permitted activities. Certain specified activities (e.g., harvesting, grazing, or other commercial uses of the forage) are permitted on CRP land under select conditions. These activities are allowed without a reduction in the annual rental rate when in response to drought, flooding, or other emergency. Managed harvesting is allowed if it is consistent with soil conservation, water quality, and wildlife habitat (including primary nesting seasons) and in exchange for not less than a 25% reduction in annual rental rates for acres covered by the activity. Managed harvesting may occur at least every five years but not more than once every three years. Routine grazing is also permitted in exchange for not less than a 25% reduction in annual rental rate, subject to nesting season restrictions, vegetation management requirements and stocking rates, and limited to not more than once every two years (accounting for regional differences). **(16 U.S.C. 3833(b))**	Expands permitted harvesting and grazing activities on CRP land. Caps the reduction in annual rental rate for managed harvesting at 25% and does not allow vegetative cover to be harvested for seed. Amends the frequency of harvesting to not more than once every three years and not more than 75 percent of the covered acres in accordance with a conservation plan. *Routine grazing* is amended to allow for grazing during periods of primary nesting season if the stocking rates are reduced by 50% in accordance with a conservation plan. Requires the frequency and duration of routine grazing to be limited to the health of established cover rather than a specific time frame. Adds a provision allowing grazing conducted as a management activity under a conservation plan to occur without a rental rate reduction. Adds a new provision that allows for grazing on CRP land during the FSA determined "normal grazing period" under the **Livestock Forage Disaster Program (LFP)** without regard to primary nesting season if there is a 50% reduction of the normal carrying capacity determined under LFP. **(§2204(b))**	Expands permitted harvesting and grazing activities on CRP land. Expands permitted harvesting, grazing, and other commercial uses of the forage on CRP acres without a reduction in annual rental rate when a state of emergency is caused by a drought or wildfire. Managed harvesting is permitted for a 25% reduction in the annual rental rate subject to: vegetation management requirements; primary nesting season restrictions; a limit of not more than once every three years; and not more than 1/3 of an owner's CRP acres in a given year. Grazing in exchange for an annual rental rate reduction of 25% is allowed subject to: vegetation management requirements and carrying capacity under LFP; timing restrictions; a limit of not more than once every three years; and a waiver of all reductions for veterans or beginning farmers or ranchers. Managed and routine grazing is not permitted during times of severe or high intensity drought (as determined by the U.S. Drought Monitor) or when determined to cause long-term damage to the vegetative cover. SAFE and CREP acres may be grazed if permitted under the related agreement. **(§2103(b))**

Current Law/Policy	House-Passed Bill (H.R. 2)	Senate-Passed Bill (H.R. 2)
No comparable provision.	Adds a new provision providing that when a natural disaster or adverse weather event has the same effect as a management practice required under a conservation plan, USDA cannot require a similar management practice if the natural disaster or adverse weather event achieved the same effect. **(§2204(c))**	No comparable provision.
No comparable provision.	No comparable provision.	Adds a new provision allowing State Technical Committees to determine years in which harvesting and grazing shall not be permitted if it would cause long- term damage to vegetative cover on that land. **(§2103(c))**
Cost-share payments. Land enrolled in CRP is eligible to receive cost-share assistance for practices implemented. Cost-share payments are limited to 50% of the actual or average cost of establishing the practice and no more than 100% of the total cost. Hardwood trees, windbreaks, shelterbelts, and wildlife corridors are eligible for additional cost-share payments. **(16 U.S.C. 3834(b))**	Reduces cost-share assistance. Cost-share payments are limited to 40% of the actual or average cost of establishing the practice except for seed, which is limited to 25% of the cost. No cost-share is available for contract management activities. No incentive payments, except those described below, are allowed beyond the cost of installing the practices. Removes the additional cost-share assistance for hardwood trees, windbreaks, shelterbelts, and wildlife corridors. **(§2205(a))**	No comparable provision.
Incentive payments. Incentive payments are allowed for up to 150% of the total cost of thinning and other practices to promote forest management or enhance wildlife habitat. **(16 U.S.C. 3834(c))**	Reduces incentive payments to not more than 100% of the total cost of thinning and other practices to promote forest management or enhance wildlife habitat. **(§2205(b))**	Adds a new provision allowing signing and practice incentive payments for continuous sign-up contracts to encourage participation. These incentive payments are limited to periods of high commodity prices. **(§2104(1)(B))**
Annual rental payments. Land enrolled in CRP is eligible to receive an annual rental payment. In determining the amount to be paid, the Secretary has discretion in determining the amount necessary to encourage enrollment. **(16 U.S.C. 3834(d)(1))**	Adds a requirement that when determining the amount of annual rental payments the Secretary must consider the impact on the local farmland rental market. **(§2205(c)(1))**	No comparable provision.
CRP enrollment is conducted through the submission of bids by owners and operators of eligible land. Annual rental payments under CRP contracts are determined by the Secretary in accordance with the rental rate criteria (see below). **(16 U.S.C. 3834(d)(2))**	Reduces annual rental payments based on enrollment type. Newly enrolled acres receive not more than 80% of the average county rental rate (described below). Reenrolled land receives not more than a percentage of the average county	No directly comparable provision. See rental rates under (§2104(2)(B) below.

Table 5. (Continued)

Current Law/Policy	House-Passed Bill (H.R. 2)	Senate-Passed Bill (H.R. 2)
	rental rate for the year of reenrollment subject to the following schedule: • First reenrollment: not more than 65%, • Second reenrollment: not more than 55%, • Third reenrollment: not more than 45%, and • Fourth reenrollment: not more than 35%. **(§2205(c)(2))**	
When accepting CRP offers, USDA may consider how the land would improve soil resources, water quality, or wildlife habitat or provide other environmental benefits. **(16 U.S.C. 3834(d)(3))**	No comparable provision.	Adds a requirement for USDA to prioritize marginal and environmentally sensitive land when evaluating offers. **(§2104(2)(A)(iii))**
Enrollment of hardwood tree acres are to be considered on a continuous basis. **(16 U.S.C. 3834(d)(4))**	Deletes provision. **(§2205(c)(3))**	No comparable provision.
Rental rates. CRP rental rates are based on soil productivity and the county average rental rate. USDA may use the National Agricultural Statistics Service's (NASS) survey estimates relating to dryland cash rental rates when determining annual rental rates. NASS is required to conduct a survey no less than once a year on county average market dryland and irrigated cash rental rates. **(16 U.S.C. 3834(d)(5))**	Requires NASS to conduct a county average rental rate survey annually and publish the survey estimate not later than September 15 each year. Requires the Secretary to use the NASS survey estimates relating to dryland rental rates when determining annual rental rates. Deletes references to "cash" rental rates. **(§2205(c)(4))**	Requires NASS to conduct a county average rental rate survey annually. Reduces annual rental payments to not more than 88.5% of the rental rate (excluding incentive payments). **(§2104(2)(B))**
Limits on rental payments. The total amount of rental payments received directly or indirectly may not exceed $50,000. Additional payment received under a Conservation Reserve Enhancement Program (CREP) contract is not subject to the payment limit. USDA is allowed to enter into CREP agreements with States. **(16 U.S.C. 3834(g))**	Adds a limit on payments to states under CREP to 50% of the cost of activities carried out under the CREP agreement. **(§2205(d))**	Maintains the $50,000 rental payment limit. Adds a waiver of payment limits and adjusted gross income (AGI) requirements for rural water district or association land enrolled for the purpose of protecting a wellhead. Deletes reference to CREP agreements. **(§2104(3))**
Early termination. Owners and operators were allowed to terminate their CRP contracts in FY2015 without penalty if the contract had been in place for at least five years. Land not eligible for early release includes filterstrips, waterways, strips adjacent to riparian areas, windbreaks, shelterbelts,	Amends the early termination provisions to allow producers with a CRP contract in place for five or more years to terminate the contract in FY2019. **(§2206(a))**	Deletes the early termination provision. **(§2106(a)(1))**

Current Law/Policy	House-Passed Bill (H.R. 2)	Senate-Passed Bill (H.R. 2)
erodibility index of more than 15, hardwood trees, wildlife habitat, duck nesting habitat, pollinator habitat, upland bird habitat buffer, wildlife food plots, State Acres for Wildlife Enhancement, shallow water areas for wildlife, rare and declining habitat, farmable wetlands, restored wetlands, diversions, erosion control structures, flood control structures, contour grass strips, living snow fences, salinity reducing vegetation, cross wind trap strips, sediment retention structures, federally designated wellhead protection areas, an easement under CRP, an average width of a perennial stream or permanent water body, and a CREP contract. Terminations become effective upon approval and payments are prorated. Land is still eligible for future CRP contracts and, if returned to production, is subject to conservation compliance requirements. **(16 U.S.C. 3835(e))**		
Transition Incentives Program. The transition option under CRP facilitates the transfer of CRP acres from a retiring owner to a beginning/socially disadvantaged/veteran producer to return land to production, and it allows the new owner to begin land improvements or start the organic certification process one year before the CRP contract expires. In exchange, the retiring owner receives up to two additional years of annual CRP rental payments following the expiration of the CRP contract. **(16 U.S.C. 3835(f))**	Amends the CRP transition option to allow new owners to start the organic certification process up to three years before the CRP contract expires. Requires that financial and technical assistance be provided to the new owner to carry out a conservation plan. **(§2206(b))**	Amends the program to transfer land from any CRP contract holder (not limited to retiring or retired farmer or rancher) to a beginning/socially disadvantaged/veteran producer. Extends the time available for the new owner to begin land improvements or start the organic certifications contract from one year to two years before the CRP contract expires. Amends participation requirements to allow short-term leases (less than 5 years) with option to purchase. In addition, gives land enrollment priority for EQIP, CSP, and ACEP. Allows for enrollment into a CRP grassland contract. **(§2106(a)(3))**
Contracts. Landowners may enroll in Conservation Stewardship Program (CSP) and conduct activities required under CSP in the final year of the CRP contract without violating the terms of the contract. **(16 U.S.C. 3835(g))**	Amends the provision to allow for enrollment in EQIP and conduct EQIP practices in the final year of the CRP contract without violating the terms of the contract. **(§2206(c))**	No comparable provision.
No comparable provision.	No comparable provision.	Adds a new reenrollment requirement for select expiring CRP contracts.

Table 5. (Continued)

Current Law/Policy	House-Passed Bill (H.R. 2)	Senate-Passed Bill (H.R. 2)
		Covered contracts include new CRP contracts entered into during the bill's authorization (through FY2023), continuous contracts with select water quality practices, and SAFE contracts. Upon expiration, covered contracts may (1) not reenroll in CRP, (2) reenroll with a 40% reduction in annual rental payments and no incentive payments, or (3) enroll in a CRP easement (see **§2107**). If the land is determined to not be suitable for a CRP easement then it may be reenrolled with the terms in effect on the date of expiration. **(§2106(a)(4))**
State laws. Land is considered ineligible for CRP if the landowner has received written notice that the land is required to have a resource concern or environmental protection measure or practices in place in accordance with tribal, state, or other local law, ordinances, or other regulation. **(7 C.F.R. 1410.6(d)(4))**	No comparable provision.	Requires USDA to amend CRP regulations prohibiting enrollment of land with existing protection measures if FSA, in consultation with the State Technical Committee, considers the enrollment to be in the best interest of the program. **(§2108)**
Conservation Stewardship Program (CSP)		
Definitions. Seven terms are defined under CSP: *agricultural operation, conservation activities, conservation stewardship plan, eligible land, priority resource concern, program,* and *stewardship threshold. Conservation activities* are defined as a conservation systems, practices, or management measures that can include structural, vegetative, and land management measures as well as planning. *Stewardship threshold* is defined as a level of management required to conserve or improve the quality and condition of a natural resource. **(16 U.S.C. 3838d(2) and (7))**	No comparable provision. Repeals CSP with transition provisions for current contracts to receive CCC funding until expiration with no option for renewal. **(§2801)**	Amends the definition of *conservation activities* to include comprehensive conservation plans, soil health planning to increase soil organic matter, and activities that will adapt or mitigate against increasing weather volatility. Amends the definition of *stewardship threshold* to include measurable resource improvements through the use of tools, models, criteria, data, and other methods. **(§2201)**
Establishment and exclusions. The purpose of CSP is to encourage producers to address priority resource concerns in a comprehensive manner by undertaking additional conservation activities and improving, maintaining,	No comparable provision.	Extends the authorization through FY2023. Extends the cropping history requirement to 4 of the 6 years preceding the date of enactment. **(§2202)**

Current Law/Policy	House-Passed Bill (H.R. 2)	Senate-Passed Bill (H.R. 2)
and managing existing conservation activities. CSP is authorized through FY2023. Eligible land may not be enrolled in other retirement or easement conservation programs (e.g., CRP and ACEP) and must have a cropping history (4 of the 6 years preceding February 7, 2014). **(16 U.S.C. 3838e)**		
Ranking of applications. Applications are ranked based on the (1) level of conservation treatment at the time of application, (2) degree of proposed increased conservation performance, (3) number of proposed priority resource concerns to be treated, (4) extent other priority resource concerns will be addressed, (5) cost effectiveness of the offer, and (6) effect of priority resource concerns when transitioning from CRP to agricultural production. **(16 U.S.C. 3838f(b)(1))**	No comparable provision.	Amends the application ranking criteria to include (1) the conservation benefits on all applicable priority resource concerns at the time of application, (2) the degree of proposed increased conservation benefits, and (3) other consistent criteria, as determined by the Secretary. Requires that similarly ranked applications be determined based on the cost- effectiveness of the offer. **(§2203(1))**
Contract renewal. CSP contracts may be renewed for an additional 5 years if the producer is in compliance with the expiring contract and agrees, at a minimum, to meet or exceed the stewardship threshold for at least two additional priority resource concerns, or exceed the stewardship threshold of two existing priority resource concerns. **(16 U.S.C. 3838f(e))**	No comparable provision.	Increases the renewal threshold requiring the adoption of new or improved conservation activities that can demonstrate continued improvement on the entire operation for the additional 5-year period. The producer must also agree, at a minimum, to meet or exceed the stewardship threshold for at least two additional priority resource concerns, or adopt or improve at least two existing priority resource concerns. **(§2203(2))**
Acreage enrollment limitation. Total acreage enrollment is limited to 10 million acres annually between February 7, 2014 and September 30, 2028. Requires a national average rate of $18 per acre (to include all costs). **(16 U.S.C. 3838g(c))**	No comparable provision.	Amends the acreage enrollment limitation to begin on the date of enactment and end on September 30, 2028. Lowers the annual acreage enrollment limit to 8,797,000. **(§2204(1))**
No comparable provision.	No comparable provision.	**Cover crop payments.** Requires that payments for cover crop activities be at least 125% of the annual payment rate. **(§2204(2))**
Crop rotation payments. Additional payments are authorized for the adoption of resource- conserving crop rotations. *Resource- conserving crop rotation* is defined and the rotation is required to provide a conservation and production benefit. **(16 U.S.C. 3838g(e))**	No comparable provision.	Authorizes additional payments for resource-conserving crop rotations and advanced grazing management. Defines *advanced grazing management* and requires that payments for these additional payments be at least 150% of the annual payment rate. **(§2204(3))**

Table 5. (Continued)

Current Law/Policy	House-Passed Bill (H.R. 2)	Senate-Passed Bill (H.R. 2)
No comparable provision.	No comparable provision.	**Comprehensive conservation plans.** Adds a new provision authorizing a one-time payment for the development of a comprehensive conservation plan. **(§2204(5))**
Payment limit. CSP payments are limited to a total of $200,000 for all contracts entered into between FY2014 through FY2023. **(16 U.S.C. 3838g(f))**	No comparable provision.	Extends the payment limit aggregate of $200,000 for all CSP contracts between FY2019 and FY2023. **(§2204(6))**
Organic certification. USDA is required to establish transparent means by which CSP participants may initiate organic certification under the Organic Foods Production Act of 1990 (7 U.S.C. 6501 *et seq.*). **(16 U.S.C. 3838g(h))**	No comparable provision.	Requires USDA to allocate CSP funding to states to support organic transition and production. Allocations must be based on the number of organic operations and organic acres within a state. **(§2204(7))**
No comparable provision.	No comparable provision.	**Additional CSP requirements.** Requires that USDA streamline and coordinate CSP and EQIP. Requires USDA to manage CSP to enhance soil health. Requires annual reports on the program. **(§2204(8))**
Environmental Quality Incentives Program (EQIP)		
Purpose. The purpose of EQIP is to promote production and environmental quality as compatible goals, and optimize environmental benefits by assisting producers: (1) with compliance with regulatory requirements; (2) avoid the need for regulation; (3) install and maintain conservation practices; and (4) make cost-effective changes to current production systems. **(16 U.S.C. 3839aa)**	No comparable provision.	Adds climate adaptation to the 3rd purpose area. Amends the 4th purpose area to address identified, new, or expected resources associated with changes to production systems and removes the cost-effective purpose. **(§2301)**
Definitions. Five terms are defined under EQIP: *eligible land*, *organic system plan*, *payment*, *practice*, and *program*. *Practice* is defined as one or more improvements (e.g., structural, land management, or vegetative practice; forest management; and other practices defined by USDA) or conservation activities (e.g., comprehensive nutrient management plans and other plans as determined by USDA). **(16 U.S.C. 3839aa-1)** Under CSP, *priority resource concern* is defined as a resource concerned that is identified at the national, state, or local level as a priority, is significant in a state or region, and	Amends the definition of *practice* by adding precision conservation management planning and the use of cover crops and resource conserving crop rotations as eligible conservation activities. Adds definitions for *priority resource concerns* and *stewardship practice*. Both new definitions are similar but not identical to the definitions for priority resource concern and stewardship threshold that are repealed under CSP. **(§2301)**	Adds a definition for *conservation planning survey* which may be developed by non-USDA entity and incorporated into the required EQIP plan. Amends the definition for *eligible land* to include land that facilitates the avoidance of crossing an environmentally sensitive area. Amends the definition of *practice* to include soil tests and soil remediation practices. Adds resource-conserving crop rotation planning, soil health planning, and

Current Law/Policy	House-Passed Bill (H.R. 2)	Senate-Passed Bill (H.R. 2)
could be addressed successfully under the program. *Stewardship threshold* is defined as a level of management required to conserve or improve the quality and condition of a natural resource. **(16 U.S.C. 3838d(5) and (7))**		conservation planning survey to the list of eligible conservation activity plans. Adds a definition for *producer*, which includes an acequia. **(§2302)**
Establishment. EQIP is authorized through FY2019. **(16 U.S.C. 3839aa-2(a))**	Reauthorizes EQIP through FY2023. **(§2302(a))**	Same as House bill. **(§2303(1))**
Contract terms. EQIP contracts are limited to 10 years. **(16 U.S.C. 3839aa-2(b)(2))**	No comparable provision.	Adds a provision allowing 10-year contracts for wildlife practices which may include incentivizing seasonal wetland development for waterfowl and migratory birds. **(§2303(2))**
Advanced payments. EQIP contracts are paid upon the completion of the approved conservation practice. USDA is authorized, however, to make up to 50% of the cost of the practice available in advance for a limited resource, socially disadvantaged, veteran, or beginning farmer or rancher. Advanced funds must be used to purchase materials within 90-days or the funds must be returned. **(16 U.S.C. 3839aa-2(d)(4)(B))**	No comparable provision.	Increases advanced payments to at least 50% of the practice cost. Extends the fund return period to 180-days and adds an opt-out option for eligible producers. **(§2303(3)(A))**
No comparable provision.	No comparable provision.	Adds new sections requiring review and guidance, within a year of enactment, on the cost effectiveness of cost-share rates and the flexibility of conservation practice standards. Also requires that each state, in consultation with the State Technical Committee, identify ten high-priority practices that will be eligible for up to 90% of the practice cost. **(§2303(3)(B))**
Funding allocation. Requires that 60% of payments go to practices related to livestock production and that a minimum of 5% of annual funds go to payments benefiting wildlife habitat through FY2018. **(16 U.S.C. 3839aa-2(f))**	Deletes carve-out for livestock related practices. Reauthorizes the wildlife habitat payment minimum (5%) through FY2023. **(§2302(b))**	Reauthorizes and reduces the carve-out for livestock related practices to 50% through FY2023 and includes grazing management practices. Reauthorizes and increases the wildlife habitat payment minimum to 10% through FY2023. Adds a requirement for USDA, within a year of enactment, to review the annual funding allocation process. **(§2303(4))**

Table 5. (Continued)

Current Law/Policy	House-Passed Bill (H.R. 2)	Senate-Passed Bill (H.R. 2)
Water conservation. EQIP may fund irrigation efficiency practices. Priority is given for applications that reduce water use on the operation or those in which the producer agrees not to use the water savings to bring new land into irrigation. **(16 U.S.C. 3839aa-2(h))**	Amends the provision by specifying that payments may be provided for water conservation scheduling technology or management, irrigation-related structural practices, use of existing or upgrade of drainage systems, or transition to water-conservation crops or rotations. Adds a new provision allowing USDA to contract with irrigation districts, irrigation associations, drainage districts, and acequias if the watershed-wide project will effectively conserve water. Only eligible land or land owned by the irrigation entity is eligible. USDA may waive income and payment limits and impose additional limits. Priority is amended to include the new irrigation entity land. **(§2302(c))**	Allows EQIP payments to be made to producers or selected eligible entities for water conservation or irrigation efficient practices. Eligible entities may be a state, irrigation district, groundwater management district, acequia, or similar entity. Practices must be implemented on eligible land of the producer or land under the control of the eligible entity. AGI and payment limits may be waived for eligible entities. Priority is given to applications that reduce water use. **(§2303(5))**
Organic payment limits. Payments for conservation practices related to organic production are limited to a total of $20,000 per year or $80,000 during any 6-year period. **(16 U.S.C. 3839aa-2(i))**	No comparable provision.	Amends the payment limit to a total of $160,000 from FY2019 through FY2023. **(§2303(6))**
No directly comparable provision. Under CSP, contracts (five years in length with the option of renewal) are based on meeting or exceeding a stewardship threshold on the entire agricultural operation. Participants must meet two priority resource concerns upon entry and meet or exceed one additional priority resource concern by the end of the contract. Contract renewal participants must meet the threshold for two additional priority resources concerns or exceed the threshold for two existing priority resource concerns. CSP provides two possible payments: (1) an annual payment for installing new conservation activities and maintaining existing activities and (2) a supplemental payment for adopting a resource-conserving crop rotation. Enrollment is offered through a continuous sign-up and applications are accepted year-round.	**Stewardship contracts.** Establishes a new stewardship contract based on priority resource concerns within a state. No more than three priority resource concerns are identified in each state. Contracts are for five to 10 years and provide annual payments to incentivize increased conservation stewardship and the adoption, installation, management, and maintenance of conservation practices. Payment amounts are to consider the level and extent of the practice, cost, income forgone, and longevity of the practice. Payments are limited to $50,000 per fiscal year. Not more than 50% of total EQIP funds may be used for stewardship contracts. **(§2302(d))**	No comparable provision.

Current Law/Policy	House-Passed Bill (H.R. 2)	Senate-Passed Bill (H.R. 2)
CSP payments are limited to not more than $200,000 total between FY2014 and FY2018. **(16 U.S.C. 3838d-3838g)**		
No comparable provision.	No comparable provision.	**Pilot program.** Establishes a pilot program, in not more than ten states, for small-scale agricultural operations. The pilot includes a payment criteria, application requirements, program coordinator, and a report to Congress. **(§2303(7))**
Evaluation of applications. USDA is required to develop criteria for evaluating applications that will ensure that national, state, and local conservation priorities are effectively addressed. **(16 U.S.C. 3839aa-3(a))**	No comparable provision.	Adds a requirement that the evaluation criteria give priority to the most effective conservation practices. **(§2304)**
EQIP plans. All EQIP contracts require an approved plan of operations. For confined livestock feeding operations, the plan provides for the development and implementation of a comprehensive nutrient management plan (CNMP). **(16 U.S.C. 3839aa-5(a)(3))**	No comparable provision.	Amends the EQIP plan of operation for confined livestock feeding operations to develop and *progressively* implement a CNMP. **(§2306)**
Duties of the Secretary. The Secretary is required to assist with the implementing of an EQIP plan and provide payments for one or more conservation practices. **(16 U.S.C. 3839aa-6)**	No comparable provision.	Requires that USDA streamline and coordinate CSP and EQIP. Requires USDA to manage EQIP to enhance soil health. **(§2305)**
Limitation on payments. An EQIP participant's payments are limit to an aggregate of $450,000 between FY2014-FY2018. **(16 U.S.C. 3839aa-7)**	Extends the EQIP payment limit ($450,000) for FY2019-FY2023 **(§2303)**	Same as House bill. **(§2307)**
Conservation Innovation Grants (CIG) and payments. CIG is a competitive grant program within EQIP. Grants are provided, on a matching basis, to implement innovative conservation projects. **(16 U.S.C. 3839aa-8(a))**	Limits CIG to no more than $25 million annually. Amends eligible uses to include persons participating in an educational activity through an institution of higher education. **(§2304(a))**	Expands the type of conservation projects to include urban agriculture and edge of field monitoring. **(§2308(1))**
Requires that $25 million of EQIP funds annually (through FY2018) be used to address air quality concerns. **(16 U.S.C. 3839aa-8(b))**	Reauthorizes and increases the air quality funding carve-out to $37 million of EQIP annually between FY2019 and FY2023. **(§2304(b))**	Reauthorizes the air quality funding carve-out of $25 million through FY2023. **(§2308(2))**
No comparable provision.	Requires up to $25 million of EQIP funds for FY2019-FY2023 be used for on-farm conservation innovation trials to test new or innovative conservation approaches either directly with producers or with eligible entities. **(§2304(c))**	No comparable provision.

Table 5. (Continued)

Current Law/Policy	House-Passed Bill (H.R. 2)	Senate-Passed Bill (H.R. 2)
Report. A report is required no later than December 31, 2014, and every two years thereafter, to Congress regarding CIG funding, project results, and technology transfer efforts. **(16 U.S.C. 3839aa-8(c))**	Adds a requirement that USDA use the required CIG reports to establish and maintain a public conservation practice database. **(§2304(c))**	No comparable provision.
No comparable provision.	No comparable provision.	**Soil health demonstration pilot.** Authorizes a new pilot project to provide financial assistance for soil health practices. A study and a report are required. Authorizes $15 million of EQIP funding annually between FY2019 and FY2023 to be used for the pilot. **(§2309)**
Other Conservation Programs		
Conservation of Private Grazing Land Program. Authorizes appropriations of $60 million annually through FY2018. **(16 U.S.C. 839bb(e))**	Extends authorization of appropriations at $60 million annually through FY2023. **(§2401)**	Similar to House bill, but adds a provision requiring education and outreach through partnership with land-grant colleges and universities and nongovernmental organizations. **(§2403)**
No comparable provision.	No comparable provision.	**Soil health and income protection program.** Creates a new program providing annual rental payments of 50% of the county average rental rate for less productive farm land to be taken out of production and planted to a low-cost perennial cover crop. At least 15% of the eligible land on the farm must be enrolled for 3-5 years. Higher annual rental rates of 75%, and cost-share assistance is available for beginning, small, socially disadvantaged, young, or veteran farmers and ranchers. Harvesting, haying, and grazing are allowed outside of the local nesting and brood-rearing period. Such sums as necessary are authorized to be appropriated. **(§2404)**
Grassroots Source Water Protection Program. Authorizes appropriations of $20 million annually through FY2018 and a one-time authorization for $5 million in mandatory funding to remain available until expended. **(16 U.S.C. 3839bb-2(b))**	Extends authorization of appropriations at $20 million annually through FY2023 and authorizes an additional $5 million in mandatory funding in FY2019 to remain available until expended. **(§2402)**	Extends and increases the authorization of appropriations at $25 million annually through FY2023. Does not reauthorize mandatory funding. **(§2405)**

Current Law/Policy	House-Passed Bill (H.R. 2)	Senate-Passed Bill (H.R. 2)
No comparable provision.	No comparable provision.	**Soil testing and remediation.** Creates a new program to assist small-scale producers with soil contaminant mitigation. USDA, in consultation with EPA, is required to create a contaminated soil testing protocol and provide technical assistance for remediation and assessment. At the request of the producer, USDA may refer the producer to EPA for additional assistance. **(§2406)**
Voluntary Public Access and Habitat Incentive Program. Authorizes $50 million in mandatory funds for FY2009-FY2012 and $40 million in mandatory funds for FY2014-2018. **(16 U.S.C. 3839bb-5(f))**	Adds authorization for $50 million in mandatory funding for FY2019-FY2023. **(§2403)**	Amends and moves the program under EQIP. Authorizes $40 million of EQIP funding for FY2019-FY2023. **(§2407)**
Agriculture Conservation Experienced Service Program (ACES). Authorizes USDA to enter into agreements with organizations to provide technical assistance (excludes administrative tasks) using qualified individuals 55 years or older. Funding from farm bill conservation programs (excluding CRP) may be used to carry out the ACES program. **(16 U.S.C. 3851)**	No comparable provision.	Amends and expands the program in the Miscellaneous title see **§12305** of **Table 15**). Adds a sunset date on the provision of October 1, 2023. **(§2408)**
No comparable provision.	No comparable provision.	**Remote telemetry data system.** Requires that the use of remote telemetry data systems for irrigation scheduling be considered a best management practice under EQIP. **(§2409)**
Funding and Administration		
Commodity Credit Corporation (CCC). Authorizes the use of funds (mandatory), facilities, and authorities of the CCC to carry out conservation programs between FY2014 and FY2018 and through FY2019 for EQIP. **(16 U.S.C. 3841(a))**	Extends the CCC authority between FY2014 and FY2023. Specific funding levels for programs are outlined below. **(§2501(a)(1))**	Same as House bill. Specific funding levels for programs are outlined below. **(§2501(a)(1))**
CRP funding. Authorizes $10 million for thinning activities and $33 million for transition contracts between FY2014 and FY2018. Total funding for CRP is limited by enrolled acres, not total dollars. See above. **(16 U.S.C. 3841(a)(1))**	Extends the specific authorizations of $10 million for thinning incentive payments and $33 million for transition contracts between FY2014 and FY2023. **(§2501(a)(1) & (a)(2))**	Extends the specific authorization of $11 million for thinning incentive payments and $50 million for transition contracts between FY2019 and FY2023. Limits outreach and technical assistance for transition contracts to $5 million. **(§2501(a)(2))**

Table 5. (Continued)

Current Law/Policy	House-Passed Bill (H.R. 2)	Senate-Passed Bill (H.R. 2)
ACEP funding. Authorizes $400 million in FY2014, $425 million in FY2015, $450 million in FY2016, $500 million in FY2017, and $250 million in FY2018. **(16 U.S.C. 3841(a)(2))**	Reauthorizes the authority for the CCC to fund ACEP for $500 million annually between FY2019 and FY2023. **(§2501(a)(3))**	Reauthorizes the authority for the CCC to fund ACEP for $400 million annually in FY2019 through FY2021, $425 million in FY2022, and $450 million in FY2023. **(§2501(a)(3))**
Conservation Security Program funding. Authorizes contracts (enrolled prior to FY2009) with such sums as necessary. **(16 U.S.C. 3841(a)(3))**	Deletes provision. **(§2501(a)(4))**	No comparable provision.
CSP funding. Total funding for CSP is limited by enrolled acres, not total dollars between FY2014 and FY2018. **(16 U.S.C. 3841(a)(4))**	Authorizes the CCC to carry out CSP contracts enrolled prior to enactment. **(§2501(a)(5))**	No comparable provision.
EQIP funding. Authorizes $1.35 billion in FY2014, $1.6 billion in FY2015, $1.65 billion in each FY2016 and FY2017, and $1.75 billion in each FY2018 and FY2019. **(16 U.S.C. 3841(a)(5))**	Reauthorizes the authority for the CCC to fund EQIP, including: $2 billion in FY2019, $2.5 billion in FY2020, $2.75 billion in FY2021, $2.935 billion in FY2022, and $3 billion in FY2023. **(§2501(a)(6))**	Reauthorizes the authority for the CCC to fund EQIP, including: $1.473 billion in FY2019, $1.478 billion in FY2020, $1.541 billion in FY2021, $1.571 billion in FY2022, and $1.595 billion in FY2023. **(§2501(a)(4))**
Availability of funds. Mandatory funding made available for CRP, ACEP, CSP, and EQIP between FY2014 and FY2018 (FY2019 for EQIP) are authorized to remain available until expended. **(16 U.S.C. 3841(b))**	Reauthorizes mandatory funding made available for CRP, ACEP, CSP, and EQIP between FY2019 and FY2023 to remain available until expended. **(§2501(b))**	Same as House bill. **(§2501(b))**
Technical assistance. USDA is required to give priority to producers who request technical assistance to comply with highly erodible land conservation (sodbuster) and wetland conservation (swampbuster) for the first time because of the changes made in the 2014 farm bill that tied crop insurance subsidies to compliance requirements. Requires reports to Congress related to the effect of conservation compliance on specialty crop producers and requested technical assistance. **(16 U.S.C. 3841(c))**	Deletes reporting requirements. **(§2501(c))**	No comparable provision.
Regional equity. Requires regional equity through proportional distribution of conservation program funds based on historical funding levels. Allows states in the first quarter of the fiscal year to establish that they can use a total of 0.6% of certain conservation funds. If established, those states may receive 0.6% of funds. **(16 U.S.C. 3841(d))**	Deletes provision. **(§2501(d))**	No comparable provision.

Current Law/Policy	House-Passed Bill (H.R. 2)	Senate-Passed Bill (H.R. 2)
Allocations. USDA is required to review all conservation program allocation formulas no later than January 1, 2012. Updates are required to reflect the cost of carrying out the programs. **(16 U.S.C. 3841(g))**	No comparable provision.	Amends the allocation review to require an update of all conservation program allocation formulas. **(§2501(c))**
Assistance to certain farmers or ranchers for conservation access. Establishes an annual set-aside in EQIP and CSP from FY2014 to FY2018—5% to beginning farmers or ranchers and 5% to socially disadvantaged farmers or ranchers. Unobligated funds for EQIP and unobligated acres for CSP under this provision may be repooled and obligated in accordance with the respective program. Preference is provided for veteran farmers or ranchers eligible under the provision. **(16 U.S.C. 3841(h))**	Reauthorizes the EQIP set-aside through FY2023 and deletes the reference to CSP. **(§2501(e))**	Reauthorizes the EQIP and CSP set-asides through FY2023 and increases the percentage set-aside to 15% to beginning farmers or ranchers and 15% to socially disadvantaged farmers or ranchers. **(§2501(d))**
Report on program enrollments and assistance. Reports are required for program enrollments and assistance under conservation programs, including significant payments, waivers, and exceptions. **(16 U.S.C. 3841(i))**	Reauthorizes reporting requirements through FY2023, adds reports on annual and current enrollment statistics, and removes references to CSP. **(§2501(f))**	Similar to House bill, but does not add reports and does not remove CSP. **(§2602)**
No comparable provision.	No comparable provision.	**Conservation standards.** Establishes the Natural Resources Conservation Service (NRCS) as the lead agency for developing technical standards and requirements for farm bill conservation programs. Requires the Farm Service Agency (FSA) to use standards consistent with NRCS. Allows local flexibility for standards and requirements. **(§2501(e))**
Delivery of technical assistance. All producers participating in conservation programs must be provided technical assistance either by USDA or through an approved third party. **(16 U.S.C. 3842(a))**	Adds a definition of third-party provider: a commercial entity, nonprofit entity, state or local government, or federal agency that has expertise in the technical aspect of conservation planning. **(§2502(a))**	Same as House bill. **(§2502(1))**
Technical service providers (TSP). TSPs are third-party providers (individuals or businesses) that have technical expertise in conservation planning and design for a variety of conservation activities. Farmers, ranchers, private businesses, nonprofit organizations, or public agencies hire TSPs to provide these services on behalf of NRCS. NRCS certifies and approves TSPs. **(16 U.S.C. 3842(e))**	Adds an alternative certification process for TSPs requiring the acceptance of other professional certification criteria that meets or exceeds the TSP certification criteria. **(§2502(b))**	TSPs may be certified through NRCS or a non-Federal entity approved by USDA to perform the certification. Requires USDA to streamline the certification process for select specialty certification, specifically the American Society of Agronomy's 4R nutrient management and sustainability specialty certification. **(§2502(2))**

Table 5. (Continued)

Current Law/Policy	House-Passed Bill (H.R. 2)	Senate-Passed Bill (H.R. 2)
Review of conservation practice standards. USDA is required to periodically review all conservation practice standards. USDA must consult with local interest and expedite required revisions. **(16 U.S.C. 3842(h))**	No comparable provision.	Requires USDA to develop, within one year of enactment, an administrative process to expedite the revision of conservation practice standards and consideration of innovative conservation measures. Requires a report to Congress every two years on the process. **(§2502(3))**
Incentives for certain producers. USDA may provide additional incentives through farm bill conservation programs for certain farmers and ranchers, including beginning, socially disadvantaged, limited resource, and veteran farmers or ranchers, and Indian tribes. **(16 U.S.C. 3844(a))**	No comparable provision.	Adds acequias to the list of farmers and ranchers eligible for additional incentives. **(§2503(a))**
Acreage limitations. No county may enroll more than 25% of the cropland into CRP or wetland reserve easements under ACEP. Not more than 10% of a county may be enrolled as a wetland reserve easement under ACEP. In select situations, USDA may waive this limitation. **(16 U.S.C. 3844(f))**	No comparable provision.	Increases the percentage limitation on wetland reserve easements to 15%. **(§2503(b))**
Pollinator habitat. See **(§12613)** of **Table 15**. **(16 U.S.C. 3844(h))**	No comparable provision.	**§12613**
Funding for Indian tribes. USDA may use alternative funding arrangements with Indian tribes for CSP and EQIP contracts. **(16 U.S.C. 3844(l))**	No comparable provision.	Requires USDA to use alternative funding arrangements with Indian tribes for CSP and EQIP contracts. **(§2503(c))**
Stipulates that select federal grant financial reporting requirements for producers (defined as producers and landowners eligible to participate in any USDA conservation program) should not apply to NRCS conservation programs. **(16 U.S.C. 3844(m)).**	Deletes provision and adds a similar provision to Section 1611 of the Commodities title (see **Table 4**),which expands the federal grant financial reporting requirement exemption for NRCS conservation programs to all USDA commodity and conservation programs administered by the Farm Service Agency and the NRCS. **(§2503(1))**	Similar to House bill. Retains the provision in the conservation title, but expands the exemption to all USDA commodity and conservation programs administered by the Farm Service Agency and the NRCS. **(§2503(d))**
No comparable provision.	**Source water protection carve-out.** Requires USDA to encourage conservation practices related to water quality and quantity that protect source waters for drinking through all farm bill conservation programs. Producers can receive incentives and high payments for such practices. USDA must	Similar to House bill. Limits applicability to CSP and EQIP. Incentives are subject to program limitations. Does not specify a percentage carve-out of each program. **(§2305(e))**

Current Law/Policy	House-Passed Bill (H.R. 2)	Senate-Passed Bill (H.R. 2)
	collaborate with community water systems and NRCS State Technical Committees to identify local priority areas. Requires 10% of all funding for conservation programs (except CRP) be used annually between FY2019 and FY2023. **(§2503(2))**	
No comparable provision.	No comparable provision	**Acequias payments.** Waives the adjusted gross income (AGI) requirement and payment limits under EQIP for contracts with acequias. If a waiver is granted, USDA must impose a separate payment limitation to the contract. **(§2305(f))**
Establishment of State Technical Committees. Requires each state technical committee be composed of representatives from: NRCS, FSA, Forest Service, the National Institute of Food and Agriculture (NIFA), state fish and wildlife agency, state forester, state water resources agency, state department of agriculture, state soil and water conservation district, agriculture producers, nonindustrial private forest landowners, nonprofit organizations working with producers, and agribusinesses. **(16 U.S.C. 3861(c))**	Adds land-grant colleges to the list of required representatives. **(§2504)**	No comparable provision.
State Technical Committees are required to meet regularly to provide information and recommendations to USDA officials regarding implementation of conservation programs and provisions. Committees are advisory in nature and exempt from Federal Advisory Committee Act requirements. **(16 U.S.C. 3862)**	No comparable provision.	Adds a requirement that State Technical Committees regularly review new and innovative technologies and practices, and provide recommendations on the development and incorporation of those practices into conservation practice standards. **(§2508)**
Agricultural Conservation Easement Program (ACEP)		
Establishment and purpose. ACEP provides financial and technical assistance through two types of easements: agricultural land easements that limit nonagricultural uses on productive farm or grasslands and wetland reserve easements that protect and restore wetlands. **(16 U.S.C. 3865)**	Amends the purpose of ACEP agricultural land easements by adding that the purpose of protecting agricultural use by limiting nonagricultural uses applies specifically for those uses that negatively affect agricultural uses and conservation values. For grasslands, the purpose is amended from protecting grasslands by restoring *and* conserving land to restoring *or* conserving land. **(§2601)**	Similar to House bill. Amends the purpose of ACEP agricultural land easements by adding that the purpose of protecting agricultural use by limiting nonagricultural uses applies specifically for those uses that negatively affect agricultural uses and conservation values. Does not amend grasslands purpose. **(§2410(a))**

Table 5. (Continued)

Current Law/Policy	House-Passed Bill (H.R. 2)	Senate-Passed Bill (H.R. 2)
Definitions. Five terms are defined under ACEP: *agricultural land easement*, *eligible entity*, *eligible land*, *program*, and *wetland reserve easement*. *Agricultural land easement* is defined as an easement that protects the natural resources and the agricultural nature of the land while maintaining production. *Eligible entity* is defined as a state or local government, Indian tribe, or conservation organization. *Eligible land* is defined separately for agricultural land easements and wetland reserve easements. Agricultural land easements include land with a pending easement offer; with prime, unique, or productive soils; that contains historical or archaeological resources; that would protect grazing uses; that furthers a similar state or local policy; that is cropland, rangeland, grassland, area historically dominated by grassland, pastureland, or nonindustrial private forest land. Wetland reserve easements include farmed or converted wetlands; cropland or grassland that has prior flooding from a closed basin lake or pothole if the state or other entity is willing to provide a 50% cost-share of the easement; wetlands that are enrolled in the CRP, have high wetland functions, and are likely to return to production after CRP; riparian areas that link protected wetlands; and wetlands determined by USDA to be significant. **(16 U.S.C. 3865a)**	Amends the definition of *agricultural land easement* by removing the requirement that landowners farm according to an approved agricultural easement plan. Amends the definition of *eligible land.* Increases the percentage of nonindustrial private forest land that may be enrolled in an agricultural land easement to 100%. Removes the requirement under wetland reserve easements that USDA consult with the Department of the Interior on the wildlife benefits and wetland functions and values. Adds a definition for *monitoring report* for agricultural land easements. **(§2602)**	Amends the definition of *agricultural land easement* by removing the requirement that landowners farm according to an approved agricultural easement plan. Amends the definition of *eligible entity* by adding acequias. Amends the definition of *eligible land* to include land owned by an organization, subject to the timely transfer of ownership to a farmer or rancher following the acquisition of the agricultural land easement. **(§2410(b))**
Agricultural land easements. ACEP funds are provided for the purchase of agricultural land easements by eligible entities and for technical assistance pursuant to an agricultural land easement plan. **(16 U.S.C. 3565b(a))**	Deletes the requirement that technical assistance be used pursuant to an agricultural land easement plan and instead be used to implement the program. **(§2603(a))**	Requires USDA to facilitate and implement the program, including technical assistance. **(§2410(c)(1))**
Eligible entities are required to provide contributions equivalent to the federal share or at least 50% of the federal share if the entity includes contributions from the private landowner. Grasslands of special environmental significance are allowed up to 75% of the fair market for the federal share.	Amends the nonfederal share of agricultural land easements. Removes the requirement that an eligible entity's contribution be equal to the federal share or at least 50% of the federal share if the entity includes contributions from the private landowner.	Similar to House bill. Amends the nonfederal share of agricultural land easements, but not the exception authority. **(§2410(c)(2)(A) & (c)(2)(B))**

Current Law/Policy	House-Passed Bill (H.R. 2)	Senate-Passed Bill (H.R. 2)
USDA is authorized to waive any portion of the eligible entity cash contribution requirement for projects of special significance subject to an increase of private landowner donation equal to the amount of the waiver if donation is voluntary. **(16 U.S.C. 3865b(b)(2)(B) & (b)(2)(C))**	Allows the eligible entity to use cash contributions, landowner contributions, or other non-USDA federal funding. Deletes the exception authority for USDA to waive an eligible entity's cash contribution for projects of special significance. **(§2603(b)(1))**	
No comparable provision.	No comparable provision.	Adds a new cost-share assistance requirement for eligible entities to develop an agricultural land easement plan. **(§2410(c)(2)(C))**
The evaluation and ranking criteria for agricultural land easement applications is required to maximize the benefit of federal investment under ACEP. **(16 U.S.C. 3865b(b)(3))**	Adds a requirement that USDA adjust the evaluation and ranking criteria for geographic differences among states. **(§2603(b)(2))**	Similar to the House bill with minor differences. **(§2410(c)(2)(D)(i))**
No comparable provision.	No comparable provision.	Adds a new provision allowing USDA to prioritize applications that maintain agricultural viability. **(§2410(c)(2)(D)(ii))**
ACEP agricultural land easement enrollment is through eligible entities that enter into cooperative agreement of three to five years in length with USDA. The entities acquire easements and hold, monitor, manage, and enforce the easements. Entities agree to a minimum level of terms and conditions for agricultural land easements including the effect of a violation. **(16 U.S.C. 3865b(b)(4))**	Amends the minimum terms and conditions by limiting the right of enforcement for USDA and removing the requirement that an agricultural land easement be subject to an agricultural land easement plan unless the land is highly erodible. Adds new provisions allowing mineral development and preventing USDA from limiting participation in environmental services markets. **(§2603(b)(3))**	Amends the minimum terms and conditions by limiting the right of inspection and removing the requirement that an agricultural land easement be subject to an agricultural land easement plan. Adds the ability for eligible entities to add additional terms and conditions to an agricultural land easement. **(§2410(c)(2)(E))**
USDA certifies eligible entities through a certification process and according to a criterion. **(16 U.S.C. 3865b(b)(5))**	Amends the certification process to allow certified entities to use their own terms and conditions for agricultural land easements. Adds to the certification criteria for land trusts accredited by the Land Trust Accreditation Commission with more than five agricultural land easements under ACEP. **(§2603(b)(4))**	Adds to the certification criteria for land trusts accredited by the Land Trust Accreditation Commission with more than ten successful agricultural land easements under ACEP, and state agencies with more than ten successful agricultural land easements under ACEP. Allows certified entities to use their own terms and conditions for agricultural land easements. **(§2410(c)(2)(F))**
USDA, if requested, may provide technical assistance for compliance with the terms and conditions of the easements and to implement an agricultural land easement plan. **(16 U.S.C. 3865b(d))**	Deletes reference to the agricultural land easement plan. **(§2603(c))**	No comparable provision.

Table 5. (Continued)

Current Law/Policy	House-Passed Bill (H.R. 2)	Senate-Passed Bill (H.R. 2)
Wetland reserve easements. ACEP wetland reserve easements may enroll land through 30-year easements, permanent easements, or 30-year contracts for Indian tribes. **(16 U.S.C. 3865c(b)(1))**	No comparable provision.	Makes acequias eligible for 30-year contracts. **(§2410(d)(1)(A))**
When evaluating ACEP wetland reserve easement applications USDA may consider (1) the benefits of obtaining the easement and removing the land from production, (2) the cost effectiveness of the easement, (3) the leveraging of federal funds, and (4) other factors determined by USDA. **(16 U.S.C. 3865c(b)(3)(B))**	No comparable provision.	Adds the ability to sequester carbon to the list of considerations that may be used when evaluating ACEP wetland reserve easement applications. **(§2410(d)(1)(B)(i))**
USDA is required to give priority to ACEP wetland reserve easements based on the value of protection and enhancement of wildlife and migratory bird habitat. **(16 U.S.C. 3865c(b)(3)(C))**	No comparable provision.	Adds water quality improvement to the wildlife and migratory bird priority. **(§2410(d)(1)(B)(ii))**
ACEP wetland reserve easements may include grazing rights if it complies with the wetland reserve easement plan. **(16 U.S.C. 3865c(b)(5)(D)(III))**	Adds that a grazing management plan may be used if consistent with the wetland reserve easement plan and is reviewed at least every five years. **(§2604)**	No comparable provision.
No comparable provision.	No comparable provision.	Adds a provision allowing for the establishment or restoration or an alternative vegetative community on the entirety of the wetland reserve easement if it would benefit wildlife or meet local resource needs. **(§2410(d)(4))**
Administration. Certain land is ineligible for ACEP easements, including land owned by the federal government, land owned by a state, land subject to an easement or deed restriction, or land where an ACEP easement would be undermined due to on- and off-site conditions (e.g., hazardous substances, proposed or existing rights of way, infrastructure development, or adjacent land use). **(16 U.S.C. 3865d(a))**	Amends ineligible land where an ACEP easement would be undermined to consider only on- site conditions. **(§2605(a))**	Allows easement acquisition on lands owned by an acequia. **(§2410(e)(1))**
USDA may subordinate, exchange, modify, or terminate any ACEP easement if it is in the federal government's interest, will address a compelling public need where there is no alternative or further the administration of ACEP, and will result in a comparable	Amends the subordination, exchange, modification, and termination requirements by providing separate criteria for modifications and terminations.	No comparable provision.

Current Law/Policy	House-Passed Bill (H.R. 2)	Senate-Passed Bill (H.R. 2)
conservation value and greater or equivalent economic value to the United States. **(16 U.S.C. 3865d(c))**	Modifications may be made if they would have a neutral or increased conservation effect and are consistent with the original intent of the easement and purposes of ACEP.	
	Terminations may be made if the current land owner and easement holder agree and the termination would be in the public interest. **(§2605(b))**	
A CRP contract may be terminated or modified if the land is transferred into ACEP. **(16 U.S.C. 3865d(d))**	No comparable provision.	Limits the CRP transfer option to enrollment as an ACEP wetland reserve easement. Adds a new provision allowing land with an ACEP agricultural land easement to participate in CRP. **(§2410(e)(2))**
No comparable provision.	Waives the AGI limitation for ACEP landowners. **(§2605(c))**	No comparable provision.
Regional Conservation Partnership Program (RCPP)		
Establishment and purpose. Establishes the Regional Conservation Partnership Program (RCPP). Combines the purposes of four repealed conservation programs to further conservation, restoration, and sustainability on a regional or watershed scale, and encourage partners to cooperate with producers in meeting or avoiding regulatory requirements and implementing projects. **(16 U.S.C. 3871)**	No comparable provision.	Expands the establishment of RCPP to include grant agreements with eligible partners. The purpose of RCPP is expanded to include the flexible delivery of conservation assistance, the coordination of conservation partnership projects, the engagement of eligible producers, and the advancement of conservation and rural development goals. **(§2411(a))**
Definitions. Six terms are defined under RCPP: *covered program*, *eligible activity*, *eligible land*, *eligible partner*, *partnership agreement*, and *program*. *Covered program* is defined as ACEP, EQIP, CSP, and the Healthy Forests Reserve Program (HFRP). *Eligible activity* is defined as activities for water quality and quantity improvement, drought mitigation, flood prevention, water retention, air quality improvement, habitat conservation, erosion control and sediment reduction, forest restoration, and others defined by USDA. *Eligible land* is defined as land on which agricultural commodities, livestock, or forest-related products are produced, including cropland, grassland, rangeland, pastureland, nonindustrial private forest land, and other incidental land.	Amends the definition of *covered program* by adding CRP and Watershed Protection and Flood Prevention operations and removing CSP. Amends the definition of *eligible activity* by adding resource-conserving crop rotations and protection of source waters for drinking water. **(§2701)**	Amends the definition of *covered program* by adding CRP and Watershed Protection and Flood Prevention. Replaces the definition of *eligible activity* by including all activities under the statutory authority of the covered programs and any other related activities, including source water protection for drinking water, soil health, or drought resilience. Replaces the definition of *eligible land* by including all land eligible under the statutory authority of the covered programs and other land as determined by the Secretary.

Table 5. (Continued)

Current Law/Policy	House-Passed Bill (H.R. 2)	Senate-Passed Bill (H.R. 2)
Eligible partner is defined as producer groups, state or local governments, Indian tribes, farmer cooperatives, water district, irrigation district, rural water district or association, municipal water or waste treatment entity, institutes of higher education, and other nongovernmental entity or organizations with a history of working with producers on conservation projects. **(16 U.S.C. 3871a)**		Adds acequia, conservation districts, and eligible entities under ACEP to the definition of *eligible partner*. Adds a definition of *eligible producer* to mean a person, legal entity, or Indian tribe that owns or operates the land. Adds a definition of *program contract*. **(§2411(b))**
Regional conservation partnerships. Under RCPP, USDA enters into partnership agreements with eligible partners for a period not to exceed five years with a possible one-year extension. **(16 U.S.C. 3871b(b))**	Amends the length of partnership agreements to include agreements longer than five years. **(§2702(a))**	Amends the length of partnership agreements to no more than five years, except when a concurrent deadline established under a state or federal program is longer than five years, or when an extension is granted due to delayed implementation. Adds a renewal option for projects that have made progress in addressing natural resource concerns. **(§2411(c)(2))**
Partners define the scope of RCPP projects, conduct outreach, act on behalf of producers to apply for assistance, leverage financial and technical assistance, conduct assessments, and report results. Partners must provide a "significant portion" of the overall cost of the project. **(16 U.S.C. 3871b(c))**	Amends the project assessments to require partners to quantify the project's environmental outcomes. **(§2702(b))**	Amends what may be in the scope of a project. Partner contributions may be through direct funding, in-kind support or a combination of both, and can include the salaries of staff required to develop the partnership agreement. Adds requirements for the Secretary that include (1) establishing a timeline for USDA under the partnership agreement, (2) appointing a designated USDA coordinator within each state to assist partners and producers with RCPP, (3) establishing guidance for assessments, (4) providing reports to partners, (5) allowing new or modified conservation practice standards, and (6) ensuring the effectiveness of eligible activities. **(§2411(c)(3) & (c)(5))**
RCPP applications are competitive, and the selection criteria are publicly available. Priority is given to applications that assist producers meeting or avoiding the need for regulation, include a large percentage of	Adds a renewal option for projects that have met or exceeded the project's objectives. **(§2702(c))**	Amends the application criteria to evaluate the engagement between the lead eligible partner and local conservation district. Requires a simplified application process. Adds priority requirements for

Current Law/Policy	House-Passed Bill (H.R. 2)	Senate-Passed Bill (H.R. 2)
producers in the project area, provide significant resource leverage, deliver a high percentage of applied conservation to priorities or conservation initiatives, or provide innovative conservation methods and delivery. **(16 U.S.C. 3871b(d))**		stakeholder diversity, and watershed and habitat plan development. Requires USDA to provide feedback to applicants throughout the annual application process. **(§2411(c)(6))**
Assistance to producers. Directs USDA to enter into contracts to provide technical and financial assistance to producers participating in projects with eligible partners, or producers within a project area or critical conservation area not working through an eligible partner. Program rules, requirements, and payments are to be consistent with the covered programs (ACEP, EQIP, CSP, and HFRP). Provides USDA the authority to adjust the rules of a covered program, including operational guidance and requirements in order to simplify the application and evaluation process. Prohibits the adjustment of statutory requirements for a covered program, including appeals, payment limits, conservation compliance, and prior irrigation history. Authorizes no more than 20 alternative funding arrangements with multi-state water agencies or authorities. **(16 U.S.C. 3871d(a) & (b))**	No comparable provision.	Amends the contracting and agreement language. Requires USDA to enter into program contracts with eligible producers to conduct activities on eligible land under conditions defined by USDA. Priority may be given to partnership applications that include bundles of program contracts with producers. **(§2411(d)(2)**
Five-year payments may be made for conversion to dryland farming and nutrient management. AGI limits may be waived to fulfill the objectives of the program. **(16 U.S.C. 3871c(c)(2) & (c)(3))**	Extends the payments for dryland farming conversion and nutrient management to match the extended partnership agreements. Expands the AGI waiver to also waive a covered program's payment limitation. **(§2703)**	Minor amendments referencing new funding language. **(§2411(d)(3))**
No comparable provision.	No comparable provision.	Adds a new section for funding arrangements through grant agreements. Allows for USDA to enter into grant agreements directly with partners. Activities through these agreements must benefit agricultural producers and address resource concerns on a regional scale, such as water infrastructure, watershed plans, leveraging federal and private funds, piloting new technologies, and transferring land to select farmers and ranchers. Limits grants to 30% of RCPP funding and waives AGI requirements for recipients. Annual reports are required. **(§2411(d)(4))**

Table 5. (Continued)

Current Law/Policy	House-Passed Bill (H.R. 2)	Senate-Passed Bill (H.R. 2)
Funding. Authorized to receive $100 million in mandatory funding annually for FY2014-FY2018 to remain available until expended. The program utilizes a percentage of other conservation program funding (ACEP, EQIP, CSP, and HFRP). Annually reserves 7% of covered program funds and acres until April 1each year, after which time uncommitted funds are returned to the covered program. Allocates 25% for a state competition, 40% for a national competition, and 35% for critical conservation areas. Administrative expenses of eligible partners are not covered. **(16 U.S.C. 3871d)**	Increases mandatory funding authority to $250 million annually for FY2019-FY2023. **(§2704)**	Increases funding to $200 million annually for FY2019-FY2023. Requires 7% of funds and acres under EQIP, CSP, and ACEP to be transferred to and obligated through RCPP only. Funding is to be distributed to projects of similar purposes to the covered programs. Amends allocations to 40% for state and multi-state competition, and 60% for critical conservation areas. Allows for funding to be advanced to eligible partners for outreach activities and reimbursed for agreement development. Adds new technical assistance requirements, including USDA reporting, limiting expenses for USDA, and third-party provider assistance. **(§2411(e))**
Administration. USDA is required to make information on selected projects publicly available and report to Congress by December 31, 2014 (and every two years thereafter) on the status of projects funded. **(16 U.S.C. 3871e)**	Adds a requirement for USDA to provide partners and producers guidance on how to quantify and report environmental outcomes associated with conservation practice adoption. Requires a report on the progress of quantification. **(§2705)**	Extends reporting requirement to December 31, 2018 (and every two years thereafter) and adds a progress requirement. Adds a prohibition on providing assistance to producers out of compliance with highly erodible cropland and wetland conservation compliance requirements. Adds a requirement to maintain benefits for historically underserved producers and requires USDA to issue regulations for RCPP. **(§2411(f))**
Critical conservation areas. USDA is required to use 35% of the funds and acres available for partnership agreements in no more than eight critical conservation areas that expire after five years, subject to redesignation. Areas are selected based on: multi-state areas with significant agricultural production; existing agreement or plan in place; water quality concerns; water quantity concerns; or subject to regulatory requirements. Partner agreements and producer contracts are administered according to the applicable covered program and, where possible,	Deletes the authority to use the Watershed Protection and Flood Prevention program in critical conservation areas. **(§2706)**	Adds a definition of *critical conservation areas* and *critical conservation condition*. Adds a requirement that USDA identify one or more critical conservation condition for each critical conservation area. Allows USDA to review critical conservation areas every five years and withdraw the designation if no longer critical. Requires outreach to partners and producers in critical conservation areas. Adds reporting requirements on critical conservation areas and conditions. **(§2411(g))**

Current Law/Policy	House-Passed Bill (H.R. 2)	Senate-Passed Bill (H.R. 2)
complement existing water quality and quantity strategies. Allows the use of authorities granted under the Watershed Protection and Flood Prevention program in critical conservation areas. **(16 U.S.C. 3871f)**		
Programs and Provisions in Other Laws		
Repeals and Transitional Provisions; Technical Amendments		
Conservation Security Program. Authorized in the 2002 farm bill and replaced by the Conservation Stewardship Program in the 2008 farm bill. The program enrolls acres in five- to 10-year stewardship contracts, the last of which will expire in FY2018. **(16 U.S.C. 3838 – 16 U.S.C. 3838c)**	Repeals the program. **(§2801)**	Same as House. **(§2402)**
Desert terminal lakes. USDA is required to transfer $150 million of CCC funds to the Bureau of Reclamation to purchase water for at- risk desert terminal lakes. Includes a voluntary land purchase grant program authorized to receive $25 million through appropriations and to remain available until expended. **(16 U.S.C. 3839bb-6)**	Repeals the program. **(§2802)**	No comparable provision.
Conservation Corridor Demonstration Program. Authorized in the Farm Security and Rural Investment Act of 2002 (2002 farm bill, P.L. 107-171). Permits one or more states, along with local governments on the Delmarva Peninsula, to develop and implement over three to five years, a conservation corridor plan to improve the economic viability of agriculture and the environmental integrity of watersheds. Funding was never appropriated. **(16 U.S.C. 3801 note)**	No comparable provision.	Repeals the program. **(§2417)**
Cranberry Acreage Reserve Program. Authorized in the 2002 farm bill to purchase permanent wetland easements on and around cranberry-producing land. Funding was never appropriated. **(16 U.S.C. 3801 note)**	No comparable provision.	Repeals the program. **(§2418)**
National Natural Resources Foundation. Authorized in the Federal Agricultural Improvement and Reform Act of 1996 (1996 farm bill, P.L. 104-127) to establish a non-profit corporation to promote and assist the conservation efforts of NRCS. Funding was never appropriated. **(16 U.S.C. 5801 *et seq.*)**	No comparable provision.	Repeals the foundation. **(§2419)**

Table 5. (Continued)

Current Law/Policy	House-Passed Bill (H.R. 2)	Senate-Passed Bill (H.R. 2)
Flood risk reduction. Authorized in the 1996 farm bill to contract with Market Transition Program participants to retire frequently flooded cropland. Related programs were repealed in subsequent legislation and funding was not appropriated. **(7 U.S.C. 7334)**	No comparable provision.	Repeals the program. **(§2420)**
Study of land use for expiring contracts and extension authority. Authorized in the Food, Agriculture, Conservation and Trade Act of 1990 (1990 farm bill, P.L. 101-624) requiring USDA to create a report on expiring CRP contracts. **(16 U.S.C. 3831 note)**	No comparable provision.	Repeals the study. **(§2421)**
Integrated Farm Management Program. Authorized in the 1990 farm bill to encourage producers to adopt integrated, multiyear, site- specific farm management plans by not reducing the farm program payments of participants who use a resource conserving crop as part of a rotation on payment acres. Related programs were repealed in subsequent legislation. **(7 U.S.C. 5822)**	No comparable provision.	Repeals the program. **(§2422)**
Definition of agricultural lands. The 1996 farm bill defined the term *agricultural lands* as related to a 1994 memorandum of agreement among USDA, the Environmental Protection Agency, and the Department of the Army (Corps) for the delineation of wetlands. USDA and the Corps withdrew from the agreement in 2005. **(110 Stat. 992)**	No comparable provision.	Repeals the provision. **(§2423)**
Resource Conservation and Development (RC&D) program. Provided local coordinators of conservation activities in 375 designated areas. FY2014 appropriations act permanently cancelled any remaining funds. **(16 U.S.C. 3451 *et seq.*)**	No comparable provision.	Adds a sunset authority to the program of October 1, 2023. **(§2424)**
No comparable provision.	Provides technical amendments and spelling corrections. **(§2803)**	Similar to House bill. **(§§2601, 2603, 2604)**
New Conservation Programs and Provisions		
No directly comparable provision. **National Feral Swine Damage Management Program.** APHIS administers the program to manage damage caused by feral swine in the United States. APHIS works with states, tribes, federal agencies, universities, organizations, and the public and	Creates a new **Feral Swine Eradication and Control Pilot Program**. USDA is required to study the extent of damage from feral swine, develop eradication and control measures and restoration methods, and provide cost-share	No comparable provision.

Current Law/Policy	House-Passed Bill (H.R. 2)	Senate-Passed Bill (H.R. 2)
coordinates with Mexico and Canada on feral swine disease monitoring and control activities. **Feral Swine Initiative.** Administered by NRCS in select states through EQIP. The initiative offers planning and management practice implementation to affected landowners.	funding to agricultural producers in established pilot areas. NRCS and APHIS must coordinate the pilot through NRCS State Technical Committees. Cost-share assistance is limited to 75% of the cost of eradication and control measures or restoration. Authorizes $100 million in mandatory funding for the period FY2019-FY2023. Requires funding to be split equally between NRCS and APHIS with no more than 10% for administrative expenses. **(§2405)**	
No comparable provision.	Adds a sense of Congress statement encouraging partnerships at the watershed level between nonpoint sources and regulated point sources to advance the goals of the Federal Water Pollution Control Act (Clean Water Act). **(§2407)**	Identical to the House bill. **(§2428)**
No comparable provision. Under the **Working Lands for Wildlife Initiative**, USDA NRCS and the Department of the Interior (DOI) U.S. Fish and Wildlife Service (FWS), through a partnership agreement, provide voluntary targeted financial and technical assistance for wildlife habitat improvement on private land in exchange for regulatory predictability relative to the Endangered Species Act.	No comparable provision.	Codifies the Working Lands for Wildlife initiative as in effect on the day before enactment. Allows for a similar agreement to be developed between FWS and FSA. The period of regulatory predictability may be extended if agreed to. Authorizes USDA to provide technical assistance under the farm bill conservation programs to support regulatory assurances for producers and landowners, under select conditions. **(§2425)**
No comparable provision.	No comparable provision.	**Conservation easement modification.** Adds a provision outlining requirements for modifying a wetland reserve easement under ACEP. Allows for the landowner to request the modification of an easement if it is jointly agreed to by the State Technical Committee and the relevant state department of natural resources, or is exchanged for land of equal or greater conservation value. The modification is required to facilitate administration of the easement and not adversely affect the functions and values of the easement as established. The modification cannot result in a net loss of wetland reserve easement

Table 5. (Continued)

Current Law/Policy	House-Passed Bill (H.R. 2)	Senate-Passed Bill (H.R. 2)
		acres or an increase in payments to any party. The party requesting the modification is responsible for all costs associated with the modification. **(§2429)**
No comparable provision.	No comparable provision.	**Report on land access, tenure, and transition.** Requires USDA, within one year of enactment, to report on barriers to farmland acquisition, how federal programs improve access to farmland, and required changes to improve access. **(§2506)**
No comparable provision.	No comparable provision.	**Report on small wetlands.** Requires NRCS to submit a report to Congress describing the number of wetlands measuring less than one acre in size in North Dakota, South Dakota, Minnesota, and Iowa. All wetlands included in the report must be described in 1/10 of an acre increments and be based on available science. **(§2507)**
Amendments to Existing Conservation Programs		
Watershed Protection and Flood Prevention (Watershed Operations). Provides technical and financial assistance to states and local organizations to plan and install watershed projects. Such sums as necessary are authorized to be appropriated for the program. **(16 U.S.C. 1001 *et seq.*)**	Adds a new section authorizing $100 million annually in mandatory funding between FY2019 and FY2023 to remain available until expended. **(§2404(b))**	Limits and sunsets authorization for appropriation to $200 million annually from FY2019-FY2023. **(§2415)**
No watershed project may exceed 250,000 acres, and no structure may exceed more than 12,500 acre-feet of floodwater detention capacity, or 25,000 acre-feet of total capacity. Assistance is provided according to a plan. **(16 U.S.C. 1002, 1003)**	No comparable provision.	Waives the 250,000-acre limit for regional drought projects. Waives the watershed planning requirements when considered unnecessary or duplicative. **(§2427)**
Small Watershed Rehabilitation Program. Authorizes appropriations of up to $85 million annually for FY2008-FY2018 and $250 million in mandatory funding for FY2014 to remain available until expended. **(16 U.S.C. 1012(h)(2)(E))**	Extends annual authorization of appropriations of $85 million annually through FY2023. **(§2404(a))**	Extends and decreases annual authorization of appropriations to $20 million annually through FY2023. **(§2416)**

Current Law/Policy	House-Passed Bill (H.R. 2)	Senate-Passed Bill (H.R. 2)
Water Bank Program. Offers 10- year, nonrenewable rental agreements to landowners in Minnesota, North Dakota, and South Dakota to maintain wetlands in lieu of draining the land for agricultural production. The program is authorized to be appropriated such sums as necessary without fiscal year limitation. Annual payments to landowners are limited to $30 million. No more than 15% of authorized funding may be used for agreements in any one state. **(16 U.S.C. 1310)**	No comparable provision.	Amends funding authorization to $5 million annually between FY2019 through FY2023, to remain available until expended. **(§2505)**
Emergency Conservation Program. Provides emergency funding and technical assistance to producers to rehabilitate farmland damaged by natural disasters. **(16 U.S.C. 2201)** Payments are made to individual producers based on a share of the cost of completing the practice. This can be up to 75% of the cost or up to 90% of the cost if the producer is considered to be a limited-resources producer. Total payments may not exceed 50% of the agricultural value of the affected land. Payments are made following completion and inspection of the practice. **(7 C.F.R. 701.126)**	Adds a reference to wildfires in a list of natural disasters. Adds a new provision allowing producers repairing or replacing damaged fences the option of accepting payment (percentage of the fair market value of the cost) before repairing or replacing the fence rather than following the completion and inspection of the practice. Adds a new section similar to existing regulations limiting the cost-share to 75% of the total allowable cost or up to 90% of the total allowable cost if the producer is considered limited resource, socially disadvantaged, or beginning farmer or rancher. Requires that total payments for a single event may not exceed 50% the agricultural; value of the land. **(§2406)**	Similar to House bill, except for the provision of advanced payment, which limits advanced payments to 25% of the total payment and requires that funds not expended after 60 days be returned. Amendments are in the Miscellaneous title, See **Table 15**. **(§12614)**
Emergency Watershed Protection (EWP) program. Assists sponsors, landowners, and operators in implementing emergency recovery measures for runoff retardation and erosion prevention to relieve imminent hazards to life and property created by natural disasters. **(16 U.S.C. 2203)**	No comparable provision.	Adds a payment limitation of $500,000 for agricultural producers. **(§2414(b))**
EWP is authorized to be appropriated such sums as necessary, to remain available until expended. Facilities, services and authorities of the CCC may be used when funding is specifically appropriated. **(16 U.S.C. 2204)**	No comparable provision.	Amends funding authority to include a set-aside of 25% of all available funding to repair and replace fencing. **(§2414(c))**
Soil and Water Resources Conservation Act of 1977 (RCA). The RCA provides USDA with broad natural resource strategic assessment and planning authority.	Amends the RCA to require USDA to conduct two comprehensive appraisals of soil, water, and related natural resources (completed by year-end 2022).	No comparable provision.

Table 5. (Continued)

Current Law/Policy	House-Passed Bill (H.R. 2)	Senate-Passed Bill (H.R. 2)
USDA is required to conduct a nationwide *appraisal* of soil, water, and related resources. USDA is also required to develop a *national conservation program* to guide the department's administration of conservation activities. Appraisals and program statements are due to Congress on a fixed schedule. **(16 U.S.C. 2001 *et seq.*)**	Adds a new requirement for assessing and monitoring USDA programs and initiatives and their progress in reaching natural resource and environmental objectives. Requires a report in the third fiscal year after enactment, and periodically thereafter. Authorizes appropriations equal to 1% of all mandatory conservation program funding (excluding CRP). **(§2408)**	
Healthy Forests Reserve Program. See **Table 11 (16 U.S.C. 6571 *et seq.*)**	**§8107**	**§2426**

Table 6. Trade

Current Law/Policy	House-Passed Bill (H.R. 2)	Senate-Passed Bill (H.R. 2)
Food for Peace Act (All section references in this subsection are to this act.)		
Labeling. Commodity donations shall, to the extent practicable, be clearly identified with appropriate markings on the package or container of such commodity in the language of the locality in which such commodities are distributed as being furnished by the people of the United States of America. **(7 U.S.C. 1722(g))**	Extends the labeling requirement to commodities and food procured outside of the United States or on printed material that accompanies other assistance. **(§3002)**	Continues current law.
Food aid quality assurance. The administrator of USAID shall use the funds made available annually from FY2014 onwards to carry out Food for Peace programs to assess types and quality of agricultural commodities donated as food aid, adjust products and formulation as necessary to meet nutrient needs of target populations, test prototypes, adopt new specifications or improve existing specifications for micronutrient food aid products based on latest development in food and nutrition science, develop new program guidance for cooperators to facilitate improved matching of products to purposes, develop improved guidance on how to address nutritional efficiencies among long- term food-aid recipients, and evaluate the performance and cost-effectiveness of new/modified food products and program approaches to	Extends authority to fund this section through FY2023. **(§3003)**	Same as House provision. **(§3101)**

Current Law/Policy	House-Passed Bill (H.R. 2)	Senate-Passed Bill (H.R. 2)
meet nutritional needs of vulnerable groups. Authorizes not more than $4.5 million of funds be made available for FY2014-FY2018 to carry out this section. **(7 U.S.C. 1722(h)(3))**		
Local sale and barter of commodities. An agreement between the administrator of USAID and a private voluntary organization or cooperative (i.e., nongovernmental organization) to provide U.S.-donated commodities for sale or barter in recipient countries, or a neighboring region, to generate proceeds for use as provided in this section. Such an agreement must involve a minimum level of local sales equal to not less than 15% of all commodities distributed under non-emergency Food for Peace programs for each fiscal year. **(7 U.S.C. 1723)**	Amends this section to provide for administrator discretion in the levels of local sales and to remove the requirement for a minimum level of monetization for nonemergency programs in recipient country or neighboring regional markets. **(§3004)**	Same as House provision. **(§3102)**
Minimum levels of assistance. The Administrator of USAID shall make available not less than 2.5 million metric tons (mt) of agricultural commodities for food distribution each fiscal year through FY2018, including not less than 1,875,000 mt for nonemergency food distribution through eligible organizations. The Administrator may waive this requirement if sufficient quantities of donated commodities are not available. **(7 U.S.C. 1724(a))**	Extends authority, with waiver authority, for requiring minimum levels of food quantities be available for emergency and nonemergency assistance through FY2023. **(§3005)**	Extends authority through FY2023. **(§3103)**
Food Aid Consultative Group. Establishes a Food Aid Consultative Group to review and address issues concerning the effectiveness of the regulations and procedures that govern food assistance programs established and implemented under Title II of the Food for Peace Act. The group shall terminate on December 31, 2018. **(7 U.S.C. 1725(f))**	Extends the authority for the Food Aid Consultative Group through FY2023. **(§3006)**	Extends the authority for the Food Aid Consultative Group through FY2023, and amends the consultation period for proposed regulations, handbooks, or guidelines concerning this subchapter to 30 days. **(§3104)**
Regulations and guidance. Not later than 270 days after enactment of the Agricultural Act of 2014, the administrator shall issue all necessary regulations and revisions to agency guidelines with respect to changes in the operation or implementation of the U.S. food assistance programs. **(7 U.S.C. 1726a(c)(1))**	Requires that the Administrator shall issue all necessary regulations and revisions to agency guidelines with respect to changes in the operation or implementation of the U.S. food assistance programs not later than 270 days after enactment of the Agricultural and Nutrition Act of 2018. **(§3007)**	Continues current law.

Table 6. (Continued)

Current Law/Policy	House-Passed Bill (H.R. 2)	Senate-Passed Bill (H.R. 2)
Program oversight, monitoring, and evaluation. The Administrator shall establish systems and carry out activities to determine the need for food assistance and to improve, monitor, and evaluate the effectiveness and efficiency of the assistance provided so as to maximize its impact. The Administrator may contract with cooperators for such services to be performed in recipient countries or regions. In addition to other funds made available for monitoring of emergency food assistance, the Administrator may use up to $17 million of the funds made available under Title II of the Food for Peace Act for each of FY2014 through FY2018, subject to an annual $500,000 maximum for maintenance of information technology systems, and an annual maximum of $8 million for early warning assessments and systems to help prevent famines (provided at least $8 million are available under chapter 1 of part I of the Foreign Assistance Act of 1961). **(7 U.S.C. 1726a(f)(4))**	Extends authority to fund this section through FY2023. Amends this section by replacing the $17 million cap on funds with a maximum of 1.5% of the funds made available under Title II of the Food for Peace Act for each of FY2019-FY2023 for monitoring of emergency food assistance subject to an annual $500,000 maximum for maintenance of information technology systems and an annual maximum of $8 million for early warning assessments and systems to help prevent famines (provided at least $8 million is available under the Foreign Assistance Act of 1961). **(§3008)**	Extends authority to fund this section through FY2023. Amends this section by replacing the $17 million cap on funds with a maximum of 1.5% of the funds made available under Title II of the Food for Peace Act, but not less than $17 million, for each of FY2019-FY2023 for monitoring of emergency food assistance subject to an annual $500,000 maximum for maintenance of information technology systems. **(§3105)**
Assistance for stockpiling and rapid transportation, delivery, and distribution of shelf-stable pre-packaged foods. The administrator may provide grants to qualifying cooperators for preparation of shelf-stable prepackaged foods and establishment and maintenance of stockpiles of the foods in the United States and for the rapid transportation, delivery, and distribution of shelf-stable prepackaged foods to needy individuals in foreign countries. **(7 U.S.C. 1726b)**	Changes the heading of this section to "International Food Relief Partnership" and extends the program authority to FY2023. **(§3009)**	Extends the program authority to FY2023. **(§3106)**
Impact on local farmers and economy. Under general provisions governing the implementation of Title II of the Food for Peace Act, no agricultural commodity shall be made available unless it is determined that (1) adequate storage facilities will be available in the recipient country at the time of the arrival of the commodity to prevent the spoilage or waste of the commodity; and (2) the distribution of the commodity in the	Amends this section to ensure that no modalities of assistance—importation of donated commodities or food vouchers, cash transfers, or local and regional procurement of food outside of the United States—are distributed in a recipient country where adequate storage facilities are not available or where distribution would create a substantial disincentive to, or interference with,	Continues current law.

Current Law/Policy	House-Passed Bill (H.R. 2)	Senate-Passed Bill (H.R. 2)
recipient country will not result in a substantial disincentive to, or interference with, domestic production or marketing in that country. Also, the Secretary or the administrator, as appropriate, shall ensure that the donation of U.S. agricultural commodities and the use of local currencies for development purposes will not have a disruptive impact on the farmers or local economy of the recipient country. **(7 U.S.C. 1733(a))**	domestic production or marketing or where it would have a disruptive impact on the farmers or local economy of a recipient country. **(§3010)**	
Allowance of Distribution Costs. USDA's Commodity Credit Corporation (CCC) may pay various related acquisition and distribution costs associated with food assistance as specified under this title. In particular, in the case of commodities for urgent and extraordinary relief requirements (including pre- positioned commodities) the transportation costs incurred in moving the commodities from designated points of entry or ports of entry abroad to storage and distribution sites and associated storage and distribution costs. **(7 U.S.C. 1736(b)(6))**	No comparable provision.	Amends this section to clarify allowable distribution costs specified as "the types of activities for which costs were paid under this subsection prior to fiscal year 2017." **(§3107)**
Prepositioning of agricultural commodities. The administrator may use funds made available for FY2001-FY2018 to carry out Title II (subchapter III) and Title III (subchapter III-A) of the Food for Peace Act to procure, transport, and store agricultural commodities for prepositioning within the United States and in foreign countries, except that for each of FY2014-FY2018 not more than $15 million of such funds may be used to store agricultural commodities for prepositioning in foreign countries. **(7 U.S.C. 1736a)**	Extends authority for prepositioning of donated agricultural commodities through FY2023. **(§3011)**	Same as House provision. **(§3108)**
Annual report on food aid programs and activities. The administrator and the Secretary shall jointly prepare and submit to the appropriate committees of Congress, by April 1 of each fiscal year, a report regarding each program and activity carried out under U.S. international food assistance programs—Food for Peace, Section 416(b), Food for Progress, and McGovern-Dole programs—during the prior fiscal year including funds spent, quantities distributed, number of beneficiaries,	Amends this section to allow the administrator and the Secretary to file the annual report either jointly or separately. In addition, this section requires that, where the annual report is not filed by the April 1 deadline, the administrator and the Secretary notify the relevant congressional committees of any delay and the reasons for such delay. In addition, Section 407(f) is updated to combine an existing annual report with more detailed	Amends this section to allow the administrator and the Secretary to file the annual report either jointly or separately. **(§3109)**

Table 6. (Continued)

Current Law/Policy	House-Passed Bill (H.R. 2)	Senate-Passed Bill (H.R. 2)
progress made in reducing food insecurity in recipient populations, description of the Food Aid Consultative Group efforts, an assessment of progress made as relates to food assistance quality, and finally an assessment of the program oversight, monitoring, and evaluation system and its impact on program effectiveness. **(7 U.S.C. 1736a(f)(1))**	information about the utilization of funds by cooperators and recipient countries under each program and the rate of return for each commodity monetized (sold to generate cash to fund cooperator projects) in recipient countries. The rate of return is defined as the ratio of the proceeds generated from monetization and the cost to procure and ship a commodity to the recipient country for monetization. **(§3012)**	
Agreements to finance sales or to provide other assistance. No agreements to finance sales or to provide other assistance under the Food for Peace Act shall be entered into after December 31, 2018. **(7 U.S.C. 1736b)**	Extends the deadline for agreements to finance sales or to provide other assistance until December 31, 2023. **(§3013)**	Same as House provision. **(§3110)**
Minimum level of nonemergency food assistance. In general, of the amounts made available to carry out emergency and nonemergency food assistance programs under Title II (subchapter III) of the Food for Peace Act, not less than 20% nor more than 30% for each of FY2014-FY2018 shall be expended for nonemergency food assistance programs but subject to a minimum level of not less than $350 million for any fiscal year that shall be made available to carry out nonemergency food assistance programs. **(7 U.S.C. 1736f(e))**	Extends this section through 2023 and amends it to provide a minimum annual outlay for nonemergency food assistance of not less than $365 million nor more than 30% of the amounts made available to carry out Title II (subchapter III) of the act. Further, certain community development funds that are made available through grants or cooperative agreements and that assist in implementing certain activities— income-generating, community development, health, nutrition, cooperative development, agricultural and other development—may be deemed to have been expended on nonemergency food assistance programs for the purposes of this section. **(§3014)**	Renames this section as "Nonemergency food assistance" and extends it through FY2023. Amends this section to provide a minimum outlay for nonemergency food assistance of not less than 20% nor more than 30% for each fiscal year, of the amounts made available to carry out Title II (subchapter III) of the Act, but subject to a minimum level of not less than $365 million for any fiscal year. Amends this section to specify that outlays for the Farmer-to-Farmer program (7 U.S.C. 1737) and funds appropriated to carry out Part I of the Foreign Assistance Act of 1961 as amended (22 U.S.C. 2151 *et seq.*) may be considered as being expended for nonemergency food assistance under this section. **(§3111)**
Micronutritient fortification programs. The administrator shall establish micronutrient fortification programs to assist developing countries in correcting micronutrient dietary deficiencies among segments of the populations of the countries and to assess and apply technologies and systems to	Extends authority for the micronutrient fortification program through FY2023. **(§3015)**	Same as House provision. **(§3112)**

Current Law/Policy	House-Passed Bill (H.R. 2)	Senate-Passed Bill (H.R. 2)
improve and ensure the quality, shelf life, bioavailability, and safety of fortified food aid agricultural commodities and products of those agricultural commodities. Under the program, grains and other commodities made available to a participating developing country may be fortified with micronutrients (such as vitamin A, iron, iodine, and folic acid) with respect to which a substantial portion of the population in the country is deficient. The commodity may be fortified in the United States or in the developing country. The authority to carry out programs established under this section shall terminate on September 30, 2018. **(7 U.S.C. 1736g-2)**		
John Ogonowski and Doug Bereuter Farmer-to-Farmer (F2F) Program. The F2F program is established to implement assistance between the United States and qualifying countries—developing and middle income countries, emerging markets, and in Sub-Saharan Africa (SSA) and the Caribbean Basin (CB)— to increase farm production and farmer incomes. The F2F program may use U.S. agricultural producers, agriculturalists, colleges and universities, private agribusinesses, private organizations, private corporations, and nonprofit farm organizations to work in conjunction with agricultural producers and farm organizations in those countries on a voluntary basis. Not less than the greater of $15 million or 0.6% of total Food for Peace program funds available for each of FY2014-FY2018, shall be used to carry out F2F programs with not less than 0.2% for programs in developing countries and not less than 0.1% for programs in SSA and CB countries. There are authorized to be appropriated for each of FY2008-FY2018 $10 million for SSA and CB countries and $5 million for other developing or middle-income countries or emerging markets not included in SSA or CB countries. **(7 U.S.C. 1737)**	Amends the F2F program to add specificity to the types of technical assistance provided by American volunteers. Extends volunteer eligibility to retired USDA extension staff, and encourages long-term and sequenced assignments that contribute to institutional capacity-building. Continues minimum fiscal year funding of not less than the greater of $15 million or 0.6% of amounts made available to carry out the Food for Peace Act through FY2023—with continued set-asides for certain geographic locations: not less than 0.1% for programs in developing countries, and not less than 0.1% for programs in SSA and CB countries. Provides that funds used to carry out F2F programs shall be counted toward the minimum level of nonemergency food assistance of the Food for Peace Act. Reauthorizes the authorization of appropriations until 2023. Establishes both a geographically defined crop yield metrics system for evaluating the degree of F2F program success, and a grant program to facilitate new partnerships and innovative activities under the F2F program. **(§3016)**	Amends this section to allow employees or staff of a State cooperative institution to volunteer under the F2F program. Reauthorizes the authorization of appropriations through FY2023. **(§3113)**

Table 6. (Continued)

Current Law/Policy	House-Passed Bill (H.R. 2)	Senate-Passed Bill (H.R. 2)
Other Food Aid Programs		
Local and Regional Food Aid Procurement Program. Establishes a local and regional procurement program with appropriations of $80 million authorized for each of FY2014- FY2018. Preference in carrying out this program may be given to eligible organizations that have, or are working toward, projects under the McGovern-Dole International Food for Education and Child Nutrition Program. Requires an annual report to Congress on the program's implementation time frame, costs, and impact on local and regional producers, markets, and consumers. **(7 U.S.C. 1736c)**	Extends authority to fund this section through FY2023. **(§3201)**	Same as House provision. **(§3309)**
Bill Emerson Humanitarian Trust. Establishes a reserve of commodities and cash to meet emergency food needs in developing countries when there are unanticipated needs or when U.S. domestic supplies are short. The trust can be held as a combination of cash and commodities. The commodities in the trust may be exchanged for funds available under Title II or the McGovern-Dole Program or for sale in the market. The funds in the trust can be invested in low-risk short-term securities or instruments. **(7 U.S.C. 1736f-1 note)**	Amends Section 302 of the Bill Emerson Humanitarian Trust to reauthorize the trust through 2023. **(§3203)**	Same as House provision. **(§3302)**
Food for Progress Program. Provides donated commodities to participating cooperators (under agreement with the U.S. government and subject to presidential approval) to support countries that have made commitments to expand free enterprise in their agricultural economies. Authorized through FY2018. **(7 U.S.C. 1736o)**	Expands eligible program cooperators to include a college or university as defined in 7 U.S.C. 3103(4). Extends authority to implement and fund the Food for Progress program through FY2023. **(§3204)**	Extends authority to implement and fund the Food for Progress program through FY2023. Amends this section to replace presidential approval with secretarial approval throughout. Expands eligible program cooperators to include land grant universities. Adds flexibility in use of funding: a percentage of program assistance to come directly from cash rather than monetization of commodities, supplemented by an additional $26 million of CCC funding each fiscal year. USDA shall issue implementing regulations and begin consultations with relevant congressional committees within 270 days of enactment. **(§3301)**

Current Law/Policy	House-Passed Bill (H.R. 2)	Senate-Passed Bill (H.R. 2)
McGovern-Dole International Food for Education and Child Nutrition. Makes available U.S. agricultural commodities and financial and technical assistance to carry out food for education and child nutrition programs in foreign countries. Authorizes such sums as may be necessary during FY2008-FY2013. **(7 U.S.C. 1736o-1 note)**	Amends this section to ensure, to the extent practicable, that assistance will be provided on a timely basis so as to coincide with the beginning of the school year and when needed during the relevant school year. Extends authority to fund this program through FY2023. **(§3205)**	Extends authority to implement and fund the McGovern-Dole program through FY2023. Amends this section to permit up to 10% of funding for this program be used to purchase commodities produced in developing recipient countries or developing countries within the same regions of the recipient countries that meet nutritional, quality and labeling standards of the recipient countries, and provides for associated costs of transporting those commodities. Also amends this section to direct the Secretary of Agriculture to ensure that assistance under this section is provided in a timely manner and is made available when needed throughout the applicable school year. **(§3307)**
Other International Agricultural Programs		
Cochran Fellowship Program. As established by the Secretary of Agriculture, the Cochran Fellowship Program provides a fellowships to individuals from eligible countries— (1) middle-income countries that are not receiving U.S. bilateral foreign aid assistance, (2) middle-income countries that have never received U.S. bilateral assistance but where a mutual relationship with the United States would be beneficial, or (3) a country that is transitioning to a representative type of government— who specialize in agriculture for study in the United States. Appropriations are authorized, by country category, as (1) $3 million, (2) $2 million, and (3) $5 million. **(7 U.S.C. 3293)**	Amends this section to permit study in foreign colleges or universities that have met certain criteria: have sufficient scientific and technical facilities, have established a partnership with at least one college or university in the United States, and have substantial participation by U.S. faculty in the design of the fellowship curriculum and classroom instruction under the fellowship. Also amends this section to clarify that the purpose of the fellowship includes trade linkages involving regulatory systems governing sanitary and phytosanitary standards for agricultural products. **(§3206)**	Reauthorizes and amends this section to clarify that the purpose of the fellowship includes trade linkages involving regulatory systems governing sanitary and phytosanitary standards for agricultural products. Amends authorized appropriations, by country category, as (1) $4 million, (2) $3 million, and (3) $6 million. **(§3304)**
Borlaug Fellowship Program. As established by the Secretary of Agriculture, the Borlaug Fellowship Program provides fellowships for scientific training and study in the United States to individuals from eligible countries (i.e., developing country, as determined by the Secretary using a gross national income per capita test) that specialize in agricultural education, research, and extension.	Amends current law to permit U.S. citizens to receive Borlaug fellowships in order to assist eligible countries in developing school-based agriculture and youth extension programs and to permit study in foreign colleges or universities that have met certain criteria. Further, Section 3207 clarifies that training or study of fellowship recipients from eligible countries outside of the United States shall occur in the	Reauthorizes and amends this section to add the development of agricultural extension services in foreign countries to the purpose of the program. Further, the section encourages the ongoing engagement of prior fellowship recipients to contribute to new or ongoing agricultural development projects, including capacity building projects. **(§3305)**

Table 6. (Continued)

Current Law/Policy	House-Passed Bill (H.R. 2)	Senate-Passed Bill (H.R. 2)
The Secretary shall— directly or via collaborating universities—manage, coordinate, evaluate, and monitor the fellowship program. There are authorized to be appropriated such sums as are necessary to carry out this section to remain available until expended. **(7 U.S.C. 3319j)**	United States or at a qualified college or university outside of the United States. Finally, Section 3207 authorizes appropriations of $6 million for the Borlaug fellowship program with $2.8 million set aside for participants from eligible foreign countries. **(§3207)**	
No comparable provision.	No comparable provision.	**International Food Security Technical Assistance.** Amends current law by adding a new section that defines "international food security" as access by any person at any time to food and nutrition that is sufficient for a healthy and productive life. It directs the Secretary to compile and make available information on the improvement of international food security. Further, the section authorizes the Secretary to provide technical assistance to certain eligible entities to implement programs for the improvement of international food security. Authorizes funding of $1 million for each of fiscal years 2019-2023. **(§3306)**
Global Crop Diversity Trust. The administrator of USAID shall contribute funds to endow the Global Crop Diversity Trust to assist in the conservation of genetic diversity in food crops through the collection and storage of germ plasm to provide for (1) maintenance and storage of seed collections; (2) documentation and cataloguing of genetics and characteristics of conserved seeds for researchers, plant breeders, and the public; (3) building the capacity of seed collection in developing countries; (4) making information regarding crop genetic data publicly available for researchers, plant breeders, and the public; (5) operation and maintenance of a backup facility in which are stored duplicate samples of seeds in the case of natural or man-made disasters; and	Amends this section to limit the aggregate contribution of U.S. funds to the trust to 33% of the total funds contributed from all sources and authorizes appropriations through FY2023. **(§3208)**	Reauthorizes appropriations for the Global Crop Diversity Trust through FY2023. **(§3308)**

Current Law/Policy	House-Passed Bill (H.R. 2)	Senate-Passed Bill (H.R. 2)
(6) oversight to ensure international coordination of those actions and efficient, public accessibility to that diversity through a cost-effective system. U.S. fund contributions to the trust shall not exceed 25% of the total funds contributed from all sources. There is authorized to be appropriated $60 million for FY2014- FY2018. **(22 U.S.C. 2220a note)**		
Export Promotion and Market Development		
Market development and export assistance programs. Provides funds and assistance to U.S. farmers and commodity exporters through the Market Access Program (MAP) **(7 U.S.C. 5623),** Foreign Market Development Cooperator Program (FMDP) **(7 U.S.C. 5721),** Emerging Markets Program (EMP) **(7 U.S.C. 5622 note)**, and Technical Assistance for Specialty Crops Program (TASC) **(7 U.S.C. 5680).** Authorizes mandatory CCC funds totaling $253.5 million annually (FY2014-FY2018) across all programs.	**International Market Development Program.** Merges USDA's four market development and export promotion programs into one program. Maintains requirements for spending for components of MAP, FMDP, EMP, and TASC. Authorizes mandatory CCC funds of $255 million annually (FY2019-FY2023). Repeals individual statutes for MAP, FMDP, EMP, and TASC. **(§3102)**	Reauthorizes MAP, FMDP, TASC and EMP. Creates the Priority Trade Fund and allows for the fund to be used when MAP, FMDP, TASC and EMP applications exceed authorized funding for those programs. Authorizes mandatory CCC funds of $260 million annually (FY2019- FY2023). Allows for MAP and FMDP funding to be used to carry out authorized programs in Cuba, although projects that contravene the directives set forth under the National Security Presidential Memorandum entitled 'Strengthening the Policy of the United States Toward Cuba' issued by the President on June 16, 2017, are prohibited. **(§3201)**
Promotion of agricultural exports to emerging markets. Authorizes direct credits or export credit guarantees of not less than $1 billion each fiscal year through 2018 for exports to emerging markets. Requires export credit guarantees be made available to establish or improve facilities and services for U.S. products. **(7 U.S.C. 5622 note)**	Reauthorizes funding through FY2023. **(§3202)**	Same as House provision. **(§3303)**
No comparable provision.	**Biotechnology and Agricultural Trade Program.** Establishes a program to assist with the removal of nontariff and other trade barriers to U.S. agricultural products produced with biotechnology and other agricultural technologies. **(§1543A)**	No comparable provision.

Table 6. (Continued)

Current Law/Policy	House-Passed Bill (H.R. 2)	Senate-Passed Bill (H.R. 2)
No comparable provision.	No comparable provision.	**Tribal representations on trade missions.** Directs the secretary to work with tribal advisors to increase the inclusion of tribal agricultural and food products in trade-related activities. Requires the establishment of goals for measuring tribal inclusion and sets a two-year deadline for a report on the department's efforts. **(§3310)**

Table 7. Nutrition

Current Law/Policy	House-Passed Bill (H.R. 2)	Senate-Passed Bill (H.R. 2)
Supplemental Nutrition Assistance Program (SNAP) — Appropriations, Implementation Funding		
Authorizes appropriations for SNAP and related programs through FY2017. **(7 U.S.C. 2027(a))**	Reauthorizes appropriations through FY2023. **(§4031)**	Same as House. **(§4112)**
Implementation funds. No comparable provision.	Provides $150 million in mandatory funding in FY2019, available until expended, to be used by the Secretary to carry out the amendments made by Subtitle A, which consists of Sections 4001 to 4036. **(§4036)**	No comparable provision.
SNAP—Eligibility, Benefit Calculation		
Thrifty Food Plan (TFP). Maximum monthly benefit allotments are tied to the cost of purchasing a nutritionally adequate low-cost diet, as measured by the USDA-created and -calculated TFP. Allotments are adjusted for food price inflation annually, each October, to reflect the cost of the TFP in the immediately previous June. Although USDA calculates the *cost* of the TFP each year to account for food price inflation, the *contents* of the TFP— often thought of as its own market basket of goods—were last revised in 2006. Maximum allotments are standard across the 48 contiguous states and the District of Columbia, but they are higher—reflecting substantially different food costs—in Alaska, Hawaii, Guam, and the Virgin Islands. **(7 U.S.C. 2012(u), 2017(a))**	Requires the Secretary to re-evaluate the current TFP market basket and publish findings by 2022. Requires subsequent re- evaluations every five years. **(§4004)**	No comparable provision.

Current Law/Policy	House-Passed Bill (H.R. 2)	Senate-Passed Bill (H.R. 2)
Broad-based categorical eligibility. In addition to regular eligibility rules of 130% of the federal poverty line and an asset limit of $2,000 or $3,000 (inflation indexed), states may opt to implement broad- based categorical eligibility. Under this option, a SNAP applicant that receives Temporary Assistance for Needy Families (TANF) cash assistance, Supplemental Security Income, state-funded general assistance cash benefits, or any TANF-funded benefit may be deemed eligible for SNAP benefits and potentially not subject to asset limits. By regulation, the TANF- funded benefit must be for households at or below 200% of the federal poverty line. **(7 U.S.C. 2014(a), 7 C.F.R. 273.2(j))**	Effective October 1, 2020, limits categorical eligibility to TANF cash assistance, Supplemental Security Income, state-funded general assistance cash benefits, or "ongoing and substantial" TANF- funded services. Limits categorical eligibility for households without elderly or disabled members to at or below 130% of the federal poverty line. Households with elderly or disabled members must be at or below 200% of the federal poverty line. **(§4006)**	No comparable provision.
Basic allowance for housing. Some active military members receive a "Basic Allowance for Housing" (BAH) within their pay **(37 U.S.C. 403)** in lieu of on-base or other in-kind housing. This payment is not excluded (and therefore counted) in income for SNAP eligibility determination. **(7 U.S.C. 2014(d))** Among SNAP deductions from gross income is an "excess shelter deduction" for which a household is eligible if housing expenses exceed a threshold set in law and adjusted annually. **(7 U.S.C. 2014(e)(5))**	Amends law to exclude from income up to $500 of BAH. Amends excess shelter deduction to include a household's BAH above $500. **(§4007)**	No comparable provision.
Earned income deduction. Applicants with earned income (i.e., from a job) have 20% of that income deducted from their gross income for net income eligibility and benefit calculations. **(7 U.S.C. 2014(e)(2))**	Increases earned income deduction to 22%. **(§4008)**	No comparable provision.
Simplified homeless housing costs. For households where all members are homeless, but the household has some housing costs and does not claim the "excess shelter deduction," states have an option to simplify SNAP's calculation of housing costs with a standard deduction of $143. **(7 U.S.C. 2014(e)(2))**	Requires states to include a deduction of $143 (indexed for inflation) for households where all members are homeless, free shelter has not been provided, and the household has not opted to use the excess shelter deduction. **(§4009)**	No comparable provision.
Standard utility allowances. A SNAP household can use a Low Income Home Energy Assistance Program (LIHEAP) payment (so long as it is greater than $20) as evidence that the household has incurred heating and cooling costs.	For households without elderly members, a LIHEAP payment (of any amount) would no longer suffice for the standard utility allowance. **(§4010)** Does not change the law for households with elderly or disabled members.	No comparable provision.

Table 7. (Continued)

Current Law/Policy	House-Passed Bill (H.R. 2)	Senate-Passed Bill (H.R. 2)
This documentation triggers a standard utility allowance, a figure that enters into the SNAP benefit calculation equation. Unless the household is already receiving the maximum SNAP benefit, a household's monthly benefit can increase if the standard utility allowance calculation results in an excess shelter deduction. LIHEAP payments are excluded from counted income. **(7 U.S.C. 2014(e)(6)(C))**		
Child support. For noncustodial parents applying for SNAP, states have the option to treat child support paid as an income exclusion (impacting eligibility and benefit calculation) or as a deduction (impacting only benefit calculation). For SNAP eligibility, states may choose to require custodial parent and/or noncustodial parent cooperation with the state's child support enforcement program. States may choose not to require either. States may also choose to disqualify applicants based on child support arrears. **(7 U.S.C. 2014(e), 2016(l)-(n))**	Requires all states to treat child support paid as an income exclusion, not a deduction. Requires all states to require child support cooperation for custodial and noncustodial parents. Eliminates disqualification for child support arrears. **(§4011)**	No comparable provision.
Asset/resource limits. Households *without* elderly or disabled members cannot have counted liquid assets above $2,000. Households *with* elderly or disabled members cannot have counted liquid assets above $3,000. Limits are adjusted annually for inflation and rounded down to the nearest $250. For FY2018, these limits are $2,250 and $3,500, respectively. **(7 U.S.C. 2014(g)(1))**	Increases asset limits to $7,000 and $12,000, respectively. Continues inflation adjustment. **(§4012)**	No comparable provision.
In calculating assets for asset limit, excludes up to $4,650 of the fair market value of any household vehicle. This amount is not adjusted for inflation. States have the option to conform how they count vehicles in SNAP with how they count vehicles in TANF. TANF frequently excludes the value of a vehicle. **(7 U.S.C. 2014(g)(2))**	Excludes up to $12,000 of the fair market value of one vehicle per licensed driver and adds inflation adjustment. Deletes the state option to use an alternative vehicle allowance that conforms with how vehicles are counted in TANF. **(§4013)**	No comparable provision.
Any savings account—regardless of whether there is a penalty for early withdrawal—is included in a household's counted assets in eligibility. **(7 U.S.C. 2014(g)(2))**	Excludes up to $2,000 (adjusted annually for inflation) of a household's savings from assets counted in eligibility determination. **(§4014)**	No comparable provision.

Current Law/Policy	House-Passed Bill (H.R. 2)	Senate-Passed Bill (H.R. 2)
Work-related requirements. *General work requirements and E&T.* Able-bodied, non-elderly (ages 16-60) SNAP applicants that are not working are required to register with the state for work opportunities. Certain individuals, such as students and those with children under six, are exempt. Each state is required to operate a SNAP Employment and Training (E&T) program. States design their respective programs' services and capacity and may offer workfare. States have the option to require SNAP participants to participate in E&T and may require a *maximum* of 120 hours per month of participation or the number of hours equal to the household's benefit amount divided by the applicable minimum wage. Individuals that do not comply with general requirements (including state-specific requirements) are, subject to exceptions for good cause, ineligible for benefits anywhere from one month to indefinitely, depending on the number of occurrences and the state's chosen options. In some cases, sanction may apply to entire household. Program requirements, uptake of these funds, and activities designed vary by state. **(7 U.S.C. 2015(d)(4), 7 U.S.C. 2025(h))** *Able-bodied adults without dependents (ABAWDs) time limit and available waivers and exemptions.* ABAWDs (ages 18-50) who do not meet specified work requirements (20 hours per week of work or comparable workfare) are limited to receiving three months of SNAP benefits in a 36-month period. Some are exempt from time limit, including pregnant women. States and portions of states may waive enforcement of the time limit if specified unemployment conditions are met. States are permitted to exempt individuals from the time limit, up to 15% of a specified caseload as defined in statute. Some individuals may be subject to general work requirements but not time limit. States are not required to provide E&T or work opportunities for individuals subject to the time limit. **(7 U.S.C. 2015(o); 7 C.F.R. 273.24)**	Amends work-related rules to combine aspects of general work requirements and time limit to create one work requirement for all states that would apply to a more expanded population than the current law time limit. Beginning in FY2021, able-bodied adults (ages 18-59) with no children or with children six years of age or older are required to work, participate in E&T, or combine work and E&T for a *minimum* of 20 hours per week (increased to 25 hours in FY2026). Certain individuals are exempt from the work requirement, including pregnant women. Nonexempt individuals who do not comply with work requirement are, subject to exceptions for good cause, ineligible for benefits for 12 months for first violation and 36 months for subsequent violations. Eligibility reinstates if individual obtains employment sufficient to meet hourly requirements or becomes exempt. If an individual becomes ineligible to participate in SNAP as a household member, "the remaining household members (including children), shall not become ineligible to apply to participate in SNAP." For geographic or labor-market-based waivers to the work requirement, includes but modifies the requirements in ABAWD time limit regulations, limiting the combining of areas and making a more stringent unemployment rate standard. Amends states' limits on individual exemptions to create different rules based on year: for FY2021-FY2025, 15% of covered individuals, as defined by bill; for FY2026 and thereafter, 12%. During transition period of FY2019 and FY2020, current law work-related requirements and ABAWD time limit would continue to apply, but the bill's changes to geographic or labor-market-based waivers would apply for the transition period. **(§4015(a),(b),(d),(e),(f),(g))**	Largely retains current law work-related requirements. Reorganizes provisions so work-related eligibility rules are located only in 7 U.S.C. 2015(d). Amends eligibility rules and E&T provisions to authorize "workforce partnerships" as a means of satisfying work requirements. "Workforce partnerships" are defined as programs run by private employers, a network of private employers, or nonprofit organizations providing workforce services that are certified to meet certain standards. These programs must use no federal funding. Requires that state E&T programs offering job search as a component must also offer at least one additional component. **(§4103)**

Table 7. (Continued)

Current Law/Policy	House-Passed Bill (H.R. 2)	Senate-Passed Bill (H.R. 2)
	Allows a state to request earned income data from the Internal Revenue Service "for purposes of ensuring equitable treatment among all households (including those containing a married couple)."**(§4015(h))**	
E&T funding. The federal government funds SNAP E&T in four ways: (1) $90 million in mandatory funds that are allocated and reallocated to states based on a formula, (2) $20 million in mandatory funding allocated to states that pledge to provide E&T to all ABAWDs, (3) open-ended matching funds for states' administrative costs for E&T, and (4) open-ended matching funds for states' reimbursement of E&T participants' dependent care and transportation costs. **(7 U.S.C. 2025(h))** *2014 farm bill E&T pilots.* USDA selected 10 states to pilot projects to test a variety of work and job readiness strategies for SNAP participants, including mandatory and voluntary strategies. Those pilots and their independent longitudinal evaluation are ongoing. Progress reports are available, but evaluation is not complete. Mandatory funding of $200 million was provided and is available until end of FY2018. **(7 U.S.C. 2025(h)(1)(F))**	Requires states to offer E&T services for individuals subject to the work requirement to get to 20 hours or otherwise reach compliance. Requires all state E&T programs to provide case management services. Modifies allowable E&T activities. For FY2020, increases to $270 million mandatory funds that are allocated and reallocated to states based on a formula. Increases to $1 billion annually in FY2021 and each fiscal year thereafter. In FY2021 and each year thereafter, reserves not more than $150 million of E&T funding for allocation to states to provide training services through providers on the state's eligible training provider list (defined in the Workforce Innovation and Opportunity Act) for SNAP participants subject to hourly requirements. Strikes authority to reallocate Employment & Training funds, instead requiring states' unspent allocated funding to be returned to the Treasury. **(§4015(a),(b),(d),(e),(f)(g))**	Authorized the Secretary to carry out eight or more additional pilot projects using a competitive grant process. The Secretary may give priority to projects targeted to specified populations, including individuals 50 years of age or older, formerly incarcerated individuals, and individuals participating in a substance abuse treatment program. States with mandatory E&T programs are eligible to run such a project only if the project provides individualized case management designed to help remove barriers to employment and participants are not assigned to activities primarily consisting of job search, job search training, or workforce activities. Provides mandatory funding of $92.5 million in each of FY2019 and FY2020 to remain available until expended. Amends 2014 farm bill pilots' funding, making it available until end of FY2023 for continuing the pilot projects currently (as of date of enactment) being carried out and also makes funding available for the additional pilot projects. **(§4103(c))**
College students. For the most part, college students (attending higher education courses half-time or more) between ages 18 and 50 are ineligible for SNAP. A student enrolled in an institution of higher education more than half-time is eligible for SNAP benefits only if the individual is (1) under age 18 or age 50 or older, (2) disabled, (3) enrolled in school because of participation in certain programs,	Amends the exception for parents of children under age six to also include care of an incapacitated person. Amends exceptions for parents to also apply to "other household member[s] with responsibility for the care of" the specified child or incapacitated person. **(§4015(c))**	No comparable provision.

Current Law/Policy	House-Passed Bill (H.R. 2)	Senate-Passed Bill (H.R. 2)
(4) employed at least 20 hours per week or participates in a work-study program during the school year, (5) a certain category of parent, *or* (6) receiving TANF cash assistance benefits. Eligible parent circumstances are a single parent enrolled in school full-time caring for a dependent under the age of 12, a parent caring for a dependent under age six, or a parent caring for a child between the ages of five and 12 for whom child care is not available to enable the parent to both attend class and work 20 or more hours per week. **(7 U.S.C. 2015(e))**		
Transitional benefits. States have the option to provide not more than five months of SNAP benefits to households that have had their cash assistance from TANF terminated. The benefit amount for these months is to equal the amount received before TANF assistance was terminated. **(7 U.S.C. 2020(s))**	Requires states to provide five months of SNAP benefits to such households. **(§4024)**	No comparable provision.
Certification period length. Length of SNAP households' certification period is based on state policy, but states must set their policy within a framework in federal SNAP law. Certification periods may not exceed 12 months, unless all adult members of a household are elderly or disabled, in which case the certification period may be up to 24 months. **(7 U.S.C. 2012(f))**	No comparable provision.	Maintains 12- and 24-month periods in current law, but adds that if each adult household member is elderly or disabled *and* the household has no earned income at the time of certification, then certification periods may not exceed 36 months. **(§4101)**
Criminal convictions. In addition to a state option to ban drug felons, current law bars individuals convicted (on or before February 7, 2014) of specified federal crimes (including murder, rape, and certain crimes against children) and state offenses determined by the Attorney General to be substantially similar, from receiving SNAP, if an individual is not in compliance with the terms of his or her sentence or who is a "fleeing felon." **(7 U.S.C. 2015(r))**.	Amends disqualification to apply to all with such convictions, not only those out of compliance with sentence or fleeing felon. **(§4039)**	No comparable provision.
SNAP— Fraud, Errors, Related State Administration Issues		
Concurrent enrollment in multiple states. Individuals are not allowed to apply for or receive benefits from more than one state agency at a time. **(7 U.S.C. 2015(j))** Some state agencies detect duplicate enrollment by exchanging enrollment data with neighboring states.	Requires the Secretary to establish a Duplicative Enrollment Database. Requires the states to use the database in eligibility determinations to prevent participants from receiving benefits concurrently in multiple states.	Requires the development of a nationwide data system (called National Accuracy Clearinghouse) to prevent participants from receiving benefits concurrently in multiple states.

Table 7. (Continued)

Current Law/Policy	House-Passed Bill (H.R. 2)	Senate-Passed Bill (H.R. 2)
Since 2013, the National Accuracy Clearinghouse (NAC), a five-state pilot, has used a database to detect and prevent duplicate enrollment. Periodically, USDA publishes a report that uses data from the U.S. Census Bureau's Survey of Income and Program Participation to analyze participants' duration of participation. The last report was published in 2014 and uses data from 2008 to 2012.	The Secretary is to establish a uniform method and format for collection and submission of data, and states are required to collect from each household member a Social Security number (or substitute), employment status, specified income, benefits, and asset information. Requires the Secretary to use the database to publish an annual report on participants' duration of participation in the program. **(§4001)**	Limits the scope of data system by requiring that the Secretary require states to make available only such information as is necessary for the multi-state duplication purpose. Specifies certain data protections, including that data shall only be used for, and shall not be retained for longer than is necessary for, the duplication prevention purpose. **(§4109)**
Data matching, verification of household information. All state agencies are required to conduct certain data matches to verify applicant information. Some states may perform additional checks using federal, state, local, or private data systems in order to verify information provided by applicants. States are required to verify household income. **(7 U.S.C. 2020(e), 7 C.F.R. 273.2(f))**	No comparable provision.	In state plans, requires state agencies to act (clarify or verify) on data matches if the information appears to significantly conflict with that provided by household, comes from specified data matches (e.g., SSA's match of deceased individuals), is fewer than 60 days old, and would have been required to be reported by the household to the state. **(§4106)** Requires the Secretary to establish a pilot program, in no more than eight states, to test strategies to improve the accuracy or efficiency of the process for verifying earned income during households' certification and recertification. Before soliciting project applications, requires Secretary to assess contract options, by reviewing, e.g., the availability and cost-effectiveness of using specified data sources. Secretary may make grants and must submit a report to Congress on the results of the pilot projects. Authorizes, in FY2019, $10 million in mandatory funding for pilot program; funds are available until expended; no more than 10% of funding may be used for assessing contract options or writing the report to Congress. **(§4107)**

Current Law/Policy	House-Passed Bill (H.R. 2)	Senate-Passed Bill (H.R. 2)
State agencies' authority to contract. States are required to use state merit system personnel to conduct SNAP certification interviews and make final decisions on eligibility determinations. **(7 U.S.C. 2020(e)(6))**	Provides states the authority to contract out certification or any other SNAP administrative function. Contractor must have no direct or indirect financial interest in an approved retail food store. **(§4043)**	No comparable provision.
Access to state systems. States are required to keep such records as may be necessary to determine compliance with SNAP law. The law requires that these records be available for audit and inspection. **(7 U.S.C. 2020(a)(3)(B))** States participate in a federally-run Quality Control (QC) system. **(7 U.S.C. 2025(c))** USDA pays half of states' computer system costs, as allowed. **(7 U.S.C. 2025(g))**	Amends to specify that records and information systems that contain records are to be made available for inspection and audit by the Secretary, subject to security protocols agreed to by the state and the Secretary. QC system reporting requirements are also amended to reflect the availability of these records and systems. Computer systems must be accessible by the Secretary for program oversight in order to receive federal cost-share funding for computer systems. **(§4023)**	Similar to House bill. Does not specify that access is subject to security protocols agreed to by the state and the Secretary. **(§4110(a))**
Error rate calculation. The SNAP QC system measures improper payments in SNAP by comparing the amounts of overpayments and underpayments that exceed the error tolerance level or threshold to total benefits issued. Error rates are used as a basis for calculating state award and liability amounts depending on high or low performance. Via statute and regulation, the threshold amount has changed over the years. Since FY2014, the quality control error threshold has been set in statute at $37 (with annual inflation adjustment). **(7 U.S.C. 2025(c))**	For FY2018 and subsequent years, reduces QC tolerance level to $0. Makes related amendments in the calculation of liability amounts in light of the changed tolerance level. **(§4028)**	Requires the Secretary to issue interim final regulations to ensure the integrity of the QC system as specified further in the provision. Requires Secretary to bar from federal procurement any person that, in carrying out the QC system, knowingly submits or causes to be submitted, false information to the Secretary. **(§4110(b))**
Performance awards. Based on QC system error rates and other data, USDA measures state performance and provides financial awards to highest performing and most improved states. Performance awards total $48 million in mandatory funding each fiscal year. **(7 U.S.C. 2025(d); 7 C.F.R. 275.24)**	Repeals authority and funding for bonus awards. Beginning FY2018, requires Secretary to establish, by regulation, performance criteria relating to actions taken to correct errors, reduce rates of error, and improve eligibility determinations and other indicators of effective administration as determined by the Secretary. **(§4029)**	Reduces amount and scope of performance bonus awards. Beginning with the awards for FY2018 performance and each year thereafter, Secretary is required to make performance bonus awards to states for high or most improved performance for application processing timeliness only, and a total of $6 million in mandatory funding is available annually. Specifies that $6 million is available in FY2019 for Secretary to make the awards for FY2018 performance. **(§4110(c))**

Table 7. (Continued)

Current Law/Policy	House-Passed Bill (H.R. 2)	Senate-Passed Bill (H.R. 2)
Adjustment to percentage of recovered funds retained by states. State agencies establish and collect claims against recipients who traffic SNAP benefits. If a state agency collects on a claim resulting from fraud, such as recipient trafficking or recipient application fraud, the state agency is entitled to retain 35% of the amount collected. **(7 U.S.C. 2025(a))**	Increases to 50% the amount of collected claims the state agency is entitled to retain. Allows states to use amounts collected only for SNAP, including investments in technology and other actions to prevent fraud. **(§4027)**	No comparable provision.
States' computer system costs are eligible for receiving federal matching funds. **(7 U.S.C. 2025(g))**	No comparable provision.	**System testing.** Requires state agencies to test automatic data processing and information retrieval systems in a live production environment prior to implementation in order to receive federal match. **(§4111)**
Retail food store and recipient trafficking. Authorizes civil penalties and SNAP disqualification penalties for retailers that engage in SNAP trafficking (the sale of SNAP benefits for money or ineligible items). USDA enforces those penalties through a variety of activities and funds from the SNAP account. Additional grant funding provided to track and prevent SNAP trafficking: $15 million in mandatory funding in FY2014, which was available until expended; authorizes up to $5 million, subject to appropriations, for each year from FY2014 through FY2018. **(7 U.S.C. §2036b)**	Extends authorization of $5 million annual funding through FY2023. **(§4034)**	No comparable provision.
SNAP—Electronic Benefit Transfer (EBT) Systems, Retailers, Eligible Foods		
EBT standards. Required state agencies to implement EBT systems by October 1, 2002, unless Secretary provided a waiver. Requires Secretary to issue final regulations that establish standards for the approval of such systems. **(7 U.S.C. 2016(h)(1)-(2))**	Requires Secretary to periodically update EBT system regulations. Requires Secretary to include "risk-based measures" to maximize system security based on what the state agency considers appropriate and cost-effective, balanced against recipients' program access. **(§4016)**	Related changes in §4104(c)-(d). **(summarized below)**
Processing fees. No "interchange fees" shall apply to EBT transactions. No bar on "switching" fees in Food and Nutrition Act, the statute authorizing SNAP. **(7 U.S.C. 2016(f)(13))** In recent years, third- party processors have been charging retailers such fees. FY2018 appropriations law provision bars charging of "switching fees" through FY2019. **(P.L. 115-141, §750)**	Bars a state or an agent or contractor of the state from charging any fee for switching or routing SNAP benefits. *Switching* is defined as "routing of an intrastate or interstate transaction that consists of transmitting the details of a transaction electronically recorded	Similar to House provision, but ban on fees is in effect through FY2022. **(§4104(a))**

Current Law/Policy	House-Passed Bill (H.R. 2)	Senate-Passed Bill (H.R. 2)
	through the use of an [EBT] card in one State to the issuer of the card that may be in the same or different State." **(§4018)**	
Replacement of EBT cards. Secretary has the authority to require states to decline, unless an explanation is provided, to issue a replacement card to a household that has made "excessive requests" for replacement cards. **(7 U.S.C. 2016(h)(8))** Current regulations require a state to contact a household after they have made four replacement requests in a 12-month period. **(7 C.F.R. 274.6(b)(6))** In December 2017, USDA's Food and Nutrition Service (FNS) granted a waiver for one state to contact recipients who request a replacement card more than two times in a 12- month period.	Amends statute to specify that "2 lost cards in a 12-month period" is an excessive number. **(§4019)**	No comparable provision.
Benefit recovery. States must store offline benefits a household has not accessed in a six-month period. States must expunge from participants' EBT cards benefits that have not been accessed after a 12-month period. **(7 U.S.C. 2016(h)(12))**	Requires benefit storage after a household has not accessed SNAP account for three months. Requires benefit expunging if the benefits have not been accessed by a household for six months or upon verification that all members of the household are deceased. **(§4020)**	No comparable provision.
Online acceptance of benefits. Requires, depending on results of a demonstration project, that USDA authorize retailers to accept benefits online. **(7 U.S.C. 2016(k))** Demonstration is ongoing.	Amends definition of *retail food store* to include "online entity." Amends pilot provision to require nationwide implementation of online benefit redemption. **(§4021)**	No comparable provision.
USDA is required to set procedures for the delivery of benefits to benefit issuers (i.e., state-contracted EBT processors). **(7 U.S.C. 2016(d))** To connect to the state's EBT processor and accept SNAP, most SNAP- authorized retailers are required to pay for their own EBT equipment and services. **(7 U.S.C. 2016(f)(2))** These retailers purchase equipment and processing services from a variety of private entities. Between the retailer and EBT processor, transactions are technologically routed through third-party processors and sometimes "gateways." A variety of third parties can hinder USDA access to and analysis of SNAP data.	**National gateway.** Expands the Secretary's EBT authority to set procedures for independent sales organizations, third-party processors, and web service providers (each defined in provision) in addition to benefit issuers. Requires, pending the completion of a feasibility study, the Secretary to establish a centralized "national gateway" through which all SNAP transactions are required to route. States are required to ensure that benefit issuers connect to the national gateway. The Secretary is required to set and collect fees, paid by benefit issuers and third- party processors, to sustain the national gateway.	Requires GAO to study EBT fees, outages, and intermediaries providing services between retailers and state-contracted EBT processors. Requires the Secretary to review state EBT contract service agreements, compatibility of systems with USDA fraud monitoring systems, and third-party applications' access to EBT systems; review is to be based on a minimum of five states. Requires Secretary, based on study and review, to promulgate regulations or guidance appropriate to prohibit the imposition of fees, minimize and update procedures for outages, and other specified topics. **(§4104(c))**

Table 7. (Continued)

Current Law/Policy	House-Passed Bill (H.R. 2)	Senate-Passed Bill (H.R. 2)
	Provision includes additional specifications for study and gateway. Authorizes funding of $10.5 million for FY2019 and $9.5 million for each of FY2020-FY2023 and allows no more than $1 million from these funds to be used for the study. **(§4022)**	Requires that the Secretary issue guidance to retailers on selecting EBT equipment and service providers that provide sufficient transaction information to minimize the risk of fraudulent transactions. Allows the Secretary to require applicant retailers to provide certain EBT-related information during retailer authorization process. **(§4104(d))**
No comparable provision. USDA undertook research on SNAP recipients' purchases using 2011 transaction data and published a report in November 2016.	**SNAP benefit transfer transaction data report.** Requires the Secretary to, not more often than every two years, collect a statistically significant sample of retailer food store transaction data, including cost and description of items purchased with SNAP, and to summarize and report that data in a manner that prevents identification of individual retailer food store chains and SNAP recipients. Provision requires specified data protections. **(§4026)**	No comparable provision.
Mobile technologies. Depending on results of an authorized demonstration project, retailers are authorized to conduct EBT transactions using mobile technologies (defined as "electronic means other than wired point of sale devices") if retailers meet certain requirements. **(7 U.S.C. 2016(h)(14))**	Amends this provision to create a different pilot to test SNAP recipients' use of mobile technology (e.g., smartphones) to redeem their SNAP benefits. Authorizes up to five states to pilot. States are to submit a plan to the Secretary that meets certain requirements including recipient privacy, access protections, and retailers (with some exemptions) bearing the costs of implementation. States are to be selected by January 1, 2020. By January 1, 2020, the Secretary is required to determine whether to implement in all states and/or whether further study is required. Participating retailers are to bear the costs of equipment and supplies for the benefit redemption, including fees. **(§4017)**	No comparable provision.
Meal providers accepting SNAP benefits. Specified facilities that serve meals to the elderly and disabled (and their spouses) may become authorized to accept SNAP benefits as payment for those meals; this includes senior citizens' centers, apartment buildings occupied	Requires Secretary to review a representative sample of those elderly- and disabled-serving facilities authorized to accept benefits and determine whether benefits are properly used by or on behalf of participating households	No comparable provision.

Current Law/Policy	House-Passed Bill (H.R. 2)	Senate-Passed Bill (H.R. 2)
primarily by the elderly and disabled, public or private nonprofit establishments that feed the elderly and disabled, and federally subsidized housing for the elderly. **(7 U.S.C. 2012(k)(3), (o)(2))** Group living arrangements and drug and alcohol treatment facilities may become authorized to accept SNAP benefits as payment for those meals provided. **(7 U.S.C. 2012(k)(5), (k)(7), (o)(2))** Treatment facilities and group living arrangements may serve as authorized representatives for SNAP participants in their care. **(7 U.S.C. 2017(e)(f))**	residing in such facilities in 7 U.S.C. 2012(k)(3). Gives the Secretary discretion to carry out similar reviews for group living arrangements and drug and alcohol treatment facilities. **(§4038)**	
In general, SNAP benefits may be redeemed for any foods for home preparation and consumption. SNAP benefits may not be redeemed for alcohol, tobacco, or hot foods intended for immediate consumption. **(7 U.S.C. 2012(k))**	Makes "multivitamin-mineral dietary supplement," as defined in the provision, eligible for purchase with SNAP benefits. **(§4037)**	No comparable provision.
SNAP authorization law refers to retailer establishments in the singular (e.g., "an establishment," "a store"). **(7 U.S.C. 2012(o); 2018(c),(d))** FNS has long interpreted this to mean one SNAP retailer authorization authorizes one location.	No comparable provision.	Allows farmer's markets and direct marketing farmers to operate EBT point of sale device at more than one location under the same SNAP retailer authorization, provided that retailer provides specified information to the Secretary. **(§4104(b))**
SNAP—Other SNAP-Related Grants		
Food Insecurity Nutrition Incentive (FINI) and other bonus incentive programs. Grant program provides grants to governmental agencies and nonprofit organizations for projects that "increase the purchase of fruits and vegetables by low-income consumers participating in [SNAP] by providing incentives at the point of purchase." Retailers often partner with grantees and retailers financially benefit from incentives, but for-profit retailers are not eligible grantees. Mandatory funding through a transfer from the CCC: $35 million for FY2014 and FY2015, $20 million for each of FY2016 and FY2017, $25 million for FY2018. FINI evaluation is ongoing. **(7 U.S.C. 7517(b))**	Renames the program **Gus Schumacher Food Insecurity Nutrition Incentive Program**. Adds new priority criteria for the awarding of grants. Certain other additional priority criteria are at the Secretary's discretion. Limits program incentives to financial incentives. Requires Secretary to consult with the director of NIFA to establish a training, evaluation, and information center for use by program grantees. Increases funding, providing $45 million for FY2019, $50 million for FY2020, $55 million for FY2021, $60 million for FY2022, and $65 million for FY2023 and each year thereafter. **(§4003)**	Renames the program **Gus Schumacher Food Insecurity Nutrition Incentive Program**. Amends definition of eligible entity to "governmental agency or nonprofit organization." Makes Puerto Rico and American Samoa eligible for grants. Allows grantees to partner or make subgrants to a list of organizational types. Allows tribal agency grantees to use certain federal funding to meet matching requirements. Requires grantees to measure fruit and vegetable purchases, except in the case of projects receiving $100,000 or less. Adds new priority criteria for the awarding of grants, some the same and some different from the House-passed bill.

Table 7. (Continued)

Current Law/Policy	House-Passed Bill (H.R. 2)	Senate-Passed Bill (H.R. 2)
For a retailer to provide bonus incentives, whether or not federally-funded, requires USDA to waive equal treatment regulations which specify that "no retailer food store may single out coupon users for special treatment in any way." **(7 C.F.R. 278.2)**	Establishes a **Retailer-Funded Incentives Pilot** through which authorized retail food stores may receive federal funding to provide bonus incentives to SNAP households for purchases of fruits, vegetables, and milk. Funding may not exceed 25% of bonuses earned by households. Retailers participating in FINI are not eligible. Aggregate value of reimbursements in a pilot project shall not exceed $120 million each fiscal year. Mandatory funding from SNAP account provided. **(§4002)**	Requires the Secretary to establish one or more training and technical centers and one or more information and evaluation centers to provide specified technical assistance and evaluation support, including information on point-of-sale technology. Requires the information and evaluation centers to use standard metrics developed in collaboration with the director of NIFA and administrator of FNS. Requires the Secretary to conduct and publish an evaluation of each project annually. Increases mandatory funding, providing $50 million for FY2019 and each fiscal year thereafter. Not more than 15% of the funding is to be allocated for the centers and evaluation. **(§4303)** Requires Secretary to promulgate regulations clarifying the process by which a retail food store may seek a waiver to offer SNAP bonus incentives for certain eligible foods (defined as "**identified for increased** consumption" in most recent Dietary Guidelines for Americans and a fruit, vegetable, low-fat dairy, or whole grain). Among other requirements for regulations, a waiver granted shall not be used to limit the use of benefits. **(§4105)** **Pilot projects to increase purchase of cow milk.** Authorizes the Secretary to carry out pilot projects to develop and test methods that would, by providing an incentive for the purchase of milk at the point of purchase, increase the purchase of fluid milk, in a manner consistent with the most recent Dietary Guidelines for Americans, by those participating in SNAP who under-consume milk.

Current Law/Policy	House-Passed Bill (H.R. 2)	Senate-Passed Bill (H.R. 2)
		Secretary may award cooperative agreements or grants to governmental agencies or non-profit organizations for this purpose, including allowing awardees to award subgrants to SNAP-authorized retailers. Funding shall not be used for any project that limits the use of SNAP benefits. Projects are to be in effect for not more than 24 months. Projects are to determine whether incentives result in improved nutritional outcomes, changes in purchasing and consumption of fluid milk, or diets more closely aligned with Dietary Guidelines for Americans. Requires an independent evaluation and reporting as further specified. Authorizes discretionary funding of $20 million to remain available until expended. **(§4108)**
Under current law and agency grant-making, some FINI grants fund "produce [fruit and vegetable] prescription programs," that provide fruits and vegetables in health care environments to SNAP participants who are patients with diet-related health conditions. Non-federal funds may also support such programs. Non-FINI-funded produce prescription programs funded by other sources of funding might serve a broader population than SNAP participants.	No comparable provision.	Establishes **Harvesting Health Pilot Projects**, a grant program to conduct pilot projects that demonstrate and evaluate the impact of "produce prescription programs" on the improvement of dietary health through increased consumption of fruits and vegetables, the reduction of individual and household food insecurity, and the reduction in health care use and associated costs. "Produce prescription program" is defined as a program that prescribes fresh fruits and vegetables to eligible individuals, and that may: provide financial or non-financial incentives for members to purchase fresh fruits and vegetables or educational resources on nutrition; or may establish additional accessible locations for members to procure fresh fruits and vegetables. Entities eligible for grants must be a nonprofit organization, state, or local government; entities must partner with one or more health care partners (defined as a hospital, federally-qualified health

Table 7. (Continued)

Current Law/Policy	House-Passed Bill (H.R. 2)	Senate-Passed Bill (H.R. 2)
		center, Veterans Affairs hospital or clinic, or a health care provider group). These projects serve individuals who, as determined by the Secretary, are eligible for SNAP or Medicaid, but the programs themselves are not to conduct an eligibility determination for SNAP or Medicaid. Provides mandatory funding of $4 million for each of FY2019 through FY2023; the Secretary may use not greater than 10% of funding to pay for administering monitoring and evaluating each pilot project. **(§4304)**
Nutrition Education and Obesity Prevention Grant Program. Formerly SNAP Nutrition Education and formerly an open-ended federal match to state funding, this program, administered by FNS, provides formula grant funding to SNAP state agencies to provide programs for SNAP (and other domestic food assistance programs) participants as well as other low-income households. Annual mandatory funding is provided, most recently $421 million in FY2018. For FY2018 and each fiscal year thereafter, 50% of funding is allocated based on states' SNAP population, and 50% of funding is allocated based on states' funding received during FY2009 (when funding for the program was an open-ended federal match). **(7 U.S.C. 2036a, P.L. 115-141)**	Makes 1862 and 1890 institutions eligible institutions for carrying out this program. Requires Secretary to act through NIFA to implement the program and to consult with FNS. Requires eligible institutions, to the extent practicable, to employ and train professional and paraprofessional aides from the target population to engage in direct nutrition education and to partner with other entities to optimize program delivery. Increases mandatory funding to $485 million beginning in FY2019. This amount is adjusted for inflation in FY2020 and subsequent years. Authorizes additional discretionary funding of $65 million for FY2019 through FY2023. Funds are allocated based solely on states' SNAP populations. Limits administrative costs for eligible institutions to 10%; makes certain administrative costs eligible for SNAP's matching administrative funds. **(§4033)**	Requires the Secretary to describe how the states shall use an electronic reporting system that measures and evaluates projects. Requires state agency to send an annual evaluation report to Secretary. Requires the Administrator of the Food and Nutrition Service to consult with the Director of the National Institute of Food and Agriculture to coordinate activities of SNAP nutrition education and the Expanded Food and Nutrition Education Program. **(§4114)**
Mandatory funding of $5 million provided for **Grants for Simple Application and Eligibility Determination Systems and Improved Access to Benefits. (7 U.S.C. 2020(s))**	Retitles to "Grants for Simple Application and Eligibility Determination Systems." Amends law to exclude projects with the purposes of reducing barriers to participation or improving methods for informing and enrolling eligible households. **(§4025)**	No comparable provision.

Current Law/Policy	House-Passed Bill (H.R. 2)	Senate-Passed Bill (H.R. 2)
No comparable provision.	**Public-Private Partnerships.** Authorizes grants for up to 10 pilot projects that support public- private partnerships addressing food insecurity and poverty. Projects are to last no more than two years and address specified objectives. Grantees shall report annually to Secretary, who shall report to congressional committees. Authorizes $5 million in discretionary funding for grants to eligible entities. **(§4030)**	No comparable provision.
Puerto Rico. Since 1982, Puerto Rico has received a block grant, Nutrition Assistance Program for Puerto Rico (NAP), in lieu of SNAP (formerly Food Stamp Program). The annual amount is based on the USDA- calculated Thrifty Food Plan, which uses data from the contiguous states. **(7 U.S.C. 2028)** In 2010, USDA published a study, required by the 2008 farm bill, on the feasibility of Puerto Rico administering SNAP. **(§4142 of P.L. 110-246)**	Authorizes discretionary funding for the Secretary to carry out a study to determine the feasibility and impact of developing a Thrifty Food Plan to specifically apply to NAP. **(§4040)** Requires the Secretary to again carry out a study of the feasibility and effects of including Puerto Rico in SNAP as opposed to the NAP block grant. Provides $1 million in mandatory funding and an authorization for additional discretionary funding. **(§4042)**	No comparable provision.
Food Distribution Programs		
Food Distribution Program on Indian Reservations (FDPIR). Commodity distribution program established to distribute agricultural commodities, in lieu of SNAP benefits, at the request of a tribal organization. $5 million in mandatory funding authorized for a traditional and locally-grown food fund. **(7 U.S.C. (2014)(b))** USDA funds 75% of program's administrative costs. **(7 C.F.R. 253.11)** Annual appropriations language provides FDPIR funding and makes it available for spending within one fiscal year. **(e.g., P.L. 115-141)** funding, the Emergency Food Assistance Act of 1983 authorizes discretionary funding for an Emergency Food Program Infrastructure Grants through FY2018. **(7 U.S.C. 7511a)**	Amends locally-grown and traditional food fund to include "regionally grown" foods. Reauthorizes fund's authorization of appropriations through FY2023. Requires that FDPIR funding be available for spending for a two-year period. **(§4005)** procure, excess fresh fruits and vegetables grown in the state or surrounding regions to be provided to emergency feeding organizations. **(§4032)**	Requires the Secretary to pay at least 80 percent of the administrative costs and that FDPIR administrative funding be available for spending for a two-year period. Establishes a demonstration project for one or more tribal organizations to enter into a self-determination contract to purchase commodities for FDPIR; to carry out this project, authorizes $5 million in discretionary funding to be available until expended. Like the House bill, reauthorizes locally-grown and traditional food fund through FY2023 and makes all FDPIR funding available for spending for a two-year period. **(§4102)** donated by agricultural producers, processors, or distributors for use by emergency feeding organizations. Provides $4 million in mandatory funding for each of FY2019 through FY2023; the federal share of project costs shall not exceed 50%

Table 7. (Continued)

Current Law/Policy	House-Passed Bill (H.R. 2)	Senate-Passed Bill (H.R. 2)
		of the total cost of the project. Requires the Secretary to allocate funds to states that have included such a project in their state plans, based on an allocation formula determined by the Secretary. **(§4115(b))** Requires states to include, in their TEFAP state plans, a plan that provides emergency feeding organizations or recipient agencies an opportunity to provide input on commodity preferences and needs. **(§4115(a))** Requires the Secretary to issue guidance outlining best practices to minimize food waste of those commodities donated by non-USDA entities. **(§4115(c))** Reauthorizes infrastructure grants through FY2023. **(§4115(d))**
Commodity Distribution Program. Authority to purchase and distribute agricultural commodities expires at the end of FY2018. **(7 U.S.C. 612c note)**	Reauthorizes through FY2023. **(§4101)**	Same as House bill. **(§4201)**
Commodity Supplemental Food Program. Various authorities expire at the end of FY2018. No minimum certification period for participants is provided in statute; a six-month minimum is in regulation. **(7 U.S.C. 612c note, 7 C.F.R. 247.16(a))** Some states currently provide temporary certifications on a month- to-month basis when clients certified for six months do not claim foods.	Reauthorizes through FY2023. **(§4102)** Requires states to establish a minimum certification period of not less than one year and allows the Secretary to approve state requests for longer certification periods if certain requirements are met. **(§4103)**	Reauthorizes through FY2023. Requires states to establish a minimum certification period of not less than one year but not more than three years (if certain requirements are met), while allowing for temporary monthly certification when other certified participants do not participate. **(§4202)**
Distribution of surplus commodities to special nutrition projects. Secretary required to encourage consumption of surplus commodities by contracting with private companies to process such commodities into end-food products. Authority expires at the end of FY2018. **(7 U.S.C. 1431e(a))**	Reauthorizes through FY2023. **(§4104)**	Same as House bill. **(§4203)**
Other Nutrition Programs and Policies		
Purchase of fresh fruits and vegetables for distribution to schools and service institutions. In addition to the minimum ($200 million per year) acquisitions required by the 2002 farm bill, USDA is required to purchase additional fruits,	Extends $50 million requirement through FY2023. **(§4201)**	Same as House bill. **(§4301)**

Current Law/Policy	House-Passed Bill (H.R. 2)	Senate-Passed Bill (H.R. 2)
vegetables, and tree nuts for use in domestic nutrition assistance programs using Section 32 funds. The added purchases required include $206 million (FY2012 and each year thereafter). Of this money for additional purchases, at least $50 million annually (for each of FY2008 through FY2018) is required for USDA fresh fruit and vegetable acquisitions for schools. **(7 U.S.C. 612c-4)**		
Senior Farmers' Market Nutrition Program (SFMNP). Authorizes and provides CCC mandatory funding of $20.6 million annually for the SFMNP through FY2018. **(7 U.S.C. 612c-4(b))**	Reauthorizes funding through FY2023. **(§4202)**	Same as House Bill. **(§4302)**
Authorizes up to $125 million to be appropriated for a "**Healthy Food Financing Initiative**" to remain available until expended. USDA is authorized to approve a community development financial institution as "national fund manager" that would administer these funds by supporting food retail projects that would "expand or preserve access to staple foods" (as defined within this section) and accept SNAP benefits. **(7 U.S.C. 6953)**	Amends appropriated funding to be available for expenditure through October 1, 2023. **(§4203)**	See Miscellaneous title, **§12409**.
Amendments to the Fresh Fruit and Vegetable Program. Provides grants to states for children at low- income elementary schools to receive fruit and vegetable snacks throughout the day. Purchases are limited to fresh fruits and vegetables. Program is permanently authorized and permanently funded. **(42 U.S.C. 1769a)** The 2014 farm bill required USDA to administer a pilot project to implement and evaluate at least five states providing frozen, canned, and dried fruits and vegetables through this program and provided $5 million for this purpose. **(42 U.S.C. 1769a note)**	Amends program to provide fresh, canned, dried, frozen, or pureed fruits and vegetables. Renames program **Fruit and Vegetable Program**. **(§4204)**	No comparable provision.
Community Food Projects. Permanently authorizes a grant program for eligible nonprofit organizations in order to improve community access to food. Grants require 50% in matching funds. For FY2015 and each year thereafter, provides $9 million annually in mandatory funding for this purpose. **(7 U.S.C. 2034)**	No comparable provision.	For FY2019 and each fiscal year thereafter, provides a total of $5 million each year (a reduction of $4 million per year). **(§4113)**

Table 7. (Continued)

Current Law/Policy	House-Passed Bill (H.R. 2)	Senate-Passed Bill (H.R. 2)
Service of Traditional Foods in Public Facilities. USDA and FDA are required to allow the donation and provision of traditional tribal foods if the food service provider meets certain conditions. Includes liability protections for the United States, Indian tribes, and tribal organizations. **(25 U.S.C. §1685)**	Amends the provision, expanding the list of specified public programs and facilities included and protected from liability. **(§4041)**	No comparable provision.
In accordance with requirements in the Healthy, Hunger-Free Kids Act of 2010 **(P.L. 111-296, §§201, 208)**, USDA published final regulations to update the nutrition standards for National School Lunch Program and School Breakfast Program in January 2012 and final regulations to set standards for other foods in the school nutrition environment in July 2016. **(77 *Federal Register* 4088; 81 *Federal Register* 50131)**	Requires the Secretary to review the 2012 and 2016 regulations that updated the school meal nutrition standards and created nutrition standards for foods served outside of the meal program, including any requirements for milk. Revised final regulations are to be based on research focused on school-age children, not add costs to the operation of the program, and maintain healthy meals for students. **(§4205)**	No comparable provision.

Table 8. Credit

Current Law/Policy	House-Passed Bill (H.R. 2)	Senate-Passed Bill (H.R. 2)
Subtitle A—USDA Farm Ownership Loans		
Eligibility. Requires, for eligibility for direct loans, at least three years of farming experience or other acceptable experience as determined by the Secretary. The applicant must also be a beginning farmer, not have received prior direct farm ownership loans, or have not received a direct farm ownership loan more than 10 years ago. **(7 U.S.C. 1922(b))**	Specifies conditions under which the Secretary may reduce the three-year farming experience requirement for beginning farmers and ranchers as follows: (A) To two years if the borrower (1) has 16 credit hours of postsecondary education in agriculture, (2) has one-year of substantive management experience in a business, (3) was honorably discharged from the military, (4) has successfully repaid an FSA youth loan, or (5) has a mentoring relationship with Service Corps Retired Executives or a local farmer, rancher, or organization approved by the Secretary. (B) To one year with military leadership or management experience from completing a military leadership course. (C) Waived entirely if the beginning farmer meets two of the options	Specifies conditions that the Secretary may count as other acceptable experience, as follows: (A) (1) At least 16 hours of post-secondary education in agriculture, (2) completing a farm management curriculum from cooperative extension, community college, adult vocational education, non-profit, or land-grant organization, (3) was honorably discharged from the military, (4) has successfully repaid an FSA youth loan, (5) has at least 1 year as hired farm labor with substantive management experience, (6) completed a mentorship, apprenticeship, or internship with emphasis on farm management, or (7) has a mentoring relationship with Service Corps Retired Executives or a local farmer, rancher,

Current Law/Policy	House-Passed Bill (H.R. 2)	Senate-Passed Bill (H.R. 2)
	(1)-(5) above, including mentoring in (5). **(§5101)**	or organization approved by the Secretary. (B) A farmer is deemed to have met the three-year requirement if he meets option (5) and (7) above. **(§5101)**
Conservation Loans. Authorizes appropriations of $150 million annually for a conservation loan and loan guarantee program for FY2014-FY2018. **(7 U.S.C. 1924(h))**	Reduces the authorization of appropriation to $75 million annually, and extends it to FY2023. **(§5102)**	Extends the current law authorization of appropriation to FY2023. **(§5102)**
Loan Limit. For guaranteed farm ownership loans, sets the loan limit per borrower at $700,000, increased beginning with FY2000 by the inflation percentage since 1996 in the NASS Index of Prices Paid by Farmers. In FY2018, USDA announced the inflation-adjusted limit at $1,399,000. For direct farm ownership loans, sets the loan limit per borrower at a constant $300,000, **(7 U.S.C. 1925)**	Raises the loan limit for guaranteed farm ownership loans to $1.75 million per borrower and adjusts it in FY2019 and thereafter for inflation. The calculation of the inflation percentage is unchanged using a 1996 base year. Thus, the inflation-adjusted limit in FY2019 may be about $3.5 million. Leaves the direct loan limit unchanged. **(§5103)**	Raises the loan limit for guaranteed farm ownership loans to $1.75 million per borrower for the 5-year period FY2019-2023, and makes it subject to an inflation adjustment. Similar to the House bill, the inflation percentage remains unchanged using a 1996 base year. Thus, the inflation-adjusted limit in FY2019 may be about $3.5 million. For direct loans, increases the limit to a constant $600,000. **(§5103)**
No comparable provision for farm loans. A similar relending program for rural development is authorized in the same section as would be amended by the Senate bill. **(7 U.S.C. 1936b)**	No comparable provision.	**Relending Program.** Authorizes a relending program for farm ownership loans on projects that assist heirs with undivided ownership interests so that they may resolve ownership and succession issues on farmland that has multiple owners. USDA would make direct loans and loan guarantees to cooperatives, credit unions and nonprofit organizations (that are certified to operate as lenders, and which have experience assisting socially disadvantaged, limited resource, and beginning farmers, ranchers and rural businesses) to relend to such projects and heirs. Preference shall be for relending entities with at least 10 years' experience, and in states that have adopted the Uniform Partition of Heirs Property Act. Borrowers are required to complete a succession plan that may be financed with the loan. **(§12624(c))**

Table 8. (Continued)

Current Law/Policy	House-Passed Bill (H.R. 2)	Senate-Passed Bill (H.R. 2)
Subtitle B—USDA Farm Operating Loans		
Loan limit. Sets the loan limit per borrower for guaranteed farm operating loans at $700,000, increased beginning with FY2000 by the inflation percentage since 1996 in the NASS Index of Prices Paid by Farmers. In FY2018, USDA announced the inflation-adjusted limit at $1,399,000. **(7 U.S.C. 1943(a))**	Raises the loan limit for guaranteed farm operating loans to $1.75 million per borrower and adjusts it in FY2019 and thereafter for inflation. The calculation of the inflation percentage remains the same using a 1996 base year; thus, the inflation-adjusted limit in FY2019 may be about $3.5 million. **(§5201)**	Raises the loan limit for guaranteed farm operating loans to $1.75 million per borrower for the 5-year period FY2019-2023. For direct loans, increases the limit to a constant $400,000. **(§5201)**
Microloans. Authorizes a microloan program for farm operating loans of less than $50,000, with streamlined application and approval processes. Includes a pilot project to deliver microloans through community development financial institutions. **(7 U.S.C. 1943(c))**	Changes the word *title* to *subsection* to clarify technical references within the statute. **(§5202)**	Reauthorizes the cooperative lending pilot project that is delivered through community development financial institutions to FY2023. **(§5202)** Authorizes the use of mandatory funds of the Commodity Credit Corporation to support up to $5 million of direct microloans for farm operating purposes, if the amount available under the ConAct or appropriations is insufficient to meet demand, and subject to notification to Congress. **(§12617)**
Subtitle C—Administrative Provisions		
Individual Development Accounts. Authorizes appropriations for the Beginning Farmer and Rancher Individual Development Account Program at $5 million per year through FY2018. This program has never received appropriations. **(7 U.S.C. 1983b)**	Reauthorizes appropriations through FY2023. **(§5301)**	Identical to House provision. **(§5301)** Reauthorizes appropriations through FY2024. **(§12624(a))**
Funding. Authorizes appropriations for loan levels of $4.226 billion through FY2018, subdivided as follows: $1.2 billion for direct loans ($350 million for farm ownership loans and $850 million for operating loans), and $3.026 billion for guaranteed loans ($1 billion for farm ownership loans and $2.026 billion for operating loans). Actual appropriations have exceeded these amounts in recent years. **(7 U.S.C. 1994(b)(1))**	Reauthorizes the same loan levels through FY2023. **(§5302)**	Reauthorizes loan levels through FY2023, and raises the total to $12 billion, subdivided as follows: $4 billion for direct loans, and $8 billion for guaranteed loans. Within the subtotals for direct and guaranteed loans, half of each is for farm ownership loans and half is for operating loans, **(§5302)**
Carve-out for beginning farmers and ranchers. Reserves 50% of each year's direct farm operating loan authority to be used for beginning farmers and ranchers for 11 months through September 1 of	Reauthorizes the carve-outs through FY2023. **(§5303)**	Identical to House provision. **(§5303)**

Current Law/Policy	House-Passed Bill (H.R. 2)	Senate-Passed Bill (H.R. 2)
each fiscal year from FY2008 to FY2018. **(7 U.S.C. 1994(b)(2)(A)(ii)(III))**		
Part of the FSA loan program is reserved for beginning farmers and ranchers. For direct loans, 75% of the funding for farm ownership loans and 50% of operating loans are reserved for the first 11 months of the fiscal year. For guaranteed loans, 40% is reserved for ownership loans and farm operating loans for the first half of the fiscal year. **(7 U.S.C. 1994 (b)(2))** Funds are also targeted to "socially disadvantaged" farmers by race, gender, and ethnicity. **(7 U.S.C. 2003)**	No comparable provision.	States the Sense of the Senate that the existing reserve amounts and targets for the farm loan program are to "incentivize participation," and that all participants should encourage beginning and socially disadvantaged farmers to use FSA loans. **(§5410)**
No comparable provision.	No comparable provision.	**Equitable relief.** Adds a new section to the Consolidated Farm and Rural Development Act (ConAct) to provide relief to a farmer whose failure to comply with the terms of the farm loan program was caused by an action of USDA. The Secretary may allow the farmer to retain the loan or provide other relief as determined appropriate. **(§5304)**
Authorizes fees to be charged for guaranteed loans. Authorizes the percentage of the loan principal that is guaranteed for repayment. Generally, guarantees are between 80% and 90%, depending on the credit risk of the borrower, except for a 95% guarantee on refinancing and the down payment loan program. **(7 U.S.C. 1929(h); and 7 C.F.R. 762.129)**	No comparable provision.	Exempts beginning farmers and ranchers, and socially disadvantaged farmers and ranchers, from the 1.5% guarantee fee that is charged on guaranteed farm ownership and farm operating loans, and raises the ratio of the loan that is guaranteed for beginning and socially disadvantaged farmers to 95%.**(§5305)**
Loan servicing. In general, prohibits making loans to farmers who are delinquent on repaying USDA farm loans, or who have received debt forgiveness. Allows exceptions for certain operating loans when there has been a restructuring or for emergency loans when the restructuring was before 1996 and there has not been debt forgiveness after 1996. **(7 U.S.C. 2008h)**	No comparable provision.	Expands the exception to allow borrowers who have received a debt write down or restructuring of a farm loan (due to circumstances beyond the control of the borrower) to maintain eligibility for an emergency loan. **(§5306)**
Farmer Loan Pilot Projects. Authorizes pilot projects of limited scope and duration for Subtitles A- D (farm real estate loans, operating loans, emergency loans and administrative provisions) of the ConAct to evaluate processes and	No comparable provision.	Authorizes (in a new section) pilot projects of limited scope and duration for Subtitles A, B, C, and D (real estate loans, operating loans, emergency loans, and administrative provisions)

Table 8. (Continued)

Current Law/Policy	House-Passed Bill (H.R. 2)	Senate-Passed Bill (H.R. 2)
techniques that may improve efficiency and effectiveness. **(7 U.S.C. 1983d)**		of the ConAct to evaluate processes and techniques that may improve efficiency and effectiveness. **(§12624(b))**
No comparable provision.	No comparable provision.	**Report Requirement.** Creates an annual reporting requirement for the USDA farm loan program. The report is to address the farm ownership and farm operating loan programs at an aggregate level, and include: borrowers' ages and length of time that borrowers have been farming; the size of farms or ranches; race, ethnicity and gender of borrowers; sizes and types of farm loans made or guaranteed; the default rates by type of loan; the number of loans by state and county, by size cohort; and loans made compared to target participation measures for beginning and socially disadvantaged farmers, by location. A comprehensive eview is also due every five years that assesses trends in the annual reports and actions that USDA will take to improve participation by underserved borrowers. **(§5409)**
Technical Corrections to the Consolidated Farm and Rural Development Act (ConAct)	**Subtitle D**	
The **Down Payment Loan Program** encourages retiring farmers and ranchers to sell their property to beginning farmers and ranchers with seller financing. The 2008 farm bill added *and socially disadvantaged farmers and ranchers* but did not specify the location and was executed with a note in Section 310E(d)(3) of the ConAct about placement to reflect the probable intent of Congress. **(7 U.S.C. 1935(d)(3))**	Clarifies the location for the addition of *and socially disadvantaged farmers and ranchers* in the statute about encouraging retiring farmers and ranchers to offer seller financing. Retroactive to the 2008 farm bill. **(§5401(a))**	No comparable provision.
For eligibility in the **Emergency Loan Program**, the 2014 farm bill added *and such other legal entities* to the first sentence. It was executed in Section 321(a) of the ConAct in the second sentence to reflect the probable intent of Congress. **(7 U.S.C. 1961(a))**	Clarifies the location in the second sentence for the addition of *and such other legal entities* to the eligibility for the Emergency Loan Program. Retroactive to the 2014 farm bill. **(§5401(b))**	No comparable provision.

Current Law/Policy	House-Passed Bill (H.R. 2)	Senate-Passed Bill (H.R. 2)
The Agricultural Credit Improvement Act of 1992 attempted to add flexibility for a state director to extend a 60-day period for a borrower to respond to notice of loan delinquency that was sent by the Secretary. The 1992 revision of Section 331D(e) of the ConAct could not be executed. **(7 U.S.C. 1981d(e))**	Clarifies that a state director may add flexibility to the time period allowed for a borrower to respond to a notice sent by the Secretary about a loan becoming delinquent. Retroactive to 1992. **(§5401(c))**	No comparable provision.
Approved lender. The definition of *approved lender* in Section 333A(f)(1)(A) of the ConAct references Section 114.	Clarifies the definition of *approved lender* with reference to Section 339 of the ConAct. Retroactive to 1992. **(§5401(d))**	No comparable provision.
Notes in the act suggest that the probable intent of Congress was likely Section 339. **(7 U.S.C. 1983a(f)(1)(A))**		
In the guaranteed loan program, the classification of "preferred certified lender" has authority to make certain decisions about loans that are not granted to all lenders that receive guarantees. **(7 U.S.C. 1989(d)(3))**	Capitalizes the spelling of Preferred Certified Lender. **(§5401(e))**	No comparable provision.
An instruction in the 2014 farm bill attempted to change the reference to *or joint operators* in Section 343(a)(11)(C) of the ConAct to *joint operator, or owners*, as noted in its execution. **(7 U.S.C. 1991(a)(11)(C))**	Clarifies in the definition of *qualified beginning farmer or rancher* that flexibility was added with the addition of *or owners* to the phrase about alternative legal entities. Retroactive to the 2014 farm bill. **(§5401(f))**	No comparable provision.
To apply certain definitions, Section 343(b) of the ConAct references Section "307(e)." Notes made during the execution suggest that the intent may have been Section 307(d). **(7 U.S.C. 1991(b))**	Deletes reference to Section 307(e), and inserts reference to Section 307(d). Retroactive to the 2014 farm bill. **(§5401(g))**	No comparable provision.
A paragraph in statute ended in an extra comma after an amendment was made in the 1996 farm bill. **(7 U.S.C. 1994(a))**	Deletes the extra comma at the end of the paragraph. **(§5401(h))**	No comparable provision.
Amendments to the Farm Credit Act of 1971 (Farm Credit System)	**Subtitle E**	**Subtitle D**
Directs the Farm Credit System to have a loan program for young, beginning, and small (YBS) farmers and ranchers, and to report to the Farm Credit Administration annually to summarize those operations. **(12 U.S.C. 2207)**	No comparable provision.	Adds "socially disadvantaged farmers and ranchers," as defined for the Farm Service Agency loan program, to the YBS requirement. **(§5402)**
Update definition of Farm Credit System (FCS) entities. Defines the entities that comprise the FCS, all of which are regulated by FCA. **(12 U.S.C. 2002(a))**	Revises the definition of entities that comprise the FCS to include more specific identification of the current types of entities and includes the Federal Farm Credit Banks Funding Corporation, FarmerMac, and service corporations, all of which	Identical to House provision. **(§5407(2))**

Table 8. (Continued)

Current Law/Policy	House-Passed Bill (H.R. 2)	Senate-Passed Bill (H.R. 2)
	shall continue to be regulated by FCA. **(§5501(a))**	
Allows a production credit association in a district with two such associations to serve borrowers who are denied credit by the other association if FCA determines that the denying association was "unduly restrictive" in granting credit. **(12 U.S.C. 2075(d))**	Deletes this section, which is no longer applicable. **(§5501(b))**	Identical to House provision. **(§5407(3))**
Establishes a system of banks for cooperatives in the FCS. **(12 U.S.C. 2121, 2123, 2128, 2130, 2131(c), 2132, 2141, 2142, 2149)**	Deletes various references to a Central Bank for Cooperatives, United Bank of Cooperatives, and/or a National Bank of Cooperatives while continuing to recognize the existence of a bank for cooperatives. **(§5501(c), (d), (e), (f), (h), (j), (k), (m), (n), (o), (p), (q), (r), (s))**	Similar to the House provisions. **(§5407(4), (5), (7), (9), (11), (12), (13), (14), (15), (16))**
Establishes provisions relating to the funding and governance of the Farm Credit Banks through referring to district banks. **(12 U.S.C. 2126, 2131(d))**	Deletes the obsolete word *district* in reference to the Farm Credit Banks, as that is no longer used following years of consolidation. **(§5501(g), (l))**	Similar to the House provisions. **(§5407(6), (10))**
Allows a bank for cooperatives to make loans to the Rural Electrification Administration. **(12 U.S.C. 2129(b)(1)(A))**	Inserts language recognizing a successor agency to the Rural Electrification Administration after the latter was absorbed into the USDA Rural Utilities Service. **(§5501(i))**	Similar to the House provisions. **(§5407(8))**
Establishes, and sets conditions for an Assistance Board, a Financial Assistance Corporation, and related funding to remediate losses within the FCS during the 1980s. **(12 U.S.C. 2278a-2278b-11, 2151, 2159, 2277a-9(b), 2162(c), 2202c, 2219c, 2254(b), 2271 (4), 2277a-7(2), 2279d(a)(4))**	Deletes references to the now-obsolete Assistance Board, Financial Assistance Corporation, and funding. Terminates the Financial Assistance Corporation after December 31, 2018. **(§5501(t), (u), (x), (bb), (ee), (ii), (jj), (mm), (nn), (oo), (qq))**	Similar to the House provisions. **(§5407(1), (17), (18), (20), (23), (26), (31), (34), (37), (38), (39), (41), (46))**
During the tenure of the Assistance Board, a member of the Assistance Board shall be a nonvoting member of the board of the Farm Credit System Funding Corporation. After termination of the Assistance Board, its successor, the Farm Credit System Insurance Corporation, shall not have a member on the Funding Corporation board. **(12 U.S.C. 2160(d)(2))**	Deletes reference to the now-obsolete Assistance Board and retains language that the Insurance Corporation shall not have a member on the board of the Funding Corporation. **(§5501(v))**	Similar to the House provisions. **(§5407(19))**
Establishes provisions and conditions for the transition of various parts of the FCS as it is created, especially from the 1980s and 1990s for FarmerMac.	Deletes provisions that are transitional in nature now that the FCS is established. **(§5501(w), (aa), (ff), (gg), (ll), (pp), (rr), (ss), (tt), (uu), (vv), (ww), (xx))**	Similar to the House provisions. **(§5407(22), (27), (29), (30), (32), (33), (36), (40), (42), (43), (44), (45), (47), (48), (49), (50), (51))**

Current Law/Policy	House-Passed Bill (H.R. 2)	Senate-Passed Bill (H.R. 2)
(12 U.S.C. 2160(e), 2202a(h), 2252(a)(2), 2253, 2275, 2279c-2(c), 2279aa(2), 2279aa(6), 2279aa(8), 2279aa-2(b), 2279aa-4(a)(1), 2279aa-6(d), 2279bb-1(a), 2279bb-4(e))		
Lists the FCS institutions that are applicable to various requirements. **(12 U.S.C. 2184(a)(1), 2205, 2207(a), 2254 (a), 2274)**	Revises the lists to more generically refer to FCS banks or associations and its current structure. **(§5501(y), (cc), (dd), (hh), (kk))**	Similar to the House provisions. **(§5407(21), (24), (25), (35))**
Defines terms relating to the restructuring of distressed loans. **(12 U.S.C.2202a(a))**	Applies the definitions that are used for distressed loans to the section about the "right of first refusal" for borrowers' rights. (12 U.S.C. 2219). **(§5501(z))**	Similar to the House provisions. **(§5407(22))**
Provides for the establishment and administration of FCA and certain of its powers to regulate entities of FCS. **(12 U.S.C. 1141b, 1141c, 1141d, 1141e, 1141f, 1141i, 1141j, 1141d-1, 1148, 1148a-4, 1148b, 1148c, 1148d, 1401-1404)**	**Conforming repeals.** Repeals sections about FCA that have been superseded by newer statutes for FCA that are in 12 U.S.C. 2241 *et seq.* and that are part of the Farm Credit Act of 1971, as amended. **(§5502)**	Similar to the House provisions. **(§5407(52), (53), (54), (55), (56), (57), (58), (59), (60), (61), (62), (63), (64))**
Headquarters. Provides for the provision of headquarters and other facilities for FCA. **(12 U.S.C. 2251)**	Directs that the principal office of FCA shall be in the Washington, DC, metropolitan area, with other offices throughout the United States as necessary. **(§5503)**	Similar to the House provisions. **(§5407(28))**
Privileged information. Instructs FCA to examine the banks and associations of the FCS, and to report on the condition of the System. Empowers FCA to share confidentially with the Farm Credit Insurance Corporation information about examinations. **(12 U.S.C. 2254)**	States that Farm Credit System institutions do not waive attorney-client privilege if they provide the content of a communication to the Farm Credit Administration as part of a regulatory or supervisory process. **(§5504)**	Identical to House provision. **(§5403)**
No comparable provision.	No comparable provision.	Allows the Farm Credit Administration, like other financial industry regulators, to prevent any individual who has been removed for violating a law, breached fiduciary duty, or participated in any unsafe or unsound practice in the FCS, from working in another sector of the financial industry. This new authority mirrors existing authority provided other regulators. **(§5404)**
Scope of FCA jurisdiction. Provides various enforcement powers to FCA against FCS entities, directors, officers, employees, and agents that engage in unsafe or unsound practices or violate the regulations of the FCS. **(12 U.S.C. 2261-2274)**	Adds a provision that the scope of FCA's jurisdiction shall include "institution-affiliated parties" (as defined in Section 5506) and that the parties may be held accountable to laws and regulations.	Similar to the House provision, although separates the provision in to multiple paragraphs. **(§5405)**

Table 8. (Continued)

Current Law/Policy	House-Passed Bill (H.R. 2)	Senate-Passed Bill (H.R. 2)
	This jurisdiction is retroactive and shall continue to apply for six years after the party ceases to be affiliated with the FCS. **(§5505)**	
Defines various terms for the enforcement powers of FCA. **(12 U.S.C. 2271)**	Adds a definition for *institution-affiliated party* (as used in Section 5505) to include the directors, officers, employees, shareholders, and agents of system institutions, including independent contractors (such as attorneys, appraisers, or accountants) and any others who participate in system affairs. **(§5506)**	Identical to House provision. **(§5406)**
FarmerMac qualified loans. Defines that the maximum size of a "qualified loan" that FarmerMac may finance is $2.5 million adjusted for inflation ($12.6 million in FY2018), except if the loan is secured by less than 1,000 acres. **(12 U.S.C. 2279aa-8(c)(2))**	Increases the acreage exception to the dollar limit to be a "qualified loan" for FarmerMac from 1,000 acres to 2,000 acres. Effective one year after the study by FCA (ordered in Section 5602(a)(2)) indicates that it is feasible to increase the limit. **(§5507)**	No comparable provision.
Compensation of bank directors. Establishes a limit for compensation of members of the boards of directors of FCS banks as $20,000 per year, adjusted for inflation. **(12 U.S.C. 2209)**	Deletes the section that establishes the limit on compensation of FCS bank boards of directors. **(§5508)**	No comparable provision.
Farm Credit System Insurance Corporation (FCSIC). Authorizes FCSIC to "act as a conservator or receiver" over a troubled FCS institution, including an FCS bank, but the statute is largely silent regarding: the FCSIC's powers and duties as a conservator or receiver, the process by which the FCSIC may administer a conservatorship or receivership, and the rights and responsibilities of parties impacted by an FCS institution being placed into a conservatorship or receivership. **(12 U.S.C. 2277a-7)**	No comparable provision.	Adds provisions that provide greater statutory guidance regarding the powers and duties of the FCSIC when acting as a conservator or receiver, the process by which the FCSIC may administer a conservatorship or receivership to resolve a troubled FCS institution, and the rights and duties of parties affected by an FCS institution being placed into a conservatorship or receivership. These authorities are largely modeled after the existing conservatorship/receivership statutory regime (12 U.S.C. 1821) that is applicable to Federal Deposit Insurance Corporation (FDIC) - insured depository institutions (e.g., banks and saving associations). The provisions at times deviate from the FDIC model to account for, among other things, the varying

Current Law/Policy	House-Passed Bill (H.R. 2)	Senate-Passed Bill (H.R. 2)
		activities of FCS institutions and insured depository institutions. Among other things, the provisions: Provide that the FCSIC, upon being appointed conservator or receiver, shall "succeed to all rights, titles, powers, and privileges" of the relevant FCS institution's officers, directors, and shareholders; Authorize the FCSIC, as conservator, to take steps "necessary to put the [FCS] institution in a sound and solvent condition," and, as receiver, to merge a failed FCS institution with a different FCS institution and sell the assets of a failed FCS institution; and Establish processes for FCSIC, as receiver, to determine and pay valid claims of failed FCS institution's creditors based on a statutorily prescribed priority scheme, and to disallow certain creditor claims against the FCS institution. **(§5408)**
Use of funds. Specifies various prohibitions and limitations about the Farm Credit System Insurance Corporation. **(12 U.S.C. 2277a-14)**	Adds a paragraph that no funds of the Farm Credit System Insurance Corporation may be used to assist FarmerMac. **(§5509)**	No comparable provision.
Miscellaneous	**Subtitle F**	**Subtitle D**
State mediation program. Authorizes a matching grant program for states that provide third-party mediation services for agricultural credit disputes. **(7 U.S.C. 5101)** Authorizes appropriations of $7.5 million annually through FY2018. **(7 U.S.C. 5106)**	Reauthorizes appropriations through FY2023. **(§5601)**	Reauthorizes appropriations through FY2023. Expands the scope of issues covered by the program to include the national organic program, leases on land and equipment, family farm transition, and disputes between a farmer and a neighbor. Allows a state secretary of agriculture to determine other issues for mediation, in addition to the USDA Secretary. Allows for mediation services before a dispute is initiated with USDA, or unrelated to USDA. Ensures notification to USDA if other issues are addressed. Directs USDA to report to Congress, within two years, about the effectiveness of the program, and recommendations for improvement. **(§5401)**

Table 8. (Continued)

Current Law/Policy	House-Passed Bill (H.R. 2)	Senate-Passed Bill (H.R. 2)
No comparable provision.	**FCA study.** Directs FCA to conduct a study that (1) analyzes and compares financial risks of loans in the FCS and by FarmerMac and how such risks are capitalized and (2) assesses the feasibility of increasing to 2,000 acres the 1,000 acre exception in the definition for *qualified loans* for FarmerMac (see 12 U.S.C. 2279aa-8). The study is to be submitted to Congress 180 days after enactment. **(§5602)**	No comparable provision.
No comparable provision.	**Report on the credit needs of Indian tribes.** Directs the Government Accountability Office (GAO) to write a report for Congress within 90 days of enactment that studies the agricultural credit needs of Indian tribes and members of Indian tribes. The report is to address whether the FCS has sufficient authority and resources to meet the credit needs of these farm, ranch, and related businesses borrowers; and to identify legislative and other recommendations that would help meet such needs. **(§5603)**	No comparable provision.
Subtitle A—USDA Farm Ownership Loans		
Eligibility. Requires, for eligibility for direct loans, at least three years of farming experience or other acceptable experience as determined by the Secretary. The applicant must also be a beginning farmer, not have received prior direct farm ownership loans, or have not received a direct farm ownership loan more than 10 years ago. **(7 U.S.C. 1922(b)(1))**	Specifies conditions under which the Secretary may reduce the three-year farming experience requirement for beginning farmers and ranchers as follows: (A) To two years if the borrower (1) has 16 credit hours of postsecondary education in agriculture, (2) has one-year of substantive management experience in a business, (3) was honorably discharged from the military, (4) has successfully repaid an FSA youth loan, or (5) has a mentoring relationship with Service Corps Retired Executives or a local farmer, rancher, or organization approved by the Secretary. (B) To one year with military leadership or management experience from completing a military leadership course. (C) Waived entirely if the beginning farmer meets two of the options	

Current Law/Policy	House-Passed Bill (H.R. 2)	Senate-Passed Bill (H.R. 2)
	(1)-(5) above, including mentoring in (5). **(§5101)**	
Funding. Authorizes appropriations of $150 million annually for a conservation loan and loan guarantee program for FY2014-FY2018. **(7 U.S.C. 1924(h))**	Extends the authorization of appropriation to FY2023 and reduces it to $75 million annually. **(§5102)**	
Loan Limit. Sets the loan limit per borrower for guaranteed farm ownership loans at $700,000, increased beginning with FY2000 by the inflation percentage since 1996 in the NASS Index of Prices Paid by Farmers. In FY2018, USDA announced the inflation-adjusted limit at $1,399,000. **(7 U.S.C. 1925)**	Raises the loan limit for guaranteed farm ownership loans to $1.75 million per borrower and adjusts it in FY2019 and thereafter for inflation. The calculation of the inflation percentage remains the same using a 1996 base year. Thus, the inflation-adjusted limit in FY2019 may be about $3.5 million. **(§5103)**	
Subtitle B—USDA Farm Operating Loans		
Loan limit. Sets the loan limit per borrower for guaranteed farm operating loans at $700,000, increased beginning with FY2000 by the inflation percentage since 1996 in the NASS Index of Prices Paid by Farmers. In FY2018, USDA announced the inflation-adjusted limit at $1,399,000. **(7 U.S.C. 1943(a))**	Raises the loan limit for guaranteed farm operating loans to $1.75 million per borrower and adjusts it in FY2019 and thereafter for inflation. The calculation of the inflation percentage remains the same using a 1996 base year; thus, the inflation-adjusted limit in FY2019 may be about $3.5 million. **(§5201)**	
Authorizes a microloan program for loans less than $50,000. **(7 U.S.C. 1943(c))**	Changes *title* to *subsection* to clarify technical references within the statute. **(§5202)**	
Subtitle C—Administrative Provisions		
Funding. Authorizes appropriations for the Beginning Farmer and Rancher Individual Development Account Program at $5 million per year through FY2018. **(7 U.S.C. 1983b)**	Reauthorizes appropriations of the same amount per year through FY2023. **(§5301)**	
Authorizes specific loan levels for direct and guaranteed farm ownership and farm operating loans through FY2018. **(7 U.S.C. 1994(b)(1))**	Reauthorizes the same loan levels through FY2023. **(§5302)**	
Carve-out for beginning farmers and ranchers. Reserves 50% of each year's direct farm operating loan authority to be used for beginning farmers and ranchers for 11 months through September 1 of each fiscal year from FY2008 to FY2018. **(7 U.S.C. 1994(b)(2)(A)(ii)(III))**	Reauthorizes the same set-aside preference for beginning farmers and ranchers through FY2023. **(§5303)**	
Subtitle D—Technical Corrections to the ConAct		
The **Down Payment Loan Program** encourages retiring farmers and ranchers to sell their property to beginning farmers and ranchers with seller financing.	Clarifies the location for the addition of *and socially disadvantaged farmers and ranchers* in the statute about encouraging retiring farmers and ranchers to offer seller financing.	

Table 8. (Continued)

Current Law/Policy	House-Passed Bill (H.R. 2)	Senate-Passed Bill (H.R. 2)
The 2008 farm bill added *and socially disadvantaged farmers and ranchers* but did not specify the location and was executed with a note in Section 310E(d)(3) of the Consolidated Farm and Rural Development Act (ConAct) about placement to reflect the probable intent of Congress. **(7 U.S.C. 1935(d)(3))**	Retroactive to the 2008 farm bill. **(§5401(a))**	
For eligibility in the **Emergency Loan Program**, the 2014 farm bill added *and such other legal entities* to the first sentence. It was executed in Section 321(a) of the ConAct in the second sentence to reflect the probable intent of Congress. **(7 U.S.C. 1961(a))**	Clarifies the location in the second sentence for the addition of *and such other legal entities* to the eligibility for the Emergency Loan Program. Retroactive to the 2014 farm bill. **(§5401(b))**	
The Agricultural Credit Improvement Act of 1992 attempted to add flexibility for a state director to extend a 60-day period for a borrower to respond to notice of loan delinquency that was sent by the Secretary. The 1992 revision of Section 331D(e) of the ConAct could not be executed. **(7 U.S.C. 1981d(e))**	Clarifies that a state director may add flexibility to the time period allowed for a borrower to respond to a notice sent by the Secretary about a loan becoming delinquent. Retroactive to 1992. **(§5401(c))**	
Approved lender. The definition of *approved lender* in Section 333A(f)(1)(A) of the ConAct references Section 114. Notes in the act suggest that the probable intent of Congress was likely Section 339. **(7 U.S.C. 1983a(f)(1)(A))**	Clarifies the definition of *approved lender* with reference to Section 339 of the ConAct. Retroactive to 1992. **(§5401(d))**	
In the guaranteed loan program, the classification of "preferred certified lender" has authority to make certain decisions about loans that are not granted to all lenders that receive guarantees. **(7 U.S.C. 1989(d)(3))**	Capitalizes the spelling of Preferred Certified Lender. **(§5401(e))**	
An instruction in the 2014 farm bill attempted to change the reference to *or joint operators* in Section 343(a)(11)(C) of the ConAct to *joint operator, or owners*, as noted in its execution. **(7 U.S.C. 1991(a)(11)(C))**	Clarifies in the definition of *qualified beginning farmer or rancher* that flexibility was added with the addition of *or owners* to the phrase about alternative legal entities. Retroactive to the 2014 farm bill. **(§5401(f))**	
To apply certain definitions, Section 343(b) of the ConAct references Section "307(e)." Notes for the execution suggest that the intent may have been Section 307(d). **(7 U.S.C. 1991(b))**	Deletes reference to Section 307(e), and inserts reference to Section 307(d). Retroactive to the 2014 farm bill. **(§5401(g))**	

Current Law/Policy	House-Passed Bill (H.R. 2)	Senate-Passed Bill (H.R. 2)
A paragraph in statute ended in an extra comma after an amendment was made in the 1996 farm bill. **(7 U.S.C. 1994(a))**	Deletes the extra comma at the end of the paragraph. **(§5401(h))**	
Subtitle E: Amendments to the Farm Credit Act of 1971 (Farm Credit System)		
Update definition of Farm Credit System (FCS) entities. Defines the entities that comprise the FCS, all of which are regulated by FCA. **(12 U.S.C. 2002(a))**	Revises the definition of entities that comprise the FCS to include more specific identification of the current types of entities and includes the Federal Farm Credit Banks Funding Corporation, FarmerMac, and service corporations, all of which shall continue to be regulated by FCA. **(§5501(a))**	
Allows a production credit association in a district with two such associations to serve borrowers who are denied credit by the other association if FCA determines that the denying association was "unduly restrictive" in granting credit. **(12 U.S.C. 2075(d))**	Deletes this section, which is no longer applicable. **(§5501(b))**	
Establishes a system of banks for cooperatives in the FCS. **(12 U.S.C. 2121, 2123, 2128, 2130, 2131(c), 2132, 2141, 2142, 2149)**	Deletes various references to a Central Bank for Cooperatives, United Bank of Cooperatives, and/or a National Bank of Cooperatives while continuing to recognize the existence of a bank for cooperatives. **(§5501(c), (d), (e), (f), (h), (j), (k), (m), (n), (o), (p), (q), (r), (s))**	
Establishes provisions relating to the funding and governance of the Farm Credit Banks through referring to district banks. **(12 U.S.C. 2126, 2131(d))**	Deletes the obsolete word *district* in reference to the Farm Credit Banks, as that is no longer used following years of consolidation. **(§5501(g), (l))**	
Allows a bank for cooperatives to make loans to the Rural Electrification Administration. **(12 U.S.C. 2129(b)(1)(A))**	Inserts language recognizing a successor agency to the Rural Electrification Administration after the latter was absorbed into the USDA Rural Utilities Service. **(§5501(i))**	
Establishes, and sets conditions for an Assistance Board, a Financial Assistance Corporation, and related funding to remediate losses within the FCS during the 1980s. **(12 U.S.C. 2278a-2278b-11, 2151, 2159, 2277a-9(b), 2162(c), 2202c, 2219c, 2254(b),**	Deletes references to the now-obsolete Assistance Board, Financial Assistance Corporation, and funding. Terminates the Financial Assistance Corporation after December 31, 2018. **(§5501(t), (u), (x), (bb),**	
2271 (4), 2277a-7(2), 2279d(a)(4))	**(ee), (ii), (jj), (mm), (nn), (oo), (qq))**	
During the tenure of the Assistance Board, a member of the Assistance Board shall be a non-voting member of the board of the Farm Credit System Funding Corporation.	Deletes reference to the now-obsolete Assistance Board and retains language that the Insurance Corporation shall not have a member	

Table 8. (Continued)

Current Law/Policy	House-Passed Bill (H.R. 2)	Senate-Passed Bill (H.R. 2)
After termination of the Assistance Board, its successor, the Farm Credit System Insurance Corporation, shall not have a member on the Funding Corporation board. **(12 U.S.C. 2160(d)(2))**	on the board of the Funding Corporation. **(§5501(v))**	
Establishes provisions and conditions for the transition of various parts of the FCS as it is created, especially from the 1980s and 1990s for FarmerMac. **(12 U.S.C. 2160(e), 2202a(h), 2252(a)(2), 2253, 2275, 2279c-2(c), 2279aa(2), 2279aa(6), 2279aa(8), 2279aa-2(b), 2279aa-4(a)(1), 2279aa-6(d), 2279bb-1(a), 2279bb-4(e))**	Deletes provisions that are transitional in nature now that the FCS is established. **(§5501(w), (aa), (ff), (gg), (ll), (pp), (rr), (ss), (tt), (uu), (vv), (ww), (xx))**	
Lists the FCS institutions that are applicable to various requirements. **(12 U.S.C. 2184(a)(1), 2205, 2207(a), 2254 (a), 2274)**	Revises the lists to more generically refer to FCS banks or associations and its current structure. **(§5501(y), (cc), (dd), (hh), (kk))**	
Defines terms relating to the restructuring of distressed loans. **(12 U.S.C.2202a(a))**	Applies the definitions that are used for distressed loans to the section about the "right of first refusal" for borrowers' rights. (12 U.S.C. 2219). **(§5501(z))**	
Provides for the establishment and administration of FCA and certain of its powers to regulate entities of FCS. **(12 U.S.C. 1141b, 1141c, 1141d, 1141e, 1141f, 1141i, 1141j, 1141d-1,**	**Conforming repeals.** Repeals sections about FCA that have been superseded by newer statutes for FCA that are in 12 U.S.C. 2241 *et seq.* and that are part of the	
1148, 1148a-4, 1148b, 1148c, 1148d, 1401-1404)	Farm Credit Act of 1971, as amended. **(§5502)**	
Headquarters. Provides for the provision of headquarters and other facilities for FCA. **(12 U.S.C. 2251)**	Directs that the principal office of FCA shall be in the Washington, DC, metropolitan area, with other offices throughout the United States as necessary. **(§5503)**	
Privileged information. Instructs FCA to examine the banks and associations of the FCS, and to report on the condition of the System. Empowers FCA to share confidentially with the Farm Credit Insurance Corporation information about examinations. **(12 U.S.C. 2254)**	Provides authority for FCS institutions to provide privileged communications that they have (e.g., with attorneys and accountants) to FCA, pursuant to its supervision and regulatory authority, without losing the ability to assert this privilege with respect to others. **(§5504)**	
Scope of FCA jurisdiction. Provides various enforcement powers to FCA against FCS entities, directors, officers, employees, and agents that engage in unsafe or unsound practices or violate the regulations of the FCS. **(12 U.S.C. 2261-2274)**	Adds a provision that the scope of FCA's jurisdiction shall include "institution-affiliated parties" (as defined in Section 5506) and that the parties may be held accountable to laws and regulations.	

Current Law/Policy	House-Passed Bill (H.R. 2)	Senate-Passed Bill (H.R. 2)
	This jurisdiction is retroactive and shall continue to apply for six years after the party ceases to be affiliated with the FCS. **(§5505)**	
Scope of FCA jurisdiction. Provides various enforcement powers to FCA against FCS entities, directors, officers, employees, and agents that engage in unsafe or unsound practices or violate the regulations of the FCS. **(12 U.S.C. 2261-2274)**	Adds a provision that the scope of FCA's jurisdiction shall include "institution-affiliated parties" (as defined in Section 5506) and that the parties may be held accountable to laws and regulations. This jurisdiction is retroactive and shall continue to apply for six years after the party ceases to be affiliated with the FCS. **(§5505)**	
Defines various terms for the enforcement powers of FCA. **(12 U.S.C. 2271)**	Adds a definition for *institution-affiliated party* (as used in Section 5505) to include the directors, officers, employees, shareholders, and agents of system institutions, including independent contractors (such as attorneys, appraisers, or accountants) and any others who participate in system affairs. **(§5506)**	
FarmerMac qualified loans. Defines that the maximum size of a "qualified loan" that FarmerMac may finance is \$2.5 million adjusted for inflation (\$12.6 million in FY2018), except if the loan is secured by less than 1,000 acres. **(12 U.S.C. 2279aa-8(c)(2))**	Increases the acreage exception to the dollar limit to be a "qualified loan" for FarmerMac from 1,000 acres to 2,000 acres. Effective one year after the study by FCA (ordered in Section 5602(a)(2)) indicates that it is feasible to increase the limit. **(§5507)**	
Compensation of bank directors. Establishes a limit for compensation of members of the boards of directors of FCS banks as \$20,000 per year, adjusted for inflation. **(12 U.S.C. 2209)**	Deletes the section that establishes the limit on compensation of FCS bank boards of directors. **(§5508)**	
Use of funds. Specifies various prohibitions and limitations about the Farm Credit System Insurance Corporation. **(12 U.S.C. 2277a-14)**	Adds a paragraph that no funds of the Farm Credit System Insurance Corporation may be used to assist FarmerMac. **(§5509)**	
Subtitle F: Miscellaneous		
State mediation program funding. Authorizes appropriations for a matching grant program for states that provide third-party mediation services for agricultural credit disputes. Appropriations authorized at \$7.5 million annually through FY2018. **(7 U.S.C. 5106)**	Reauthorizes appropriations of \$7.5 million annually through FY2023. **(§5601)**	

Table 8. (Continued)

Current Law/Policy	House-Passed Bill (H.R. 2)	Senate-Passed Bill (H.R. 2)
No comparable provision.	**FCA study.** Directs FCA to conduct a study that (1) analyzes and compares financial risks of loans in the FCS and by FarmerMac and how such risks are capitalized and (2) assesses the feasibility of increasing to 2,000 acres the 1,000 acre exception in the definition for *qualified loans* for FarmerMac (see 12 U.S.C. 2279aa-8). The study is to be submitted to Congress 180 days after enactment. **(§5602)**	

Table 9. Rural Development

Current Law/Policy	House-Passed Bill (H.R. 2)	Senate-Passed Bill (H.R.2)
Improving Health Outcomes in Rural Communities		
Project prioritization. The Secretary is authorized to coordinate a nationwide rural development program using the services of executive branch departments and agencies. **(7 U.S.C. 2204a-2204b)**	Authorizes the Secretary to announce a reprioritization of certain loan and grant programs to assist rural communities in responding to specific health emergencies (e.g., opioid abuse). Authorizes not less than 10% of the distance learning/telemedicine appropriation for telemedicine services to individuals affected by the emergency. Prioritizes the community facilities loan and grant program for developing prevention, treatment, and recovery services for individuals affected by the emergency. **(§6001)**	Requires the Secretary to give priority to applications for community facilities direct loans and grants to applicants who develop facilities providing substance use disorder (including opioid substance use disorder) prevention, treatment, and/or recovery services, and employ staff with expertise and training in identifying and treating individuals with substance abuse disorders. Loan and grant funds may also be used to develop telemedicine services and facilities to address substance use disorder treatments. **(§6105)**
Distance learning and telemedicine program. Provides grants to rural hospitals, clinics, schools, and libraries to develop and improve their telecommunications infrastructure. Authorizes funding of $75 million annually FY2014-FY2018, subject to appropriations. **(7 U.S.C. 950aaa)**	Authorizes appropriations of $82 million annually FY2019-FY2023 for the distance learning and telemedicine program. **(§6002)**	Amends the program to provide no less than 20% of the amounts made available to the program for substance abuse disorder treatments. Reauthorizes appropriations of $75 million annually for FY2019-FY2023. **(§6301)**
Farm and Ranch Stress Assistance Network. In coordination with the Secretary of Health and Human Services, the Secretary is authorized to make competitive grants to establish a Farm and Ranch Stress Assistance Network to provide stress assistance programs for –	Reauthorizes such sums as necessary for FY2019-FY2023. Requires a review of the program within two years after the first grant is awarded. **(§6003)**	Amends to designate eligible entities. Authorizes training and workshops for affected farmers and ranchers. Also authorizes the Network to enter into contracts with community-based, direct service organizations to initiate and expand programs.

Current Law/Policy	**House-Passed Bill (H.R. 2)**	**Senate-Passed Bill (H.R.2)**
those engaged in agriculture-related occupations. Such sums as necessary authorized FY2008- FY2012. **(7 U.S.C. 5936)**		Requires a report from the Secretary in coordination with the Secretary of Health and Human Services describing the mental and behavioral health of farmers and ranchers. Authorizes $10 million annually for FY2019-FY2023. **(§7511)**
No comparable provision.	**Agricultural association group health plans.** Authorizes a loan and grant program to assist in the establishment of agricultural association group health plans for rural areas. In coordination with the Secretary of Labor, the Secretary is authorized to make no more than 10 loans to establish agricultural association group health plans to qualified agricultural associations. Authorizes $65 million for the period FY2019-FY2022. **(§6004)**	No comparable provision.
Farmers Home Administration. Defines the powers and duties of the Secretary regarding agricultural credit. **(7 U.S.C. 1981)**	Amends to authorize the refinancing of debt obligations of rural hospitals as an eligible loan or loan guarantee purpose if the assistance would help preserve access to a health service in a rural area and improve the financial position of the hospital. **(§6005)**	No comparable provision.
Connecting Rural Americans to High-Speed Broadband		
No comparable provision.	**Establishing forward-looking broadband standards.** Amends Section 601 of the Rural Electrification Act of 1936. Directs the Secretary to establish minimum acceptable standards of broadband service of 25 megabits per second downstream transmission capacity and three megabits per second upstream transmission capacity and projections of broadband service five, 10, 15, 20, and 30 years into the future. Loans are conditioned on meeting the acceptable minimum standards. Requires a report to the House and Senate Agriculture Committees on the effectiveness of broadband loans for expanding broadband to rural areas. **(§6101)**	No comparable provision.
No comparable provision.	**Incentives to reach hard-to- reach communities.** Amends Title VI of the Rural Electrification Act of 1936. Establishes a method for calculating service points per road mile as a density measure.	No comparable provision.

Table 9. (Continued)

Current Law/Policy	House-Passed Bill (H.R. 2)	Senate-Passed Bill (H.R.2)
	Eligible applicants are those areas with a density of 12 or fewer homes, businesses, or institutions in a proposed service area. Authorizes appropriations of $350 million for each of FY2019-FY2023. **(§6102)**	
Access to broadband telecommunications services in rural areas. Title VI of the Rural Electrification Act of 1936. States that the Secretary "shall make or guarantee" loans to provide funds for the costs of the construction, improvement, and acquisition of facilities and equipment for broadband service in rural areas. **(7 U.S.C. 950bb *et seq.*)**	Amends Section 601 of the Rural Electrification Act to state that the Secretary "shall make loans and shall guarantee loans" for expanding broadband services. **(§6103);** Makes a rural area with an incorporated city of 20,000 or more ineligible for direct broadband loans. **(§6202);**	Amends Section 601 to (1) establish broadband application priorities; (2) identify unserved communities; (3) define broadband development costs, and set maximum levels of grant support; Further amends to require the Secretary to coordinate with the Federal Communications Commission to ensure that any grant or loan does not conflict with universal service high-cost support provided by the FCC; permits the Secretary to provide not less than 3%, nor more than 5%, of amounts appropriated for the Access to Broadband Telecommunications in Rural Areas for technical assistance and training to applicants for broadband loans and grants. **(§6205)**
No comparable provision	**Smart utility authority for broadband**. Amends the ConAct to permit any recipient of a loan or grant from USDA Rural Development to use up to 10% of the amount provided for any activity provided under the Access to Broadband Telecommunications Services in Rural Areas and to construct other broadband infrastructure in areas not served by minimum acceptable standards of broadband service. **(§6104)**	No comparable provision.
Rural gigabit network. A rural, ultra-high-speed gigabit pilot program is authorized in the 2014 farm bill (P.L. 113-79). Authorized appropriation of $10 million each of FY2014-FY2018. **(7 U.S.C. 950bb-2)**	Renames the Rural Gigabit Program Innovative Broadband Advancement. Authorizes loans and grants for the purpose of demonstrating innovative broadband technologies or methods of broadband deployment that significantly decrease the costs of broadband deployment.	No comparable provision.

Current Law/Policy	House-Passed Bill (H.R. 2)	Senate-Passed Bill (H.R.2)
	Gives priority to projects involving multiple entities and would provide service to the greatest number of rural residents at or above the minimum broadband speed. **(§6105)**	
Unified broadband reporting requirements. Authorizes loans and loan guarantees to provide funds for the costs of the construction, improvement, and acquisition of facilities and equipment for broadband service in rural areas. **(7 U.S.C. 950bb)**	Directs the Secretary to report annually to Congress on the extent of participation in the broadband loan and grant program. **(§6106)**	No comparable provision.
Rural Electrification Act's Telephone Loan Program. The Secretary is authorized to make loans to persons now providing or who may hereinafter provide telephone service in rural areas; to public bodies now providing telephone service in rural areas; and to cooperative, nonprofit, limited dividend, or mutual associations. **(7 U.S.C. 922-928)**	Authorizes the Secretary to obligate but not disburse funds for broadband projects before completion of otherwise required environmental, historical, or other reviews of the project. The Secretary is also authorized to de- obligate funds for projects if any such review will not be completed in a reasonable period of time. **(§6107)**	Identical to House provision. **(§6205)**
Evaluation period. Establishes not less than two evaluation periods for each fiscal year to compare loan and loan guarantee applications and to prioritize loans and loan guarantees to all or part of rural communities that do not have residential broadband service that meets the minimum acceptable level of broadband service. **(7 U.S.C. 950bb(c)(2)(A))**	Reduces the evaluation period from two evaluation periods to one. **(§6108)**	No comparable provision.
Priority to certain applicants. Gives priority to applicants that offer to provide broadband service not predominantly for business service if at least 25 percent of the customers in the proposed service territory are commercial. **(7 U.S.C. 950bb(c)(2))**	Removes priority for applicants that provide broadband service not predominantly for business service if at least 25% of the customers in the proposed service territory are commercial interests. **(§6109)**	Requires the Secretary to give highest priority for loans and grants to the following: • unserved rural areas that have no residential broadband service; After giving priority to unserved rural communities without any residential broadband and applications that provide the maximum level of broadband service to the greatest proportion of rural households, the Secretary will give priority to the following: • applications for projects that provide the maximum level of broadband service to the • greatest proportion of rural households in the proposed service area;

Table 9. (Continued)

Current Law/Policy	House-Passed Bill (H.R. 2)	Senate-Passed Bill (H.R.2)
		• applications to provide rapid and expanded deployment of fixed and mobile broadband on • cropland and ranchland within the proposed service areas for precision agriculture applications; • applications that provide equal consideration to all eligible entities including those that • have not previously received broadband loans or grants; • with respect to two or more applications for unserved areas that are given the same • priority, gives priority to an application that requests less grant funding than loan funding. • rural communities with a population of fewer than 10,000 permanent residents; • rural communities experiencing outmigration and have adopted a strategic community investment plan; • rural communities with a high percentage of low income families or persons; • rural communities that were developed with the participation of, and which would receive a substantial portion of project funding from, state and local government, tribal governments, non-profit entities, public libraries, elementary and secondary schools health care facilities, private entities, and philanthropic organization. **(§6205)**
Buildout requirement. Eligible applicants agree to complete buildout of the broadband service described in the loan application by not later than three years after the initial date on which proceeds from the loan made or	Amends requirements to have a broadband loan applicant agree to the buildout of the service in no later than five years rather than three years. **(§6110)**	Requires a recipient of a grant or loan to provide complete, reliable, and precise geolocation information that indicates the location of new broadband service that is being provided or upgraded within the service area not later

Current Law/Policy	House-Passed Bill (H.R. 2)	Senate-Passed Bill (H.R.2)
guaranteed under this section are made available. **(7 U.S.C. 950bb(d)(1)(A)(iii))**		than 30 days after the earlier of the date of completion of any project milestone or the date of completion of the project. **(§6205)**
Borrower refinancing options. The Secretary is authorized and empowered to make loans to persons now providing or who may hereinafter provide telephone service in rural areas; to public bodies now providing telephone service in rural areas; and to cooperative, nonprofit, limited dividend, or mutual associations. **(7 U.S.C. 922)**	Adds refinancing of loans for broadband services and other loans provided to purposes of telecommunications. **(§6111)**	Amends to include other eligible telecommunication loans (e.g., broadband). **(§6208)**
Reporting requirements. Requires reporting that provides the progress toward fulfilling the objectives for which the assistance was granted, including (I) the number and location of residences and businesses that will receive new broadband service, existing network service improvements, and facility upgrades resulting from the federal assistance; (II) the speed of broadband service; (III) the average price of broadband service in a proposed service area; (IV) any changes in broadband service adoption rates, including new subscribers generated from demand-side projects; and (V) any metrics the Secretary determines to be appropriate. **(7 U.S.C. 950bb(d)(8)(A)(ii))**	Removes a reporting requirement that borrowers report the location of residences and businesses that will receive new broadband service, existing network service improvements, and facility upgrades. **(§6112)**	No comparable provision.
Authorization of appropriations. There is authorized to be appropriated to the Secretary to carry out this section $25 million for each of FY2008-FY2018 to remain available until expended. **(7 U.S.C. 950bb(k))**	Authorizes appropriations for loans and loan guarantees at $150 million each of FY2019-FY2023. **(§6113)**	Identical to House provision. **(§6205)**
No comparable provision.	**Middle mile broadband infrastructure.** Authorizes loans for development of middle mile broadband infrastructure, defined as infrastructure that does not directly connect to end user locations. Loans and loan guarantees for middle mile infrastructure are limited to no more than 20% of the amounts made available under Section 601 of the Rural Electrification Act of 1936. **(§6114)**	No comparable provision.

Table 9. (Continued)

Current Law/Policy	House-Passed Bill (H.R. 2)	Senate-Passed Bill (H.R.2)
No comparable provision.	No comparable provision.	**Transparency in the Telecommunications Infrastructure Loan Program.** Amends Title VI of the Rural Electrification Act of 1936 to require the Secretary to publish and make available to the public a fully searchable database on the Rural Utility Service (RUS) website, a notice of each application from the Telecommunications Infrastructure Loan and Loan Guarantee Program including the applicant's identity, description of the application, type of support requested, the application status, estimated number of people in each census block group without telecommunication service, a list of census block groups the applicant proposes to service, the name of each borrower, the type of assistance each is receiving, and the purpose for which the borrower is receiving assistance. With respect for a loan application, the Secretary is required to provide an opportunity for the pubic to submit information concerning the service the borrower is offering in the census blocks proposed in the application. **(§6207)**
Rural electrification and telephone revolving fund. Authorizes the Fund in the U.S. Treasury consisting of bonds, notes, and obligations made under the Rural Electrification Act of 1936. **(7 U.S.C. 931** ***et seq.*****)**	No comparable provision.	Amends Title III of the Rural Electrification Act of 1936 to permit loan guarantees to be issued for cybersecurity and grid security improvements. **(§6210)**
No comparable provision.	**Outdated broadband systems.** Amends Section 601 of the Rural Electrification to Act of 1936 to require the Secretary to consider any portion of a broadband service area subject to an outstanding grant agreement where service is not at least 10 megabits per second and one megabit per second upstream as "unserved" for purposes of	No comparable provision.

Current Law/Policy	House-Passed Bill (H.R. 2)	Senate-Passed Bill (H.R.2)
	broadband loans, unless the broadband provider has constructed or begun to construct service that meets minimal acceptable of standards as established under Section 601(e)(1) of the Rural Electrification Act of 1936. **(§6115)**	
No comparable provision	**Federal broadband program coordination.** Directs the Secretary to coordinate with the Assistant Secretary of the National Telecommunications and Information Administration for assessment and mapping capabilities. The Secretary will consult with the Federal Communications Commission (FCC) before making a broadband loan or grant for a project to serve an area in which another entity is receiving Connect America Fun or Mobility Fund support under the federal universal service support mechanism. The FCC shall submit a report to congressional committees assessing its abilities to meet various objectives regarding long-term broadband service needs of rural residents. **(§6116)**	No comparable provision
No comparable provision.	**Effective date.** Requires that the Secretary issue final rules before any amendments in this Subtitle take effect. **(§6117)**	No comparable provision.
Community Connect Grant Program. Provides grant support for broadband transmission in rural areas eligible for the Distance Learning and Telemedicine Program. Supports broadband on a community –oriented connectivity basis to unserved rural areas for projects fostering economic development, education, health care, and public safety. **(7 U.S.C. 950bb *et seq.*)**	No comparable provision.	Amends to define eligible broadband service at speeds designated by the Secretary to service areas where current service is less that 10-Mbps downstream and 1-Mbps upstream. Defines eligible projects and the use of grant funds under the program. Requires matching funds. Also, requires grant recipients to use a portion of the grant funding to provide free broadband access to community centers. **(§6207)**
Rural Community, Business Development, and Infrastructure Programs		
Strategic Economic and Community Development. Authorizes the Secretary to give priority to applications for rural projects that support strategic community and economic development plans on a multijurisdictional basis.	Amends the ConAct to prioritize project applications that support implementation of strategic investment plans on a multi-sectoral and multi-jurisdictional basis by reserving a portion of funds available in a fiscal year for such projects.	Identical to House provision. **(§6123)**

Table 9. (Continued)

Current Law/Policy	House-Passed Bill (H.R. 2)	Senate-Passed Bill (H.R.2)
Authorizes the Secretary to reserve up to 10% of the appropriations for community facilities, water and waste disposal, business and industry loan guarantees, and rural business development grants for projects serving strategic community and regional plans. **(7 U.S.C. 2008v)**	Also authorizes assistance for developing strategic community investment plans. Authorizes an appropriation of $5 million for each of FY2019-FY2023 for developing strategic investment plans. **(§6201)**	
Rural Definitions. Defines "rural" and "rural area" as any area other than an area with a city or town of 50,000 or more, and the contiguous and adjacent urbanized area to such a city or town. For water and waste disposal applications, the population threshold is 10,000 and 20,000 for community facilities applications, **(7 U.S.C. 1991(a)(13).**	Amends the ConAct to exclude water and waste disposal guaranteed loans from the requirement of an eligible rural area being one of 10,000 or less population, and 20,000 for community facilities loans and grants, **(§6202)**	No comparable provision.
Special conditions and limitations on loans. Establishes various standards on borrowers. **(7 U.S.C. 1983)**	Authorizes the collection of loan fees for guaranteed loans in a fiscal year to equal the total subsidy costs for loan guarantees in that fiscal year. **(§6203)**	No comparable provision.
Collection of fees. Authorizes loans and loan guarantees to provide funds for the costs of the construction, improvement, and acquisition of facilities and equipment for broadband service in rural areas. **(7 U.S.C. 950bb(c))**	Authorizes the collection of loan fees for broadband guaranteed loans in a fiscal year to equal the total subsidy costs for loan guarantees in that fiscal year. **(§6203)**	No comparable provision.
Water, waste disposal, and wastewater facility grants. Authorizes grants to capitalize revolving loan funds of nonprofit association to support water and waste water projects in rural areas. Authorizes $30 million in grants annually for FY2008-FY2018, subject to annual appropriations. **(7 U.S.C. 1926(a)(2)(B))**	Raises the maximum amount of project financing from $100,000 to $200,000. Authorizes $15 million annually for FY2019-FY2023. **(§6204)**	Raises the maximum amount of project financing from $100,000 to $200,000. Authorizes $30 million annually for FY2019-FY2023. **(§6101)**
Rural water and wastewater technical assistance and training programs. Provides grants to private nonprofit organizations to provide technical assistance to rural water systems. **(7 U.S.C. 1926(a)(2)(B))**	Directs technical assistance toward identifying options to enhance long-term sustainability of rural water systems. Increases appropriations for technical assistance grants from no less than 1% or more than 3% of the water, waste disposal, and wastewater facility grant appropriation to no less than 3% or more than 5%. **(§6205)**	Directs the Secretary to give priority to private non-profit organizations that have experience providing technical assistance and training on contaminated drinking water and surface water supplies from emerging contaminants. Increases appropriations for technical assistance grants from no less than 1% or more than 3% of the water, waste disposal, and wastewater facility grant

Current Law/Policy	House-Passed Bill (H.R. 2)	Senate-Passed Bill (H.R.2)
		appropriation to no less than 3% or more than 5%. **(§6102)**
Rural Water and Waste Water Circuit Rider Program. Provides funding to support technical assistance to water rural water systems. Authorizes funding of $20 million annually in FY2014 and each fiscal year thereafter. **(7 U.S.C. 1926(a)(22))**	Authorizes funding at $25 million in FY2018 and for each fiscal year thereafter. **(§6206)**	Authorizes funding at $25 million for each of FY2019-FY2023. **(§6103)**
Tribal college and university essential community facilities. Provides grant funding to entities that are tribal colleges to provide the federal share of the cost of developing specific tribal college or university essential community facilities.	Amends the provision by authorizing funding of $5 million for each of FY2019-FY2023. **(§6207)**	Authorizes funding at $10 million for each of FY2019-FY2023. **(§6104)**
Authorizes funding of $10 million each of FY2008-FY2018. **(7 U.S.C. 1926(a)(25)(C))**		
Emergency and Imminent Community Water Assistance Program. Provides assistance to water systems in rural communities of 10,000 or less where there is a threat to potable water supplies. Authorizes funding of $35 million for each of FY2008-FY2018. **(7 U.S.C. 1926a(i)(2))**	Amends the program to reserve any funds for the program only until July 1 of the fiscal year, except where a natural disaster has threatened potable water supplies. Authorizes funding at $27 million annually for FY2019-FY2023. **(§6208)**	Provides selection criteria for projects addressing contamination that poses a threat to human health or the environment. Raises the loan rate provision from $500,000 to $1 million. Instructs the Secretary to create an "Interagency Task Force on Rural Water Quality" within 90 days of the enactment of H.R. 2. Requires a report that provides recommendations to the House and Senate agriculture committees. Authorizes funding of $50 million annually for FY2019-FY2023. **(§6106)**
Grants for water systems for rural and Native Villages in Alaska. Funding for water projects to improve sanitation and potable water in rural Alaska. Authorizes $30 million annually for FY2008- FY2013, subject to appropriations. **(7 U.S.C. 1926d)**	Reauthorizes appropriations at $30 million annually for FY2019-FY2023. **(§6209)**	Amends the definition of Alaska and Native villages by using definitions in P.L. 105-83 and 43 U.S.C. 1602. Reauthorizes appropriations of $30 million annually for FY2019-FY2023. **(§6107)**
Household water well systems. Provides funding to third-party organizations with expertise in residential well-water systems to construct, refurbish, and service individually owned household water well systems in rural areas for individuals with low or moderate incomes. Authorizes $10 million annually for FY2008-FY2018, subject to appropriations. **(7 U.S.C. 1926(e))**	Reauthorizes appropriations at $5 million annually for FY2019-FY2023. **(§6210)**	Renames the provision the "Rural Decentralized Water Systems." Redefines "eligible individual" as one who does not exceed 60% of the median nonmetropolitan household income for the state or territory. Limits grants to a maximum of $15,000 for each water well system or decentralized wastewater system. Authorizes $40 million annually for FY2019-FY2023. **(§6108)**

Table 9. (Continued)

Current Law/Policy	House-Passed Bill (H.R. 2)	Senate-Passed Bill (H.R.2)
Solid waste management grants. Provides grant assistance for communities to establish or improve solid waste management facilities. Authorizes $10 million annually for FY2008-FY2018, subject to annual appropriations. **(7 U.S.C. 1932(b))**	Reauthorizes appropriations at $10 million for each of FY2019-FY2023. **(§6211)**	Identical to House provision. **(§6109)**
Rural business development grants. Provides grants in rural areas for business opportunities and for support of business enterprises that finance small and emerging private enterprises. Authorizes $65 million for each fiscal year 2014-2018. **(7 U.S.C. 1932 (c)(4)(A))**	Reauthorizes the program at $65 million for each of FY2019-FY2023. **(§6212)**	Identical to House provision. **(§6110)**
Rural cooperative development grants. Authorizes the creation of jobs in rural areas through the development of new rural cooperatives, value-added processing, and rural businesses. Authorizes $40 million annually for FY2008-FY2013, subject to appropriations. **(7 U.S.C. 1932(e)(5))**	Reauthorizes the program at $40 million for each of FY2019-FY2023. **(§6213)**	Requests that Economic Census data (conducted by the Bureau of the Census) be utilized for analysis. Reauthorizes the program at $40 million annually for FY2019-FY2023. **(§6111)**
Locally or regionally produced agricultural food products. Provides funding to increase domestic consumption of locally and regionally produced agricultural products and to provide affordable food products in underserved rural and urban areas. Reserves not less than 5% of the funds of the Business and Industry Loan Guarantee program for support of locally and regionally produced food. Requires an annual report to Congress on the program. **(7 U.S.C. 1932(g)(9)(B)(v)(I))**	Reauthorizes the program for FY2019-FY2023. **(§6214)**	Identical to House provision. **(§6112)**
Appropriate technology transfer for rural areas. Provides grant support at an agricultural institution (e.g., universities) for information activities to agricultural producers. Authorizes $5 million annually for FY2008-FY2018, subject to appropriations. **(7 U.S.C. 1932(i)(4))**	Reauthorizes the program at $5 million for each year FY2019-FY2023. **(§6215)**	Identical to House provision. **(§6113)**
Rural Economic Area Partnership. The program assists communities dealing with geographic and economic isolation, low-density population, absence of nearby metropolitan centers, and historical dependence on agribusiness, out-migration,	Reauthorizes the program for FY2019-FY2023. **(§6216)**	Identical to House provision. **(§6114)**

Current Law/Policy	House-Passed Bill (H.R. 2)	Senate-Passed Bill (H.R.2)
and economic upheaval to develop strategies for revitalization zones. **(7 U.S.C. 1932j)**		
No comparable provision.	No comparable provision.	**Rural Business-Cooperative Service Programs Technical Assistance and Training.** Authorizes the Secretary to make grants to a variety of entities for the purpose of providing or obtaining technical assistance and training to support applications through the Rural Business-Cooperative Service. Authorizes grants to assist communities in identifying economic development needs, identify resources, prepare reports and surveys, and to prepare applications for financial assistance. Authorizes $5 million annually for FY2019-FY2023. **(§6118)**
Intermediary Relending Program. Provides direct loans at 1% interest to intermediaries to finance business facilities and community development projects in rural areas with populations of 25,000 or less. The Rural Business Service loan to an intermediary is used to establish or fund a revolving loan program to provide financial assistance to ultimate recipients for community development projects, establishment of new businesses or expansion of existing businesses. Authorizes appropriations of $25 million for each of FY2014-FY2018, subject to annual appropriations. **(7 U.S.C 1936b(e))**	Reauthorizes the program at $10 million for each of FY2019-FY2023. **(§6217)**	Limits the maximum amount of a loan by an eligible entity for projects, including the unpaid balance of any existing loans, to $400,000 and 50% of the loan to the eligibility entity. Requires the Secretary to establish a schedule consistent with the amortization schedules of the portfolio of loans made or guaranteed. Authorizes appropriations of $25 million annually for FY2019-FY2023, **(§6115)**
Definition of "rural" and "rural area." Rural and rural area are defined as any area other than a city or town with a population of 50,000 or more, and any urbanized area contiguous or adjacent to such a city or town. **(7 U.S.C. 1991(a)(13))**	Amends the definition to exclude incarcerated prison populations in determining whether an area is "rural." **(§6218)**	No comparable provision.
Definition of "rural" and "rural area." Rural and rural area are defined as any area other than a city or town with a population of 50,000 or more, and any urbanized area contiguous or adjacent to such a city or town. **(7 U.S.C. 1991(a)(13))**	Amends the definition to exclude the first 1,500 individuals who reside in housing located on a military base to determining whether an area is "rural" for eligibility for rural broadband loans. Further amends to define "rural area" for purposes of	No comparable provision.

Table 9. (Continued)

Current Law/Policy	House-Passed Bill (H.R. 2)	Senate-Passed Bill (H.R.2)
	the Distance Learning and Telemedicine Program as area other than (1) a city or town with a population of 50,000 or more, and any urbanized area contiguous or adjacent to such a city or town, and (2) a city, town, or incorporated area with a population greater than 20,000. **(§6505)**	
National Rural Development Partnership. A state-federal rural economic development coordinating entity operating through State Rural Development Councils and a National Rural Development Coordinating Committee. Authorizes appropriations of $10 million annually for FY2014-FY2018. **(7 U.S.C. 2008m)**	Reauthorizes the program at $10 million for each of FY2019-FY2023. **(§6219)**	Identical to House provision. **(§6119)**
Grants for NOAA weather radio transmitters. Provides grant funding to public and nonprofit entities for the federal share of the cost of acquiring radio transmitters to increase coverage in rural areas by the all hazards weather radio broadcast system of the National Oceanic and Atmospheric Administration. Authorizes $1 million for each of FY2014-FY2018, subject to annual appropriations. **(7 U.S.C. 2008p)**	Reauthorizes the program at $1 million for each of FY2019-FY2023. **(§6220)**	Identical to House provision. **(§6120)**
Rural Microentrepreneur Assistance Program. Provides grant support to third-party entities that assist rural entrepreneurs in establishing microenterprises in rural areas. Authorizes $40 million annually in discretionary spending for each of FY2009-FY2018, subject to appropriations, and $3 million in mandatory spending annually for FY2014-FY2018. **(7 U.S.C. 2008s)**	Reauthorizes the program at $4 million in discretionary funding for each year FY2019-FY2023. **(§6221)**	Authorizes funding at $20 million for FY2019-FY2023. **(§6121)**
Health care services. Addresses unmet health needs in the Mississippi Delta region through grants awarded to health care services and health care education programs. Authorizes $3 million in appropriations for each of FY2008-FY2018. **(7 U.S.C. 2008u)**	Reauthorizes the program at $3 million for each year FY2019-FY2023. **(§6222)**	Identical to House provision. **(§6122)**

Current Law/Policy	House-Passed Bill (H.R. 2)	Senate-Passed Bill (H.R.2)
Delta Regional Authority. An eight-state and federal regional planning and development entity that provides loan and grant support for economic development projects in rural counties in the Mississippi Delta area. Authorizes $30 million annually for FY2008-FY2018, subject to appropriations. **(7 U.S.C. 2009aa *et seq.*)**	Reauthorizes the program at $12 million for each of FY2019-FY2023. **(§6223)**	Identical to House provision. **(§6124)**
Northern Great Plains Regional Authority. Authorizes an economic development commission that develops regional plans and makes loans and grants for infrastructure and economic development in five Great Plains states. Authorizes $30 million annually for FY2008-FY2018, subject to appropriations. **(7 U.S.C. 2009bb *et seq.*)**	Reauthorizes the program at $2 million for each of FY2019-FY2023. **(§6224)**	No comparable provision.
Rural Business Investment Program. Modeled on the Small Business Administration's Small Business Investment Companies, the Rural Business Investment Program provides funding to help capitalize Rural Business Companies that, in turn, provide loans to rural businesses. Authorizes $20 million for each of FY2014-FY2018, subject to appropriations. **(7 U.S.C. 2009cc *et seq.*)**	Reauthorizes the program at $20 million for each of FY2019-FY2023. **(§6225)**	Identical to House provision. **(§6125).** See also **(§12626)**.
Rural Electrification Act of 1936		
Farmers Home Administration. Defines the powers and duties of the Secretary regarding agricultural credit. **(7 U.S.C. 1981)**	No comparable provision.	Amends to permit the Secretary to fund broadband facilities and broadband service of the Rural Electrification Act of 1936 as an incidental part of any grant, loan, or loan guarantee. Funding cannot constitute more than 10% of any loan for a fiscal year for any programs under this title. Directs the Secretary not to provide funding if it would result in competitive harm to any existing grant, loan, or loan guarantee. **(§6116)**
Guarantees for bonds and notes issued for electrification or telephone purposes. Provides for federal guarantees for bonds and notes that finance rural electrification and telephone infrastructure. **(7 U.S.C. 940c-1(f))**	Reauthorizes the program through FY2023. **(§6301)**	Directs the Secretary to continue the program until amendments restructuring payments made in the H.R. 2 are implemented. Amends to provide a guarantee term of 30 years for a loan to be repaid in periodic installments. **(§6205)**

Table 9. (Continued)

Current Law/Policy	House-Passed Bill (H.R. 2)	Senate-Passed Bill (H.R.2)
Loans for Rural Telephone Service. Authorizes the Secretary to make loans to persons now providing or who may hereafter provide telephone service in rural areas, to public bodies now providing telephone service in rural areas and to cooperative, nonprofit, limited dividend, or mutual associations. **(7 U.S.C. 922)**	No comparable provision.	Amends to make technical changes to language. **(§6203)**
General authority of the Secretary of Agriculture. Authorizes the Secretary to make loans for rural electrification and for furnishing and improving electric and telephone service to rural areas. **(7 U.S.C. 902(a)).**	No comparable provision.	Amends to provide a program for technical assistance for rural electric loans. Authorizes the Secretary to enter into a memorandum of understanding with the Secretary of the Department of Energy to provide direct advice, maps and training to implement demand-side management of electric and telephones service in rural areas, energy efficiency and conservation, and off-grid and on-grid renewable energy systems. **(§6202)**
General authority of the Secretary of Agriculture. Authorizes the Secretary to make loans for rural electrification and for furnishing and improving electric and telephone service to rural areas. **(7 U.S.C. 902(a)).**	No comparable provision.	Amends to add "or refinance" to the authorities of the Secretary. **(§6201)**
Expansion of 911access. Authorizes expanding the emergency telephone service of 911 in rural areas by using any funds otherwise made available for telephone loans for each of FY2008-FY2013. **(7 U.S.C. 940(e)d)**	Reauthorizes the program through FY2023. **(§6302)**	No comparable provision.
Improvements to the Guarantees Underwriter Program. States that a lender receiving a guarantee on a bond or note shall pay a fee to the Secretary. **(7 U.S.C. 940c-1)**	Amends the Rural Electrification Act of 1936 to authorize guaranteed payments on bonds or notes issued by cooperatives or other lenders on a not-for-profit basis if the bonds are used to make utility infrastructure loans or to refinance bonds or notes issued for such purposes. Defines the terms of such bonds or notes. **(§6303)**	No comparable provision.

Current Law/Policy	House-Passed Bill (H.R. 2)	Senate-Passed Bill (H.R.2)
Rural Economic Development Loan and Grant Program. Authorizes "cushion of credit" accounts for electric cooperative borrowers who may voluntarily forward-pay on their loans. The payments earn 5% interest for the borrowers. Total deposits in these accounts and the average interest rates certificates of outstanding beneficial ownership accrue to the Rural Economic Development subaccount and may be used to support grants and 0% interest loans for economic development projects in the RUS borrower's communities. **(7 U.S.C. 940c))**	Amends to re-designate the language of the Rural Economic Development Subaccount and to establish a new section authorizing discretionary appropriations of $10 million for each year FY2019- FY2023. **(§6304)**	Amends to terminate deposit authority into cushion of credit accounts after October1, 2018. Further amends to change a borrower's interest rate for FY2019 and thereafter to a rate equal to the average interest rate used to make payments on the 5-year Treasury note, but not greater than 5%. Authorizes $5 million in mandatory spending and $5 million in discretionary spending for FY2022 and FY2023. **(§6204)**
Miscellaneous		
Value-added agricultural product market development grants. Provides grant support to agricultural producers to undertake projects that add value to commodities and thereby increase producer income. Also supports planning and business development for value-added projects. Authorizes $40 million annually for FY2008-FY2018, subject to annual appropriations, in addition to $63 million in mandatory spending to remain available until expended. **(7 U.S.C. 1632a(b)(7))**	Eliminates mandatory funding and increases discretionary funding to $50 million annually FY2019-FY2023. **(§6501)**	Combines the Value-Added Agricultural Product Market Development Grants (7 U.S.C. 1632a(b)(7)), among other existing USDA farmers' markets and local food programs, as part of a new "Local Agriculture Market Program" with expanded mandatory funding and administrative functions. See also Horticulture title **(§10102)**
Agriculture Innovation Center Demonstration Program. Provides grant funding to producers for technical assistance in developing agricultural-based businesses based on value-added production. Authorizes funding of $1 million annually for FY2014- FY2018, subject to annual appropriations. **(7 U.S.C. 1632(b)(i))**	Reauthorizes the program through FY2023 at the current appropriation. **(§6502)**	No comparable provision.
Rural Development, Small Farm Programs authorized. Authorizes the Secretary in cooperation and coordination with colleges and universities, to conduct rural development extension, rural development extension work programs, small farm extension, and other programs. Authorizes a national program administered by NIFA to provide rural citizens with training and technical management assistance and education opportunities, including rural health and safety programs. Authorizes the Secretary to make grants for rural health	No comparable provision.	Amends rural health and safety education programs to add a new grant program on substance use and disorder education and prevention. **(§6303)**

Table 9. (Continued)

Current Law/Policy	House-Passed Bill (H.R. 2)	Senate-Passed Bill (H.R.2)
and safety education programs. **(7 U.S.C. 2662)**		
Regional economic and infrastructure development commissions. Consists of three regional development authorities: a Northern Border Regional Commission, a Southeast Crescent Regional Commission, and a Southwest Border Regional Commission.	Reauthorizes the commissions through FY2023 at the current appropriation. **(§6503)**	Identical to House provision. **(§6304)**
These commissions develop regional development plans and then make infrastructure loans and grants to eligible entities in their respective regions. **(40 U.S.C. 15101 *et seq.*)** Authorizes annual appropriations of $30 million to each of the commissions. Not more than 10% of appropriated funds to any commission can be used for administrative expenses.		
(40 U.S.C. 15751(b))		
Definition of rural area for purposes of the Housing Act of 1949. *Rural area* is defined as any area so defined between 1990 and 2010 to remain so classified until receipt of the 2020 decennial census. The provision also caps the eligible rural population threshold at 35,000 residents or less for rural areas in excess of 10,000 and with a serious lack of mortgage credit for lower and moderate-income families. **(42 U.S.C. 1490)**	Amends the definition by defining *rural area* as any area so defined between 1990 and 2020 to remain so classified until receipt of the 2030 decennial census. The provision keeps the 35,000 population threshold for areas rural in character and with a serious lack of mortgage credit for lower and moderate-income families. **(§6504)**	No comparable provision.
Program Repeals		
Elimination of unfunded programs. The following programs of the ConAct, as amended, no longer receive funding: • Multijurisdictional regional planning organizations (Section 306(a)(23) of ConAct); • Grants to broadcasting systems (Section 310B(f) of ConAct); • Rural telework organizations (Section 379 of ConAct); • Historical barn preservation (Section 379A of ConAct); • Grants to train farm workers in new technologies and to train farm workers in specialized skills necessary for higher value crops (Section 379C of ConAct);	Repeals unfunded programs. **(§6601)**	No comparable provision.

Current Law/Policy	House-Passed Bill (H.R. 2)	Senate-Passed Bill (H.R.2)
• Grants to Delta Region Agricultural Economic Development Program (Section 379D of ConAct); • Grants for expansion of employment opportunities for individuals with disabilities in rural areas (Section 379F of ConAct); Regional rural collaborative investment program (Subtitle I of ConAct). **(7 U.S.C. 1926 *et seq.*)**		
Rural Telephone Bank. Establishes a corporate body called the Rural Telephone Bank whose general purpose is securing funds and making loans to support a telephone bank in rural areas. **(7 U.S.C. 941-950b)**	Repeals the Rural Telephone Bank. **(§6602)**	No comparable provision.
Launching Our Communities' Access to Local Television Act of 2000. Facilitates access to signals of local television stations for households located in unserved areas and underserved areas by providing loans and loan guarantees. Authorizes such sums as necessary. **(P.L. 106-553)**	Amends the act by striking Sections 1001-1007 and 1009-1012 and inserting Title X—Satellite Carrier Retransmission Eligibility. **(§6603)**	No comparable provision.
Technical Corrections		
No comparable provision.	Provides technical corrections related to various provisions of the Consolidated Farm and Rural Development Act, as amended. **(§6701)**	No comparable provision.
No comparable provision. **(7 U.S.C. 901 *et seq.*)**	Provides technical corrections related to various provisions of the Rural Electrification Act, as amended. **(§6702)**	No comparable provision.
No comparable provision	**Precision agriculture connectivity.** States findings by Congress regarding precision agriculture **(§6801)** and authorizes the establishment of a task force by the Federal Communications Commission for reviewing the connectivity and technology needs of precision agriculture. The task force will collaborate with the Department of Agriculture and public and private stakeholders in the agriculture and technology fields to identify gaps in the availability broadband across agricultural land and to develop policy recommendations. **(§6802)**	Identical to House provision at **(§12516)** of the Miscellaneous title (XII).

Table 10. Research, Extension, and Related Matters

Current Law/Policy	House-Passed Bill (H.R. 2)	Senate-Passed Bill (H.R. 2)
Subtitle A—National Agricultural Research, Extension, and Teaching Policy Act of 1977(NARETP)		
Agricultural research, extension, and education. Provides support to enhance the competitiveness of the agricultural research, extension, and education capabilities of the United States. **(7 U.S.C. 3101)**	Amends to add the objective of supporting international scientific collaboration that leverages resources and advances the food and agricultural interests of the United States. **(§7101)**	Amends to add the objective of supporting international scientific collaboration that leverages resources and advances the food and agricultural interests of the United States, such as addressing emerging plant and animal diseases, improving crop varieties and animal breeds, and developing safe and nutritious food systems. **(§7101)**
Non-land-grant colleges of agriculture (7 U.S.C. 3103(14)(A))	Establishes a process of review within 90 days of enactment of each Non-Land Grant College of Agriculture (NLGCA) to ensure compliance in the colleges with appropriate study of food and agricultural sciences and to propose revocation of the designated NLGCA for noncompliance. Permits NLGCAs and Hispanic- serving agricultural colleges until FY2023 to no longer be designated as such institutions. **(§7102)**	Amends to require NLGCAs to offer at least 2 baccalaureate or higher degrees in food and agricultural sciences, rather than a single degree. Requires the Secretary to establish a process in which, not less than every 2 years, the Secretary conducts a review to ensure each NLGCA is in compliance with the new baccalaureate requirement, and removes an NLGCA that is not in compliance. **(§7102)**
National advisory board. Establishes the National Agricultural Research, Extension, Education, and Economics Advisory Board. **(7 U.S.C. 3123)**	Amends the membership composition of the Advisory Board. Directs the Advisory Board to make recommendations and to address long- and short-term national priorities consistent with various priorities of the Agriculture and Food Research Initiative and the NARETP Act. **(§7103)**	Amends to reauthorize the Board's existence through FY2023. **(§7103)**
Citrus disease subcommittee. Establishes a citrus disease subcommittee within the specialty crops committee to advise USDA on citrus research and establish priorities for grants and regularly consult and collaborate with USDA and other groups and institutions. **(7 U.S.C. 3123a(a)(2))**	Extends the citrus disease subcommittee through FY2023 and changes the composition of the subcommittee. **(§7104)**	Extends the citrus disease subcommittee through FY2023. **(§7104)**
Renewable energy committee. Establishes a renewable energy committee, directs the Advisory Board to appoint committee members, and establishes the committee's duties. **(7 U.S.C. 3121(b))**	Discontinues the renewable energy committee. **(§7105)**	No comparable provision.

Current Law/Policy	House-Passed Bill (H.R. 2)	Senate-Passed Bill (H.R. 2)
Veterinary Services Grant Program. Authorizes competitive grants to address the shortage of veterinarians. Defines "qualified entities" eligible for the grants as a for-profit or nonprofit that operates a veterinary clinic providing veterinary services. **(7 U.S.C. 3151b)**	No comparable provision.	Amends to further designate "qualified entities" as those exposing students in the 11th and 12th grades to veterinary sciences. Authorizes appropriations of $10 million through FY2023, and reserves at least two-thirds of the appropriations to qualified entities with a focus on food animals. **(§7105)**
Duties of the Secretary of Agriculture. Sets out the duties of the Secretary of Agriculture as concerns extension and agricultural research at 1890 land-grant colleges, including Tuskegee University. **(7 U.S.C. 3221, 3222)**	Directs the Secretary to transmit to Congress annually a report on the allocations made to, and matching funds received by, 1890 land-grant institutions. **(§7106)**	No comparable provision.
Grants and fellowships for food and agriculture sciences education. Authorizes the Secretary to make grants and conduct fellowships to strengthen higher education in food and agricultural sciences. **(7 U.S.C. 3152(m)(2))**	Reauthorizes appropriations for grants and fellowships for FY2019-FY2023. **(§7107)**	Identical to House provision. **(§7106)**
Agriculture and food policy research centers. Authorizes competitive grants to, or to enter into cooperative agreements with, policy research centers to conduct research and education programs that are objective, operationally independent, and external to the federal government and that concern the effect of public policies and trade agreements on agriculture. **(7 (U.S.C. 3155(e))**	Reauthorizes appropriations for FY2019-FY2023. **(§7108)**	Identical to House provision. **(§7108)**
Education grants to Alaska Native–serving institutions and Native Hawaiian–serving institutions. Authorizes competitive grants to Alaska Native–serving institutions for the purpose of promoting and strengthening the ability of Alaska Native–serving institutions to carry out education, applied research, and related community development programs. **(7 U.S.C. 3156)**	Reauthorizes appropriations for FY2019-FY2023. **(§7109)**	Identical to House provision. **(§7109)**
No comparable provision.	No comparable provision,	**Next Generation Agricultural Technology Challenge.** Directs the Secretary to establish a next generation technology challenge for the development of mobile technology that removes barriers to marketplace entry for beginning farmers and ranchers. Limits awards to no more than $1 million in the aggregate to one or

Table 10. (Continued)

Current Law/Policy	House-Passed Bill (H.R. 2)	Senate-Passed Bill (H.R. 2)
		more winners of the competition. **(§7110)**
Nutrition Education Program. Authorizes establishment of a National Education Program to disseminate results of food and human nutrition research funded by USDA. **(7 U.S.C. 3175)**	Repeals the Nutrition Education Program. **(§7110)**	Reauthorizes the Nutrition Education Program for FY2019-FY2023. **(§7111)**
Continuing animal health and disease research programs. Directs deans of accredited colleges and the state agricultural experiment station to develop a comprehensive animal health and disease research program for the state based on the animal health research capacity of each eligible institution in the state, which shall be submitted to the Secretary for approval and shall be used for the allocation of funds available to the state under this section. **(7 U.S.C. 3195(c)(1))**	Reauthorizes appropriations for FY2019-FY2023. **(§7111)**	Identical to House provision. **(§7113)**
Extension at 1890 land-grant colleges, including Tuskegee University. Limits carryover of federal funding to no more than 20% of the funds received for conducting extension activities. **(7 U.S.C. 3221(a))**	Amends by striking paragraph 4 that prohibits 1890 colleges from carrying forward to the succeeding fiscal year more than 20% of the funds they receive in a given fiscal year. **(§7112)**	No comparable provision.
Agricultural extension at 1890 land-grant universities. Authorizes such sums as Congress may determine necessary to support continuing agricultural and forestry extension at 1890 land-grant universities. **(7 U.S.C. 3222)**		Amends to require an annual report to Congress from the Secretary describing extension allocations made to, and matching funds received by, 1890 land-grant colleges. **(§7114)**
Extension at 1890 land-grant colleges, including Tuskegee University. Authorizes annual appropriations to 1890 land-grant colleges for extension activities. **(7 U.S.C. 3221)**	Amends by establishing a scholarship grant program at 1890 institutions for accepted students who intend to pursue a career in agribusiness, energy and renewable fuels, or financial management. Authorizes $19 million for each year FY2019-FY2023. **(§7114)**	Same as House provision. **(§7134)**
No comparable provision.	No comparable provision.	**Report on agricultural research at 1890 land-grant colleges, including Tuskegee University.** Requires an annual report to Congress from the Secretary describing research allocations made to, and matching funds received by, 1890 land-grant colleges. **(§7115)**

Current Law/Policy	House-Passed Bill (H.R. 2)	Senate-Passed Bill (H.R. 2)
Grants to upgrade agricultural and food sciences facilities at 1890 land-grant colleges, including Tuskegee University. (7 U.S.C. 3222b(b))	Reauthorizes appropriations for FY2019-FY2023. **(§7114)**	Identical to House provision. **(§7116)**
Grants to upgrade agricultural and food sciences facilities and equipment at insular area land- grant institutions. Authorizes appropriations of $25 million for each of FY2002-FY2018 for the acquisition and improvement of agricultural and food sciences facilities and equipment, including libraries, so that the eligible institutions may participate fully in the production of human capital. **(7 U.S.C. 3222b-2(d))**	Reauthorizes appropriations for FY2019-FY2023. **(§7115)**	Identical to House provision. **(§7117)**
No comparable provision.	No comparable provision.	**New Beginning for Tribal Students.** Amends Subtitle G of NARETP Act to authorize a competitive grant program for tribal students at land-grant colleges. Land-grant colleges may apply for grants to support tribal students through recruiting, tuition and fees, tutoring, counseling, and other services. Land-grants receiving such funds would be required to match the funding at 100%. States are limited to a maximum of $500,000 per year. Provision authorizes appropriations of $5 million each year for FY2019-FY2023. **(§7118)**
Education grants program at Hispanic-serving institutions. Authorizes competitive grants to promote and strengthen Hispanic-serving institutions to carry out education, applied research, and related community development programs. **(7 U.S.C. 3241(c))**	Reauthorizes appropriations for FY2019-FY2023. **(§7116)**	Identical to House provision. **(§7119)**
No comparable provision.	No comparable provision.	**Binational Agricultural Research and Development (BARD).** Amends 7 U.S.C. 3291(e) to name binational funding between the United States and Israel the BARD Fund. Supports agricultural research and development of mutual benefit to the United States and Israel. Supports accelerated development of drip irrigation, pesticides, aquaculture, disease control, and

Table 10. (Continued)

Current Law/Policy	House-Passed Bill (H.R. 2)	Senate-Passed Bill (H.R. 2)
		farm equipment. Encourages collaborative research with colleges, universities, and the private sector. **(§7120)**
No comparable provision.	No comparable provision.	**Partnerships to build capacity in international agricultural research, extension, and teaching.** Promotes building capacity and improving performance among 1862, 1890, 1994, NLGCA, and Hispanic-serving colleges and similar institutions in developing countries to strengthen agricultural research, teaching, and extension institutions. Establishes a program under the National Institute of Food and Agriculture to place interns from U.S. institutions to serve lower and middle income countries, and provide fellowships for study at foreign agricultural colleges and universities. Authorizes $10 million each year for FY2019-FY2023. **(§7121)**
No comparable provision.	**Land-grant designation.** Prohibits any additional entity from being designated as eligible to receive funds for agricultural research, extension, and related programs under formula funds (e.g., Hatch Act, Smith-Lever Act, and McIntire-Stennis Act). **(§7117)**	No comparable provision.
Competitive grants for international agricultural science and education programs. Authorizes grants to colleges and universities that will enhance international content of curricula, promote extension of U.S. scientists' research to international peers, and enhance collaborative research with other countries. **(7 U.S.C. 3292b(c)(2))**	Reauthorizes appropriations for FY2019-FY2023. **(§7118)**	Identical to House provision. **(§7122)**
Limitation on indirect costs for agricultural research, education, and extension programs. Sets limits on indirect cost recovery on grants awarded to support research, education, and extension activities to 22% of total federal funding. **(7 U.S.C. 3310)**	Amends the provision to allow indirect cost recovery charged against any agricultural research, education, or extension grant awarded to increase from 22% of total federal funds received to 30% of federal funding. **(§7119)**	No comparable provision.

Current Law/Policy	House-Passed Bill (H.R. 2)	Senate-Passed Bill (H.R. 2)
No comparable provision.	**Research equipment grants**. Adds new section to Section 1462 of NARETP Act establishing a competitive grants program for research equipment. Grant amounts may not exceed $500,000 to an eligible institution. Prohibits charges of indirect costs or acquisition or depreciation of equipment. Authorizes $5 million for each of FY2019-FY2023. **(§7120)**	Identical to House provision.
Authorization of appropriations for research. Authorizes formula funds for agricultural research at land-grant universities. **(7 U.S.C. 3311)**	Reauthorizes Hatch Act funding to state agricultural experiment stations at the current level for FY2019-FY2023. **(§7121)**	Identical to House provision. **(§7123)**
Authorization of appropriations for extension education. Authorizes formula funds for agricultural extension at land-grant universities. **(7 U.S.C. 33312)**	Reauthorizes such sums as necessary to carry out extension programs of USDA for FY2019- FY2023. **(§7122)**	Identical to House provision. **(§7124)**
Supplemental and alternative crops. Requires USDA to develop and implement a program to develop supplemental and alternative crops. Authorizes $1 million in appropriations for each of FY2014-FY2018. **(7 U.S.C. 3319d)**.	Extends program and funding levels through FY2023. Amends the program to include canola and alternative crops "for agronomic rotational purposes and for use as a habitat for honey bees and other pollinators," among other changes. **(§7123)**	Extends program and funding levels through FY2023. Amends the program to include canola and alternative crops "for agronomic rotational purposes and for use as a habitat for honey bees and other pollinators," among other changes. Expands eligibility to include industrial hemp. **(§7125)**
New Era Rural Technology Program Authorizes the "New Era Rural Technology Program," to make grants available for technology development, applied research, and training to aid in the development of an agriculture- based renewable energy workforce. **(7 U.S.C. 3319e.**	No comparable provision.	Amends to add precision agriculture as an eligible activity for grant support under the program. Reauthorizes the program for FY2019-FY2023. **(§7126)**
Capacity-building grants for NLGCA institutions. Authorizes competitive grants program for NLGCAs. **(7 U.S.C. 3319i(b))**	Reauthorizes appropriations for FY2019-FY2023. **(§7124)**	Identical to House provision.
No comparable provision.	No comparable provision.	**Agriculture advanced research and development authority**. Amends Subtitle K of the NARETP Act to establish the Agriculture Advanced Research and Development Authority (AGARDA) in the Department of Agriculture under the Office of Chief Scientist to assess the efficacy and applicability of authority for advanced research and development.

Table 10. (Continued)

Current Law/Policy	House-Passed Bill (H.R. 2)	Senate-Passed Bill (H.R. 2)
		Advanced research and development is defined as activities to overcome long-term and high-risk research challenges in agriculture and food. Defines "qualified product or projects" suitable for AGARDA. Directs the Secretary to develop a strategic plan for AGARDA and disseminate the plan to those who can best contribute to the activities described in the strategic plan. Outlines the duties of the Office of Chief Scientist in achieving the objectives of the strategic plan. Permits the Secretary to expedite awarding grants and entering into contracts. Permits the Secretary to appoint highly qualified individuals without regard to certain sections of the U.S. Code governing appointments in the competitive service and without regard to the General Schedule pay rates. Authorizes establishment of the AGARDA Fund in the U.S. Treasury administered by the Chief Scientist for the purpose of advanced research of qualified products and projects, agricultural technology, and research tools as described in the provision. **(§7128)**
Aquaculture assistance programs. Provides competitive grants to support aquaculture research and assistance. **(7 U.S.C. 3324(a)(2))**	Reauthorizes appropriations for FY2019-FY2023. **(§7125)**	Identical to House provision. **(§7129)**
Rangeland research programs. Provides competitive grants to support rangeland research and assistance. **(7 U.S.C. 3336(a)(2))**	Reauthorizes appropriations for FY2019-FY2023. **(§7126)**	Repeals the Rangeland research program. **(§7130)**
Special authorization for biosecurity planning and response. Authorizes $20 million annually for research, education, and extension activities for biosecurity planning and response. **(7 U.S.C. 3351)**	Authorizes appropriations of $30 million for each of FY2019-FY2023. Adds that the Secretary shall, in addition to other stated activities, use the funds to coordinate tactical science activities of USDA's mission areas to protect the agricultural system of the U.S. against	Reauthorizes the program and provides $20 million annually for FY2019-FY2023. **(§7131)**

Current Law/Policy	House-Passed Bill (H.R. 2)	Senate-Passed Bill (H.R. 2)
	biosecurity threats from pests, diseases, contaminants, and disasters. **(§7127)**	
Distance education and resident instruction grants program for insular area institutions of higher education. Authorizes distance education grants and resident instruction grants for insular area institutions. **(7 U.S.C. 3362(f)(2), 3363(c)(2))**	Reauthorizes appropriations for FY2019-FY2023. **(§7128)**	Identical to the House provision. **(§7132)**
Matching funds requirement. Requires the recipient of a competitive grant that is awarded by the Secretary under a covered law to provide funds, in-kind contributions, or a combination of both from sources other than funds provided through such grant in an amount that is at least equal to the amount of such grant. **(7 U.S.C. 3371(d))**	Strikes paragraph 5, which excludes competitive, special, and facilities research grants from the matching requirement. **(§7129)**	Amends to add a section stating that after enactment of this provision no additional entities shall be eligible to receive funds under a capacity program administered by the following "covered laws": • Title XVI of the Food, Agriculture, Conservation, and Trade Act of 1990 (7 U.S.C. 5801 *et seq.*); • The Agricultural Research, Extension, and Education Reform Act of 1998 (7 U.S.C. 7601 *et seq.*); • Part III of subtitle E of title VII of the Food, Conservation, and Energy Act of 2008; and • Section 3157 of this title. **(§7133)** Repeals Subtitle P (7 U.S.C. 3371) of the NARETP Act, subject to conforming amendments as listed in the provision. **(§7601)**
Subtitle B—Food, Agriculture, Conservation, and Trade Act of 1990		
Best utilization of biological applications. Authorizes appropriations under the Sustainable Agriculture Research and Education Program of $40 million annually for FY2013-FY2018. **(7 U.S.C. 5814)**	Reauthorizes appropriations for FY2019-FY2023. **(§7201)**	Identical to House provision. **(§7201)**
Integrated management systems. Authorizes a research and education program concerning integrated resource management and integrated crop management to enhance research related to farming operations, practices, and systems that optimize crop and livestock production potential and are environmentally sound. Authorizes $20 million annually for FY2013- FY2018. **(7 U.S.C. 5821(d))**	Reauthorizes appropriations for FY2019-FY2023. **(§7202)**	Identical to House provision. **(§7202)**

Table 10. (Continued)

Current Law/Policy	House-Passed Bill (H.R. 2)	Senate-Passed Bill (H.R. 2)
Technical guides and handbooks. (7 U.S.C. 5831(f)(2))	Reauthorizes appropriations for FY2019-FY2023. **(§7203)**	Identical to House provision. **(§7203)**
National Training Program. Authorizes a National Training Program in Sustainable Agriculture to provide education and training for Cooperative Extension Service agents and other professionals involved in the education and transfer of technical information concerning sustainable agriculture. Authorizes $20 million annually for FY2013-FY2018. **(7 U.S.C. 5832(1))**	Reauthorizes appropriations for FY2019-FY2023. **(§7204)**	Identical to House provision. **(§7204)**
National Genetics Resources Program. Establishes a National Genetics Resources Program to maintain and enhance the collection, preservation, and dissemination of genetic material of importance to American food and agriculture production. Describes the functions of the Program. **(7 U.S.C. 5841(d))**	No comparable provision.	Amends the functions of the Program to authorize the creation of a strategic germplasm and cultivar collection assessment and utilization plan that considers the resources necessary to address the backlog of characterization and maintenance of existing accessions. Requires the Secretary to make the plan available to the public. **(§7205)**
National Genetics Resources Program. Authorizes a National Genetics Resources Program with an appropriation of $1million annually for FY2013-FY2018. **(7 U.S.C. 5844(b)(2))**.	Reauthorizes appropriations for FY2019-FY2023. **(§7205)**	Amends the organization of the Advisory Council by adding 4 members and changing the appointment of members, and by adding membership from 1862, 1890, and NLGCA institutions. Instructs the Advisory Council to include recommendations on the state of public cultivar development, research gaps relating to cultivar development, and the state of commercialization of federally funded cultivars. Reauthorizes appropriations for FY2019-FY2023. **(§7206)**
National Agricultural Weather Program. Authorizes a National Agricultural Weather Program with an authorized appropriation of $1 million annually for FY2014-FY2018. **(7 U.S.C. 5855(c))**	Reauthorizes appropriations for FY2019-FY2023. **(§7206)**	Identical to House provision. **(§7207)**
Agricultural genome initiative. Establishes an Agricultural Genome Program to expand the knowledge of public and private sector entities and persons concerning genomes for species of importance to the food and agriculture	Adds the phrase *to Phenome* after *Genome*. Outlines goals of research to expand knowledge concerning genomes and phenomes of crops important to the United States.	Identical to House provision. **(§7208)**

Current Law/Policy	House-Passed Bill (H.R. 2)	Senate-Passed Bill (H.R. 2)
sectors in order to maximize the return on the investment in genomics of agriculturally important species. **(7 U.S.C. 5924)**	Authorizes appropriation of $30 million each fiscal year for FY2019-FY2023. **(§7207)**	
High-priority research and extension. Provides for "high- priority research and extension" areas and initiatives and other programs. **(7 U.S.C. 5925)**	Retains, amends, and/or adds research areas as a "high-priority." Added initiatives that cover macadamia tree health, national turfgrass research, fertilizer management, cattle fever ticks, and laying hen and turkey research. **(§7208)**	Retains, amends, and/or adds research areas as a "high-priority." Added initiatives that cover macadamia tree health, national turfgrass research, pulse crops, and training coordination. Reauthorizes research and existing annual appropriations on pollinator protection through FY2023, and expands the provision to establish a pollinator health task force to implement the 2015 National Pollinator Health Strategy, coordinate research, and cover both native and managed pollinators. **(§7209)**
Organic Agriculture Research and Extension Initiative. Establishes the Organic Agriculture Research and Extension Initiative. Provides grants to facilitate the development of organic agriculture production and processing. Provides mandatory Commodity Credit Corporation (CCC) funds of $20 million annually for FY2014- FY2018. **(7 U.S.C. 5925b)**	Reauthorizes program and increases annual CCC funding levels to $30 million for FY2019-FY2023. **(§7209)**	Reauthorizes program and increases annual CCC funding at $40 million for FY2019-FY2020, $45 million for FY2021, and $50 million for FY2022 and each fiscal year thereafter, and extends authorized appropriations through FY2023. **(§7210)**
Farm business management. Authorizes competitive research and extension grants for improving the farm management knowledge and skills of agricultural producers and for establishing and maintaining a national, publicly available farm financial management database to support improved farm management. **(7 U.S.C. 5925f)**	Amends to permit the Secretary to make competitive research and extension grants for the purpose of improving farm management knowledge and skills of agricultural producers by maintaining a national, publicly available farm financial management database to support improved farm management. **(§7210)**	Amends existing law to allow USDA to make competitive research and extension grants for the purpose of improving farm management knowledge and skills of agricultural producers by maintaining a national, publicly available farm financial management database to support improved farm management. **(§7211)**
Farm business management. Authorizes competitive research and extension grants for improving the farm management knowledge and skills of agricultural producers and for establishing and maintaining a national, publicly available farm financial management database to support improved farm management. **(7 U.S.C. 5925f)**	No comparable provision.	Amends to authorize competitive grants, in consultation with the Urban Agriculture and Innovative Production Advisory Committee, to support research and extension activities to enhance urban, indoor, and other emerging agricultural production, including facilitating urban agricultural production, harvesting, transportation, packaging, and marketing; assessing and

Table 10. (Continued)

Current Law/Policy	House-Passed Bill (H.R. 2)	Senate-Passed Bill (H.R. 2)
		developing strategies to remediate contaminated sites; analyzing means by which new agricultural sites are determined; exploring new technologies that minimize energy, lighting systems, water, and other inputs. Grants would be made under the Competitive, Special, and Facilities Research Grant Act with priority for proposals that involve cooperation with multiple entities and states and regions with significant interest in urban farms and indoor production. Authorizes mandatory funding of $4 million in mandatory CCC funding and $10 million in discretionary spending, both annually, for FY2019-FY2023 for these purposes. Directs the Secretary to conduct a follow-up study to the Census of Agriculture of 2017 on urban, indoor, and emerging agricultural production, including community gardens and farms located in urban areas, rooftop farms and vertical production, indoor farms and greenhouses, hydroponic, aeroponic, and aquaponic farm facilities. Authorizes $14 million for the period FY2019-FY2021 to carry out this provision. **(§7212)**
Centers of excellence. Requires the Secretary to prioritize centers of excellence established for purposes of carrying out research, extension, and education activities relating to the food and agricultural sciences. **(7 U.S.C. 5926)**)	No comparable provision.	Amends to add at least 3 centers of excellence, each led by an 1890 institution, to focus on one or more of the following: student success and workforce development, nutrition, health, and wellness, farming systems and rural prosperity, global food security and defense, natural resources, energy and the environment, and emerging technologies. Requires the Secretary to submit a report to Congress on the centers' work. Authorizes $10 million annually for FY2019-FY2023. **(§7213)**

Current Law/Policy	House-Passed Bill (H.R. 2)	Senate-Passed Bill (H.R. 2)
Assistive Technology Program for Farmers with Disabilities. Authorizes demonstration grants to support cooperative programs between State Cooperative Extension Service agencies and private nonprofit disability organizations to provide on-the- farm agricultural education and assistance directed at accommodating disability in farm operations for individuals with disabilities who are engaged in farming and farm-related occupations and their families. **(7 U.S.C. 5933)**	Clarifies language to make the provision apply to veterans engaged in farming or pursuing new farming opportunities. **(§7211)**	Reauthorizes the program for FY2019-FY2023. **(§7214)**
National Rural Information Center Clearinghouse. Establishes within the National Agricultural Library, in coordination with the National Institute of Food and Agriculture, a National Rural Information Center Clearinghouse to provide and distribute information and data to any industry, organization, or federal, state, or local government entity, on request, about programs and services provided by federal, state, and local agencies and private nonprofit organizations and institutions under which individuals residing in, or organizations and state and local government entities operating in, a rural area may be eligible for any kind of assistance, including job training, education, health care, and economic development assistance and emotional and financial counseling. **(7 U.S.C. 3125b(e))**	Reauthorizes appropriations for FY2019-FY2023. **(§7212)**	Identical to House provision. **(§7215)**
Subtitle C—Agriculture, Research, Extension, and Education Reform Act of 1998		
Ending limitation on funding. Limits grant funding to no more than three years and prohibits further funding after an eligible entity has received three years of funding. **(7 U.S.C. 7625(e)(3))**	Removes limitation on funding that restricts USDA from providing additional grant funding once an entity has received three years of grant funding. **(§7300)**	No comparable provision.
National food safety training. Authorizes appropriations of such sums as necessary for competitive grants to support training, education, extension, outreach, and technical assistance projects to increase the adoption of established food safety standards, guidance, and protocols. **(7 U.S.C. 7625(j))**	Reauthorizes appropriations through FY2023. **(§7301)**	Reauthorizes the training program and provides an authorized appropriation of $10 million annually for FY2019-FY2023. **(§7301)**
Integrated research, extension, and education competitive grant program. (7 U.S.C. 7626(e))	Reauthorizes appropriations for FY2019-FY2023. **(§7302)**	Identical to the House provision. **(§7302)**

Table 10. (Continued)

Current Law/Policy	House-Passed Bill (H.R. 2)	Senate-Passed Bill (H.R. 2)
Support for research regarding diseases of wheat, triticale, and barley caused *by Fusarium graminearum* or by *Tilletia indica.* Authorizes grants to consortia of land-grant colleges and universities to enhance the ability of the consortia to carry out multi- state research projects aimed at understanding and combating diseases of wheat, triticale, and barley caused by Fusarium graminearum and related fungi. **(7 U.S.C. 7628(e)(2))**	Reauthorizes appropriations for FY2019-FY2023. **(§7303)**	Amends by authorizing an appropriation of $15 million annually for FY2019-FY2023. **(§7303)**
Grants for youth organizations. Authorizes grants through the director of NIFA, which shall make grants to the Girl Scouts of the United States of America, the Boy Scouts of America, the National 4– H Council, and the National Future Farmers of America Organization to establish pilot projects to expand the programs carried out by the organizations in rural areas and small towns. **(7 U.S.C. 7630(d)(2))**	Reauthorizes appropriations for FY2019-FY2023. **(§7304)**	Identical to House provision. **(§7304)**
Specialty Crop Research Initiative. Provides mandatory CCC funds of $80 million for FY2014 and each fiscal year thereafter and authorizes appropriations of $100 million annually for FY2014-FY2018. **(7 U.S.C. 7632(b))** Reserves at least $25 million in funding for the emergency citrus disease research and extension program and includes an additional $25 million in authorized appropriations annually for FY2014-FY2018. **(7 U.S.C. 7632(j))**	Extends program and funding levels through FY2023, including funding for the emergency citrus disease research and extension program. Expands program eligibility to include "size-controlling rootstock systems for perennial crops" and "emerging and invasive species," among other production practices and technologies. **(§7305)**	Extends funding levels through FY2023. Expands program eligibility to include "size-controlling rootstock systems for perennial crops," "emerging and invasive species," and "threats to specialty crop pollinators," among other production practices and technologies. **(§7305)**
Food Animal Residue Avoidance Database Program. Establishes a database to provide livestock producers, extension specialists, scientists, and veterinarians with information to prevent drug, pesticide, and environmental contaminant residues in food animal products. **(7 U.S.C. 7642(e))**	Reauthorizes appropriations for FY2019-FY2023. **(§7306)**	Identical to House provision. **(§7306)**
Office of Pest Management Policy. Establishes the Office of Pest Management Policy to coordinate USDA's policies and activities related to pesticides and pest management tools. Authorizes appropriations of such sums as necessary through FY2018. **(7 U.S.C. 7653)**	Reauthorizes appropriations for FY2019-FY2023. **(§7307)**	Identical to House provision. **(§7307)**

Current Law/Policy	House-Passed Bill (H.R. 2)	Senate-Passed Bill (H.R. 2)
Forestry products advanced utilization research. Establishes forestry and forestry products research and extension initiative to develop and disseminate science- based tools that address the needs of the forestry sector and their respective regions; forest and timberland owners and managers; and forestry products engineering, manufacturing, and related interests. **(7 U.S.C. 7655b(f)(1))**	Reauthorizes appropriations for FY2019-FY2023. No change to current law. **(§7308)**	Identical to House provision. **(§7308)**
Subtitle D—Food, Conservation, and Energy Act of 2008 (FCE)		
Agricultural Biosecurity Communication Center. Establishes a communication center within USDA to collect and disseminate information and prepare for an agricultural disease emergency, agroterrorist act, or other threat to agricultural biosecurity and to coordinate activities among agencies and offices within the USDA. Authorizes $2 million annually for FY2013-FY2018. **(7 U.S.C. 8912(c)(2))**	Reauthorizes appropriations for FY2019-FY2023. **(§7401)**	Identical to House provision. **(§7501)**
Assistance to build local capacity in agricultural biosecurity planning, preparation, and response.	Reauthorizes appropriations for FY2019-FY2023. **(§7402)**	Identical to House provision. **(§7502)**
Authorizes a competitive grant program to support the development and expansion of advanced training programs in agricultural biosecurity planning and response for food science professionals and veterinarians. Authorizes $15 million annually for FY2013-FY2018. **(7 U.S.C. 8913)**		
Research and development of agricultural countermeasures. Authorizes a competitive grant program to encourage basic and applied research and the development of qualified agricultural countermeasures. Authorizes $15 million annually for FY2013-FY2018. **(7 U.S.C. 8921(b)(2))**	Reauthorizes appropriations for FY2019-FY2023. **(§7403)**	Identical to House provision. **(§7503)**
Agricultural Biosecurity Grant Program. Authorizes a competitive grant program to promote the development of teaching programs in agriculture, veterinary medicine, and disciplines closely allied to the food and agriculture system to increase the number of trained individuals with an expertise in agricultural biosecurity. **(7 U.S.C. 8922(e)(2))**	Reauthorizes appropriations for FY2019-FY2023. **(§7404)**	Identical to House provision. **(§7504)**

Table 10. (Continued)

Current Law/Policy	House-Passed Bill (H.R. 2)	Senate-Passed Bill (H.R. 2)
Grazinglands Research Laboratory. Establishes a research laboratory for grazingland research. **(§7502, P.L. 110-246)**	Amends provision to state that the Grazinglands Research Laboratory shall not be declared excess or surplus federal property for the 15-year period beginning on the date of enactment of the FCE Act. The amendment increases the time period from 10 years to 15 years. **(§7405)**	No comparable provision.
Natural products research program. Authorizes a natural products research program to improve human health and agricultural productivity through the discovery, development, and commercialization of products and agrichemicals from bioactive natural products, including products from plant, marine, and microbial sources. Authorizes $7 million annually for FY2014-2018. **(7 U.S.C. 5937(e))**	Reauthorizes appropriations for FY2019-FY2023. **(§7406)**	Identical to House provision. **(§7512)**
Sun grant program. Establishes six sun grant centers and authorizes competitive grants to enhance national energy security through the development, distribution, and implementation of biobased energy technologies. Authorizes $75 million annually through FY2018. **(7 U.S.C. 8114(g))**	Reauthorizes appropriations for FY2019-FY2023. **(§7407)**	Identical to House provision. **(§7513)**
No comparable provision.	No comparable provision.	**Mechanization and automation for specialty crops**. Directs the Secretary to conduct a review of programs in the Department that affect the production or processing of specialty crops. **(§7514)**
Subtitle E—Amendments to Other Laws		
Critical Agricultural Materials Act. Authorizes a research program into the use of agricultural materials that are of strategic and industrial importance to the United States. Authorizes $2 million annually for FY2014-FY2018. **(7 U.S.C. 178n(a)(2)**.	Reauthorizes appropriations for FY2019-FY2023. **(§7501)**	
Section 5(b)(9) of the act provides for basic and applied research, technology development, and technology transfer. **(7 U.S.C. 178c(b)(9))**	No comparable provision.	Expands scope of the program to study the economic feasibility of developing native agricultural crops to include industrial hemp. **(§7401)**

Current Law/Policy	House-Passed Bill (H.R. 2)	Senate-Passed Bill (H.R. 2)
Equity in Educational Land- Grant Status Act of 1994. Establishes land-grant aid to colleges. **(7 U.S.C. 301 note)**	Amends provision to define 36 tribal colleges as "1994 land-grant institutions." Reauthorizes endowment funding, capacity-building grants, and research grants for the 36 tribal colleges for FY2019-FY2023. **(§7502)**	Identical to House provision. **(§7402)**
Research Facilities Act. Defines and authorizes funding for agricultural research facilities. **(7 U.S.C. 390 *et seq.*)**	Amends the Research Facilities Act (7 U.S.C. 390(1)) by striking *a college, university, or nonprofit institution* and inserting *an entity eligible to receive funds under a capacity and infrastructure program as defined in Section 251(f)(1)(C) of the 1994 Agriculture Reorganization Act.* Adds a new section authorizing competitive grants appropriation and limiting those funds made available to no more than 25% for any one project. Limits an eligible entity to receiving funds for only one project at a time. **(§7503)**	Reauthorizes the provision for FY2019-FY2023. **(§7403)**
Competitive, Special, and Facilities Research Grant Act. Authorizes a competitive grants program at USDA to address various areas of importance to the agricultural production, food, and nutrition sectors. **(7 U.S.C. 3157(b))**	Amends the act by making technical corrections and adding clauses that accelerate research in the use of automation or mechanization for labor-intensive tasks in crop production and distribution and remove barriers to entry for young, beginning, socially disadvantaged veteran, and immigrant farmers and ranchers. **(§7504)**	Similar to House provision. Also amends to add soil health as an environmental research area. Does not include the House provision regarding socially disadvantaged farmers and ranchers. **(§7404)**
Competitive, Special, and Facilities Research Grant Act. Authorizes a competitive grants program at USDA to address various areas of importance to the agricultural production, food, and nutrition sectors. **(7 U.S.C. 3157(b))**	No comparable provision.	Amends to create an extension design and demonstration initiative to encourage the design of adaptive prototype systems for extension and education that seek to advance the application, translation, and demonstration of scientific discoveries and other agricultural research for the adoption and understanding of food, agricultural, nd natural resources practices. Authorizes competitive grants to land-grant institutions and agricultural experiment stations for up to 5 years for the design of extension and education prototypes, Provides $5 million annually for FY2019-FY2023. **(§7405)**

Table 10. (Continued)

Current Law/Policy	House-Passed Bill (H.R. 2)	Senate-Passed Bill (H.R. 2)
Renewable Resources Extension Act of 1978. Authorizes $30 million annually for FY2002-FY2018 for forestry-related extension activities. **(16 U.S.C. 1675, 1671)**	Reauthorizes appropriations for FY2019-FY2023. **(§7505)**	Identical to House provision. **(§7406)**
National Aquaculture Act of 1980. Authorizes appropriations of $1 million annually for FY1991- FY2018 to the Departments of Agriculture, Commerce, and the Interior to support research on aquaculture. **(16 U.S.C. 2809)**	Reauthorizes appropriations for FY2019-FY2023. **(§7506)**	Identical to House provision. **(§7407)**
Purposes of agricultural research, extension, and education. Describes the objectives and purposes of federal support for agricultural research, extension, and education. **(7 U.S.C. 3101, note)**	No comparable provision.	Repeals a review of the Agricultural Research Service authorized by Section 7404 of P.L. 107-171. Review would have evaluated the merits of establishing one or more national institutes focused on disciplines important to the progress of food and agricultural science. **(§7408)**
MxIntire-Stennis Cooperative Forestry Research Act. Provides funding to schools of forestry for research and extension activities. **(16 U.S.C. 582a-1)**	No comparable provision.	Amends to add 1994 institutions (tribal land grant colleges) that offer an associate's degree or a baccalaureate degree in forestry as eligible to participate in McIntire-Stennis funding under terms determined by the Secretary. **(§7414)**
Smith-Lever Act. Provides formula funding to land-grant institutions to support extension activities. **(7 U.S.C. 343(d))**	No comparable provision.	Amends the Smith-Lever Act to permit the Secretary to provide competitive grant funding to 1890 colleges and Tuskegee University, and 1994 institutions (tribal colleges of agriculture) for the Children, Youth, and Families at Risk program and the Federally Recognized Tribes Extension Program. **(§7419)**
Agriculture innovation center demonstration program. Directs the Secretary to establish a demonstration program under which agricultural producers are provided technical assistance, assistance in marketing, market development, and business planning; and organizational, outreach, and development assistance. Authorizes appropriations of $1 million annually FY2014-2018. **(7 U.S.C. 1632b)**	No comparable provision.	Amends to provide "such sums as necessary to carry out this section." **(§7418)**

Current Law/Policy	House-Passed Bill (H.R. 2)	Senate-Passed Bill (H.R. 2)
Legitimacy of industrial hemp research. Allows an institution of higher education or State department of agriculture to grow or cultivate industrial hemp for research purposes, if allowed under the laws of the State in which the institution is located. Establishes a definition for "industrial hemp" to mean the plant Cannabis sativa with a delta-9 tetrahydrocannabinol concentration of not more than 0.3% on a dry weight basis." **(7 U.S.C. 5940)**	No comparable provision.	Requires USDA to conduct a study of agricultural pilot programs, assessing the economic viability of the domestic production and sale of industrial hemp, and review the hemp pilot program and any other agricultural or academic research relating to industrial hemp. **(§7415)** Other provisions regarding industrial hemp are contained in the Horticulture title (XII) **(§§10111, 10112),** Crop Insurance title (XI) **(§§11101, 11106, 11112, 11120, 11101, 11121),** Miscellaneous title (XII) **(§12608),** and elsewhere in the Research title (XII) **(§§7125, 7401**).
No comparable provision.	No comparable provision.	**Collection of data relating to barley area planted and harvested**. Directs the Secretary through the National Agricultural Statistics Service to include New York in the states surveyed for the table entitled "barley area planted and harvested" in those reports. **(§7416)**
No comparable report.	No comparable provision.	**Collection of data relating to the size and location of dairy farms.** Requires the Administrator of the Economic Research Service (ERS) to update the report entitled "Changes in the Size and Location of US Dairy Farms" contained in the report of the ERS entitled "Profits, Costs, and the Changing Structure of Dairy Farming" and published in September 2007. Requires an expanded table containing the full range of herd sizes. **(§7417)**
Beginning Farmer and Rancher Development Program. Authorizes a beginning farmer and rancher development program to provide training, education, outreach, and technical assistance initiatives for beginning farmers or ranchers. Authorizes $20 million in mandatory funding annually for FY2014-FY2018 and $30 million annually for FY2014-FY2018 in discretionary spending.	Reauthorizes mandatory and discretionary appropriations for FY2019-FY2023. Amends to require that grant recipients provide a match in the form of cash or in-kind contributions equal to 25% of the grant funds provided. The Secretary is authorized to waive the matching requirement to effectively reach an underserved area or population.	No comparable provision.

Table 10. (Continued)

Current Law/Policy	House-Passed Bill (H.R. 2)	Senate-Passed Bill (H.R. 2)
(7 U.S.C. 3319f)	Amendment adds new subsection outlining the purposes of the competitive grants. Requires that not less than 5% of the funds be made available to socially disadvantaged farmers and ranchers, limited resource farmers and ranchers, and farm workers who desire to become farmers and ranchers. Also requires not less than 5% of the funds be made available to support programs and services that address the needs of veteran farmers. **(§7507)**	
Federal agricultural research facilities. Provides funding for federal agricultural research facilities. **(Title XIV, P.L. 99-198; 99 Stat. 1556; 128 Stat. 900))**	Reauthorizes appropriations for FY2019-FY2023. No change to current law. **(7508)**	Identical to House provision. **(§7112)**
Biomass research and development. Establishes a research initiative between USDA and the Department of Energy to coordinate research and development programs and activities relating to biofuels and biobased products that are carried out by their respective departments. Authorizes $20 million in discretionary funding annually for FY2014-FY2018. **(7 U.S.C. 8108(h))**	Reauthorizes appropriations of $20 million for each fiscal year for FY2019-FY2023. **(§7509)**	Amends to add carbon dioxide intended for permanent sequestration to be considered a biobased product. Adds an expert in carbon sequestration to the membership of the Advisory Council. Reauthorizes $3 million mandatory spending and $20 million in discretionary spending for FY2019-FY2023. **(§7409)**
Foundation for Food and Agriculture Research A non-profit corporation established to advance the research mission of USDA by supporting research activities focused on key problems of national and international significance. The Foundation is governed by an elected Board of Directors of 15 members selected from a list of candidates provided by the National Academy of Sciences and a list provided by industry. Provides $200 million in mandatory spending to remain available until expended. Federal funding is matched on a 1:1 basis. **(7 U.S.C. 5939)**		Amends to include that the Board of Directors shall actively solicit and accept any funds, gifts, grants, devises, or bequests of real or personal property made to the Foundation, including from private entities. Requires publication of an annual notice to stakeholders of agricultural research priorities for the coming year, including a schedule for funding competitions and a description of how funding applications will be evaluated. Describes how the Foundation will improve transparency in the application review process. Requires the Secretary to transfer $200 million of mandatory funding to the Foundation. **(§7413)**

Current Law/Policy	House-Passed Bill (H.R. 2)	Senate-Passed Bill (H.R. 2)
Subtitle F—Other Matters		
Enhanced Use Lease Authority Program. Concerns the National Agricultural Library's authority under a pilot program to lease nonexcess property. **(7 U.S.C. 3125a note)**	Transitions the lease authority program from a pilot program to a permanent program and changes the dates of report submission requirements. **(§7601)**	Amends the Federal Crop Insurance Reform and Department of Agriculture Reorganization Act of 1994 to terminate the lease authority program in FY2023, and to require reporting by FY2021.**(§7411)**
Functions and duties of the Under Secretary for Research, Education, and Economics. (7 U.S.C. 6971(d)(2))	Declares that certain duties of the Secretary with respect to coordination of research across disciplines and to address the priority research areas of the Agriculture and Food Research Initiative. **(§7602)**	No comparable provision.
Reinstatement of District of Columbia matching requirement for certain land- grant university assistance. (P.L. 93-471, §38-1202.09(e), D.C. Official Code)	Amends Section 208(c) of the District of Columbia Postsecondary Education Reorganization Act to pay no more than one-half of the total cost of providing certain extension work. **(§7603)**	Identical to House provision. **(§7410)**
No comparable provision.	**Farmland tenure, transition, and entry data initiative.** Directs the Secretary to collect and report annually data and analysis on farmland ownership, tenure, transition, and entry of beginning farmers. Authorizes $2 million each fiscal year for FY2019-FY2023. **(§7604)**	No comparable provision.
No comparable provision.	**Transfer of administrative jurisdiction, portion of Henry A. Wallace Beltsville Agricultural Research Center, Beltsville, Maryland.** Authorizes the Secretary to transfer a parcel of real property at the Henry A. Wallace Beltsville Agricultural Research Center to the administrative jurisdiction of the Secretary of the Treasury and specifies the conditions of the transfer. **(§7605)**	Identical to House provision. **(§7412)**
Smith-Lever Act of 1916, Sections 3 and 4; Hatch Act of 1887, Section 3; National Agricultural Research, Extension, and Teaching Policy Act, Sections 1444 and 1445. (7 U.S.C. 343(h)(2)); (7 U.S.C 344); (7 U.S.C 366(c)); (7 U.S.C 361g); (7 U.S.C> 3221(d)); (7 U.S.C. 3222(e))	Amends provisions requiring submission of plans of work by land-grant institutions with respect to the use of formula funds and state matching funds provided under the Hatch Act, Smith-Lever Act, and similar formula funds provided to the 1890 land-grant universities.	No comparable provision.

Table 10. (Continued)

Current Law/Policy	House-Passed Bill (H.R. 2)	Senate-Passed Bill (H.R. 2)
	Provides that the procedures of such plans of work are not subject to audits to determine their sufficiency. **(§7606)**	
Department of Agriculture Reorganization Act of 1994, Section 251. (7 U.S.C. 6971(f)(1)(C))	Exempts entities receiving certain funds from time and effort reporting requirements under Part 200 of Title 2 of the *Code of Federal Regulations* with respect to the use of such funds. **(§7607)**	No comparable provision.
No comparable provision	Provides that USDA, in consultation with the Food and Drug Administration (FDA), shall develop and carry out a national science-based education campaign to increase public awareness regarding the use of biotechnology in food and agriculture production. **(§7608)**	No comparable provision.

Table 11. Forestry

Current Law/Policy	House-Passed Bill (H.R. 2)	Senate-Passed Bill (H.R. 2)
Forestry Assistance and Research		
Program Reauthorizations and Modifications		
Authorizes up to $10 million in annual appropriations between FY2008 and FY2018 to implement the requirements for **statewide forest resource assessments** and strategies. **(16 U.S.C. 2101a)**	Reauthorizes funding at the current authorized level of up to $10 million annually through FY2023. **(§8101)**	No comparable provision.
Permanently authorizes such sums as necessary to be appropriated to carry out the **Forest Legacy Program**, which was created to protect forests from conversion to nonforest uses and received average annual appropriations of approximately $59 million from FY2014 through FY2018. **(16 U.S.C. 2103c)**	Eliminates permanent authority to receive annual appropriations of such sums as necessary and instead authorizes the program to receive $35 million annually through FY2023, subject to appropriations. **(§8102)**	No comparable provision.
Permanently authorizes such sums as necessary to be appropriated to carry out the **Community Forest and Open Space Conservation** program. The program provides financial assistance to local governments, federally recognized Indian tribes, and nonprofit organizations to establish community forests by acquiring and protecting private forests threatened by conversion to nonforest uses.	Eliminates permanent authority to receive annual appropriations of such sums as necessary and instead authorizes the program to receive $5 million annually through FY2023, subject to appropriations. **(§8103)**	No comparable provision.

Current Law/Policy	House-Passed Bill (H.R. 2)	Senate-Passed Bill (H.R. 2)
It received an average of $2.4 million annually in appropriations between FY2014 and FY2018. **(16 U.S.C. 2103d)**		
Permanently authorizes up to 5% of the funds made available for all CFAA programs to be appropriated to carry out a program to support innovative regional or national forest restoration projects that address priority landscapes. The **Landscape Scale Restoration** program received average annual appropriations of $14 million from FY2014 through FY2018. **(16 U.S.C. 2109a)**	Eliminates the existing program and establishes a State and Private Forest Landscape-Scale Restoration program to provide financial assistance for landscape-scale restoration projects that cross landownership boundaries (e.g., federal, state, tribal, and/or private forest land). Specifies that half of the program funding is to be allocated for a competitive grant program and the other half proportionally allocated to the states. Establishes a national and optional regional process for reviewing proposals for the competitive grant program and requires up to a 50% cost-share match, unless waived by the Secretary. Requires the development of performance metrics to measure the results of the program. Authorizes the program to receive $10 million annually through FY2023, subject to appropriations. **(§8104)**	Establishes a competitive grant program similar to the House bill, but does not include the requirement to allocate half of the program funding to the states. Also defines private forest land and state forest land differently; requires a 50% cost-share match without exceptions; does not establish a review process; requires proposals to be accessible by wood- processing infrastructure and based on best available science; and requires the Chief of the Forest Service to consult with the Chief of the NRCS and relevant stakeholders regarding program administration. Establishes the State and Private Forest Landscape-Scale Restoration Fund to administer program funds and authorizes the fund to receive $20 million annually through FY2023, subject to appropriations. **(§8101)**
Establishes the **Healthy Forests Reserve Program** (HFRP) to assist private and tribal landowners in restoring and enhancing forest ecosystems using 10-year agreements, 30-year contracts, 30-year easements, and permanent easements for the purposes of species recovery, improving biodiversity, and enhancing carbon sequestration as outlined in restoration plans. Authorizes appropriations for HFRP of $12 million annually through FY2018. **(16 U.S.C. 6571-6578)**	Expands the purposes, eligibility requirements, and enrollment priorities of the program to include species recovery and habitat conservation considerations. Authorizes federally recognized Indian tribes to sell permanent easements on lands they own in fee simple. Specifies that restoration plans may include a variety of land management practices if necessary to achieve habitat restoration objectives. Reauthorizes HFRP at the current authorized level through FY2023, subject to appropriations. **(§8107(a))**	Similar to House bill, except for the inclusion of practices to improve biological diversity or to increase carbon sequestration in the definition of practices, and measures required in the restoration plan. **(§2426, §8407)**
Authorizes such sums as necessary from FY2004 through FY2008, subject to annual appropriations, for **rapid forest insect and disease assessments** on federal and nonfederal lands **(16 U.S.C. 6556)**	No comparable provision.	Removes the authorization for appropriations and specifies that the authority terminates in FY2023. **(§8406)**

Table 11. (Continued)

Current Law/Policy	House-Passed Bill (H.R. 2)	Senate-Passed Bill (H.R. 2)
Establishes a **semiarid agroforestry research center** in Lincoln, NE and authorizes appropriations of $5 million annually **(16 U.S.C. 1642 note)**	No comparable provision.	Eliminates permanent authority to receive annual appropriations and instead authorizes the program to receive $5 million in annual appropriations through FY2023. **(§8502)**
Authorizes the Secretary of Agriculture to provide matching funds to the **National Forest Foundation** (NFF) for administrative expenses through FY2018. Section 410(b) authorizes $3 million in annual appropriations through FY2018 to provide matching funds for the NFF. **(16 U.S.C. 583j)**	Reauthorizes the Secretary's authority to provide matching funds for NFF administrative expenses and appropriations at the current authorized level of $3 million hrough FY2023. **(§8108)**	Same as the house bill. **(§8503)**
Establishes a competitive grant program for **forestry research**. Entities eligible for funding include state agricultural experiment stations, colleges and universities, research organizations, federal agencies, private organizations, and corporations capable of conducting forestry research. **(16 U.S.C. 582a-8)**	Adds forest restoration as a funding priority in addition to forestry research. Forest restoration grants are to be competitively awarded and may be used to support programs that restore native tree species. **(§8511)**.	No comparable provision.
Program Repeals		
Authorizes a **Wood Fiber Recycling Research** program and authorized appropriations up to $10 million annually through FY1996. **(16 U.S.C. 1648)**	No comparable provision.	Repeals the Recycling Research program. **(§8201)**
Authorizes a **Forestry Student Grant** program to assist minority and female undergraduate and graduate students and authorizes appropriations of such sums as may be necessary without a sunset date. **(16 U.S.C. 1649)**	No comparable provision.	Repeals the Forestry Student Grant program. **(§8202)**
Requires the Secretary to revise the **strategic plan for forest inventory and analysis** within 180 days of enactment of the 2014 farm bill **(16 U.S.C. 1642 note)**	No comparable provision.	Repeals the requirement to revise the forest inventory and analysis strategic plan. **(§8501)**
Wood Energy and Construction Assistance: Program Reauthorizations, Modifications, and Repeals		
Authorizes up to $5 million annually through FY2018 for the **Rural Revitalization Technologies** program to provide technical and financial assistance to facilitate biomass and other small-diameter wood product development and use, specifically for small-scale or community-based business enterprises. The program is funded through allocations from FS's hazardous fuels management program. **(7 U.S.C. 6601(d)(2))**	Reauthorizes the program at the current authorized level of up to $5 million annually through FY2023. **(§8105)**	No comparable provision.

Current Law/Policy	House-Passed Bill (H.R. 2)	Senate-Passed Bill (H.R. 2)
Authorizes financial assistance for communities to plan and install wood energy systems in public buildings and authorizes appropriations of $5 million annually through FY2018. The program has never received appropriations. **(7 U.S.C. 8113)**	Changes the name to the **Community Wood Energy and Wood Innovation Program** and expands it to provide financial assistance for the installation of public or private wood energy systems or the construction of manufacturing or processing plants that use or produce innovative wood products, including mass timber. Cost-share grants may cover up to 35% of the capital cost for installing a community wood energy system or building an innovative wood product facility, capped at a total of $1 million, or up to 50% if special circumstances, as established by the Secretary, apply, such as if the project involves a school or hospital in a low- income community, capped at a total of $1.5 million. A maximum of 25% of the annual grant funds may go to projects proposing innovative wood products facilities. Authorizes the program to receive $25 million annually through FY2023, subject to appropriations. **(§8106)**	Establishes a 50% cost-share grant program to advance the use of innovative wood products as described in a 2015 request for proposals Forest Service Request for Proposals: 2016 Wood Innovations Funding Opportunity" (80 *Federal* ("*Register* 63498, October 20, 2015)) to expand and accelerate wood energy and wood product markets to support forest management needs on NFS and other forested lands. Specifies that proposals which use or retrofit sawmill facilities located in counties with average annual unemployment above the national average shall be prioritized for funding. **(§8643)**
No comparable provision.	Establishes a research, development, education, and technical assistance program— including a competitive grant program—to facilitate the use of innovative wood products for building and construction purposes. **(§8501)**	Same as the House bill. **(§8641, §8642)**
Authorizes the Secretary of Agriculture, upon an agreement with the Secretary of Defense, to study and develop a program to manage forests for biomass growth and carbon sequestration on military installations. **(7 U.S.C. 6708)**	No comparable provision.	Removes the requirement to manage for biomass growth and carbon sequestration and authorizes the Secretary of Agriculture, upon an agreement with the Secretary of Defense, to develop a program to manage forests and lands on military installations. **(§8302)**
Authorizes the Secretary of Agriculture, in consultation with the Secretary of Energy, to carry out **Biomass Energy Demonstration Project** program to demonstrate the potential of short-rotation silvicultural methods to produce wood for energy. **(7 U.S.C. 6708)**	No comparable provision.	Repeals the Biomass Energy Demonstration Project program. **(§8301)**

Table 11. (Continued)

Current Law/Policy	House-Passed Bill (H.R. 2)	Senate-Passed Bill (H.R. 2)
Authorizes the Secretary to provide financial assistance to offset the cost of biomass for owners or operators of facilities which use biomass for as a raw material to produce energy. The **Biomass Commercial Utilization Program** was authorized up to $5 million in appropriations annually through FY2008. **(16 U.S.C. 6531)**	No comparable provision.	Repeals the Biomass Commercial Utilization Program. **(§8403)**
Hazardous Fuels Reduction on Federal and Nonfederal Land: Funding Priorities and Assistance for Cross-Boundary Projects		
Directs the Secretary to develop an annual program of work which prioritizes hazardous fuel reduction projects on NFS that would protect at-risk communities that have developed a community wildfire protection plan (CWPP) and encourages the Secretary to allocate funding for assistance programs to prioritize hazardous fuel reduction projects recommended by those communities. Defines the wildland urban interface (WUI) as an area within, adjacent, or within 0.5 mile to a community identified as at-risk for large-scale wildland fire disturbance event in a CWPP.	Encourages the Secretary to use any funds appropriated for hazardous fuels reduction activities in excess of $300 million annually for cross-boundary hazardous fuel reduction projects on federal and nonfederal land. Also encourages the Secretary to use up to $20 million or 20% of any excess funds appropriated annually to provide financial assistance grants to states to implement hazardous fuel reduction projects on nonfederal land.	Authorizes appropriations up to $20 million annually through FY2023 to provide financial assistance grants to states for cross-boundary hazardous fuels reduction projects. Reduces the authorization of appropriations for hazardous fuel reduction activities to $660 million annually through FY2023. Directs the Secretary to prioritize hazardous fuels funding for projects within the WUI. **(§8401, §8402, §8625)**
Authorizes up to $760 million annually in appropriations for hazardous fuel reduction activities on federal and nonfederal land and specifies that at least 50% of the funds should be allocated to projects on federal lands within the WUI. **(16 U.S.C. 6511, 6513, 6518)**	Further directs the Secretary to use any excess funds to support cross-boundary hazardous fuel reduction projects using existing authorities to cooperate or provide technical and financial assistance to states and authorizes the Secretary to allocate some of the excess funds for GNA projects. **(§8332)**	
Federal Forest Management		
National Forest System (NFS) Insect and Disease Treatment Area Designation and National Environmental Policy Act (NEPA) Provisions		
Authorizes the Secretary, upon request from the Governor, to designate landscape-scale **insect and disease treatment areas** on at least one national forest within the state. Designated areas must be experiencing substantially increased tree mortality or dieback due to insect or disease infestations. Authorizes the use of procedures intended to expedite the environmental analysis, administrative review, and judicial review for specified priority forest health	Adds invasive vegetation to the definition of a forest that is experiencing declining forest health, adds hazardous fuels reduction projects as a priority project category, and permanently authorizes the use of the procedures intended to expedite priority projects. **(§8107(b), §8109)**	Removes the authorization of appropriations for the insect and disease treatment areas. **(§8408)**

Current Law/Policy	House-Passed Bill (H.R. 2)	Senate-Passed Bill (H.R. 2)
projects within designated areas through FY2018. Authorizes appropriations up to $200 million annually through FY2024. The program has never received appropriations although the program has been implemented using other authorized funding sources. **(16 U.S.C. 6591a)**		
Categorically excludes (CE) priority projects from the requirements to produce an environmental assessment or environmental impact statement under the National Environmental Policy Act (NEPA, P.L. 91-109) if the project was: developed through a collaborative process; maximizes the retention of old-growth and large trees to the extent practicable; considers best available science; is located within designated insect and disease treatment areas and either the WUI or in areas classified as Condition Class 2 or 3 in Fire Regime groups I, II, or III; and involves less than 3,000 acres. **(16 U.S.C. 6591a-6591b)**	Expands the availability of the NEPA categorical exclusion (CE) to projects up to 6,000 acres and to projects located in areas classified as Condition Class 2 or 3 in Fire Regimes IV and V. **(§8107(b)-(c), §8321)**	Requires the Secretary to apply the extraordinary circumstances procedures under 36 C.F.R. Part 220.6 when using the insect and disease treatment CE. (**§8409**, see also **§8611** below)
NEPA and Endangered Species Act (ESA, P.L. 93-205) Provisions		
No comparable provision.	Defines relevant terms and specifies that the Secretary concerned refers to the Secretary of Agriculture for NFS lands or the Secretary of the Interior for the public lands. **(§8301)**	No comparable provision.
No comparable provision.	Excludes from the authorities established in the subtitle NFS or public lands that are designated wilderness areas, inventoried roadless areas except under specific conditions, or lands on which timber harvesting is prohibited by law. **(§8302)**	No comparable provision.
The Endangered Species Act (ESA, P.L. 93-205) requires consultation with the Secretary of the Interior to determine if a federal action may adversely impact a species - or its habitat -listed as endangered or threatened. **(16 U.S.C. 1536)**	Provides for an expedited ESA consultation for forest management activities carried out under this subtitle on NFS or public lands or, if the Secretary concerned determines that the activity is not likely to adversely affect a listed species or designated critical habitat, removes the requirement for consultation. **(§8303)**	No comparable provision.
No comparable provision.	Authorizes the Secretary to choose which categorical exclusion (CE) to use if a forest management activity on NFS or public lands qualifies for multiple CEs under this subtitle. **(§8304)**	No comparable provision.

Table 11. (Continued)

Current Law/Policy	House-Passed Bill (H.R. 2)	Senate-Passed Bill (H.R. 2)
No comparable provision.	Establishes a CE for projects up to 6,000 acres and for any combination of addressing an insect or disease infestation; reducing hazardous fuel loads; protecting a municipal water source; maintaining, enhancing, or modifying critical habitat to protect it from catastrophic disturbances; or increasing water yield on NFS or public lands. **(§8311)**	No comparable provision.
No comparable provision.	Establishes a CE for projects to prevent wildfire as a result of a catastrophic event or to use and generate revenue from the sale of forest products impacted by a catastrophic event on NFS or public lands, subject to a maximum project size of 6,000 acres and a requirement to prepare a reforestation plan. **(§8312)**	No comparable provision.
No comparable provision.	Establishes a CE for projects up to 6,000 acres to improve, enhance, or create early successional forests for wildlife habitat improvement and other purposes on NFS or public lands. Projects should maximize production and regeneration of priority species. **(§8313)**	No comparable provision.
No comparable provision.	Establishes a CE for projects to remove hazardous trees to protect public health or safety, water supply, or public infrastructure on NFS or public lands. **(§8314)**	No comparable provision.
No comparable provision.	Establishes a CE for forest restoration or improvement projects up to 6,000 acres to reduce the risk of wildfire on NFS or public lands, including the removal of specified vegetation, including conifer trees, through livestock grazing, prescribed burns, and mechanical treatments; performance of hazardous fuels management; creation of fuel and fire breaks; modification of fences for livestock grazing; installation of erosion control devices; construction and maintenance of livestock grazing infrastructure; various specified soil treatments; and use of	No comparable provision.

Current Law/Policy	House-Passed Bill (H.R. 2)	Senate-Passed Bill (H.R. 2)
	herbicides in accordance with applicable land and resource management plan and agency procedures. **(§8315)**	
No comparable provision.	Establishes a CE for projects up to 6,000 acres to improve forest resiliency, reduce hazardous fuels, or improve wildlife and aquatic habitat on NFS or public lands, including timber, salvage, and regeneration harvests; prescribed burning; stream restoration and erosion control; and road and trail decommissioning activities. Projects may include permanent roads up to three miles or temporary roads for up to three years. **(§8316)**	No comparable provision.
No comparable provision.	Establishes a CE for projects on NFS lands to construct, reconstruct, or decommission NFS roads up to three miles; reclassify or add NFS roads; reconstruct, rehabilitate, or decommission bridges; remove dams; or maintain facilities through the use of pesticides according to federal and state requirements. **(§8317)**	No comparable provision.
No comparable provision.	Establishes a CE for projects to operate, maintain, modify, reconstruct, or decommission existing developed recreation sites on NFS lands, including activities related to facility and site maintenance and road and trail construction, reconstruction, maintenance or decommissioning, subject to a maximum of three miles for permanent roads or three years for temporary roads. **(§8318)**	No comparable provision.
No comparable provision.	Establishes a CE for projects on NFS lands to construct, reconstruct, maintain, decommission, relocate, or dispose of an administrative site. Projects may include road and trail construction, reconstruction, or maintenance activities, subject to a maximum of three miles for permanent roads or three years for temporary roads. **(§8319)**	No comparable provision.
No comparable provision.	Establishes a CE for projects on NFS lands to issue new special use authorizations or renew or modify existing or expired special use authorizations for the use or	No comparable provision.

Table 11. (Continued)

Current Law/Policy	House-Passed Bill (H.R. 2)	Senate-Passed Bill (H.R. 2)
	occupancy of NFS lands under certain specified conditions. Specifies that the Secretary of Agriculture is not required to prepare a project file for such actions. **(§8320)**	
No comparable provision.	No comparable provision.	Directs the Secretary of Agriculture, for NFS lands, and the Secretary of the Interior, for the public lands managed by the Bureau of Land Management (BLM), to establish a CE for specified projects of up to 3,000 acres to protect, restore, or improve habitat for **greater sage-grouse and/or mule deer habitat** within one year of enactment. Projects must protect, restore, or improve habitat for either species, or concurrently for both species if the project is located in both mule deer and sage- grouse habitat. Projects must be consistent with the existing resource management plan and may not occur in designated wilderness areas, inventoried roadless areas, or any area where the removal of vegetation is restricted or prohibited. Projects may not include any new permanent roads, but may repair existing permanent roads. Temporary roads shall be decommissioned within three years of project completion, or when no longer needed. On NFS lands, projects may only occur within designated *insect and disease treatment areas* (see above section) and the Secretary of Agriculture is required to apply the extraordinary circumstances procedures under 36 C.F.R. Part 220.6 when using the CE. On public lands, the Secretary of the Interior is required to apply the extraordinary circumstances procedures under 43 C.F.R. Part 46.215 when using the CE. **(§8601, §8611)**

Current Law/Policy	House-Passed Bill (H.R. 2)	Senate-Passed Bill (H.R. 2)
No comparable provision.	Prohibits the Forest Service from considering certain criteria when considering if extraordinary circumstances exist that would potentially require further review and documentation under NEPA than would normally be required under a CE, such as wilderness designations, sensitive species, cumulative impacts, threatened or endangered species, or critical habitat. Eliminates the requirements to prepare an environmental impact statement for activities that would substantially alter a potential wilderness area. Directs the Forest Service to initiate rulemaking to implement these procedures within 60 days of enactment and issue final regulations within 120 days of enactment. **(§8503)**	No comparable provision.
No comparable provision.	Requires the Secretary of Agriculture or the Secretary of the Interior to consider only the **proposed action and no-action alternative** while preparing an environmental assessment pursuant to NEPA for a forest management activity that is: developed through a collaborative process; proposed by a RAC; on lands identified as suitable for timber production; within areas designated as insect and disease treatment areas under HFRA; or covered by a community wildfire protection plan. **(§8335)**	No comparable provision.
No comparable provision.	Requires the Secretary of Agriculture or the Secretary of the Interior to complete the environmental assessment for a **salvage operation** or reforestation activity within 60 days after the conclusion of a catastrophic event with specified time frames for public scoping, comments, and objections. Prohibits federal courts from issuing restraining orders or injunctions for any salvage operation or reforestation activity in response to a large-scale catastrophic event. **(§8334)**	No comparable provision.

Table 11. (Continued)

Current Law/Policy	House-Passed Bill (H.R. 2)	Senate-Passed Bill (H.R. 2)
No comparable provision.	Directs any court reviewing a forest management activity as an agency action to balance the short- and long-term effects of undertaking and not undertaking the action when considering a request for an injunction. **(§8336)**	No comparable provision.
Secure Rural Schools and Community Self-Determination Act of 2000 Amendments		
The **Secure Rural Schools and Community Self- Determination Act of 2000** (SRS, P.L. 106-393), as amended, requires that 50% of the funds authorized by Title II of SRS are used on (1) road maintenance, decommissioning, or obliteration or (2) stream or watershed restoration projects. **(16 U.S.C. 7124(f))**	Changes the requirements to provide that 50% of the funds are to be used on timber or forest product sales, fire risk reduction, water supply, or forest stewardship projects. **(§8201)**	No comparable provision.
Establishes local **Resource Advisory Committees** (RACs) to coordinate, review, and recommend Title II projects to the Secretary to implement on NFS lands through FY2018 and specifies that RACs shall consist of 15 members, with five members representing a balance of specified community interests. Members must reside within the state in which the RAC has jurisdiction. **(16 U.S.C. 7125)**	Extends the authorization for RACs through FY2023 and reduces the membership requirement to nine members, with three members representing the specified community interests. Restricts membership to the county or adjacent counties within the RAC jurisdiction. Authorizes the Secretary to designate an appointee to perform certain functions. **(§8202)**	No comparable provision.
No comparable provision.	Adds a new Section 209 to SRS, establishing a program for 10 select RACs to retain and use the revenues generated by projects they propose, through FY2023. **(§8203)**	No comparable provision.
Tribal Forestry Provisions		
Authorizes the Secretary concerned to enter into an agreement with federally recognized Indian tribes to implement forest or rangeland projects on tribal lands or on federal lands adjacent to tribal lands. **(25 U.S.C. 3115a(b))**	Requires the Secretary concerned to respond to a tribal request within 120 days and, if the project is accepted, requires the project analysis to be completed within two years. **(§8401)**	No comparable provision.
No comparable provision.	Authorizes the Secretary concerned and federally recognized Indian tribes, on a demonstration basis, to enter into contracts to allow tribes to perform administrative, management, and other functions of the Tribal Forest Protection Act. **(§8402)**	No comparable provision.

Current Law/Policy	House-Passed Bill (H.R. 2)	Senate-Passed Bill (H.R. 2)
NFS Land Conveyances, Exchanges, and Leases		
Establishes the Forest Service **Facility Realignment and Enhancement** program to authorize the conveyance of administrative sites or up to 10 undeveloped parcels of up to 40 acres of NFS land. Authorization expired FY2016. **(16 U.S.C. 580d note)**	No comparable provision.	Reauthorizes the program from FY2019 through FY2023. **(§8504)**
No comparable provision.	No comparable provision.	Authorizes the Secretary to **lease administrative sites** on up to ten isolated, undeveloped parcels of up to 40 acres per fiscal year, through FY2023. Requires the Secretary to consult with local and state government officials and provide public notice of the proposed lease, and to provide the local or county government the right of first refusal on the lease. The lease must be for market value, but may be paid in cash or in-kind considerations. Authorizes the Secretary to retain any cash consideration and use for other leases or management of administrative sites. Excludes areas such as designated wilderness and national monuments, among others. Requires the Secretary to submit a list of anticipated and executed leases to Congress annually. **(§8623)**
Authorizes the Secretary to sell, exchange, or interchange NFS lands for lands of equal value or cash payment and to dispose of **small tracts** of NFS land, through sale or exchange, of up to $150,000 in value, to improve management efficiencies where NFS lands are interspersed with nonfederal mineral rights owners (40 acres maximum), relieve encroachments due to erroneous surveys (10 acres maximum), or dispose of unneeded federal rights-of-way surrounded by nonfederal lands (no specified acreage limitation). **(16 U.S.C. 521d and 521e)**	No comparable provision.	Increases the maximum value of lands eligible for disposal to $500,000. Adds additional purposes for the Secretary to dispose of NFS lands: parcels which are isolated, inaccessible, or have lost NFS character (40 acres maximum), relieve encroachments due to unintentionally erroneous surveys (10 acres maximum), or parcels which are used as a cemetery, landfill, or for sewage treatment under a special use authorization (no maximum specified). Specifies that proceeds are to be deposited into the Sisk Fund (as established by 16 U.S.C. 484a) and used for acquisition of land for administrative sites in the state

Table 11. (Continued)

Current Law/Policy	House-Passed Bill (H.R. 2)	Senate-Passed Bill (H.R. 2)
		from which the amounts were derived, for acquisitions to enhance recreational access, or to reimburse costs incurred by other small tract sales. **(§8621)**
No comparable provision.	Authorizes the Secretary, through the Chief of the Forest Service, to convey 1,520 acres of NFS land to the Village of Santa Clara, NM, upon request, and at fair market value. Authorizes the Secretary to charge cost recovery fees for the conveyance and to collect payment in periodic installments. **(§8506)**	No comparable provision.
No comparable provision.	Authorizes the Secretary to convey 3.61 acres of NFS land (the West Fork Fire Station Conveyance Parcel), upon request from Dolores County, CO, for specified purposes, subject to a reversionary clause, and for no consideration. **(§8510)**.	No comparable provision.
Authorizes the Secretary to exchange NFS lands for nonfederal land of equal value and in the same state, if it serves the public interest. Cash equalization payments of up to 25% are authorized if the land values are not equal. **(43 U.S.C. 1716(b))**	No comparable provision.	Authorizes the Secretary to sell or exchange 30 tracts of NFS lands in Georgia, totaling 3,841 acres and identified on maps, for disposal at market value. Authorizes cash equalization payment above 25% and specifies that proceeds are to be used for acquisition of NFS land in the state. **(§8626)**
No comparable provision.	No comparable provision.	Authorizes the conveyance of specified NFS land in the Kisatchie National Forest in Louisiana. Requires the Secretary to first offer the sale to the Collins Camp Properties and authorizes the Secretary to collect cost-recovery fees from the Collins Camp Properties. Requires the Collins Camp Properties to administer any existing special use authorizations according to the terms of the permit unless the permit holder agrees to relinquish rights. **(§8629)**
No comparable provision.	No comparable provision.	Directs the Secretary to sell, at appraised value, 8.75 acres of land (including improvements) administered by NRCS to the Riverside Corona Resource

Current Law/Policy	House-Passed Bill (H.R. 2)	Senate-Passed Bill (H.R. 2)
		Conservation District in CA. Specifies that the Secretary is not required to take any remediation or abatement efforts but is required to meet the disclosure requirements under the Comprehensive Environmental Response, Compensation, and Liability Act of 1980 and the Solid Waste Disposal Act for hazardous substances, pollutants, or contaminants. Further authorizes the Secretary to enter into non-competitive leases, contracts, and cooperative agreements with the Conservation District. **(§8630)**
No comparable provision.	No comparable provision.	Directs the Secretary to convey 150 acres of NFS land in Mississippi to the Scenic Rivers Development Alliance, upon their request, for cash consideration at fair market value. Authorizes the Secretary to collect cost recovery fees and retain the sale proceeds. **(§8633)**
Miscellaneous NFS-specific Provisions		
Establishes the **Collaborative Forest Landscape Restoration Program** (CFLRP) to select and fund the implementation of collaboratively-developed restoration projects for priority forest landscapes. The priority forest landscapes must be at least 50,000 acres and consist primarily of NFS lands, but may include other federal, state, tribal, or private land within the project area. Only 10 proposals may be selected in any given fiscal year, and the Secretary has the discretion to limit the number of proposals selected based on funding availability. Once selected, Requires the publication of an annual accomplishments report and submission of 5-year status reports to specified congressional committees. Establishes a fund for to pay for up to 50% of the costs to implement and monitor projects on selected proposals and authorizes up to $40 million in annual appropriations to the fund through FY2019.	Reauthorizes the program through FY2023 at the current funding level and authorizes the Secretary to fund proposals for more than 10 fiscal years **(§8509)**.	Reauthorizes $80 million annually through FY2023 and adds the House and Senate Committees on Agriculture as recipients of the 5-year program status reports. **(§8631)**

Table 11. (Continued)

Current Law/Policy	House-Passed Bill (H.R. 2)	Senate-Passed Bill (H.R. 2)
Appropriations to the fund may not be used on project planning and may only fund up to $4 million per proposal per year for up to 10 years. The program received $40 million annually in appropriations between FY2014 and FY2018 and 23 proposals have been selected and funded since the program was established in FY2010. **(16 U.S.C. 7301-7304)**		
No comparable provision.	No comparable provision.	Authorizes the Secretary to establish a **water source protection program** on NFS land. Watershed restoration or protection projects proposed under a water source management plan must be consistent with the forest plan and any required environmental analyses may be conducted through a single analysis. Authorizes the Secretary to accept cash or in-kind donations from specified non-federal partners. Authorizes $10 million in annual appropriations through FY2023. **(§8404)**
No comparable provision.	No comparable provision.	Requires the Secretary to establish a **Watershed Condition Framework** for NFS land. Under the framework, the Secretary is required to identify up to 5 priority watersheds in each national forest and develop an action plan, in coordination with interested nonfederal landowners and other governments, to prioritize protection and restoration activities. **(§8405)**
No comparable provision.	Establishes a pilot program through December 21, 2027, for owners or operators of rights-of-way on NFS land to develop, and implement vegetation management plans and pay for and perform projects on specified NFS lands within and up to 75 feet from the right-of-way. Authorizes the Secretary to waive or modify provisions of the Federal Acquisition Regulation to provide non-competitive contracts to implement the pilot program.	Similar to the House bill, except authorizes the pilot program through FY2023. **(§8632)**.

Current Law/Policy	House-Passed Bill (H.R. 2)	Senate-Passed Bill (H.R. 2)
	Authorizes the Secretary to contribute funds to approved projects if determined to be in the public interest, and to retain any proceeds from the pilot for program costs. **(§8502)**	
Authorizes the Secretary to issue special use authorizations for the use and occupancy of NFS lands and charge cost recovery fees for processing and monitoring applications and an annual land use rental fee based on fair market value. Directs the Secretary of the Interior to update the fair market value rental fee schedule by August 8, 2006 and directs the Secretary of Agriculture to adopt the same revised fee schedule for NFS lands. **(43 U.S.C. 1761, 42 U.S.C. 15925)**	Directs the Secretary of Agriculture to promulgate regulations revising the process to issue special use authorizations for communications sites or rights-of-ways on NFS lands within 1 year of enactment. Specifies that the new process must be streamlined, uniform, and standardized across the NFS to the extent practicable; that applications are to be considered and granted on a competitively neutral, technology neutral, and non- discriminatory basis; lease terms must be a minimum of 15 years and shall renew automatically unless revoked for good cause; and a fee structure based on the cost of processing and monitoring applications and approvals. **(§8507)**	No comparable provision.
No comparable provision.	Directs the Secretary to make vacant grazing allotments on NFS lands available to holders of existing grazing permits, under certain conditions. **(§8338)**	No comparable provision.
No comparable provision.	No comparable provision.	Requires the Chief of the Forest Service to issue a report on the extent to which prairie dogs are present in grazing allotments on NFS lands within 180 days of enactment and to take appropriate action based on the report findings. **(§8634)**
Authorizes the Secretary, through the Chief of the Forest Service, to participate in the Agriculture Conservation Experienced Services Program to provide technical services for conservation-related programs on NFS lands. **(16 U.S.C. 3851a)**	No comparable provision.	Terminates the authority at the end of FY2023. **(§8622)**
Export prohibition. Prohibits the foreign export of unprocessed logs from the contiguous federal lands west of the 100th Meridian unless the Secretary concerned determines through a rulemaking process that certain grades or species of lumber are surplus to domestic needs. **(16 U.S.C. 620a)**	Directs the Secretary to undertake a rulemaking to issue a determination exempting unprocessed dead and dying trees on NFS lands in California from the export prohibition for 10 years. **(§8333)**	No comparable provision.

Table 11. (Continued)

Current Law/Policy	House-Passed Bill (H.R. 2)	Senate-Passed Bill (H.R. 2)
No comparable provision.	Creates a pilot research program on the Lincoln, Cibola, and Gila National Forests to study the effectiveness of silvicultural management technique to address natural resource concerns. Projects in the pilot program are subject to the refusal of the county government in which the project is located. Establishes an arbitration program as an alternative dispute resolution process for challenges to projects in the pilot program. **(§8339)**	No comparable provision.
No comparable provision.	Exempts all NFS land in Alaska from the Forest Service Roadless Area Conservation Rule as published in 66 *Federal Register* 9, January 12, 2001. **(§8337)**	No comparable provision.
No comparable provision.	No comparable provision.	Designates the Upper Bald River **Wilderness** and adds land to the Big Frog, Little Frog, Sampson Mountain, Big Laurel Branch, and Joyce Kilmer-Slickrock Wilderness areas on NFS lands in Tennessee. **(§8627)**
No comparable provision.	No comparable provision.	Adds land to the Rough Mountain and Rich Hole **Wilderness** areas on the George Washington National Forest in Virginia. **(§8628)**
Miscellaneous Provisions Affecting NFS and BLM lands		
Authorizes Forest Service and BLM to enter into **stewardship end- result contracts** (stewardship contracts) with entities to combine timber sale contracts and service contracts to achieve specified land management goals. Revenue generated through a stewardship contract may be retained by the agency and is not considered monies received from the NFS, making those receipts exempt from various revenue-sharing laws. Contracts may be awarded on a best-value basis. **(16 U.S.C. 6591c)**	Establishes that receipts from Stewardship Contracting projects shall be considered monies received from the NFS, making those receipts subject to any applicable revenue-sharing laws. **(§8107(d))**	No comparable provision.
Permanently authorizes the Forest Service and BLM to enter into **Good Neighbor Agreements** (GNAs) with states to perform authorized forest restoration activities on NFS or public lands and non-federal land. **(16 U.S.C. 2113a)**	Expands the availability of GNAs to include federally recognized Indian tribes and county governments. **(§8331)**	Similar to the House bill, except specifies that proceeds from GNAs are not considered monies received from the NFS, and thus not subject to any applicable revenue-sharing laws. **(§8624)**

Current Law/Policy	House-Passed Bill (H.R. 2)	Senate-Passed Bill (H.R. 2)
No comparable provision.	States that nothing in this title or any amendments made to the title would impact the availability of funds or other resources for wildfire suppression. **(§8504)**	No comparable provision.
The Wildfire Suppression Funding and Forest Management Activities Act, enacted as Title I of Division O of the FY2018 Consolidated Appropriations Act (P.L. 115-141), establishes a new mechanism for funding federal wildfire suppression activities.	Makes technical amendments. **(§8505)**	No comparable provision.
No comparable provision.	Directs the Secretary of Agriculture and Secretary of the Interior to submit annual reports to Congress on specified wildfire and forest management metrics. **(§8508)**	No comparable provision.

Table 12. Energy

Current Law/Policy	House-Passed Bill (H.R. 2)	Senate-Passed Bill (H.R.2)
Farm Security and Rural Investment Act of 2002 (Bio-Energy Provisions)		
Definitions		
Definition of *biobased product.* A commercial or industrial product that is composed of biological products or an intermediate ingredient or feedstock. **(7 U.S.C. 8101(4))**	Same as current law. **(§9001)**	Expands the term to include renewable chemicals. **(§9101)**
Definition of *biorefinery.* A facility (including equipment and processes) that converts renewable biomass into biofuels and biobased products, and may produce electricity. **(7 U.S.C. 8101(7))**	Same as current law. **(§9001)**	Expands the term to include renewable biomass and the conversion of an intermediate ingredient or feedstock of renewable biomass into biofuels, renewable chemicals, or biobased products. **(§9101)**
Definition of *renewable energy system.* A system that produces useable energy from a renewable energy source and may include distribution components necessary to move energy produced by the system to an initial point of sale. A renewable energy system may not include a mechanism for dispensing energy at retail. **(7 U.S.C. 8101(16))**	Same as current law. **(§9001)**	Changes the definition to mean a system that produces useable energy from a renewable source, including the distribution components necessary to move energy produced by the system to the initial point of sale, and other components and ancillary infrastructure such as a storage system. **(§9101)**
Authorized Programs		
Rural Energy Savings Program. Extends program through FY2018. Provides loans to rural families and small businesses to implement durable cost-effective energy efficiency measures.	Adds two requirements to the loans for eligible entities section—eligibility for other loans and accounting. Increases the loan interest to not exceed 5 percent.	Extends the program through FY2023. Expands the definition of energy efficiency measures to include cost-effective on- or off-grid renewable energy or energy storage systems.

Table 12. (Continued)

Current Law/Policy	House-Passed Bill (H.R. 2)	Senate-Passed Bill (H.R.2)
Authorized to be appropriated $75 million annually for FY2014- FY2018. **(7 U.S.C. 8107a)**	Authorizes to be appropriated $75 million annually for FY2019-FY2023. **(§6401)**	Amends the program so that any debt a borrower may incur under the program cannot be applied to eligibility for loans for programs authorized by the Rural Electrification Act of 1936. Requires the Secretary to streamline accounting requirements for borrowers of the program while simultaneously maintaining adequate assurance of loan repayment. Increases the interest limits for loans to not exceed 6%. Requires the Secretary to publish annually the number of applications received for the program, the number of loans made, and the recipients of the loans made. Authorizes to be appropriated $75 million annually through FY2023. **(§6302)**
Biobased Markets Program. Extends program through FY2018. Requires federal agencies to purchase products with maximum biobased content (explicitly including forest products) subject to availability, flexibility, and performance standards. Minimum biobased content standards applied to federal contracts on case-by- case basis. Continued voluntary labeling. Authorized mandatory funding of $3 million annually for FY2014-FY2018 for biobased products testing and labeling. Authorized to be appropriated $2 million annually for FY2014- FY2018. **(7 U.S.C. 8102)**	Extends program through FY2023. Authorizes to be appropriated $2 million annually for FY2014-FY2023. No mandatory funding is authorized. Prohibits federal agencies from placing limitations on the procurement of wood and wood-based products. **(§6402)**	Extends the program through FY2023, and assigns it to the rural development mission area. Requires the Secretary to update the criteria for determining which renewable chemicals are eligible to receive a "USDA Certified Biobased Product" label. Requires the Secretary and the Secretary of Commerce to develop North American Industry Classification System (NAICS) codes for both renewable chemical manufacturers and biobased product manufacturers. Adds an education and outreach component to the program for stakeholders, and establishes an expedited approval process for products to be determined eligible for the procurement program and to receive a biobased product label. Prohibits an agency from establishing procurement guidelines for biobased products that are more restrictive than what the Secretary has established. Provides mandatory funding of $3 million annually through FY2023,

Current Law/Policy	House-Passed Bill (H.R. 2)	Senate-Passed Bill (H.R.2)
		and authorizes to be appropriated $3 million annually through FY2023. **(§9102)**
Biorefinery, Renewable Chemical, and Biobased Product Manufacturing Assistance Program. Extends program through FY2018. Assists in development of new and emerging technologies for advanced biofuels, renewable chemicals, and biobased products by providing loan guarantees—not to exceed 80% of project costs— for development, construction, and/or retrofitting of commercial- scale biorefineries. Authorizes mandatory funding of $100 million in FY2014 and $50 million each for FY2015 and FY2016. Authorizes to be appropriated $75 million annually for FY2014-FY2018. **(7 U.S.C. 8103)**	Extends program through FY2023. Amends the definition of eligible technology to include a technology that is being adopted in a viable commercial-scale operation of a biorefinery that produced advanced biofuel *or* a technology that has been demonstrated to have technical and economic potential for commercial application in a biorefinery that produces advanced biofuel. Authorizes to be appropriated $75 million annually for FY2019-FY2023. No mandatory funding is authorized. **(§6403)**	Extends the program through FY2023. Expands the definition of eligible technology to include technologies that produce 1or more of the following, or a combination thereof: an advanced biofuel, a renewable chemical, or a biobased product. Provides mandatory funding of $100 million for FY2019 and $50 million for FY2020. Authorizes to be appropriated $75 million annually through FY2023. **(§9103)**
Repowering Assistance Program. Extends program through FY2018. Provides funds to replace the use of fossil fuels used to produce heat or power to operate biorefineries in existence as of the 2008 farm bill enactment date. Authorizes mandatory funding of $12 million for FY2014, available until expended. Authorizes to be appropriated $10 million annually for FY2014- FY2018. **(7 U.S.C. 8104)**	Extends program through FY2023. Authorizes to be appropriated $10 million annually for FY2019-FY2023. No mandatory funding is authorized. **(§6404)**	Repeals the program. **(§9104)**
Bioenergy Program for Advanced Biofuels. Extends program through FY2018. Provides payments to producers to support and expand production of advanced biofuels by entering into contracts to pay producers for production of eligible advanced biofuels. Provides mandatory funding of $15 million annually for FY2014- FY2018. Authorizes to be appropriated $20 million annually (FY20014-FY2018) **(7 U.S.C. 8105)**	Extends program through FY2023. Modifies the equitable distribution portion of the program by limiting the amount of payments for advanced biofuel produced from a single eligible commodity to not exceed one-third of the total program funding available in a fiscal year. Authorizes to be appropriated $50 million annually for FY2019-FY2023. No mandatory funding is authorized. **(§6405)**	Extends program through FY2023. Provides mandatory funding of $15 million annually for FY2019-FY2023. Authorizes to be appropriated $15 million annually for FY2019-FY2023. **(§9105)**
Biodiesel Fuel Education Program. Extends program through FY2018. Awards competitive grants to nonprofit organizations that educate fleet operators and the public on biodiesel benefits. Provides mandatory funding of $1 million annually (FY2008-FY2018). Authorizes to be appropriated $1 million annually for FY2014- FY2018. **(7 U.S.C. 8106)**	Extends program through FY2023. Authorizes to be appropriated $2 million annually for FY2019-FY2023. No mandatory funding is authorized. **(§6406)**	Extends program through FY2023. Authorizes to be appropriated $1 million annually through FY2023. No mandatory funding is authorized. **§9106)**

Table 12. (Continued)

Current Law/Policy	House-Passed Bill (H.R. 2)	Senate-Passed Bill (H.R.2)
Rural Energy for America Program. Authorization does not expire. Provides grants to conduct energy audits and for renewable energy development assistance and provides loan guarantees and grants for energy efficiency improvement projects and renewable energy systems. Provides mandatory funds of $50 million in FY2014 and each fiscal year thereafter. Authorizes to be appropriated $20 million annually for FY2014-FY2018. **(7 U.S.C. 8107)**	Extends program through FY2023. Limits mandatory funding to FY2014-FY2018. Authorizes to be appropriated $20 million annually for FY2014-FY2023. No mandatory funding is authorized for FY2019-FY2023. Provides a categorical exclusion for electric generating facilities with a capacity of 10 megawatts or less in the program from having to prepare an environmental assessments or an environmental impact statement. **(§6407)**	Extends program through FY2023. Expands the program to provide financial assistance for the purchase and installation of efficient energy equipment or systems. Authorizes to be appropriated $50 million annually through FY2023. Retains mandatory funding of $50 million for FY2014 and each FY thereafter. **(§9107)**
Biomass Research and Development Initiative. Extends program through FY2018. Requires the Secretaries of Agriculture and Energy to coordinate research, development, and demonstration of technologies and processes for biofuels and biobased products. **(7 U.S.C. 8108)**	Extends program through FY2023. Authorizes to be appropriated $20 million annually for FY2019-FY2023. No mandatory funding is authorized. **(§7509)**	Extends program through FY2023. Amends the definition of biobased product to include carbon dioxide. Requires the Initiative's technical advisory committee to consist of an individual with expertise in carbon capture, utilization, and storage. Expands the objectives and technical areas of the Initiative to include carbon dioxide utilization and sequestration. Provides mandatory funding of $3 million annually for FY2019-FY2023. Authorizes to be appropriated $20 million annually through FY2023. **(§7409)**
Rural Energy Self-Sufficiency Initiative. Not included in the 2014 farm bill—funding authority expired after FY2013. Established in the 2008 farm bill to provide financial assistance to increase the energy self-sufficiency of such communities. **(7 U.S.C. 8109)**	Repeals the initiative. **(§6408)**	Repeals the initiative. **(§9108)**
Feedstock Flexibility Program. Extends program through FY2018. Allows the CCC to purchase surplus sugar from processors for resale to ethanol producers for fuel ethanol. **(7 U.S.C. 8110)**	Extends program through FY2023. **(§6409)**	Extends the program through FY2023. **(§9109)**
Biomass Crop Assistance Program. Extends program through FY2018. Provides payments to owners and operators of agricultural land and nonindustrial private forest land that establish, produce, and deliver biomass feedstocks to eligible processing plants.	Extends program through FY2023. Authorizes to be appropriated $25 million annually for FY2019-FY2023. No mandatory funding is authorized. **(§6410)**	Extends the program through FY2023. Amends the definition of eligible material to include algae. Amends the definition of eligible material to not exclude oilseeds.

Current Law/Policy	House-Passed Bill (H.R. 2)	Senate-Passed Bill (H.R.2)
Modifies enrolled land eligibility requirements, limits one-time establishment payments, reduces the matching payment rate, and stipulates how much funding—10-50%—may be used for collection, harvest, storage, and transportation. **(7 U.S.C. 8111)**		Expands the collection, harvest, storage and transportation portion of the program to include material harvested for hazardous woody fuel reduction. Removes the relationship to other laws providing for technical assistance funding. Retains mandatory funding of $25 million through FY2023. Authorizes to be appropriated $20 million annually through FY2023. **(§9110)**
No comparable provision.	No comparable provision.	Establishes a Biogas Research and Adoption of Biogas Systems initiative. Requires the Secretary to form an Interagency Biogas Opportunities Task Force to coordinate policies, programs, and research to accelerate biogas research and investments in cost-effective biogas systems. Requires the Secretary to enter into an agreement with the National Renewable Energy Laboratory to conduct a biogas study that examines the barriers and opportunities of biogas systems, among other things. Requires the Secretary to collect and analyze data pertaining to biogas systems to develop markets for biogas and biogas system products. **(§9111)**
No comparable provision.	No comparable provision.	Establishes a Carbon Utilization Education Program under the energy title. The program would provide competitive funding for eligible entities to provide education to the public and biogas producers about the benefits of carbon utilization and sequestration and the opportunities to aggregate multiple sources of organic waste into a single biogas system, respectively. Mandatory funding is provided at $2 million annually through FY2023. Authorizes to be appropriated $2 million annually through FY2023. **(§9113)**

Table 13. Horticulture

Current Law/Policy	House-Passed Bill (H.R. 2)	Senate-Passed Bill (H.R. 2)
Specialty Crop, Organic Agriculture, and Local Foods Programs		
Specialty crop market news. Authorizes support for the collection and dissemination of market news for specialty crops. Authorized appropriations of $9 million annually through FY2018 to remain available until expended. **(7 U.S.C. 1622b(b))**	Reauthorizes program and funding levels through FY2023. **(§9001)**	Similar to House bill. **(§10101)**
Farmers' Market and Local Food Promotion Program; Value-Added Producer Grants. Authorizes the promotion of (1) farmers' markets, community- supported agriculture programs, and other direct producer-to-consumer market opportunities and (2) local and regional food business enterprises. Authorizes CCC funding of $30 million annually (FY2014 through FY2018) and authorized appropriations of $10 million each year (FY2014-FY2018). **(7 U.S.C. 3005)** Provides for Agricultural Product Market Development Grants supporting agricultural producers that add value to commodities, and support planning and business development projects. Authorizes $40 million annually for FY2008- FY2018, subject to annual appropriations, in addition to $63 million in mandatory spending to remain available until expended. **(7 U.S.C. 1632a(b)(7))**	Amends 7 U.S.C. 3005(g)(3) only, which authorizes discretionary appropriations for these programs. Reorganizes the paragraph and authorizes appropriations of $30 million annually for FY2019-FY2023. Does not make changes to the mandatory funding Section in (g)(1) and does not add any mandatory funding beyond FY2018. **(§9002)** Does not reauthorizes mandatory funding for Value-Added Producer Grants, but instead increases discretionary funding to $50 million annually FY2019-FY2023. **(§6501)**	Combines and expands the existing Farmers' Market and Local Food Promotion Program (7 U.S.C. 3005) and the Value-Added Agricultural Product Market Development Grants (7 U.S.C. 1632a(b)(7))to create a new "Local Agriculture Market Program" with expanded mandatory funding and administrative functions. Expanded mission would also support regional partnerships, developmental grants, and cooperative extension support, while also simplifying application and reporting requirements, and requiring program evaluation. Provides mandatory funding of $60 million for FY2019 and each year thereafter, and authorized appropriations of $20 million for FY2019 and each year thereafter. Funds would be allocated as follows: 10% for regional partnerships, 35% for producer grants, 47% for development grants for other eligible entities, and 8% for administrative expenses. Funding would also cover a pilot program (Agricultural Marketing Resource Center). **(§10102)**
Food safety education initiatives. Amends the Agricultural Research, Extension, and Education Reform Act of 1998 (P.L. 105-185) to implement a program to educate fresh produce industry personnel and consumers on ways to reduce pathogens in fresh produce. Authorizes appropriations of $1 million annually to remain available until expended. **(7 U.S.C. 7655a(c))**	Reauthorizes program and funding levels through FY2023. **(§9003)**	Similar to House bill. **(§10106)**.

Current Law/Policy	House-Passed Bill (H.R. 2)	Senate-Passed Bill (H.R. 2)
Block grants to states. The Specialty Crops Competitiveness Act of 2004 (P.L. 108-465), as amended, authorizes block grants to states to support projects in marketing, research, pest management, and food safety, among other purposes. Authorizes CCC funding of $72.5 million annually (FY2014-FY2017) and $85 million for FY2018 and each fiscal year thereafter. Funding for multi- state project grants shall remain available until expended, rising from 1 million (FY2014) to $5 million (FY2018). **(7 U.S.C. 1621 note)**	Reauthorizes program and funding levels through FY2023. Requires USDA enter into a cooperative agreement to conduct program evaluation with state government and industry stakeholders **(§9004)**	Reauthorizes program and funding levels through FY2023, including funding for approved multistate projects. Requires that performance measures be developed by the State agriculture departments for evaluation purposes, as well as best practices to enhance the competitiveness of specialty crops across multiple commodities, types of production, and geographic locations. Requires an audit of the program. Requires USDA provide guidance to States regarding best practices and national and regional priorities. **(§10107)**
National Organic Program (NOP). The Organic Foods Production Act (OFPA) of 1990 authorizes NOP to develop and enforce national standards for organically produced agricultural products. Authorizes the creation of National Organic Standards Board (NOSB) and the creation of the "National List of Approved and Prohibited Substances for Organic Farming and Handling Operations." Authorized appropriations were $15 million annually (FY2014- FY2018). **(7 U.S.C. 6522)** Provides $5 million in CCC funding for technology upgrades. **(7 U.S.C. 6519)** Section 7407(d) of the 2002 farm bill, as amended, requires USDA to collect data under the Organic Production and Market Data Initiatives (ODI), providing $5 million in mandatory CCC funds in FY204 (to remain available until expended). **(7 U.S.C. 5925c)** Section 10606 establishes the National Organic Certification Cost Share Program (NOCCSP) to help producers and handlers of organic products obtain certification. Provides $11.5 million in FY2014, to remain available until expended. **(7 U.S.C. 6523)**	Amends OFPA to include provisions in H.R. 3871 (Organic Farmer and Consumer Protection Act of 2017), including the following: limits the types of operations excluded from NOP certification; requires electronic import documentation; establishes mechanisms for collaborative investigations and enforcement; requires increased documentation; increases accreditation authority of NOP over certifying agents; requires audits of satellite offices; ensures coordination to data; and requires additional reporting. **(§9006(a),(e)-(f))** Reauthorizes NOP appropriations, increasing from $16.5 million (FY2019) to $24 million (FY2023), and provides $5 million for technology upgrades to improve tracking and verification of organic imports (FY2019). **(§9006(g)-(h))** Reauthorizes ODI funds at current levels. **(§9006(i))** Funding for NOCCSP is not reauthorized. Requires USDA to establish procedures for expedited petitions for postharvest handling substances related to food safety pertaining to the NOP's "National List of Approved and Prohibited Substances." **(§9006(b))** Amends the eligibility and consultation requirements of the NOSB. **(§9006(c)-(d))**	Amends OFPA to include limits the types of operations excluded from NOP certification; requires import certification, modernization of tracking and data collection; requires increased documentation and traceability; increases accreditation authority of NOP over certifying agents; requires audits of satellite offices; ensures coordination to data; and requires additional reporting, investigations, and data collection related to organic imports. **(§10104(a)-(d), (f)-(g))** Requires the establishment of an Organic Agricultural Product Imports Interagency Working Group, and submission of an organic trade enforcement interagency coordination report. **(§10104(h))** Reauthorizes NOP appropriations, increasing from $15 million (FY2018) to $24 million (FY2023), and provides $5 million to improve tracking and verification of organic imports (FY2019). **(§10104(i))** Reauthorizes ODI funds to receive $5 million for the period from FY2019 through FY2023. **(§10103)** Reauthorizes mandatory funding for NOCCSP of $11.5 million annually for FY2019 through FY2023, to remain available until expended.

Table 13. (Continued)

Current Law/Policy	House-Passed Bill (H.R. 2)	Senate-Passed Bill (H.R. 2)
		(§10105) Amends the eligibility and consultation requirements of the NOSB. **(§10104(e))**
Pecan marketing orders. Section 8e of the Agricultural Marketing Agreement Act of 1937 requires U.S. import of fruit, vegetable, and specialty crops to meet the same or comparable grade, size, quality, and maturity standards as domestic products covered by federal marketing orders. **(7 U.S.C. 608e–1(a))**	Adds pecans to the list of products with import prohibitions regulating the grade, size, quality, or maturity of certain crops. **(§9202)**	No comparable provision.
Food labeling. The Nutrition Labeling and Education Act of 1990 (P.L. 101-535) amended the Federal Food, Drug, and Cosmetic Act and provides the FDA with the authority to require nutrition labeling on most packaged foods. **(21 U.S.C. 343(q))**	Requires USDA to submit a report to the House and Senate Agriculture Committees examining the effect of a final FDA regulation, "Food Labeling: Revision of the Nutrition and Supplement Facts Labels" (81 *Federal Register* 33742) and whether the nutrition facts panel on the labeling of packaged food regarding "added sugar" should apply for foods with added honey and maple syrup. **(§9203)**	No comparable provision.
Plant Variety Protection Act. Provides legal intellectual property rights protection to breeders of new varieties of plants that are sexually reproduced (by seed) or tuber-propagated. USDA issues Certificates of Protection that protect varieties for 20 years (25 years for vines and trees). **(7 U.S.C. 2401(a), 2402(a), 2541(a)(3), and 2568(a))**	Amends the Plant Variety Protection Act to include certain protections for sexually reproduced varieties. **(§9005)**	Similar to House bill. **(§10108)**
Section 11 Cap. The Commodity Credit Corporation (CCC) is a government-owned financial institution that provides most of the mandatory payments administered by various agencies of USDA. CCC may reimburse other government agencies for administrative services in connection with authorized activities. Total allotments and transfers of CCC funds for these services may not exceed FY1995 levels. This is commonly referred to as the section 11 cap. **(15 U.S.C. 714i)**	No comparable provision.	Excludes funds for technical assistance from the CCC section 11 cap. **(§10110)**

Current Law/Policy	House-Passed Bill (H.R. 2)	Senate-Passed Bill (H.R. 2)
Industrial Hemp		
Legitimacy of industrial hemp research. Allows an institution of higher education or State department of agriculture to grow or cultivate industrial hemp for research purposes, if allowed under the laws of the State in which the institution is located. Establishes a definition for "industrial hemp" to mean "the plant *Cannabis sativa* L. and any part of such plant, whether growing or not, with a delta-9 tetrahydrocannabinol concentration of not more than 0.3 percent on a dry weight basis." **(7 U.S.C. 5940)**	No comparable provision.	Incorporates provisions in S. 2667 (Industrial Hemp Farming Act of 2018). Creates a new "Hemp Production" subtitle under the Agricultural Marketing Act of 1946 (7 U.S.C. § 1621 *et seq.*). The new program expands upon the existing statutory definition of hemp to and to expand eligibility of other producers and groups, including tribes and territories. States or Indian tribes wanting primary regulatory authority over hemp production would be required to implement a "plan" to further monitor and regulate hemp production. State and tribal plans would require grower information collection, procedures for testing, disposal (of hemp grown in violation and the law), and compliance. Authorizes appropriations "such sums as are necessary" for USDA to support and enforce state and tribal plans, specifies requirements regarding the plan approval process, USDA technical assistance to develop plans, and necessary corrective action for plan violations. **(§10111, §10112)** Other provisions regarding hemp are contained in the bill's Crop Insurance title **(§§11101, 11106, 11112, 11120, 11101, 11121)**, Research title **(§§ 7415, 7125, 7401)**, and Miscellaneous title **(§12608)**.
Chemical Regulation and Information Collection		
Pesticide registrations; experimental use permits. FIFRA Section 3 specifies criteria for the registration of a pesticide by EPA, establishes a process for the periodic review of existing pesticide registrations, and authorizes EPA to conditionally grant the registration of a pesticide if it meets certain criteria. FIFRA Section 5 governs the issuance of experimental use permits for pesticides. **(7 U.S.C. 136a, 136c, 136d)** ESA authorizes federal agencies, such as EPA, to consult with the Interior Department's	Amends FIFRA to require EPA to determine that certain agency actions are not likely to jeopardize the survival of a federally listed threatened or endangered species or alter critical habitat in a way that affects the survival and recovery of such species and expressly states that EPA is not required to consult with FWS and NMFS under ESA unless requested by an applicant for a pesticide registration.	No comparable provision.

Table 13. (Continued)

Current Law/Policy	House-Passed Bill (H.R. 2)	Senate-Passed Bill (H.R. 2)
Fish and Wildlife Service (FWS) and the Commerce Department's National Marine Fisheries Service (NMFS) when federal agency actions may likely jeopardize the continued existence of any endangered or threatened species or adversely modify their critical habitat. **(16 U.S.C. 1536)**	Requires EPA to consider certain information when making such a determination and engage in collaboration with other federal agencies. **(§9111, 9112)**	
Administrative review; suspension. FIFRA Section 6 governs the cancellation, change in classification, or suspension of a pesticide registration. **(7 U.S.C. 136d)**	Authorizes EPA to initiate proceedings to cancel a pesticide registration or change a pesticide's classification if the agency determines that the proper use of the registered pesticide jeopardizes the survival of a federally listed species or alters critical habitat in a way that affects the survival and recovery of such species. **(§9113)**	No comparable provision.
Unlawful acts. FIFRA Section 12 specifies unlawful acts that are subject to civil or criminal penalties. **(7 U.S.C. 136j)**	Clarifies that any taking of federally listed species incidental to the lawful use of a pesticide that EPA has determined not to jeopardize the survival of such species or alter their critical habitat shall not be considered unlawful under ESA. **(§9114)**	No comparable provision.
Authority of states. FIFRA Section 24 authorizes a state to register EPA-registered pesticides for additional uses to meet special local needs within the state if EPA had not previously disapproved such uses. **(7 U.S.C. 136v)**	Amends requirements regarding state pesticide registrations and federally listed species considerations. Repeals EPA authority to suspend the authority of a state to register pesticides for not exercising adequate controls. **(§9115)**	No comparable provision.
No comparable provision.	Directs EPA to publish, and revise as appropriate, a work plan and processes for completing determinations on whether the registration of a pesticide would jeopardize the survival of federally listed threatened or endangered species or would alter their critical habitat. **(§9116)**	No comparable provision.
Use and discharges of authorized pesticides. FIFRA Section 3 directs EPA to register pesticides that have a pesticidal effect and, when used in conformance with labeling directions, do not present unreasonable adverse effects on human health or the environment. 9	Amends FIFRA to prohibit EPA or a state from requiring a permit for point source discharges of a pesticide registered under FIFRA into navigable waters except in specific circumstances provided under new CWA Section 402(s).	No comparable provision.

Current Law/Policy	House-Passed Bill (H.R. 2)	Senate-Passed Bill (H.R. 2)
Pesticide registrations govern the sale, distribution, and use of a pesticide. **(7 U.S.C. 136a)** The Clean Water Act (CWA) makes it unlawful to discharge any pollutant into navigable waters unless specifically authorized by a permit, such as a permit for the discharge of a pollutant or group of pollutants from a point source into navigable waters under Section 402. Any person who unlawfully discharges a pollutant is subject to civil/criminal penalties. **(33 U.S.C. 1342)** Pesticide general permits cover most discharges of biological and chemical pesticides into navigable waters.	**(§9117)** Amends the CWA to prohibit EPA or a state from requiring a permit for point source discharges of a pesticide registered under FIFRA into navigable waters. Defines circumstances where a permit would be required (e.g., pesticide applications in violation of FIFRA, stormwater discharges, industrial or treatment works effluents, and certain vessel discharges). **(§9118)**	
Pesticide registration fees reauthorization. FIFRA authorizes EPA to collect fees from pesticide manufacturers for the maintenance of existing pesticide registrations and evaluation of applications to register new pesticides, amend existing registrations, or related activities. **(7 U.S.C. 136 *et seq.*)**	Enacts into law H.R. 1029 of the 115th Congress, entitled the Pesticide Registration Improvement Enhancement Act of 2017. As passed by the House on March 20, 2017, H.R. 1029 would amend FIFRA to extend the authority to collect pesticide fees and for other purposes. **(§9119)**	No comparable provision.
Collection of Pesticide Use Information. Requires USDA coordinate with EPA in designing surveys of farmers on the use of pesticides to control pests and diseases of major crops, including fruits and vegetables, and make results available to EPA. **(7 U.S.C. 136i–2)**	No comparable provision.	Requires USDA, acting through the Office of Pest Management Policy (see §7306), to conduct a multiple crop and pesticide use survey of farmers to collect data for risk assessment modeling and mitigation for an active ingredient. Requires USDA to submit the survey to EPA. Authorizes appropriations of $2.5 million to remain available until expended. **(§10109)**
Methyl bromide. Section 419 of the Plant Protection Act provides that USDA—in consultation with state, local and tribal authorities— shall establish a program to identify alternatives to methyl bromide for treatment and control of plant pests and weeds. For uses where no registered, effective, economically feasible alternatives available can currently be identified, USDA shall initiate research programs to develop alternative methods of control and treatment. **(7 U.S.C. 7719)**	Requires USDA to establish a process to determine authorized methyl bromide uses in response to an emergency event. Amends the definition of an emergency event. Sets limitations on use per emergency event to allow for up to 20 metric tons of methyl bromide to be used per event at a specific location. **(§9121)**	No comparable provision.

Table 13. (Continued)

Current Law/Policy	House-Passed Bill (H.R. 2)	Senate-Passed Bill (H.R. 2)
Definition of *retail facilities*. Occupational Safety and Health Act of 1970 (OSHA) regulations exempt retail facilities from its standards for Process Safety Management (PSM) of Highly Hazardous Chemicals. While current regulations do not define the term *retail facility*, OSHA, in accordance with a ruling of the U.S. Court of Appeals, considers a facility to be a retail facility if more than half of the facility's income is obtained from direct sales to end users. **(29 U.S.C. 655)**	Requires OSHA to revise the PSM standard to formally define *retail facility* in accordance with its current, income-based definition. **(§9131)**	No comparable provision.
Report on regulation of plant biostimulants. *Plant biostimulant* is not defined in current law or regulation. Plant biostimulants that meet the definition of a "plant regulator" under FIFRA (7 U.S.C. §136 *et seq.*) are subject to requirements under the act.	Requires USDA—in consultation with EPA, states, and stakeholders—to submit a report to the President and Congress that identifies potential regulatory and legislative reforms to ensure the expeditious and appropriate review, approval, uniform national labeling, and availability of plant biostimulant products to agricultural producers. Defines *plant biostimulant* for purposes of the section. **(§9201)**	No comparable provision.

Table 14. Crop Insurance

Current Law/Policy	House-Passed Bill (H.R. 2)	Senate-Passed Bill (H.R. 2)
Definitions		
The Federal Crop Insurance Act lists defined terms used in the statute. **(7 U.S.C. 1502(b))**	No comparable provision.	**Cover crop termination:** a practice that historically and under reasonable circumstances results in the termination of the growth of a cover crop. **Hemp**: the meaning given the term in section 297A of the Agricultural Marketing Act of 1946. **(§11101)**
Data Collection and Sharing of Records		
Data Collection. Requires the Federal Crop Insurance Corporation (FCIC) to assemble data for the purpose of establishing sound actuarial bases for insurance of agricultural commodities. **(7 U.S.C. 1506(h)(2))**	No comparable provision.	Requires the National Agricultural Statistics Service (NASS) to share data in aggregate form with FCIC for the purpose of providing insurance and to maintain the confidentiality of the data in the same manner and extent required under section 1770 of the Food Security Act of 1985 (7 U.S.C. 2276) and the Confidential

Current Law/Policy	House-Passed Bill (H.R. 2)	Senate-Passed Bill (H.R. 2)
		Information Protection and Statistical Efficiency Act of 2002 (44 U.S.C. 3501). Requires USDA to ensure that "appropriate data" are collected by the Farm Service Agency (FSA) in the noninsured crop disaster assistance program, that FSA shares that data with FCIC, and that FCIC considers the data at least once a year. **(§11102)**
Sharing of Records. Requires sharing of records with USDA agencies and local offices, appropriate state and federal agencies and divisions, and Approved Insurance Providers (AIPs) in carrying out certain crop insurance and noninsured crop assistance (NAP) functions, subject to certain statutory limitations. **(7 U.S.C. 1506(h)(3))**	No comparable provision.	Requires the Secretary of Agriculture to share records for program purposes with private developers of crop insurance products who have received payment under section 522(b)(2)(E) of the Federal Crop Insurance Act (FCIA) (7 U.S.C. 1522(b)(2)(E)). **(§11103)**
Specifies resources the FCIC Board should use: in (1) classifying land as to risk and production capability and in the development of acceptable conservation practices, (2) developing a timber insurance plan, (3) in determining individual producer yields, and (4) consulting federal agencies as necessary. **(7 U.S.C. 1507(f))**	No comparable provision.	Updates how the FCIC Board should use resources, data, and collaborate with USDA agencies, and other federal agencies for multiple purposes, including: (1) working with FSA to determine individual producer yields, to share information on disadvantaged farmers and ranchers, to investigate potential waste, fraud, and abuse, and to share information to support the transition of crops from the noninsured crop disaster assistance program to crop insurance; (2) working with the NRCS to classify land as to risk and production capacity, to assess long-term trends and impacts from weather variability, and to consider acceptable conservation practices; and (3) working with other federal agencies as necessary. **(§11104)**
Specialty Crops		
Specialty Crops Coordinator. Requires FCIC to establish the position of Specialty Crops Coordinator with the primary responsibility of addressing the needs of specialty crop producers, among other duties related to specialty crops. Requires the Specialty Crops Coordinator to use information collected from FCIC field office directors and	No comparable provision.	Requires the Specialty Crop Coordinator to: (1) designate a Specialty Crops Liaison in each regional field office, (2) share the contact information of the Specialty Crops Liaisons with specialty crop producers, and (3) establish a website focused on

Table 14. (Continued)

Current Law/Policy	House-Passed Bill (H.R. 2)	Senate-Passed Bill (H.R. 2)
other sources, including extension service and colleges and universities, in states in which specialty crops have a significant economic effect. **(7 U.S.C. 507(g))**		crop insurance for specialty crop producers. The website must include an online mechanism to provide comments or feedback, a calendar of opportunities and events related to specialty crops, and a plan for examining potential new crops to be added to existing policies or plans of insurance for specialty crops, opportunities to expand existing policies or plans, and the potential for providing additional policies or plans of insurance for specialty crops, such as adding a revenue option or endorsement.
Addition of New and Specialty Crops. Requires data collection, reporting to Congress on progress and timetable for expanding coverage to new and specialty crops, reporting to Congress on the feasibility of crop insurance offerings for specialized producers of vegetables and other perishable crops who market through direct marketing channels, and completion of a feasibility study and limited pilot program on the feasibility of insuring nursery crops. **(7 U.S.C. 508(a)(6))**	No comparable provision	Requires the FCIC Manager (usually the RMA Administrator) to annually present research and development to the FCIC Board for not less than two of the following: (1) an insurance policy or plan for a new crop; (2) expansion of existing insurance to additional counties or states, including malting barley endorsements or contract options; and (3) research and development for a new policy or plan of insurance for crops with existing insurance, such as dollar plans. **(§11105)**
Treatment of Forage and Grazing		
Catastrophic risk protection. Requires FCIC to offer catastrophic risk protection (high-deductible coverage) for all crops except for "crops and grasses used for grazing." **(7 U.S.C. 1508(b)(1))**	Strikes the exception that catastrophic risk protection plans shall not be available for crops and grasses used for grazing. **(§10001(a))**	No comparable provision.
Ineligible producers. Makes producers ineligible to receive both catastrophic risk protection benefits and other assistance for the same loss under any program administered by USDA, with the exception of certain emergency loans. **(7 U.S.C. 1508(n)(1),(2))**	Provides an exception to the limitation on multiple benefits for the same loss for coverage described in the new Section 508D of the FCIA. **(§10001(b))**	No comparable provision.
No comparable provision.	**Expanded coverage for forage and grazing.** Adds a new Section 508D, which permits separate crop insurance policies, including a catastrophic risk protection plan,	No comparable provision.

Current Law/Policy	House-Passed Bill (H.R. 2)	Senate-Passed Bill (H.R. 2)
	to be purchased for crops that can be both grazed and mechanically harvested on the same acres during the same growing season. Such separate policies can be independently indemnified for each intended use. **(§10001(c))**	
Insurance Policy Provisions		
Prohibits coverage of post- harvest losses, except for tobacco, potatoes, and sweet potatoes. **(7 U.S.C. 508(a)(2))**	No comparable provision.	Adds hemp to the crops for which post-harvest losses may be covered. **(§11106)**
Consideration for Good Farming Practices. Excludes coverage for losses due to the failure of the producer to follow good farming practices, including scientifically sound sustainable and organic farming practices. **(7 U.S.C. 508(a)(3)(A)(iii))**	No comparable provision.	Clarifies conditions for voluntary conservation practices, including cover crop termination, to be considered as good farming practices. Specifies that cover crop termination shall not affect the insurability of a subsequently planted insurable crop if the cover crop termination is carried out according to guidelines approved by the Secretary of Agriculture, NRCS, or an agricultural expert recognized by FCIC. **(§11107)**
Defines Adequately Served. Requires the FCIC Board to review polices and plans of insurance to determine if each state is adequately served, requires the FCIC Board to report to Congress on its review and provide recommendations to increase participation in states that are not adequately served. **(7 U.S.C. 508(a)(7))**	No comparable provision.	Defines underserved producer as a beginning farmer or rancher, a veteran farmer or rancher, or a socially disadvantaged farmer or rancher. Requires the FCIC Board to examine the types of production common among underserved producers, and to publish reports to the public and Congress on its findings and recommendations on the needs of underserved producers at least once every 3 years. **(§11108)**
CAT fees. Sets the administrative fee for catastrophic risk protection (commonly referred to as CAT fees) at $300 per crop per county. **(7 U.S.C. 1508(b)(5)(A))**	Increases the administrative basic fee to $500 per crop per county. **(§10002)**	No comparable provision.
Additional Coverage Options. Requires FCIC to offer insurance plans that provide additional coverage, including additional coverage based on an individual yield and loss basis, an area yield and loss basis, an individual yield and loss basis supplemented with coverage based on an area yield and loss basis, or a margin basis. **(7 U.S.C. 1508(c)(1))**	Provides that crops for which the producer has elected agriculture risk coverage (ARC) or that are enrolled in the stacked income protection plan (STAX) are ineligible for coverage based on an area yield and loss basis or coverage based on the supplemental coverage option (SCO). **(§10003(a))** Adds conforming amendments. **(§10003(b))**	No comparable provision.

Table 14. (Continued)

Current Law/Policy	House-Passed Bill (H.R. 2)	Senate-Passed Bill (H.R. 2)
Performance-based premium discounts. Authorizes FCIC to provide performance-based premium discounts to producers with "good insurance or production experience relative to other producers" of the same crop in the same area. **(7 U.S.C. 1508(d)(3))**	Repeals the authority for performance-based discounts for producers. **(§10004(a))** Adds conforming amendments. **(§10004(b))**	Authorizes FCIC to offer discounts for risk-reducing practices. Specifies types of practices FCIC shall consider for discounts for the 2020 reinsurance year, including precision irrigation or fertilization, crop rotations, and cover crops. Requires FCIC to seek expert opinions and consider additional practices based on new evidence on an annual basis. **(§11109)**
Enterprise Units. Authorizes FCIC to pay premium subsidies for plans or polices of insurance with whole farm or enterprise units, specifies parameters for the premium subsidy percentages for whole farm or enterprise units, including a maximum of 80% of premium, and requires FCIC to offer separate enterprise units for irrigated and nonirrigated acreage of crops in counties beginning in crop year 2015. An enterprise unit consists of all insurable acreage of the same insured crop in the county in which the insured has a share. Enterprise units receive a premium discount compared to smaller units. **(7 U.S.C. 1508(e)(5))**	No comparable provision.	Authorizes FCIC to allow a producer to establish a single enterprise unit by combining enterprise units or enterprise units with basic units and optional units in one or more other counties. **(§11110)**
Federal Premium Subsidies. Sets premium subsidy percentages by insurance plans, coverage levels, and practices. **(7 U.S.C. 508(e))**	No comparable provision.	Sets premium subsidies for a member of an Indian tribe for the first-time purchase of pasture, rangeland, and forage insurance at 90% of premium. **(§11111)**
Calculation of APH yields. Details how FCIC determines yields and provides exceptions to the calculation of actual production history (APH) yields, such as transitional yields and yield exclusion options. **(7 U.S.C. 1508(g))**	Requires FCIC to establish underwriting rules that would give producers the choice to limit their APH decreases to 10% of the previous year's APH. Requires actuarially sound premiums to cover the additional risk. **(§10005)**	No comparable provision.
Submission of Policies and Materials to FCIC Board. Authorizes the FCIC Board to review and evaluate private submissions for new crop insurance policies or provisions, or premium rates. Approved submissions are eligible for cost reimbursement, premium subsidies, administrative and operating subsidy, and reinsurance by FCIC.	No comparable provision.	Authorizes FCIC to waive certain viability and marketability requirements in the case of a policy or pilot program relating to the production of hemp. **(§11112)**

Current Law/Policy	House-Passed Bill (H.R. 2)	Senate-Passed Bill (H.R. 2)
Requires private submitters to show that proposed submissions are viable and marketable, among other requirements. **(7 U.S.C. 1508(h))**		
Whole Farm Revenue Agent Incentives. Sets maximum administrative and operating subsidies at 24.5% of premium. **(7 U.S.C. 1508(k)(4))** Approved Insurance Providers (AIPs) may not pay more than 80% of administrative and operating subsidy (A&O) and catastrophic loss adjustment expense subsidy (CAT LAE) as a base commission to agents. However, if certain conditions are met, AIPs may pay up to 100% of A&O and CAT LAE to agents. **(2011 and subsequent Standard Reinsurance Agreements, §III(a)(4))**	No comparable provision.	Requires FCIC to pay additional administrative and operating subsidy (A&O) to Approved Insurance Providers (AIPs) to pay to agents selling Whole Farm Revenue Policies in certain circumstances. Sets a minimum of $1,000 in agent compensation for selling a Whole Farm Revenue Policy and an additional $300 for sales to first- time purchasers of the Whole Farm Revenue policy. To the extent that this provision allows for compensation that is higher than what is allowed in the Standard Reinsurance Agreement (SRA), the additional amount is not subject to agent compensation limits under the SRA. **(§11113)**
Crop production on native sod ("Sodsaver"). During the first four years of planting, crop insurance and NAP benefits are reduced on native sod acreage in Minnesota, Iowa, North Dakota, South Dakota, Montana, and Nebraska. Provisions include: (1) a reduction in the crop insurance premium subsidy by 50 percentage points, and NAP fee is doubled; (2) annual data for actual production history are equal to 65% of the transitional yield for all four years rather than the higher, variable percentage applicable for other cropland; and (3) for crop insurance, yield substitutes are not allowed; that is, low farm yields must be used in the actual production history rather than replacing them with potentially higher transitional yield (T-yield). (On other cropland, producers can substitute 60% of the T-yield for any actual yield below 60% of the T- yield). **(7 U.S.C. 1508(o))**	No comparable provision.	Amends the Sodsaver provision to require the loss of four cumulative years of crop insurance and NAP benefits following planting on native sod. Differentiates between land tilled between enactment of the 2014 farm bill and enactment of this bill, and land tilled subsequent to enactment of this bill. Non-hay and non-forage insurable crops tilled on native sod after enactment are subject to four cumulative years of reduced benefits. For insurable hay and forage crops planted on native sod, benefits are reduced for four cumulative years during each crop year of planting. Producers must certify all tillage on native sod using an FSA acreage report form and maps. Annual reports to Congress are required on total certified acres by state and county. Governors of states outside of the six covered under the provision may elect to apply Sodsaver in their state. **(§11114)**

Table 14. (Continued)

Current Law/Policy	House-Passed Bill (H.R. 2)	Senate-Passed Bill (H.R. 2)
Use of NASS data to combat waste, fraud, and abuse. Requires USDA to develop and implement a coordinated plan for FSA to assist FCIC in the ongoing monitoring of the federal crop insurance program to identify potential fraud, waste, or abuse. **(7 U.S.C. 1515(d)(1))**	No comparable provision.	Authorizes FCIC to use NASS data in existing data mining efforts to detect anomalies and identify potential fraud for audits and other enforcement actions. **(§11115)**
Submission of Policy Information to FCIC. Requires the Secretary of Agriculture to establish procedures outlining required information and deadlines for AIPs to submit policy information to FCIC. **(7 U.S.C. 1515(g))**	No comparable provision.	Requires AIPs to submit the actual production history used to establish insurable yields to FCIC not later than 30 days after the applicable production reporting date for the crop to be insured. **(§11116)**
Acreage Report Streamlining Initiative. Requires the Secretary of Agriculture to develop and implement an acreage report streamlining initiative project to allow producers to report acreage and other information directly to USDA. **(7 U.S.C. 1515(j)(1)(B)(ii)).**	No comparable provision.	Requires the Risk Management Agency and the Farm Service Agency to implement a consistent method for determining crop acreage, acreage yields, farm acreage, property descriptions, and other common informational requirements, including measures of common land units. Requires FCIC to require Approved Insurance Providers to accept reports of crop acreage, acreage yields, and other information from producers or authorized agents in an electronic format. **(§11117)**
No comparable provision.	No comparable provision.	**Continuing Education for Loss Adjusters and Agents.** Requires FCIC to establish requirements for continuing education on conservation and agronomic practices, including organic and sustainable practices, for loss adjusters and agents of AIPs. **(§11118)**
Information Technology. Requires the Secretary of Agriculture to maintain and upgrade information management systems used to administer the federal crop insurance program. **(7 U.S.C. 1515(j)(1)).**		Provides $1,000,000 in annual funding for information technology in fiscal years 2019 and 2020. **(§11119)**
Funding for reviews, compliance, and program integrity. Provides up to $9,000,000 per fiscal year from the insurance fund for expenses, including	Reduces the funds available for review, compliance, and program integrity from $9 million to $7 million per fiscal year. **(§10006)**	No comparable provision.

Current Law/Policy	House-Passed Bill (H.R. 2)	Senate-Passed Bill (H.R. 2)
operating and reviewing plans of insurance (including actuarial and related information) and for maintaining the actuarial soundness and financial integrity of the program. Allows the Secretary to merge some or all of the funds into the accounts of the RMA and to obligate the funds. **(7 U.S.C. 1516(b)(2)(C)(i) and (ii))**		
Defines Agricultural Commodities. Defines *agricultural commodity* as "wheat, cotton, flax, corn, dry beans, oats, barley, rye, tobacco, rice, peanuts, soybeans, sugar beets, sugar cane, tomatoes, grain sorghum, sunflowers, raisins, oranges, sweet corn, dry peas, freezing and canning peas, forage, apples, grapes, potatoes, timber and forests, nursery crops, citrus, and other fruits and vegetables, nuts, tame hay, native grass, aquacultural species (including, but not limited to, any species of finfish, mollusk, crustacean, or other aquatic invertebrate, amphibian, reptile, or aquatic plant propagated or reared in a controlled or selected environment), or any other agricultural commodity, excluding stored grain, determined by the Board, or any one or more of such commodities, as the context may indicate." **(7 U.S.C. 1518)**	No comparable provision.	Adds *hemp* to the definition of *agricultural commodity*. **(§11120)**
Research, development, and maintenance costs. Authorizes FCIC to contract with private submitters to research and develop new crop insurance policies. FCIC may approve up to 75% of the projected total research and development costs to be paid in advance to an applicant. Provides for reimbursement of "reasonable research and development costs." **(7 U.S.C. 1522(b))**	Allows for reimbursement of "reasonable and actual research and development costs" related to policies that have been approved by the FCIC board. Defines *reasonable and actual costs* as costs based on (1) wage rates equal to two times Bureau of Labor Statistics hourly wage rates plus benefits or (2) actual documented costs incurred by the applicant. Prohibits disapproval of a user fee based on (1) it being compared to a maintenance fee or (2) the potential for the fee to result in a financial gain/loss to the applicant. Limits discretion of the FCIC board in approval of user fees. **(§10007(a))**	Authorizes the FCIC Board to waive the viability and marketability requirements for reimbursement of research and development relating to a policy to insure the production of hemp. **(§11121)**

Table 14. (Continued)

Current Law/Policy	House-Passed Bill (H.R. 2)	Senate-Passed Bill (H.R. 2)
No comparable provision.	**Resubmission of reimbursement requests.** Provides that this section applies to reimbursement requests made on or after October 1, 2016, and that requests for reimbursement previously denied between October 1, 2016, and the date of enactment of this act may be resubmitted. **(§10007(b))**	No comparable provision.
Research and Development Authority		
Priorities. Authorizes FCIC to conduct activities or contract for research and development efforts to maintain or improve existing policies or develop new policies. Directs FCIC to conduct or contract for specific types of coverage for specific crops or livestock. **(7 U.S.C. 1522(c))**	Strikes 16 completed studies and research and development contracts. **(§10008(a))** Defines *beginning farmer or rancher* for the purposes of research and development of whole farm insurance plans as having actively operated and managed a farm or ranch for less than 10 years. **(§10008(b))** Requires FCIC to contract with one or more qualified entities to conduct research and development on (1) a policy to insure certain crops due to losses due to tropical storms or hurricanes; (2) create a separate practice for subsurface irrigation; (3) the difference in rates, average yields, and coverage levels of grain sorghum policies as compared to other feed grains within a county (with a reporting requirement of sorghum study results within a year of enactment) and; (4) establish an alternative (and optional) method of adjusting for quality losses that does not impact the APH of producers. **(§10008(c))**	Requires FCIC to conduct activities or enter into contracts to carry out research and development to maintain or improve existing policies or develop new policies. Provides direction for the following priorities: effectiveness of whole farm plans, irrigated grain sorghum, limited irrigation practices, quality loss, citrus, greenhouses, hops, local foods, irrigation practices for rice, and batture lands. **(§11122)**
Funding. Under Sections 522 and 523 of the FCIA, FCIC may enter into contracts to carry out research and development for new crop insurance policies but may not conduct research itself. **(7 U.S.C. 1522)**	Amends the act to discontinue partnerships for risk management development and implementation and to reduce CCC funding for research and development contracting from $12.5 million to no more than $8 million for FY2019 and each subsequent fiscal year. **(§10009)**	

Current Law/Policy	House-Passed Bill (H.R. 2)	Senate-Passed Bill (H.R. 2)
Education and Risk Management Assistance		
Underserved states. Authorizes FCIC to establish a program for crop insurance education and information to producers in states where federal crop insurance participation and availability are low and producers are underserved by the federal crop insurance program. **(7 U.S.C. 1524(a)(2))**	Eliminates the crop insurance education and information program for targeted states carried out by RMA and AMA and reauthorizes the risk management education and assistance carried out through NIFA. Directs the FCIC insurance fund to transfer $5 million for FY2018 and each fiscal year thereafter to fund partnerships for risk management education. **(§10010)**	Adds conservation activities to the list of risk management activities that are eligible for competitive educational grants. **(§11123)**
Partnerships for risk management education. Authorizes the Secretary, through NIFA, to establish a program of competitive grants for public and private entities to educate agricultural producers about the full range of risk management activities, including futures, options, agricultural trade options, and crop insurance, among others. **(7 U.S.C. 1524(a)(3))**		
Agricultural Management Assistance (AMA) Program. Authorizes the AMA program, which provides financial and technical to producers in 16 specified states for conservation practices, risk mitigation, and market diversification. Provides $15 million in annual mandatory funding in FY2008-FY2014 and $10 million each fiscal year thereafter. Requires 50% to NRCS, 40% to RMA, and 10% to AMS. **(7 U.S.C. 1524(a)(2) and 1524(b))**		
Cropland Report Annual Updates		
Requires the Secretary of Agriculture to provide annual reports each January 1 to the House and Senate Agriculture Committees on changes in cropland acreage in each applicable county and state, from on January 1, 2015 through January 1, 2018. **(11014(c)(2) of 2014 farm bill, Public Law 113-79)**	No comparable provision.	Extends authority to January 1, 2023. **(§11124)**

Table 15. Miscellaneous

Current Law/Policy	House-Passed Bill (H.R. 2)	Senate-Passed Bill (H.R. 2)
Livestock		
Animal Health Protection Act (AHPA). AHPA contains provisions to prevent, detect, control, and eradicate diseases and pests to protect animal health. **(7 U.S.C. 8301 *et seq.*)** The 2014 farm bill (P.L. 113-79) establishes a National Animal Health Laboratory Network to develop and enhance national veterinary diagnostic capabilities, with an emphasis on surveillance planning, vulnerability analysis, and technology development and validation. Authorizes appropriations of $15 million per year for FY2014- FY2018. **(7 U.S.C. 8308a)**	Requires USDA to establish the **National Animal Disease Preparedness and Response Program** to address the risk of the introduction and spread of animal pests and diseases that affect the U.S. livestock and related industries, including export expansion. Directs USDA to sign cooperative agreements or other legal agreements with state departments of agriculture, offices of the chief animal health state official, land- grant colleges or universities or non-land-grant colleges of agriculture, colleges of veterinary medicine, state or national livestock producer organizations, state emergency agencies, veterinarian organizations recognized by the American Veterinary Medical Association, Indian tribes, federal agencies, or a combination of entities. To the extent practicable, activities include enhancing animal pest and disease analysis and surveillance; expanding outreach and education; targeting domestic inspection at vulnerable points; strengthening threat identification; improving biosecurity; enhancing emergency response capabilities; conducting technology development (veterinary biologics, diagnostics, animal drugs, and animal medical devices); enhancing electronic sharing of health data and risk analysis; and other activities as determined by USDA. USDA will notify entities of information required to enter into cooperative agreements, requirements for the use of funds, and criteria to evaluate the activities. USDA may consider entities' ability to contribute nonfederal funds but may not require entities to contribute funds. Requires recipients to use funds according to cooperative agreements.	Similar to House bill. Establishes the **National Animal Disease Preparedness Response, and Recovery Program. (§12103)**

Current Law/Policy	House-Passed Bill (H.R. 2)	Senate-Passed Bill (H.R. 2)
	Recipients may enter sub-agreements with state entities responsible for animal disease prevention, surveillance, and response. Requires recipients to submit to USDA reports describing the purposes and results of activities no later than 90 days after completion of activities. Requires USDA to establish a **National Animal Health Vaccine Bank** to protect U.S. agriculture and food systems against terrorist attack, major disaster, and other emergencies. Requires the Vaccine Bank to maintain sufficient quantities of animal vaccine, antiviral, therapeutic, or diagnostic products for rapid response to animal disease outbreak that would have a damaging effect on human health or the economy. Directs it to leverage existing mechanisms and infrastructure of the National Veterinary Stockpile of APHIS. Also requires USDA to prioritize the acquisition of sufficient quantities of foot-and-mouth disease vaccine and consider contracting with one or more entities capable of producing foot- and-mouth disease vaccines and having surge production capacity.	Similar to the House bill. Establishes the **National Animal Vaccine and Veterinary Countermeasures Bank**. **(§12103)**
	For FY2019, requires mandatory funding of $250 million from the CCC, of which $30 million is for **the National Animal Health Laboratory Network**, $70 million for the **National Animal Disease**	Authorizes appropriations of $30 million per year for FY2019-FY2023 for the **National Animal Health Laboratory Network**. **(§12102)**
	Preparedness and Response Program, and $150 million for the **National Animal Health Vaccine Bank**. In FY2020-FY2023, $50 million per year in mandatory CCC funds is available for the three programs, of which not less than $30 million per year is for the National Animal Disease Preparedness and Response Program. In addition, authorizes appropriations of $15 million per year for FY2019-FY2023 for the National Animal Health Laboratory Network. Funds made available may be used until expended. **(§11101)**	Authorizes appropriations for such sums as necessary to carry out the preparedness program and the vaccine bank. **(§12103)**

Table 15. (Continued)

Current Law/Policy	House-Passed Bill (H.R. 2)	Senate-Passed Bill (H.R. 2)
National Aquatic Animal Health Plan. Authorizes USDA to enter into cooperative agreements for the purpose of detecting, controlling, or eradicating diseases of aquaculture species and promoting species-specific best management practices on a cost-share basis. The Secretary may use authorities from AHPA **(7 U.S.C. 8301 *et seq.*)** to carry out the plan. Authorizes such sums as necessary to be appropriated in each of FY2008- FY2018. **(7 U.S.C. 8322)**	Authorizes appropriations of such sums as necessary to administer the program through FY2023. **(§11102)**	No comparable provision.
Veterinary Training. Allows USDA to develop a program to maintain a sufficient number of federal and state veterinarians who are trained in the recognition and diagnosis of exotic and endemic animal diseases. **(7 U.S.C. 8318)**	Amends the section to include "veterinary teams, including those based at colleges of veterinary medicine" and inserts *and who are capable of providing effective services before, during, and after emergencies* at the end of the section. **(§11103)**	No comparable provision.
No comparable provision.	**Report on FSIS Guidance and Outreach to Small Meat Processors.** Requires the USDA inspector general to provide the Secretary of Agriculture a report on the effectiveness of existing FSIS guidance materials and tools for small and very small establishments. The report is to include (1) an evaluation of the outreach conducted by FSIS, (2) an evaluation of guidance materials and tools used by FSIS, (3) an evaluation of FSIS responsiveness to inquiries and issues, and (4) recommendations FSIS should take to improve regulatory clarity and consistency. **(§11104)**	No comparable provision.
No comparable provision.	**Regional Cattle and Carcass Grading Correlation and Training Centers.** USDA is required to establish not more than three regional Centers to provide education and training for cattle and carcass beef graders of the Agricultural Marketing Service, cattle producers, and other professionals involved in the reporting, delivery, and grading of feeder cattle, live cattle, and	No comparable provision.

Current Law/Policy	House-Passed Bill (H.R. 2)	Senate-Passed Bill (H.R. 2)
	carcasses. The Centers are to be located near cattle feeding or slaughtering areas, provide intensive training, and coordinate the existing resources of USDA, state agricultural extension and research centers, relevant contract markets, and producers. Funding for the Centers may not be used for new construction or remodeling of facilities, but may be used for rental space. The Centers may also accept in-kind donations to cover such spaces. **(§11105)**	
Sheep Production and Marketing Grant Program. Establishes a competitive grant program through USDA's Agricultural Marketing Service to improve the sheep industry, including infrastructure, business, resource development, or innovative approaches for long- term needs. Provided $1.5 million in CCC mandatory funds for FY2014 to remain available until expended. **(7 U.S.C. 1627a)**	Authorizes $2 million of CCC funds for FY2019 for the purposes of strengthening and enhancing the production of sheep and sheep products in the United States, with funds remaining available until expended. **(§11304(e)(3))** Included in the Textile Trust Fund subtitle of the House bill.	Authorizes appropriations of $1.5 million per year for FY2019-FY2023. **(§12101)** The provision is in the livestock subtitle of the Senate bill.
No comparable provision.	No comparable provision.	**Study on Livestock Dealer Statutory Trust.** Requires USDA to conduct a study on the feasibility of establishing a livestock dealer statutory trust, and to submit a report to the House Committee on Agriculture and the Senate Committee on Agriculture, Nutrition, and Forestry no later than 540 days after enactment. The study is to cover: (1) the effects of a trust on buyer and seller market behavior; (2) the effect on credit availability, including impacts on lenders and lending behavior; (3) unique circumstances common to livestock dealers and how they impact the functioning of a statutory trust; (4) the feasibility of electronic transfer of funds or other expeditious payments to provide sellers protection for nonsufficient funds payments; (5) the effectiveness of statutory trusts in other agricultural segments; and (6) the effects of setting a de minimis annual sales threshold exemption. **(§12104)**

Table 15. (Continued)

Current Law/Policy	House-Passed Bill (H.R. 2)	Senate-Passed Bill (H.R. 2)
Emergency Livestock Feed Assistance Act of 1988. Under the Act, USDA provides emergency feed assistance to preserve and maintain livestock in any state or area of a state because of disease, insect infestation, flood, drought, fire, hurricane, earthquake, storm, hot weather, or other natural disaster. **(7 U.S.C. 1471 and 1471a)**	No comparable provision.	**Definition of Livestock.** Amends the act to include llamas, alpacas, live fish, crawfish, and other animals. **(§12105)**
Agriculture and Food Defense		
Office of Homeland Security. The 2008 farm bill (Section 14111 of P.L. 110-246) established the office to coordinate and advise the Secretary on homeland security activities for agricultural disease emergencies, agro-terrorist acts, and other threats to agricultural biosecurity. The office is the primary liaison with other federal departments and agencies on the coordination of efforts and interagency activities pertaining to agricultural biosecurity. **(7 U.S.C. 8911)**	No comparable provision.	Repeals the Office of Homeland Security as established. **(§12201)**
The Department of Agriculture Reorganization Act of 1994. Authorizes the Secretary to streamline, reorganize, and manage USDA programs and activities. **(7 U.S.C. 6901 *et seq.*)** Similar provisions to those in the Agriculture and Food Defense subtitle exist in various forms in other laws. For example, the National Agriculture and Food Defense Strategy (21 U.S.C. 2202) in the Food Safety Modernization Act (P.L. 111-353).	No comparable provision.	USDA is required to establish an **Office of Homeland Security** under the 1994 Act. The office is to be headed by an executive director whose duties include (1) serve as principal advisor to the Secretary on homeland security issues; (2) coordinate the department's homeland security activities; (3) act as the primary liaison with other federal departments and agencies; (4) coordinate USDA's information gathering on early warning and threats and risks to critical infrastructure; (5) liaise with the Director of National Intelligence; (6) coordinate exercises to identify and eliminate gaps in preparedness; (7) produce a department-wide strategic coordination plan; and (8) carry out other duties as determined by the Secretary.

Current Law/Policy	House-Passed Bill (H.R. 2)	Senate-Passed Bill (H.R. 2)
		USDA is required to carry out an *Agriculture and Food Threat Awareness Partnership Program* with the intelligence community to share personnel and information in order to improve communications and analysis. This program is to be conducted in collaboration with federal, state, and local authorities. **(§12202)**
No comparable provision.	No comparable provision.	**Agriculture and Food Defense.** Provides definitions relevant to the section. **(§12203(a))** USDA is required to conduct *Disease and Pest of Concern Response Planning* that includes establishing a list of diseases and pests using expert opinion and evidence related to the diseases and pests, and to develop a comprehensive response plan for them. The response plans are to be developed on a state or regional basis and include a concept of operations, and the appropriate interactions between federal, state, local, and tribal governments, and animal and plant industry partners. The plans are to include a decision matrix and performance metrics. **(§12203(b))**
Special Authorization for Biosecurity Planning and Response. Land-grant universities, federal and state agencies, state departments of agriculture, and other stakeholders established a National Plant Diagnostic Network (NPDN) in 2002 to enhance agricultural security. Under the National Agricultural Research, Extension, and Teaching Policy Act (NARETPA), the USDA National Institute of Food and Agriculture (NIFA) provides funding to the network through authorized appropriations. **(7 U.S.C. 3351)**	No comparable provision.	USDA is required to establish a *National Plant Diagnostic Network* to monitor threats to plant health from diseases or pests. The network is to provide increased awareness and early identification, coordinate between USDA and state agencies, establish diagnostic standards, establish regional hubs of expertise and leadership, and establish a national repository of records of endemic or emergent diseases and pests of concern. **(§12203(c))** The Director of NIFA would lead the network, and coordinate and collaborate with land-grant colleges and universities, and partner with the Administrator of the Animal and Plant Health

Table 15. (Continued)

Current Law/Policy	House-Passed Bill (H.R. 2)	Senate-Passed Bill (H.R. 2)
		Inspection Service. **(§12203(c)(3) and (4))** Authorizes appropriations for the network of $15 million per year for FY2019-FY2023. **(§12203(c)(5))** USDA is to establish a *National Plant Disease Recovery System* for strategic long-term planning on high- consequence plant transboundary diseases. The recovery system is to coordinate response operations, make long-range plans for research projects for long-term recovery, identify specific genotypes, cultivars, breeding liens and disease-resistant materials for crop stabilization and improvement, and establish a watch list of transboundary diseases for long-term planning. **(§12203(d))**
Agricultural Bioterrorism Protection Act of 2002. Under the act, USDA established and maintains a list of biological agents and toxins that potentially pose a severe threat to animal or plant health, or animal or plant product. **(7 U.S.C. 8401(a)(1)(B)(i))**	No comparable provision.	**Biological Agents and Toxins List.** Amends the criteria to be considered for adding a biological agent or toxin to the list, as follows: (1) whether adding to the list would have a substantial negative impact on the research and development of solutions for animal or plant diseases, and (2) whether the negative impact substantially outweighs the risk posed by not adding it to the list. **(§12204)**
No comparable provision.	No comparable provision.	**Authorization of Appropriations.** Authorizes appropriations of $5 million of each fiscal year for FY2019-FY2023. **(§12205)**
Beginning, Socially Disadvantaged, and Veteran Producers		
Outreach and Assistance for Socially Disadvantaged Farmers and Ranchers and Veteran Farmers and Ranchers. Provides for an outreach and technical assistance program to assist socially disadvantaged farmers and ranchers and veteran farmers and ranchers in owning and operating farms and ranches and in participating equitably in the full range	Reauthorizes $10 million in mandatory spending each year for FY2019-FY2023. Prioritizes grants under the program for agricultural education for youth under the age of 18, for agricultural employment and volunteer opportunities for youth under the age of 18, and for projects that demonstrate experience in	No comparable provision

Current Law/Policy	House-Passed Bill (H.R. 2)	Senate-Passed Bill (H.R. 2)
of agricultural programs offered by USDA. **(7 U.S.C. 2279(a)(4))**	providing such education and opportunities to socially disadvantaged youth. Reauthorizes appropriations of $20 million each for FY2019-FY2023. **(§11201)**	
Established the **Office of Advocacy and Outreach** which leads USDA in implementing outreach and assistance to socially disadvantaged farmers and ranchers and veteran farmers and ranchers. Also carries out the functions and duties of the Office of Outreach and Diversity under the Assistant Secretary for Civil Rights, oversees the Office of Small Farms Coordination, and coordinates with NIFA on the administration of the beginning farmer and rancher development program. **(7 U.S.C. 6934)**	Requires the Secretary to designate a **State Beginning Farmer and Rancher Coordinator** from among existing employees of Farm Service Agency, the Natural Resources Conservation Service, the Risk Management Agency, the Rural Business-Cooperative Service, and the Rural Utilities Service. Requires USDA to coordinate the development of a training plan for each state coordinator, to work with various outreach coordinators in state offices, and to work with the Office of Partnership and Public Engagement, the successor agency of the Office of Advocacy and Outreach. **(§11202)**	Similar to House bill. Requires the Secretary to establish the position of National Beginning Farmer and Rancher Coordinator to who is required as to establish a State Beginning Farmers and Ranchers Coordinator. **(§12306)**
	Renames the Office of Advocacy and Outreach as the **Office of Partnerships and Public Engagement**. Amends the section to improve access to USDA programs to limited resource producers, veteran farmers and ranchers, and tribal farmers and ranchers. Also adds "promoting youth outreach" as an objective of the newly named office. Reauthorizes appropriations funding of $2 million each fiscal year FY2019-FY2023. **(§11203)**	Reauthorizes appropriations of $2 million each fiscal year for FY2019- FY2023 for the Office of Advocacy and Outreach. **(§12303)**
Establishes the **Office of Tribal Relations** in the Office of the Secretary to advise the Secretary on policies related to Indian tribes. **(7 U.S.C. 6921)**	Amends the section to require the Secretary of Agriculture to (1) establish an Office of Tribal Relations within the Office of Partnerships and Public Engagement to advise the Secretary on policies related to Indian tribes and (2) establish the "New Beginnings Initiative," under which the Secretary shall provide funds to a land-grant college or university in the amount equal to the amount such land-grant college or university expends for providing educational programs and services for, or tuition paid with respect to, Indians at a land-grant college or university. **(§11204)**	No comparable provision.

Table 15. (Continued)

Current Law/Policy	House-Passed Bill (H.R. 2)	Senate-Passed Bill (H.R. 2)
No comparable provision.	**Commission on Farm Transition—Needs for 2050.** Establishes a commission to conduct a study on issues affecting the transition of agricultural operations from established farmers and ranchers to the next generation of farmers and ranchers. Outlines the composition and operation of the commission. Not later than one year from enactment, the commission is required to submit to the House Committee on Agriculture and the Senate Committee on Agriculture, Nutrition, and Forestry a report on the study results and recommendations the commission considers appropriate. **(§11205)**	No comparable provision.
Department of Agriculture Reorganization Act of 1994. Authorizes the Secretary to streamline, reorganize, and manage USDA programs and activities. **(7 U.S.C. 6911 *et seq.*)**	Amends the 1994 Act to establish the position of **Agricultural Youth Organization Coordinator** to promote the role of youth-serving organizations and school-based agricultural education. Outlines contracts and cooperative agreements the coordinator may engage in with land-grant universities, research centers of the Agricultural Research Service, and nonprofit organizations. **(§11206)**	Similar to House bill. Requires USDA to establish the position of **Agricultural Youth Coordinator** to promote school-based agricultural education and youth-serving agricultural organizations in motivating and preparing young people to pursue careers in the agriculture, food, and natural resources systems, and to coordinate outreach programs within the Department to work with schools and youth-serving organizations to develop joint programs and initiatives **(§12306)**
Farm Security and Rural Investment Act of 2002. Established a *beginning farmer and rancher development program*. Authorized a competitive grant program to support new and established local and regional training and technical assistance initiatives for beginning farmers and ranchers. **(7 U.S.C. 3319f)** **Food, Agriculture, Conservation, and Trade Act of 1990.** Established the Outreach and Assistance for Socially Disadvantaged Farmers and Ranchers and Veteran Farmers and Ranchers program. Authorized the Secretary to carry out an outreach and technical assistance program to encourage and assist socially disadvantaged farmers and	No comparable provision.	Repeals the beginning farmer and rancher development program in the 2002 Act. Amends the 1990 Act by renaming the development program **Farming Opportunities Training and Outreach.** Gives priority in making grants and entering into contract to nongovernmental and community-based organizations with an expertise in working with socially disadvantaged farmers and ranchers or veteran farmers and ranchers. Directs the Secretary to ensure the geographical diversity of eligible entities.

Current Law/Policy	House-Passed Bill (H.R. 2)	Senate-Passed Bill (H.R. 2)
ranchers and veteran farmers or ranchers in owning and operating farms and ranches; and in participating equitably in the full range of agricultural programs offered by the Department. **(7 U.S.C. 2279)**		Authorizes USDA, NIFA, to make competitive grants, and enter contracts or agreements, to support new and established local and regional training, education, outreach, and technical assistance initiatives for beginning farmers and ranchers. Grants, contracts, or agreements can be for three years or less, and may provide not more than $250,000 per year. Partnerships and collaborations that are led by or include nongovernmental, community-based organizations and school-based educational organizations with expertise in new agricultural producer training and outreach are to receive priority. Requires USDA to establish beginning farmer and rancher education teams to develop curricula and conduct educational programs and workshops for beginning farmers and ranchers in diverse geographical areas of the United States. The material is to be online and may include online courses for direct use by beginning farmers and ranchers. Authorizes $50 million in mandatory spending for FY2018 and each fiscal year thereafter. Authorizes $50 million discretionary spending each year for FY2018-2023. Of the funds authorized, 50% is reserved for the beginning farmer and rancher development grants, and 50% for farming opportunities training and outreach. Of those amounts, 5% of beginning farmer and rancher outreach and assistance, education teams, and curriculum and training clearinghouse funds are reserved for veteran farmers, and 5% for limited resource farmers, socially disadvantaged farmers and ranchers, and farmworkers who desire to become farmers. **(§12301)**

Table 15. (Continued)

Current Law/Policy	House-Passed Bill (H.R. 2)	Senate-Passed Bill (H.R. 2)
Urban Agriculture. Previous farm bills expanded federal support for local and regional food systems, mostly in the form of new or expanded grants and loans across a range of USDA programs and agencies.	No comparable provision.	**Urban Agriculture.** Amends existing law to incorporate provisions introduced in S. 3005 (Urban Agriculture Act of 2018), including establishing: (1) an Office of Urban Agriculture and Innovative Production at USDA to encourage and promote urban, indoor, and other emerging agricultural practices; (2) an Urban Agriculture and Innovative Production Advisory Committee; (3) new grant authority for USDA to support the development of urban agriculture and innovative production; and (4) new pilot programs and reporting requirements. Authorizes $25 million in annual appropriations for FY2019 and each for fiscal year thereafter. **(§12302)** Other provisions from S. 3005 are included in the Conservation title (**§2405**, Soil Testing and Remediation Assistance), Research title (**§7212**, Urban, Indoor, and Other Emerging Agricultural Production Research, Education, and Extension Initiative); Crop Insurance (**§11122**, Research and Development Authority); and provisions within **§1601** (Noninsured Crop Assistance Program).
Establishes the **Office of Tribal Relations** in the Office of the Secretary to advise the Secretary on policies related to Indian tribes. **(7 U.S.C. 6921)**	No comparable provision.	**Tribal Advisory Committee.** Direct the Secretary to create the Tribal Advisory Committee to provide advice and guidance to the Secretary on matters relating to Tribal and Indian affairs. The Committee will facilitate but not supplant government-to-government consultation between USDA and Indian tribes. The Council would be composed of 9 members, 7 appointed by the Secretary and one each by the Chair of the Senate Committee on Indian Affairs and the ranking member. Members would be

Current Law/Policy	House-Passed Bill (H.R. 2)	Senate-Passed Bill (H.R. 2)
		appointed for 3- year terms, with the first 7 appointments appointed to 2-year terms. A member of the Office of Tribal Relations and the Assistant Secretary for Indian Affairs of the Department of the Interior shall attend each meeting of the Committee. The Committee will identify issues relating to programs of USDA and Indian tribes and submit recommendations and solutions to such identified issues. The Committee will identify priorities and provide advice on strategies to Tribal consultation on issues at the Tribal, regional, or national level that concern USDA. The Committee will submit an annual report describing the activities and recommendations for legislative or administrative action, and the Secretary shall respond in writing to that report. **(§12304)**
Agriculture Conservation Experienced Service Program (ACES). Authorizes USDA to enter into agreements with organizations to provide technical assistance (excludes administrative tasks) using qualified individuals 55 years or older. Funding from farm bill conservation programs (excluding CRP) may be used to carry out the ACES program. **(16 U.S.C. 3851)**	No comparable provision.	**Experienced Services Program.** Amends and expands the ACES program to include technical, professional, and administrative services for the research, education, and economics mission area at USDA. Renames the program the *Experienced Services Program* and includes a sunset date of October 1, 2023. **(§12305)**
No comparable provision.	House bill Sections 11202 and 11206 are similar to the Senate bill.	**Youth Outreach and Beginning Farmer Coordination.** Amends Subtitle D of title VII of the Farm Security and Rural Investment Act of 2002 by adding a new section 7405 that requires the Secretary to establish the position of National Beginning Farmer and Rancher Coordinator to advise the Secretary on issues affecting beginning farmers and ranchers, and in consultation with state food and agriculture councils, to assess plans submitted by a state beginning farmers and ranchers coordinator, which the National

Table 15. (Continued)

Current Law/Policy	House-Passed Bill (H.R. 2)	Senate-Passed Bill (H.R. 2)
		Coordinator is authorized to establish. The National Coordinator will report at least annually on actions taken to assist beginning farmers and ranchers. Permits the Coordinator to enter into contacts and agreements with universities or nonprofits to conduct research on the profitability of new farms, to develop educational materials, to conduct workshops, and to conduct mentoring activities. **(§12306)**
Outreach and Assistance for Socially Disadvantaged Farmers and Ranchers and Veteran Farmers and Ranchers. Requires the Secretary of Agriculture to carry out an outreach and technical assistance program to encourage and assist socially disadvantaged farmers and ranchers and veteran farmers or ranchers (A) in owning and operating farms and ranches; and (B) in participating equitably in the full range of agricultural programs offered by the Department. **(7 U.S.C. 2279)**	No comparable provision.	**Availability of Department of Agriculture Programs for Veteran Farmers and Ranchers.** Amends provisions of the Federal Crop Insurance Act, the Consolidated Farm and Rural Development Act, Agricultural Research, Extension, and Education Reform Act of 1998, the Federal Agriculture Improvement and Reform Act of 1996, the Food Security Act of 1985, and Agricultural Act of 2014 to define veteran farmer and rancher in those statutes and to designate veteran farmers and ranchers as "covered producers" and "covered farmers and ranchers" and to insert "and "veterans" as specifically eligible farmers and ranchers for various forms of agriculture assistance and support under these statutes. **(§12307)**
Textiles		
Pima Agriculture Cotton Trust Fund. Establishes a trust fund in the Treasury of the United States for the purpose of reducing the injury to domestic manufacturers resulting from tariffs on cotton fabric that are higher than tariffs on certain apparel articles made of cotton fabric. The Secretary may make payments to nationally recognized associations that promote pima cotton use, yarn spinners who produce ring spun	Repeals the Pima Cotton Trust Fund. **(§11301)**	Reauthorizes the trust fund in the Treasury of the United States for the purpose of reducing the injury to domestic manufacturers resulting from tariffs on cotton fabric that are higher than tariffs on certain apparel articles made of cotton fabric. The Secretary may make payments to nationally recognized associations hat promote pima cotton use,

Current Law/Policy	House-Passed Bill (H.R. 2)	Senate-Passed Bill (H.R. 2)
cotton yarns, and manufacturers that cut and sew cotton shirts in the United States and that certify that they used imported cotton fabric in 2013. Payments to spinners and manufacturers are based on a production ratio and must be certified through affidavit. The Secretary shall transfer $16 million for each of the calendar years 2014-2018 from the Commodity Credit Corporation (CCC) to the trust fund, and are to remain available until expended. **(7 U.S.C. 2101 note)**		yarn spinners who produce ring spun cotton yarns, and manufacturers that cut and sew cotton shirts in the United States and that certify that they used imported cotton fabric in the prior calendar year. A yarn spinner shall not receive more than the cost of pima cotton that was purchased during the prior calendar ear and was used in spinning any cotton yarns. The Secretary shall reallocate any amounts to spinners using the new ratio. The Secretary shall transfer $16 million for each of the calendar years through 2023 from the CCC to the trust fund to remain available until expended. **(§12603)**
Agriculture Wool Apparel Manufacturers Trust Fund. Establishes a trust fund in the Treasury of the United States for the purpose of reducing the injury to domestic manufacturers resulting from tariffs on wool fabric that are higher than tariffs on certain apparel articles made of wool fabric. Annual payments based on one of four funding mechanisms are to be made to eligible domestic manufacturers of wool fabric and processors of wool material. The Secretary shall transfer up to $30 million in CCC funds for each of the calendar years 2014-2019 to the Agriculture Wool Trust. The funds remain available until expended. **(7 U.S.C. 7101 note)**	Repeals the Wool Apparel Manufacturers Trust Fund. **(§11302)**	Reauthorizes the trust fund in the Treasury of the United States and directs the Secretary shall transfer up to $30 million in CCC funds for each of the calendar years through 2023 to the Agriculture Wool Trust to remain available until expended. **(§12604)**
Wool Research, Development, and Promotion Trust Fund. Establishes a trust fund for the purpose of assisting U.S. wool producers to improve the competitiveness of the American wool market. The trust fund sunsets effective January 1, 2015. Section 12316 of the 2014 farm bill provided $2.25 million of CCC funds for grants as defined in the trust fund for each of the calendar years 2015-2019. The funds remain available until expended. **(7 U.S.C. 7101 note)**	Repeals Wool Research and Promotion Grants Funding. **(§11303)**	**Wool Research and Promotion.** Reauthorizes grants funding for the purpose of assisting U.S. wool producers to improve the competitiveness of the American wool market providing $2.25 million of CCC funds for each of the calendar years 2020 through 2023 to remain available until expended. **(§12605)**

Table 15. (Continued)

Current Law/Policy	House-Passed Bill (H.R. 2)	Senate-Passed Bill (H.R. 2)
No comparable provision.	Establishes the **Textile Trust Fund** for the purpose of reducing injury for domestic manufacturers resulting from tariffs on pima fabric and wool products that are higher than tariffs on certain apparel items made of pima cotton fabric and wool. The Secretary may make payments to nationally recognized associations who promote pima cotton use, yarn spinners who produce ring spun cotton yarns in the United States and certify through affidavit that they used pima cotton during the year in which the affidavit is filed and the previous calendar year, and manufacturers that cut and sew cotton shirts in the United States and that certify through affidavit that they used imported cotton fabric during the previous calendar year. In addition, the Textile Trust Fund is established for the purpose of reducing economic injury to domestic manufacturers resulting from tariffs on wool fabric that are higher than tariffs on certain apparel articles made of wool fabric. Payments to eligible wool manufacturers and processors must be certified through affidavit. For each of the calendar years 2019-2023, the Secretary shall transfer $8 million of CCC funds to the Textile Trust Fund for eligible manufacturers of pima cotton, $15 million to eligible wool manufacturers, and $2.25 million in grants for wool research and promotion. Funds are to remain available until expended. **(§11304)**	No comparable provision.
Sheep Production and Marketing Grant Program. Establishes a competitive grant program through USDA's Agricultural Marketing Service to improve the sheep industry, including infrastructure, business, resource development, or innovative approaches for long- term needs.	Authorizes $2 million of CCC funds for FY2019 for the purposes of strengthening and enhancing the production of sheep and sheep products in the United States, with funds remaining available until expended. **(§11304(e)(3))**	Authorizes appropriations of $1.5 million per year for fiscal years 2019-2023. **(§12101)**

Current Law/Policy	House-Passed Bill (H.R. 2)	Senate-Passed Bill (H.R. 2)
Provided $1.5 million in CCC mandatory funds for FY2014 to remain available until expended. **(7 U.S.C. 1627a)**		
United States Grains Standards Act		
United States Grain Standards Act (USGSA). Establishes official marketing standards for grains and oilseeds and sets procedures for grain inspection and weighing services. Authorizes user fees for services. **(7 U.S.C. 71 *et seq.*)** **Exceptions to Geographic Areas for Official Agencies Under the USGSA.** Revises USGSA regulations to establish criteria to allow more than one designated official agency to inspect or weigh grain within a single geographic area. Criteria to consider for exceptions are (1) timely service, (2) nonuse of service, and (3) barge probe service. The rule enhances the orderly marketing of grain by providing segments of the grain industry with more cost-effective and responsive official grain inspection and weighing services without undermining the integrity of the official system. **(68 *Federal Register* 19137 (April 18, 2003))**	Restores exceptions created in the 2003 regulation **(7 C.F.R. 800.117)** that were revoked on or after September 30, 2015, upon the reauthorization of the USGSA (Title III of P.L. 114-54). Grain handling facilities must request the restoration of exceptions within 80 days of enactment. **(§11401)**	No comparable provision.
Noninsured Crop Disaster Assistance Program		
Noninsured Crop Disaster Assistance Program (NAP). Authorized to receive such sums as necessary in mandatory funding to provide financial assistance to producers of crops that are not insurable under the federal crop insurance program. Basic, or catastrophic coverage, provides a payment to an eligible producer whose actual production is less than 50% of the established (historical) yield for the crop. Producers pay a fee of $250 per crop per county or $750 per producer per county, not to exceed $1,875 per producer. Additional, or buy-up coverage, may be purchased for an additional premium to cover increments up to 65% of production. Total NAP payments are limited to $125,000 per crop year, per individual or entity. **(7 U.S.C. 7333)**	Amends the definition of *eligible crop* to include those crops that may be insurable under the crop insurance program but only for whole farm plans or policies that provide coverage for specific intervals based on weather indexes. **(§11501)** Increases the service fees to $350 per crop per county or $1,050 per producer per county, not to exceed $2,100 per producer. **(§11502)** Reauthorizes buy-up coverage through FY2023 and amends the premium for additional coverage to be proportional to a producer's share of the crop. **(§11503)**	Adds a data collection and coordination requirement. Amends benefit reductions on native sod to include all "eligible" crops rather than "annual" crops for four years. Adds an annual reporting requirement for benefits reduced by the native sod provision. Provides flexibility for NAP application deadlines and requires a streamlined process for submitting records and acreage reports for diverse production systems. Adjusts the payment formula to include the total number of acres devoted to the eligible crop. Separates the payment limit for catastrophic coverage ($125,000) and additional coverage ($300,000). Increases service fees to $325 per crop per county, or $825 per producer per county, not to exceed $1,950 per producer. Deletes sunset dates for buy-up coverage. **(§1601)**

Table 15. (Continued)

Current Law/Policy	House-Passed Bill (H.R. 2)	Senate-Passed Bill (H.R. 2)
		Adds a new requirement for certain producers that suffered losses due to volcanic activity stating that USDA must provide NAP assistance, less fees, to cover losses of eligible crops in counties with a qualifying disaster declaration. **(§1602)**
USDA Reorganization		
In May 2017, USDA announced an agency reorganization that created an Under Secretary for Trade and Foreign Agricultural Affairs, an Under Secretary for Farm Production and Conservation, and an Assistant to the Secretary for Rural Development. The duties of the new Under Secretaries were previously assigned to the Under Secretary of Farm and Foreign Agricultural Affairs and the Under Secretary for Natural Resources and Environment. The duties of the Assistant to the Secretary were formerly assigned to the Under Secretary for Rural Development USDA used authorities under the Department of Agriculture Reorganization Act of 1994 **(7 U.S.C. 6911 et seq)** and the Reorganization Plan No. 2 of 1953 **(7 U.S.C. 2201 note)**.	Reorganization provisions are in **Subtitle F—Other Matters** in the House bill.	Reorganization provisions are in **Subtitle D—Department of Agriculture Reorganization Act of 1994 Amendments** in the Senate bill.
Department of Agriculture Reorganization Act of 1994. **(7.S.C. 6933(d)(1))**	Removes Under Secretary of Agriculture for Farm and Foreign Agricultural Services and inserts Under Secretary of Agriculture for Production and Conservation in the Office of Risk Management. **(§11601(a))**	Identical to House bill. **(§12405(a))**
Department of Agriculture Reorganization Act of 1994. **(7 U.S.C. 6952(b)(3))**	Removes Under Secretary of Agriculture for Farm and Foreign Agricultural Services and inserts Under Secretary for Trade and Foreign Agricultural Affairs in the Multiagency Task Force. **(§11601(a))**	Removes Under Secretary of Agriculture for Farm and Foreign Agricultural Services and inserts Under Secretary for Agriculture for Farm Production and Conservation in the Multiagency Task Force. **(§12405(b))**
Food for Peace Act. **(7 U.S.C. 1725(b))**	Removes Under Secretary of Agriculture for Farm and Foreign Agricultural Services and inserts Under Secretary for Trade and Foreign Agricultural Affairs in the Food Aid Consultative Group. **(§11601(a))**	Identical to House bill. **(§12405(c))**

Current Law/Policy	House-Passed Bill (H.R. 2)	Senate-Passed Bill (H.R. 2)
Higher Education Act of 1965. **(20 U.S.C. 1131c(c)(1)(A))**	Removes Under Secretary of Agriculture for Farm and Foreign Agricultural Services and inserts Under Secretary of Agriculture for Trade and Foreign Agricultural Affairs in the Interagency Committee on Minority Careers in International Affairs. **(§11601(a))**	Identical to House bill. **(§12405(d))**
Agricultural Act of 1961 and Consolidated Farm and Rural Development Act. **(7 U.S.C. 1991(a)(13)(D))**	In the definitions, inserts *or other official designated by the Secretary of Agriculture* after *Under Secretary for Rural Development* where it appears and inserts *or designated official* after *Under Secretary* where it appears. **(§11601(b))**	No comparable provision
Agricultural Marketing Act of 1946. **(7 U.S.C. 1627b(f)(3)(B)(i))**	Inserts *or other official designated by the Secretary* after *Under Secretary of Agriculture for Rural Development* in the National Sheep Industry Improvement Center. **§11601(b))**	No comparable provision.
Native American Business Development, Trade Promotion, and Tourism Act of 2000. **(25 U.S.C. 4305(a)(2)(A))**	Inserts *or other official designated by the Secretary of Agriculture* after *Under Secretary of Agriculture for Rural Development* in the Intertribal Tourism Demonstration Projects. **(§11601(b))**	No comparable provision.
Rehabilitation Act of 1973. **(29 U.S.C. 721(a)(11)(C))**	Inserts *or other official designated by the Secretary of Agriculture* after *Under Secretary for Rural Development of the Department of Agriculture* in the State Plans for Vocational Rehabilitation Services. **(§11601(b))**	No comparable provision.
Establishes the **Assistant Secretaries of Agriculture** under the Department of Agriculture Reorganization Act of 1994. **(7 U.S.C. 6918)**	No comparable provision.	Amends the 1994 Act to change the name of the Assistant Secretary of Agriculture for Congressional Relations to Assistant Secretary of Agriculture for Congressional and Intergovernmental Affairs. Any official serving in the position on the date of enactment, and who has been confirmed by the Senate, is not required to be reconfirmed. **(§12401)**
Establishes the **Military Veterans Agricultural Liaison** under the Department of Agriculture Reorganization Act of 1994. **(7 U.S.C. 6919)**	No comparable provision	Amends the duties of the liaison to require the establishment and periodic update of a website that identifies available apprenticeships for veterans in USDA, job and skills training opportunities.

Table 15. (Continued)

Current Law/Policy	House-Passed Bill (H.R. 2)	Senate-Passed Bill (H.R. 2)
		The information should be designed to assist businesses, nonprofits, educational institutes, and farmers that want to create apprenticeship programs for veterans and have them approved by a state approving agency under 38 U.S.C. Chapter 36. The liaison is required to consult with and give technical assistance to the Department of Defense, Department of Veteran Affairs, the Small Business Administration, and the Department of Labor. Requires USDA to conduct a study on the effectiveness of the website. The liaison is required to submit an annual report on beginning farmer training for veterans and agricultural vocational and rehabilitation programs for veterans. **(§12402)**
Department of Agriculture Reorganization Act of 1994. Authorizes the Secretary to streamline, reorganize, and manage USDA programs and activities. **(7 U.S.C. 6911 *et seq.*)**	No comparable provision.	Amends the 1994 Act to require **Civil Rights Analyses.** Defines civil rights analysis as a review to analyze and identify actions, policies and decisions that may have an adverse impact on employees, contractors, or beneficiaries of any USDA program or activity based on membership in a group protected by federal law. Before implementing actions, policy, or decision documents, USDA is to conduct a civil rights analysis. These include entries into the Federal Register, charters for advisory committees, councils, or boards, any regulations or new or revised instructions, procedures, or guidance, reductions- in-force, or transfer of functions, or any policy, program, or activity that might have an adverse civil rights impact The Assistant Secretary for Civil Rights may grant expedited review or waivers in certain cases.

Current Law/Policy	House-Passed Bill (H.R. 2)	Senate-Passed Bill (H.R. 2)
		No later than 2 years after enactment, the Comptroller General is required to conduct a study on the effectiveness of USDA in processing and resolving civil rights complaints, minority participation rates in farm programs, the realignment of civil rights functions under Secretarial Memorandum 1076-023 (March 9, 2018) and whether the realignment has had negative implications, efforts of USDA to identify actions, programs, or activities that may have an adverse effect, and efforts to strategically plan actions to decrease discrimination and civil rights complaints. The Comptroller General is to submit the report to the House and Senate agriculture committees no later than 60 days after completion of its study on civil rights. **(§12403)**
Establishes **Consolidated Farm Service Agency (FSA)** under the Department of Agriculture Reorganization Act of 1994. **(7 U.S.C. 6932)**	No comparable provision.	**Farm Service Agency.** Amends the section, and other related sections in the 1994 Act, by removing the term "consolidated." **(§12404)**
Establishes the **Under Secretary of Agriculture for Rural Development** under the Department of Agriculture Reorganization Act of 1994. **(7 U.S.C. 6941)** The May 2017 USDA reorganization replaced the Under Secretary of Agriculture for Rural Development with an Assistant to the Secretary for Rural Development.	No comparable provision.	Requires USDA to re-establish the position of **Under Secretary of Agriculture for Rural Development.** The authority in this provision does not terminate. **(§12406)**
Establishes the **Rural Utilities Service (RUS)** under the Department of Agriculture Reorganization Act of 1994. **(7 U.S.C. 6942)** Rural Electrification Act of 1936 **(7 U.S.C. 918b)** Consolidated Farm and Rural Development Act **(7 U.S.C.2008p(a))** Farm Security and Rural Investment Act of 2002 **(7 U.S.C. 8107a(b)(a))** Launching Our Communities' Access to Local Television Act of 2000 **(47 U.S.C. 1103)**	No comparable provision.	**Administrator of RUS.** Amends compensation for the RUS administrator. The base pay is not to exceed the maximum amount of compensation payable to a member of the Senior Executive Service under 5 U.S.C. 5382, except the certification requirement does not apply. Removes the RUS administrator from Level IV Executive Schedule (5 U.S.C. 5315). Makes conforming amendments to various laws by striking *Administrator of RUS* and inserting *Secretary of Agriculture*.

Table 15. (Continued)

Current Law/Policy	House-Passed Bill (H.R. 2)	Senate-Passed Bill (H.R. 2)
		(§12407)
Department of Agriculture Reorganization Act of 1994. Authorizes the Secretary to streamline, reorganize, and manage USDA programs and activities. **(7 U.S.C. 6911 *et seq.*)**	No comparable provision.	Requires USDA to establish the position of **Rural Health Liaison**. The liaison is to (1) consult with the Secretary of Health and Human Services and coordinate USDA's role in rural health; (2) integrate USDA rural health strategic planning and activities; (3) improve communications within USDA and other federal agencies; (4) advocate for health care and infrastructure needs; (5) provide stakeholders with relevant information on USDA programs for rural health; (6) maintain communication with public health, medical, occupational safety, and other stakeholders on current and upcoming issues; (7) consult on programs, pilot projects, research, and training; (8) provide expertise on rural health as Chair of the Interagency Task Force on Agriculture and Rural Prosperity, and (9) provide technical assistance and guidance to USDA outreach, extension, and county offices. **(§12408)**
Establishes the **Healthy Foods Financing Initiative** under the Department of Agriculture Reorganization Act of 1994. **(7 U.S.C. 6953)**	No comparable provision.	Amends the Initiative by adding enterprises after retailers in the section, and adding the conditional clause "as applicable" in the subsection (c)(2)(B)(ii) on eligible projects. **(§12409)**
Establishes the **Natural Resources Conservation Service (NRCS)** under the Department of Agriculture Reorganization Act of I 994. **(7 U.S.C. 6962)**	No comparable provision.	Adds a section on field offices, by prohibiting USDA from closing an NRCS field office unless the House Committee on Agriculture and the Senate Committee on Agriculture, Nutrition, and Forestry are notified no later than 60 days before closure. Prohibits, without 60-day committee notification, the permanent relocation of NRCS field employees if the result is two or fewer employees. **(§12410)**

Current Law/Policy	House-Passed Bill (H.R. 2)	Senate-Passed Bill (H.R. 2)
Establishes the **Under Secretary of Agriculture for Research, Education, and Economics (REE)** under the Department of Agriculture Reorganization Act of 1994. **(7 U.S.C. 6971)**	No comparable provision.	Amends the Research, Education, and Extension Office under REE by renaming it the **Office of Chief Scientist**, and changes the names where they appear. Amends the term of service of division chiefs in the Office to "not less than 3 years." In addition, the Under Secretary of REE is to select personnel to oversee the implementation, training, and compliance with USDA scientific integrity policy, integrate strategic planning and evaluation, prepare an annual report to Congress, and coordinate international engagements with the Department of State, other federal offices, and international agencies. Authorizes appropriations of such sums as necessary to fund the costs of division personnel. Amends the Rotation of Personnel clause by adding (iii) provides strong staff continuity to the Office of Chief Scientist. **(§12411)**
Department of Agriculture Reorganization Act of 1994. Authorizes the Secretary to streamline, reorganize, and manage USDA programs and activities. **(7 U.S.C. 6911 *et seq.*)**	No comparable provision.	Amends the 1994 Act to establish Subtitle J—Trade and Foreign Agricultural Affairs, and the Under Secretary of Agriculture for Trade and Foreign Agricultural Affairs. The Under Secretary is appointed by the President, by and with the advice and consent of the Senate. The Under Secretary's principal functions are trade and foreign agricultural affairs, and whatever other duties may be required by law or prescribed by the Secretary. **(§12412)**
Termination of Authority. Ends the Secretary of Agriculture's authority to reorganize USDA two years after the enactment of the Department of Agriculture Reorganization Act of 1994. Lists functions that are not affected by the two-year termination date. **(7 U.S.C. 7014)**	Adds to provisions that do not terminate *Section 772 of the Agriculture, Rural Development, Food and Drug Administration, and Related Agencies Appropriations Act, 2018, or the Agriculture and Nutrition Act of 2018* in 7 U.S.C. 7014(b). **(§11602)** Section 772 establishes the position of Under Secretary of Farm Production and Conservation, which replaces the	Similar to House bill. Amends the section to insert the *Agriculture Improvement Act of 2018* in 7 U.S.C. 7014(b). **(§12416)**

Table 15. (Continued)

Current Law/Policy	House-Passed Bill (H.R. 2)	Senate-Passed Bill (H.R. 2)
	Under Secretary of Agriculture for Farm and Foreign Agricultural Services. Section 772 also amends 5 U.S.C. 5314, which lists Level III positions of the Executive Schedule, by striking *Under Secretary for Farm and Foreign Agricultural Services* and inserting *Under Secretary of Farm Production and Conservation* and *Under Secretary of Agriculture for Trade and Foreign Agricultural Affairs*.	
Department of Agriculture Reorganization Act of 1994. Authorizes the Secretary to streamline, reorganize, and manage USDA programs and activities. **(7 U.S.C. 6911 *et seq.*) Agriculture Act of 2014 (P.L. 113-79)**	No comparable provision.	Repeals several sections of the 1994 Act and one in the 2014 farm bill that are in 7 U.S.C. 6901 *et seq.* as follows: Transfer of Department Functions to Secretary of Agriculture (§6911); Reductions in Number of Department Personnel (§6913); Consolidation of Headquarters Offices (§6914);
		Reports by Secretary (§6917); Reorganization of Forest Service (§6963); Program Staff (§6972); Proposed Conforming Amendments (§7013); and Under Secretary of Agriculture for Trade and Foreign Agricultural Affairs (§6935) in the 2014 farm bill. **(§12413)**
Establishes the **Office of Risk Management** under Department of Agriculture Reorganization Act of 1994. **(7 U.S.C. 6933)**	No comparable provision.	**Technical Corrections.** Strikes the first clause in section (a), which refers to a nonexistent paragraph. **(§12414(a))**
Establishes **Assistant Secretaries of Agriculture** under Department of Agriculture Reorganization Act of 1994. **(7 U.S.C. 6918)**	No comparable provision.	Amends some language in sections (b) and (c) to correct an error. Amends the effective date language. **(§12414(b))**
No comparable provision.	No comparable provision.	**Effect of Subtitle.** The effective date for the provisions in Subtitle D—Department of Agriculture Reorganization Act of 1994 Amendments (excluding 12407(a)(1)(B) and 12414(b)(2)) take effect upon enactment. The subtitle provisions do not affect the authority of the Secretary or the authorities delegated. **(§12415)**

Current Law/Policy	House-Passed Bill (H.R. 2)	Senate-Passed Bill (H.R. 2)
Other Organizational Changes		
USDA conference transparency. Requires USDA to provide annual reports to the House Committee on Agriculture and the Senate Committee on Agriculture, Nutrition, and Forestry on conferences sponsored or held by USDA or attended by USDA employees. Conferences that cost the federal government less than $10,000 are excluded from reporting requirements. **(7 U.S.C. 2255b(a)(3)(A))**	Amends the subsection by raising the exclusion to $75,000. **(§11603)**	No comparable provision
No comparable provision	**National Agriculture Imagery Program.** Requires USDA, through the Farm Service Agency, to carry out a national agriculture imagery program to annually acquire aerial imagery during the agricultural growing season. Requires the data to (1) include high resolution processed digital imagery; (2) be available in a format that can be provided to federal, state, and private sector entities; (3) be technologically compatible with geospatial information technology; and (4) be consistent with the standards of the Federal Geographic Data Committee. Authorizes an appropriation of $23 million for FY2019 and each fiscal year thereafter. **(§11604)**	No comparable provision
Commodity Promotion, Research, and Information Act of 1996. Authorizes the establishment of commodity promotion and research programs (i.e., checkoff programs). **(7 U.S.C. 7401 *et seq.*)**	**Report on Inclusion of Natural Stone Products in Commodity Promotion, Research, and Information Act of 1996.** Requires that not later than 180 days after enactment, USDA is required to submit a report to the House Committee on Agriculture that examines the effects of establishing a promotion and research program for natural stone. The report is to cover the effects a program would have on (1) research and promotion of natural stone, (2) development and expansion of domestic markets, (3) economic activity of the natural stone industry subject to a promotion board, (4) economic development in rural areas, and (5) benefits to U.S. consumers of natural stone. **(§11605)**	No comparable provision.

Table 15. (Continued)

Current Law/Policy	House-Passed Bill (H.R. 2)	Senate-Passed Bill (H.R. 2)
Peanuts Standards Board. Establishes a board consisting of producers and industry representatives from peanut-producing states. Board members are appointed from three regions: Southeast (Alabama, Georgia, and Florida); Southwest (Texas, Oklahoma, and New Mexico); and Virginia/Carolina (Virginia and North Carolina). Members of the board are to advise the Secretary on quality and handling standards for domestic and import peanuts. **(7 U.S.C. 7958(c))**	**South Carolina inclusion in Virginia/Carolina peanut-producing region.** Amends the designated Virginia/Carolina region by adding South Carolina as a state represented on the Peanut Standards Board. **(§11606)**	Identical to House bill. **(§12502)**
Department of Agriculture Reorganization Act of 1994. Authorizes the Secretary to streamline, reorganize, and manage USDA programs and activities. **(7 U.S.C. 6911 *et seq.*)**	Amends the 1994 Act to require USDA to establish, within the Office of the Secretary, a **Food Loss and Waste Reduction Liaison** to coordinate federal programs to measure and reduce the incidence of food loss and waste, provide information and resources, and raise awareness of the liability protections for donated foods. **(§11607)**	No comparable provision.
Department of Agriculture Reorganization Act of 1994. Authorizes the Secretary to streamline, reorganize, and manage USDA programs and activities. **(7 U.S.C. 6911 *et seq.*)**	Amends the 1994 Act to require USDA to establish a **Food Access Liaison** within the Office of the Secretary. The Liaison is to coordinate USDA programs to reduce barriers to food access, and provide information and outreach. The Liaison is to submit an annual report to Congress on USDA efforts to reduce barriers to food access. **(§11608)**	No comparable provision.
Cotton classification services. Authorizes USDA to make cotton classification and classification fee collection services available to cotton producers. **(7 U.S.C. 473a)**	Amends the cotton classification section by allowing employees who are hired to classify cotton to work up to 240 days in a service year and be rehired noncompetitively every year for the same position, or a successor position, if they meet performance standards. **(§11609)**	No comparable provision.
No comparable provision.	**Century Farms Program.** Establishes a program under which the Secretary of Agriculture recognizes any farm or ranch, as defined in Cooperative Services Grant Programs, which has been in continuous operation for at least 100 years, and has been owned by the same family for at least 100	Identical to House bill. **(§12512)**

Current Law/Policy	House-Passed Bill (H.R. 2)	Senate-Passed Bill (H.R. 2)
	consecutive years, as verified through appropriate documentation. **(§11610)**	
Reports, Studies and Initiatives		
Commodity Promotion, Research, and Information Act of 1996. Authorizes the establishment of commodity promotion and research programs (i.e., checkoff programs). **(7 U.S.C. 7401 *et seq.*)**	**Report on Inclusion of Natural Stone Products in Commodity Promotion, Research, and Information Act of 1996.** Requires that not later than 180 days after enactment, USDA is required to submit a report to the House Committee on Agriculture that examines the effects of establishing a promotion and research program for natural stone. The report is to cover the effects a program would have on (1) research and promotion of natural stone, (2) development and expansion of domestic markets, (3) economic activity of the natural stone industry subject to a promotion board, (4) economic development in rural areas, and (5) benefits to U.S. consumers of natural stone. **(§11605)**	No comparable provision.
No comparable provision.	**Report on Agricultural Innovation.** Requires USDA, in consultation with EPA and FDA, to prepare and submit a report to the House Committee on Agriculture and the Senate Committee on Agriculture, Nutrition, and Forestry on plans for improving federal government policies and procedures with respect to gene editing and other precision plant breeding methods. **(§11611)**	No comparable provision.
No comparable provision.	No comparable provision.	**Study on Food Waste.** Requires USDA to conduct a study to evaluate and determine methods of measuring food waste; standards for the volume of food waste; and factors that reate food waste. **(§12506)**
No comparable provision.	No comparable provision.	**Report on Business Centers.** Requires the Comptroller General of the United States to provide House and Senate agriculture committees a report evaluating USDA business centers. The report is to examine the effectiveness on customer service and on funding in the Natural Resources Conservation Service, the Farm Service Agency, and the

Table 15. (Continued)

Current Law/Policy	House-Passed Bill (H.R. 2)	Senate-Passed Bill (H.R. 2)
		Risk Management Agency; the impact on information technology modernization, on human resources; and concerns, and positive or negative impacts of the centers. The report is due no later than 365 days after enactment. **(§12507)**
No comparable provision.	No comparable provision.	**Information Technology Modernization.** The Comptroller General is to examine USDA efforts related to information technology for business centers and conservation, and efforts to modernize other information technology projects. An initial report including a detailed description, a justification, a cost-benefit analysis, and a description of concerns on each project is due to the House and Senate agriculture committees no later than 180 days after enactment. The Comptroller General is to provide the committees regular briefings and, no later than two years after enactment, the Comptroller General is to provide a comprehensive report that reviews awarded contracts and activities, a description of any problems or inadequacies, and recommendations. **(§12508)**
No comparable provision.	No comparable provision.	**Report on Personnel.** USDA is required to provide the House and Senate agriculture committees a biannual report on the number of staff years and employees for each agency for each fiscal year 2019 through 2023. **(§12509)**
No comparable provision.	No comparable provision.	**Report on Absent Landlords.** USDA is required to provide Congress a report on the effects of absent landlords on agricultural production, including land valuation, soil health, and the economic stability of rural communities. The report is due no later than one year from enactment. **(§12510)**

Current Law/Policy	House-Passed Bill (H.R. 2)	Senate-Passed Bill (H.R. 2)
No comparable provision.	No comparable provision.	**Study of Marketplace Fraud of Unique Traditional Foods.** Requires the U.S. Comptroller General to conduct a study (within one year of enactment) of the market impact of traditional and tribally produced foods and products; the marketplace fraud of foods that mimic tribal foods; and an analysis of federal laws administered by USDA, intellectual property laws,
No comparable provision.	No comparable provision.	**Dairy Business Innovation Initiatives.** The USDA Agricultural Marketing Service (AMS) is required to establish at least three regionally located dairy business innovation initiatives to encourage the use of regional milk production, create higher-value use of dairy products, promote processing and marketing innovation, diversify markets to reduce risk, and use of federal resources. The initiatives are to provide direct nonmonetary assistance (e.g., technical assistance, training, informational websites, and conferences) and grants for modernization, specialization, updates to the value chain, and product development and marketing. Within one year of enactment, USDA is to provide a report to Congress describing the implementation of the initiatives. Authorizes appropriations of $20 million each fiscal year. **(§12519)**
No comparable provision.	No comparable provision.	**Report on Funding for the National Institute of Food and Agriculture (NIFA) and Other Extension Programs.** Within two years of the date that the 2017 Census of Agriculture is released, USDA is to submit a report to the House and Senate agriculture committees that describes the funding requirements that would enable NIFA to address extension and research needs to further address the growth and economics of rural and farming communities based on changing demographics.

Table 15. (Continued)

Current Law/Policy	House-Passed Bill (H.R. 2)	Senate-Passed Bill (H.R. 2)
		(§12520)
Animal Welfare		
No comparable provision.	**Report on Dog Importation.** USDA, in consultation with the Secretaries of Commerce, Health and Human Services, and Homeland Security, is to submit a report to the House Committee on Agriculture and the Senate Committee on Agriculture, Nutrition, and Forestry on the importation of dogs. The report is to include (1) an estimate of the number of dogs imported annually, (2) the number of dogs imported for resale, (3) the number imported for resale but denied importation due to failure of Animal Welfare Act (7 U.S.C. 2148) requirements, and (4) Secretary recommendations of federal statutory changes needed for importation for resale. **(§11612)**	Identical to House bill. **(§12513)**
No comparable provision.	**Prohibition on Slaughter of Dogs and Cats for Human Consumption.** Amends the Animal Welfare Act (7 U.S.C. 2131 *et seq.*) to prohibit knowingly slaughtering dogs or cats for human consumption. Also prohibits the transporting, possessing, buying, selling, or donation of a dog or cat for such purposes and imposes penalties for violations. The provision does not limit any state or local law to protect animal welfare. **(§11613)**	Identical to House provision. **(§12521)**
Animal Welfare Act. The Act regulates the transportation, purchase, sale, housing, care, handling, and treatment of animals by carriers, persons, or organizations using them for research, experimental purposes, exhibition purposes, holding them for sale as pets or for any such purpose or use. **(7 U.S.C. 2131 *et seq.*)**	**Extending Prohibition on Animal Fighting to the Territories.** Amends Section 26 of the Animal Welfare Act (7 U.S.C. 2156) by removing the exemption for states where animal fighting would not be a violation of the law. Makes it unlawful to sell, buy, or transport in interstate or foreign commerce any knife or sharp object to be used on the leg of a bird as a weapon in animal fighting. **(§11616)**	No comparable provision.

Current Law/Policy	House-Passed Bill (H.R. 2)	Senate-Passed Bill (H.R. 2)
Wildlife		
Control of Depredating and Otherwise Injurious Birds. Under the authority of the Migratory Bird Treaty (7 U.S.C. 703 *et seq.*), regulates how a person may take, possess, or transport migratory birds for depredation control purposes. **(50 C.F.R. Subpart D)**	**Depredation Permits for Black Vultures.** Allows the Secretary of the Interior, in conjunction with the Director of the United States Fish and Wildlife Service, to authorize the issuance of depredation permits to livestock farmers for black vultures, otherwise prohibited by Federal law, to prevent black vultures from taking livestock during the calving season. The permits are allowed only in states or regions where producers are affected by black vultures. Producers are required to report takings to the proper enforcement agencies. **(§11615)**	No comparable provision.
Prohibited Acts. Under the authority of the Endangered Species Act (ESA; 16 U.S.C. 1531 *et seq.*) all individuals are required to obtain permission from the Secretary of the Interior prior to engaging in the import or export of fish, wildlife, or raw or worked African elephant ivory. Exemptions for this requirement are provided for individuals engaging in the import or export of shellfish and fishery products for species not listed as threatened or endangered under the ESA. The section is enforced by the U.S. Fish and Wildlife Service and implemented through title 50 C.F.R. Part 14, which requires all individuals, who are not exempted, to obtain an import/export license prior to engaging in business. **(16 U.S.C. 1538(d)(1))**	No comparable provision.	**Expedited Exportation of Certain Species.** Within 180 days of enactment, requires the Director of the U.S. Fish and Wildlife Service to issue a proposed rule to amend 50 C.F.R. 14.92 to establish expedited procedures relating to the export of sea urchin and sea cucumber species. To be eligible for an exemption, the sea urchin and sea cucumber species intended for export must not require permits under 50 C.F.R. Parts 16, 17, or 23; must have been harvested from waters under U.S. jurisdiction; and must be exported for the purpose of animal or human consumption. As part of the proposed rulemaking, the Director may provide an exemption from the requirements to obtain permission under 16 U.S.C. 1538(d)(1), or an export license under 50 C.F.R. Part 14. Prior to providing such an exemption, the Director must find that an exemption will not have a negative impact on the conservation of the species. Additionally, an entity is not eligible to receive an exemption if they have been convicted of violating a federal law related to the import, transport, or export of wildlife within not less than five

Table 15. (Continued)

Current Law/Policy	House-Passed Bill (H.R. 2)	Senate-Passed Bill (H.R. 2)
		years prior to the date on which the entity applies for the exemption. **(§12601)**
Interagency Cooperation. Under the authority of the Endangered Species Act (ESA; 16 U.S.C. 1531 *et seq.*), directs all federal agencies to aid in the conservation of species listed as threatened or endangered under the. Requires federal agencies to consult with the relevant Secretary responsible for implementing of the ESA on agency actions, including actions in which the agency provides funding or permitting to nonfederal partners, to ensure that the actions are not likely to jeopardize a listed species or adversely modify designated critical habitats. Outlines the consultation process between federal agencies and the respective Secretary. Requires the consultation process, when necessary, to be completed within 90 days or a timeline that is otherwise agreed to pursuant to the requirements under the section. Following the conclusion of the consultation, requires the Secretary to promptly issue a biological opinion with the findings. The biological opinion may find that either the action is unlikely to jeopardize the species or adversely modify critical habitat or, in the event that jeopardy or adverse habitat modification is likely, the opinion may include reasonable and prudent alternatives for the agency action. Provides for an exemption process and identifies the process by which an exemption can be applied for and granted. **(16 U.S.C. 1536(b)(3))**	**Consideration of the Totality of Conservation Measures.** Requires the responsible Secretary to consider off-setting effects of avoidance, minimization, and other species-protection or conservation measures already in place or proposed to be implemented as part of a federal action when determining if an action is likely to jeopardize a listed species or adversely impact critical habitat during the consultation process between a federal agency and the responsible Secretary required pursuant to the ESA. Conservation measures may include the development, improvement, protection, or management of species habitat whether or not it is designated as critical habitat of such species. **(§11614)**	No comparable provision.
Taking, Killing, or Possessing Migratory Birds Unlawful. Prohibits any person to take any migratory game bird by the aid of baiting, or on or over a baited area, when an individual knows or should reasonably know an area is baited under authority of the Migratory Bird Treaty (16 U.S.C. 703 *et seq.*). The prohibition also extends to the baiting of or causing the baiting of an area to aid in the taking of a migratory game bird.	No comparable provision.	**Baiting of Migratory Game Birds.** Within 30 days of the enactment of this Act, requires the Secretary of the Interior, in consultation with the Secretary of Agriculture, to revise 50 C.F.R. Part 20 to clarify that rice ratooning and post-disaster flooding, when carried out as part of a normal agriculture operation, do not constitute baiting with

Current Law/Policy	House-Passed Bill (H.R. 2)	Senate-Passed Bill (H.R. 2)
The prohibition is implemented through 50 C.F.R. 20.21(i), which clarifies that areas that have seeds or grains spread through normal agricultural practices are not considered baited and that the inadvertent scattering of grain or other feed as the result of a hunter entering an area does not constitute baiting. **(16 U.S.C. 703)**		regard to migratory game bird hunting. Defines "rice ratooning" and "post-disaster flooding." Requires the Secretary of Agriculture to, not less than once a year, provide a report to the Secretary of the Interior that describes any changes to normal agricultural operations across the United States. Requires the Secretary of Agriculture, in consultation with the Secretary of the Interior and after seeking input from state departments of fish and wildlife or the Regional Migratory Bird Flyway Councils of the U.S. Fish and Wildlife Service, to publicly post a report on the impact of rice ratooning and post-disaster flooding on the behavior of migratory game birds that are hunted in areas where these practices have occurred. **(§12602)**
Other Provisions		
Clean Water Rule: Definition of *Waters of the United States*. A final rule issued on June 29, 2015, by the Environmental Protection Agency and the Secretary of the Army. It defines the scope of the waters protected under the Clean Water Act (33 U.S.C. 1251 *et seq.*). **(80 *Federal Register* 37054)**	Repeals the final rule, and any regulation or policy revised under the rule is to be applied as if the rule had not been issued. **(§11617)**	No comparable provision.
Acer Access and Development Program. Authorizes grants to state and tribal governments to promote the domestic maple syrup industry. Authorizes appropriations of $20 million per year for FY2014 through FY 2018. **(7 U.S.C. 1632c)**	No comparable provision.	Reauthorizes appropriations of $20 million per year through FY2023. **(§12501)**
No comparable provision.	No comparable provision.	**Pet and women safety.** Adds various provisions of Title 18 of the U.S. Code to address domestic violence and stalking, interstate stalking, interstate violation of protection orders, and restitution (Sections 2261, 2262, 2264A, and 2266) that also involve the pets of abuse victims. Authorizes the Secretary, acting in consultation with the Office of the Violence Against Women of the Department of Justice, the Secretary of Housing and Urban

Table 15. (Continued)

Current Law/Policy	House-Passed Bill (H.R. 2)	Senate-Passed Bill (H.R. 2)
		Development, and the Secretary of Health and Human Services, to award grants to eligible entities to carry out programs to provide assistance to victims of domestic violence, dating violence, sexual assault, or stalking and the pets of such victims. Grants may be used to provide emergency and transitional shelter and housing assistance for domestic violence victims with pets, short-term shelter and housing assistance, support services to victims fleeing a situation of domestic violence, and provide pet-related services such as transportation, veterinary services, and pet care. The provision describes conditions of an award, such as being bound to the nondisclosure of confidential information requirements of the Violence Against Women Act of 1994 (34 U.S.C. 1229(a)). Assistance to victims is limited to no more than 24 months, although there is provision for an extension of up to 6 months. A report to Congress is required which will be transmitted to the Office of Violence Against Women, the Office of Community Planning and Development, and the Administration for Children and Families. Authorizes an appropriation of $3 million each year for FY2019- FY2023. **(§12503)**
No comparable provision.	No comparable provision.	**Data on conservation practices.** Adds a new provision requiring USDA to collect and analyze select conservation practices and their effect on crop yields, soil health, risk, and profitability. Establishes privacy and confidentiality requirements and creates a data warehouse accessible by academic institutions or researchers. Requires technical assistance and the development of internet-based

Current Law/Policy	House-Passed Bill (H.R. 2)	Senate-Passed Bill (H.R. 2)
		tools to assist producers in improving sustainable production practices. Authorizes USDA to utilize existing authorities and funds. **(§12504)**
Import prohibitions on specified foreign produce. Requires that certain imported produce comply with marketing order grade, size, quality, and maturity provisions or comparable marketing order restrictions. **(7 U.S.C. 608e-1(a))**	No comparable provision.	**Marketing orders.** Amends the section by adding cherries and pecans. **(§12505)**
No comparable provision.	No comparable provision.	**Restrictions on use of certain poisons for predator control.** Sodium cyanide is a public safety, national security, environment, and accidental contact risk when used to control predatory animals. The provision prohibits the use of sodium cyanide as a predator control device unless used in accordance with the February 27, 2018 Wildlife Services Directive Number 2.415 of the Animal and Plant Health Inspection Service, and the implementing guidelines. **(§12511)**
Native American Housing Assistance and Self- Determination Act of 1996. Authorizes the Secretary of Housing and Urban Development to make grants on behalf on Indian tribes to carry out affordable housing activities. **(25 U.S.C. 4103)**	No comparable provision.	**Establishment of technical services.** Authorizes the Secretary of Agriculture to establish a technical assistance program to improve access by Tribal entities to rural development programs funded by USDA through available cooperative agreement authorities of the Secretary. The technical assistance program established under subsection (b) shall address the unique challenge of Tribal governments, Tribal producers, Tribal businesses, Tribal business entities, and tribally designated housing entities in accessing Department of Agriculture supported rural infrastructure, rural cooperative development, rural business and industry, rural housing, and other rural development activities. **(§12514)**

Table 15. (Continued)

Current Law/Policy	House-Passed Bill (H.R. 2)	Senate-Passed Bill (H.R. 2)
Native American Housing Assistance and Self- Determination Act of 1996. Authorizes the Secretary of Housing and Urban Development to make grants on behalf on Indian tribes to carry out affordable housing activities. **(25 U.S.C. 4103)**	No comparable provision.	**Promise Zones.** Authorizes the Secretary, after consultation with other Departments, to designate "Tribal Promise Zones" nominated by 1 or more Indian tribes. Designations of Tribal Promise Zones shall occur before January 1, 2020. Designation as a Promise Zone is for the purpose of priority consideration in federal grant programs upon execution of the Tribal Promise Zone agreement with the Secretary. Designation as a Tribal Zone requires a competitiveness plan to address the needs of the nominated zone to attract investment and jobs and improve educational opportunities, demonstrate collaboration across a wide range of stakeholders, outline a strategy that connects the nominated zone to drivers of regional economic growth, and proposes a strategy for focusing on increased access to high quality affordable housing and improved public safety. From the list of nominated sites, the Secretary shall designate Tribal Promise Zones based on the effectiveness of the competitiveness plan, unemployment rates, poverty rates, vacancy rates, crime rates, and other factors determined by the Secretary. Tribal Zones will receive priority for each federal grant program, technical assistance, and capacity building competitive funding application opportunity. Tribal Zone designation will terminate after 10 years, or the date of revocation of such designation. **(§12515)**
No comparable provision.	Similar to §6801 and §6802 in the Rural Development title.	**Precision agriculture connectivity.** States the congressional findings on precision agriculture and authorizes the establishment of a task force by the Federal

Current Law/Policy	House-Passed Bill (H.R. 2)	Senate-Passed Bill (H.R. 2)
		Communications Commission for reviewing the connectivity and technology needs of precision agriculture. The task force will collaborate with USDA and public and private stakeholders in the agriculture and technology fields to identify gaps in the availability of broadband across agricultural land and to develop policy recommendations. **(§12516)**
No comparable provision. The **U.S. Drought Monitor** is a collaboration between the USDA, National Oceanic and Atmospheric Administration (NOAA), and the National Drought Mitigation Center at the University of Nebraska-Lincoln. Weekly maps are released based on measurements of climatic, hydrologic, and soil conditions and are combined with local impacts and observations across the country. The drought monitor is used to determine drought relief for USDA programs (e.g., Livestock Forage Program (LFP) and the Non-Fat Dry Milk Program) and by the Internal Revenue Service (IRS) to determine the replacement period for livestock sold because of drought. Funding is not directly appropriated for these efforts.	No comparable provision.	**Improved soil moisture and precipitation monitoring.** Requires the Secretary to develop and implement a cost-effective strategy to improve the accuracy of the U.S. Drought Monitor within one year of enactment. USDA is required to prioritize the implementation of soil moisture monitoring stations (up to 50 per state) in drought prone states. Authorizes an appropriation of $5 million annually between FY2019 through FY2023 for these stations. USDA is also required to standardize soil moisture data collection and data derived from *citizen science* (as defined in 15 U.S.C. 3724, and including the Cooperative Observer Program at the National Weather Service). For Livestock Forage Program (LFP) and federal crop insurance policies, USDA is required to use the U.S. Drought Monitor, soil moisture data from the aforementioned stations, data from the Cooperative Observer Program, and any other applicable data to determine grazing losses and grazing rates. USDA may coordinate with other federal, state, and local governments, and non-federal entities. **(§12517)**
Specialty Crop Research Initiative. A specialty crop research and extension initiative established within USDA addresses the critical needs of the specialty crop industry. It provides mandatory CCC funds of $80 million for FY2014 and each fiscal year thereafter and authorizes appropriations of $100	No comparable provision.	**Emergency Citrus Disease Research and Development Trust Fund.** Establishes a trust fund in the Treasury of the United States to address domestic or invasive citrus diseases and pests, including huanglongbing and the

Table 15. (Continued)

Current Law/Policy	House-Passed Bill (H.R. 2)	Senate-Passed Bill (H.R. 2)
million annually for FY2014-FY2018. At least $25 million is reserved for the emergency citrus disease research and extension program. An additional $25 million is authorized to be appropriated annually for FY2014-FY2018. **(7 U.S.C. 7632 *et seq.*)**		Asian Citrus Psyllid. USDA may make payments to entities engaged in scientific research on diseases and pests, and the dissemination and commercialization of relevant information, techniques, or technology to solve citrus production disease or pest problems. Authorizes mandatory CCC funding of $25 million annually (FY2019-FY2023), to remain available until expended. **(§12606)**
United States-Korea Free Trade Agreement Implementation Act (KORUS; P.L. 112-41). Section 503 of the act includes the rate and ending date for merchandise processing fees in the KORUS agreement. **(19 U.S.C. 3805 note)**	No comparable provision.	**Merchandise processing fees.** Amends the ending date in Section 503 of the Act from February 24, 2027 to May 26, 2027. **(§12607)**
Controlled Substances Act (CSA). Schedule I of the CSA (21 U.S.C. §§801 *et seq.*) includes all cannabis varieties under the term "marihuana" that is defined to mean "all parts of the plant *Cannabis sativa,"* covering both marijuana and industrial hemp. **(21 U.S.C. §802(16))**	No comparable provision.	**Conforming changes to Controlled Substances Act (CSA).** Amends Section 102 of the CSA (21 U.S.C. 802(16)) to exclude "industrial hemp" from the statutory definition of marijuana. Industrial hemp is defined as containing a delta-9 tetrahydrocannabinol (marijuana's primary psychoactive chemical) concentration of not more than 0.3% on a dry weight basis content. **(§12608)** Other provisions regarding industrial hemp are contained in the bill's Horticulture title **(§10111 and 10112)**, Research title **(§7415, §7125, and §7401)**, and Crop Insurance title **(§11101, §11106, §11112, §11120, §11101, and §11121)**
National Flood Insurance Program. Offers primary flood insurance to properties with significant flood risk, and aims to reduce flood risk through the adoption of floodplain management standards. **(42 U.S.C. 4001 *et seq.*)**	No comparable provision.	Reauthorizes financing for the program (42 U.S.C. 4016(a)) and extends the termination date for entering new flood insurance contracts (42 U.S.C. 4026) until January 31, 2019. **(§12609)**

Current Law/Policy	House-Passed Bill (H.R. 2)	Senate-Passed Bill (H.R. 2)
Emergency Assistance for Livestock, Honey Bees, and Farm-Raised Fish. Provides payments to producers of livestock, honey bees, and farm- raised fish as compensation for losses due to disease, adverse weather, feed or water shortages, or other conditions (such as wildfires) that are not covered under Livestock Indemnity Program (LIP) or LFP. **(7 U.S.C. 9081(d)(2))**	No comparable provision.	Amends the program to add the cost of inspecting for cattle tick fever to the list of approved costs covered by the program **(§12610)**
Agriculture Act of 2014. Establishes Agriculture Risk Coverage (ARC) program. **(7 U.S.C. 9017)**	No comparable provision.	**Administrative units.** Amends current law to allow, under certain circumstances, for the division of a county into two separate administrative units for determining ARC payments. To be eligible, a county must be: (1) larger than 1,400 square miles; (2) contained within a state that is larger than 140,000 square miles; and (3) contains more than 190,000 base acres. Prior to any ARC payments for the 2019 crop, the FSA state committee, in consultation with the FSA county committee, may make a one-time election to divide a county into two administrative units to better reflect differences in weather patterns, soil types, or other factors. The election is in effect for the 2019 through 2023 crop years. **(§12611)**
No comparable provision.	No comparable provision.	**Drought and water conservation agreements.** Adds a section to the Conservation Reserve Enhancement Program (CREP) under the Conservation Reserve Program (CRP) allowing dryland farming on CREP acres if the purpose of the CREP agreement is to address regional drought concerns. **(§12612)**
Pollinator habitat. USDA may encourage the development of habitat for native and managed pollinators, and use conservation practices to maximize the benefits for honey bees when carrying out farm bill conservation programs. **(16 U.S.C. 3844(h))**	No comparable provision.	**Encouragement of pollinator habitat development and protection.** Adds new considerations for pollinators under farm bill conservation programs, including planning for biological control methods of pest control and producer training related to biological control methods. **(§12613)**

Table 15. (Continued)

Current Law/Policy	House-Passed Bill (H.R. 2)	Senate-Passed Bill (H.R. 2)
Emergency Conservation Program (See **Table 5**).	See House bill. (**§2406**)	Similar to House bill. (**§12614**)
Bill Emerson Good Samaritan Food Donation Act provides protection from liability for people or entities donating apparently wholesome food to non-profit organizations as well as protection from liability for non-profit organizations receiving such foods. **(42 U.S.C. 1791)**	No comparable provision.	**Food donation standards.** Requires Secretary to issue guidance to promote awareness of donations of apparently wholesome food, as defined by the Bill Emerson Good Samaritan Food Donation Act, by qualified direct donors, a term defined in the bill provision. Requires the Secretary to encourage State agencies and emergency feeding organizations to share the guidance with qualified direct donors. **(§12615)**
No comparable provision.	No comparable provision.	Establishes the **Micro-Grants for Food Security** program, which is intended to increase the quality and quantity of locally grown foods in food insecure communities. USDA is to distribute funds to agricultural departments or agencies in eligible states (states of Alaska and Hawaii, American Samoa, Commonwealth of the Northern Mariana Islands, Commonwealth of Puerto Rico, Federated States of Micronesia, Guam, Republic of the Marshall Islands, Republic of Palau, and the U.S. Virgin Islands) to competitively issue subgrants to eligible entities (individuals, Indian tribes, nonprofits engaged in food insecurity, federally funded educational facilities, and local or Tribal government). The subgrants may not be greater than $5,000 for an individual and $10,000 of the other eligible entities. The entities must provide 10% in matching funds. The funds must be used for activities (e.g., purchasing gardening tools and equipment, seeds, plants, composting units; expanding cultivated land; building fencing for livestock; purchasing and equipping slaughter and

Current Law/Policy	House-Passed Bill (H.R. 2)	Senate-Passed Bill (H.R. 2)
		processing facilities; and attending education programs) that increase the quantity and quality of local foods. Entities that receive grants must submit a report to the eligible state on the quantity of food grown and the number of people fed as a result of the grant; the states must provide the reports to USDA. Authorizes appropriations of $10 million for FY2019 and each fiscal year thereafter. The funds remain available until expended. The states of Alaska and Hawaii will each receive 40% of the funds, and each of the other eligible states will receive 2.5%. **(§12616)**
Microloans. Authorizes a microloan program for farm operating loans of less than $50,000, with streamlined application and approval processes. **(7 U.S.C. 1943(c))**	No comparable provision.	**Use of additional Commodity Credit Corporation funds for direct operating microloans under certain conditions.** Authorizes the use of mandatory funds from the Commodity Credit Corporation to support up to $5 million of direct microloans for farm operating loan purposes, if the amount available under the Consolidated Farm and Rural Development Act (ConAct), or if appropriations are insufficient to meet demand, and subject to notification to Congress. **(§12617)**
Consolidated Farm and Rural Development Act (ConAct). Authorizes the Secretary to make and guarantee loans and grants to support essential community facilities in rural areas. **(7 U.S.C. 1926(a))**	No comparable provision.	**Business and innovation services essential community facilities.** Amends to make business and innovation services, such as incubators, co-working spaces, markerspaces, and residential entrepreneur and innovation centers eligible for funding as essential community facilities. **(§12618)**
Consolidated Farm and Rural Development Act (ConAct). Outlines powers of the Secretary and authority to make loans and grants, enter into partnerships and cooperative agreements, among other powers. **(7 U.S.C. 1981 *et seq.*)**	No comparable provision.	**Rural Innovation Stronger Economy Grant Program.** Amends Subtitle D of the ConAct to establish a new grant program for a "rural jobs accelerator partnership," an entity that organizes key community and regional stakeholders that focuses on shared goals and needs of industry clusters that are existing,

Table 15. (Continued)

Current Law/Policy	House-Passed Bill (H.R. 2)	Senate-Passed Bill (H.R. 2)
		emerging, or declining. The partnership will represent a region and includes one or more representatives of a higher education institution, a private entity, a government entity, and may include an economic development or labor organization, financial institution, cooperative, or philanthropic organization. The competitive grant program will award grants to entities to establish job accelerators to improve the ability of distressed rural communities to create high-wage jobs, accelerate the formation of new businesses, help rural communities identify and maximize local assets, and connect to regional opportunities, networks, and industry clusters. The Secretary will provide grants for job accelerators in not fewer than 25 states at a time. The federal share of the cost of any activity carried out under the grant shall no greater than 80%. Criteria for selecting eligible entities to receive grants are specified. Grants may be used to construct or equip a building to serve as an innovation center, construct housing for business workers or owners, co- working spaces, job training centers, linking small businesses into a supply chain, and for other job development and business innovation purposes.
		Grants shall be no less than $500,000 nor more than $2 million. Indirect costs are limited to no more than 10%. The term of a grant shall be 4 years, with the possibility of a 2-year renewal. Activity reports are required. The Secretary is required to establish an interagency task force to support the network of job accelerators by establishing a

Current Law/Policy	House-Passed Bill (H.R. 2)	Senate-Passed Bill (H.R. 2)
		federal support team to provide dedicated support services to job accelerators. The task force is to be co-chaired by the Secretary of Commerce and include the Secretaries of Energy, Health and Human Services, Labor, Transportation, the Treasury, the Administrators of the Environmental Protection Agency, and the Small Business Administration, co-chair of the Appalachian Regional Commission, Delta Regional Authority, and the federal co-chair of the Northern Borders Regional Commission, and representatives of local and regional organizations. **(§12619)**
High-priority research and extension initiatives. Provides competitive grant support for high- priority research and extension areas. **(7 U.S.C. 5925(d))**	No comparable provision.	**Dryland farming agricultural systems.** Amends to make research and extension grants for carrying out, or enhancing, research on the use of big data for more precise management of dryland farming agricultural systems. **(§12620)**
Forest and Rangeland Renewable Resources Research Act of 1978. Established a program to inventory and analyze, in a timely manner, public and private forests and their resources in the United States. **(16 (U.S.C. 1642(e))**	No comparable provision.	**Remote sensing technologies.** Requires the Chief of the Forest Service to find efficiencies in the inventory and analysis program through improved use and integration of remote sensing technologies. The Chief is to partner with state and interested stakeholders. **(§12621)**
National School Lunch Program. Requires that state agencies and school food authorities follow Buy American provisions to the maximum extent possible. **(7 C.F.R. 210.21(d)**	No comparable provision.	No later than 180 days after enactment, USDA must enforce the **Buy American** provisions applicable to domestic food assistance purchases administered by the Food and Nutrition Service including fish from a state, the District of Colombia, and an Exclusive Economic Zone of the United States, and tuna harvested by a U.S. flagged vessel. USDA is to submit a report to Congress on actions taken and plans to comply with the provision. **(§12622)**

Table 15. (Continued)

Current Law/Policy	House-Passed Bill (H.R. 2)	Senate-Passed Bill (H.R. 2)
No comparable provision.	No comparable provision.	**Eligibility for operators on heirs property land to obtain a farm number.** In the case of a farm operator that has inherited farmland and seeks assignment of a farm number for purposes of farm identification and assignment of farm program payments, the operator must provide eligible documentation including: (1) in states that have adopted the Uniform Partition of Heirs Property Act, a court order verifying the land meets the definition of heirs property or certification from the local recorder of deeds that the recorded landowner is deceased and not less than one heir has initiated a procedure to retitle the land; (2) a tenancy-in-common agreement that sets out ownership rights and responsibilities among all of the land owners; (3) tax returns for the preceding five years; (4) self- certification that the farm operator has control of the land; and (5) any other documentation identified by the Secretary as an alternative form of eligible documentation. **(§12623)**
Individual Development Accounts. Authorizes appropriations for the Beginning Farmer and Rancher Individual Development Account Program at $5 million per year through FY2018. This program has never received appropriations. **(7 U.S.C. 1983b)**	Reauthorizes appropriations through FY2023. **(§5301)**	Reauthorizes appropriations through FY2024, a one-year extension beyond that reauthorized by §5301. **(§12624(a))**
Farmer loan pilot projects. Authorizes pilot projects of limited scope and duration for Subtitles A- D (farm real estate loans, operating loans, emergency loans and administrative provisions) of the ConAct to evaluate processes and techniques that may improve efficiency and effectiveness. **(7 U.S.C. 1983d)**	No comparable provision.	Authorizes (in a new section) pilot projects of limited scope and duration for Subtitles A, B, C, and D (real estate loans, operating loans, emergency loans, and administrative provisions) of the ConAct to evaluate processes and techniques that may improve efficiency and effectiveness. **(§12624(b))**

Current Law/Policy	House-Passed Bill (H.R. 2)	Senate-Passed Bill (H.R. 2)
No comparable provision for farm loans. A similar relending program for rural development is authorized in the same section as would be amended by the Senate bill, i.e., §12624. **(7 U.S.C. 1936b)**	No comparable provision.	**Loans to purchasers of land with undivided interest and no administrative authority relending program.** Authorizes a relending program for farm ownership loans on projects that assist heirs with undivided ownership interests so that they may resolve ownership and succession issues on farmland that has multiple owners. USDA would make direct loans and loan guarantees to cooperatives, credit unions and nonprofit organizations (that are certified to operate as lenders, and have experience assisting socially disadvantaged, limited resource, and beginning farmers, ranchers and rural businesses) to relend to such projects and heirs. Preference shall be for relending entities with at least 10 years' experience, and in states that have adopted the Uniform Partition of Heirs Property Act. Borrowers are required to complete a succession plan that may be financed with the loan. **(§12624)**
Outreach and assistance for socially disadvantaged farmers and ranchers and veteran farmers and ranchers. Requires the Secretary to carry out an outreach and technical assistance program to encourage and assist socially disadvantaged farmers and ranchers and veteran farmers or ranchers in (A) owning and operating farms and ranches; and (B) in participating equitably in the full range of agricultural programs offered by the Department. **(7 U.S.C. 2279)**	No comparable provision.	**Farmland ownership data collection.** Amends to require the Secretary to report, at least once every 5 years, data and analysis on farmland ownership, tenure, transition, and entry of beginning farmers and ranchers and socially disadvantaged farmers and ranchers. The Secretary will collect and distribute comprehensive reporting of trends in farm ownership, tenure, barriers to entry, profitability, and viability of beginning and socially disadvantages farmers and ranchers; develop surveys and report statistical and economic analysis on these variables; and require the National Agricultural Statistics Service to include tenure, ownership, and transition of agricultural land survey questions in a follow-up survey to the Census of Agriculture.

Table 15. (Continued)

Current Law/Policy	House-Passed Bill (H.R. 2)	Senate-Passed Bill (H.R. 2)
		The survey will include questions on the extent to which non-farming landowners are purchasing and holding onto farmland for the sole purpose of real estate investment, the impact of these farmland ownership trends on the successful entry and viability of beginning and socially disadvantaged farmers and ranchers, and the impact of land tenure patters by race, gender, and ethnicity. **(§12625)**
Rural Business Investment Program. Authorizes the establishment of Rural Business Investment Companies to be certified by USDA for purposes of generating "developmental venture capital" with the objective of fostering economic development in rural areas **(7 U.S.C. 29009cc *et seq.*)**	No comparable provision.	**Rural Business Investment Program.** Amends to strike the term *venture capital* and replace with *equity capital* defined as common or preferred stock or a similar instrument, including subordinated debt with equity features. Strikes sentence regarding fees from "does not exceed $500" to "such fees as the Secretary considers appropriate." Under the section "Limitation on rural business investment companies controlled by Farm Credit System institutions" increases that limit to 50% before the rural business investment company is prohibited from providing equity investments to companies that are not otherwise eligible to receive financing from the Farm Credit System. The provision is further amended to state that the Secretary may not require that an entity applying to become a certified rural business investment company provide investment or capital that is not required of other companies eligible to apply to operate as a rural business investment company. **(§12626)**
National Oilheat Research Alliance Act of 2000 (NORA). Established an oilheat industry alliance to develop projects for the research, development, and demonstration of clean and efficient	No comparable provision.	Repeals the sunset clause of the 2000 Act. Amends the act to limit the amount of assessment funds the Alliance can obligate in a fiscal year to 75% of the assessments.

Current Law/Policy	House-Passed Bill (H.R. 2)	Senate-Passed Bill (H.R. 2)
oilheat utilization equipment; and to operate programs that enhanced consumer and employee training. **(42 U.S.C. 6201 note; P.L. 106-469)**		Excess amounts over the 75% limit are to be deposited in an escrow account, and interest earned must be deposited in the account and not be obligated. After the covered period, the Alliance may obligate up to one-fifth of the amount in the escrow account on the last day of the covered period. For estimating the amount of assessment to be collected for a fiscal year, the estimate is to be 62% of the actual amount collected in the most recent fiscal year that has been audited as of the beginning of the fiscal year for which funds are being obligated. Fiscal years are the 9th and 10th fiscal years after enactment and the covered period begins upon enactment and ends on the last day of the 11th fiscal year. **(§12627)**
Rural Emergency Medical Training and Equipment Assistance Program. Authorizes grants to eligible entities to provide for improved emergency medical services in rural areas under Section 330J of the Public Health Service Act (42 U.S.C. 201 *et seq.*) An entity shall use amounts received under a grant made under subsection (a), either directly or through grants to emergency medical service squads that are located in, or that serve residents of, a nonmetropolitan statistical area, an area designated as a rural area by any law or regulation of a State, or a rural census tract of a metropolitan statistical area (as determined under the most recent Goldsmith Modification, originally published in a notice of availability of funds in the *Federal Register* on February 27, 1992, 57 *Fed. Reg.* 6725). Authorizes such sums as necessary for FY2002-FY2006. **(42 U.S.C. 254c-15)**	No comparable provision.	Reauthorizes and amends the program to add a new section, 'Supporting and Improving Rural EMS Needs Act of 2018." Eligible grant recipients are emergency medical services agencies operated by a local or tribal government, including fire-based and non-fire based. Funds may be used to train emergency medical service personnel to obtain and maintain licenses and certifications, conduct courses that qualify graduates to serve in an emergency medical services agency, fund specific training to meet federal and state licensing or certification requirements, to acquire emergency medical services equipment, recruit and retain emergency medical services personnel. Grants cannot exceed $200,000, and require a 25% match from the recipient. Eligible rural areas are defined. Funding of such sums as necessary is authorized to be appropriated annually for FY2019-FY2023. **(§12628)**

Table 15. (Continued)

Current Law/Policy	House-Passed Bill (H.R. 2)	Senate-Passed Bill (H.R. 2)
Protecting Interstate Commerce		
No comparable provision.	**Prohibition Against Interference by State and Local Governments With Production of Agricultural Products from Other States.** Prohibits any state or local government from setting standards or conditions on the production or manufacture of agricultural products from other states if the products are produced or manufactured according to federal law or the laws of the state or locality. **(§11701)**	No comparable provision.
	Federal Cause of Action to Challenge State Regulation of Interstate Commerce. Empowers producers, consumers, trade organizations, governments, and others affected by a state standard or condition for products sold in interstate commerce to bring action in the appropriate court to invalidate the state standard or condition and to seek damages for economic losses, subject to a 10-year statute of limitations. Requires courts to issue a preliminary injunction on the state standard or condition unless the state provides convincing evidence it would prevail in the case or the injunction would cause irreparable harm. **(§11702)**	No comparable provision.

INDEX

A

abatement, 213
acquisitions, 144, 145, 212
adjusted gross income (AGI), ix, 12, 24, 25, 29, 77, 80, 92, 98, 105, 109, 111
adjustment, 24, 50, 51, 61, 65, 68, 78, 83, 111, 130, 135, 147, 233
Administration for Children and Families, 270
adverse weather, 77, 91, 275
agencies, 32, 40, 44, 46, 82, 85, 88, 89, 103, 107, 111, 114, 133, 134, 135, 136, 139, 141, 142, 144, 162, 191, 193, 202, 218, 224, 225, 226, 229, 238, 242, 243, 248, 258, 259, 267, 268, 276, 279, 283
agricultural commodities, vii, 8, 13, 14, 29, 49, 109, 118, 119, 121, 123, 125, 143, 144, 228
agricultural conservation, vii, 13, 26
agricultural policy, vii, 13
agricultural producers, 111, 115, 117, 123, 143, 172, 177, 189, 196, 222, 228, 237
agricultural programs, viii, 2, 3, 16, 245, 247, 250, 281
Agricultural Risk Coverage program (ARC), ix, 12, 22, 23, 24, 48, 50, 51, 52, 53, 54, 57, 58, 59, 60, 61, 62, 63, 64, 66, 78, 80, 82, 83, 231, 275
agriculture, vii, viii, 11, 13, 36, 39, 40, 44, 45, 62, 99, 105, 113, 125, 146, 155, 156, 163, 166, 171, 179, 180, 181, 185, 186, 188, 189, 193, 196, 197, 200, 222, 223, 225, 231, 238, 239, 243, 246, 248, 249, 250, 257, 261, 263, 264, 265, 268, 272, 273
Agriculture and Nutrition Act of 2018, vii, viii, 11, 13, 55, 259
Agriculture Committee, vii, 1, 3, 41, 44, 82, 83, 163, 224, 237
Agriculture Improvement Act of 2018, vii, viii, 11, 13, 71, 259
American Samoa, 139, 276
animal disease, ix, 12, 48, 180, 239, 240
animal welfare, 49, 266
Appropriations Act, 83, 217, 259
assessment, 42, 76, 101, 117, 122, 169, 188, 205, 209, 227, 282, 283
audits, 75, 200, 220, 223, 234
authorized programs, 127

B

banks, 152, 153, 154, 159, 160, 161
barriers, 30, 116, 127, 132, 142, 181, 195, 221, 262, 281
barriers to entry, 195, 281
base, 24, 35, 37, 48, 50, 51, 53, 54, 55, 56, 57, 58, 62, 63, 64, 82, 83, 125, 129, 147, 148, 157, 173, 233, 246, 247, 257, 275
base year, 147, 148, 157
benefits, ix, 8, 12, 24, 27, 31, 32, 33, 34, 44, 45, 47, 64, 66, 67, 78, 80, 81, 82, 84, 85, 86, 92, 95, 96, 106, 108, 112, 129, 131, 132, 133, 134, 135, 136, 137, 138, 139, 140, 141, 143, 145, 219, 221, 230, 233, 235, 253, 261, 263, 275
biodiesel, 6, 219
biodiversity, 201
bioenergy, x, 13, 19, 69
biological control, 275

biomass, 42, 202, 203, 204, 217, 220
Biomass Crop Assistance Program, 22, 44, 220
biotechnology, 30, 44, 127, 200
borrowers, 36, 38, 149, 150, 152, 153, 156, 159, 160, 167, 170, 176, 218
breeding, 244, 263
broadband, x, 6, 12, 36, 37, 163, 164, 165, 166, 167, 168, 169, 170, 173, 175, 179, 273
Bureau of Labor Statistics, 235
Bureau of Land Management, 41, 208
Bush, President George Walker, 7, 87
businesses, 38, 79, 103, 147, 156, 164, 167, 172, 173, 175, 177, 217, 256, 271, 278, 281

C

carbon, 44, 108, 198, 201, 203, 220, 221
cash, 14, 29, 30, 43, 88, 89, 92, 107, 120, 122, 124, 129, 133, 197, 211, 212, 213, 214
cattle, 39, 189, 240, 241, 275
Census, 40, 134, 172, 190, 265, 281
certification, 28, 32, 33, 44, 93, 96, 103, 107, 133, 134, 135, 144, 223, 257, 280, 283
challenges, 186, 216
chemical, 45, 76, 218, 219, 227, 274
children, 33, 34, 131, 132, 133, 145, 146
citizens, 77, 125, 138, 177
civil rights, 256, 257
classification, 151, 158, 226, 262
Clean Water Act (CWA), 15, 46, 115, 227, 269
Code of Federal Regulations, 200
collaboration, 140, 179, 226, 243, 272, 273
colleges, 39, 100, 105, 123, 125, 171, 177, 180, 181, 182, 183, 184, 192, 195, 196, 202, 230, 238, 240, 243
commercial, ix, 12, 28, 45, 63, 89, 90, 103, 165, 217, 219
commodity, viii, ix, 2, 3, 4, 5, 6, 7, 11, 12, 13, 14, 16, 23, 24, 50, 51, 52, 54, 55, 56, 57, 58, 59, 60, 61, 62, 63, 64, 65, 66, 67, 69, 80, 81, 82, 83, 84, 91, 104, 118, 120, 122, 123, 127, 144, 219, 235, 261, 263
Commonwealth of the Northern Mariana Islands, 276
communities, x, 12, 36, 37, 38, 162, 163, 164, 165, 166, 171, 172, 173, 177, 203, 204, 220, 264, 265, 276, 278
compensation, 35, 85, 154, 161, 233, 257, 275
competitive grant program, 99, 183, 191, 193, 201, 202, 203, 241, 246, 252, 278
competitiveness, 68, 179, 223, 251, 272
compliance, 63, 81, 84, 85, 93, 95, 96, 102, 107, 111, 112, 132, 133, 135, 180, 225, 234, 259
composition, 180, 246
Congress, vii, viii, 1, 2, 5, 7, 8, 11, 13, 14, 99, 100, 102, 104, 112, 115, 116, 118, 121, 124, 134, 148, 150, 151, 155, 156, 158, 162, 165, 172, 179, 181, 182, 190, 211, 217, 227, 228, 230, 231, 233, 259, 262, 264, 265, 270, 277, 279
Congressional Budget Office, viii, 11, 13
connectivity, 36, 169, 179, 272, 273
conservation, vii, viii, ix, 2, 3, 4, 7, 11, 12, 13, 14, 15, 16, 17, 18, 19, 20, 22, 23, 26, 27, 28, 29, 41, 45, 49, 54, 55, 58, 63, 64, 65, 80, 83, 84, 85, 86, 88, 89, 90, 91, 92, 93, 94, 95, 96, 97, 98, 99, 100, 101, 102, 103, 104, 105, 106, 109, 110, 111, 112, 113,114, 115, 116, 117, 118, 126, 147, 157, 176, 187, 193, 200, 201, 213, 215, 216, 229, 231, 234, 237, 245, 246, 248, 249, 254, 258, 259, 260, 263, 264, 267, 268, 270, 275, 276
Conservation Reserve Program (CRP), ix, 7, 12, 20, 22, 28, 54, 85, 86, 87, 88, 89, 90, 91, 92, 93, 94, 95, 101, 102, 104, 105, 106, 109, 114, 118, 249, 275
Conservation Stewardship Program (CSP), ix, 12, 20, 22, 27, 93, 94, 95, 96, 98, 99, 102, 103, 104, 109, 111, 112, 113
conserving, 28, 63, 85, 95, 96, 98, 105, 109, 114
construction, 42, 164, 165, 170, 203, 206, 207, 219, 241
consumers, 14, 49, 124, 139, 222, 261, 263, 284
contaminant, 101, 192
contaminated sites, 190
cooperative agreements, 122, 141, 181, 213, 238, 240, 246, 277
coordination, 49, 82, 109, 127, 162, 163, 169, 177, 189, 191, 199, 214, 223, 242, 253
cost, viii, 11, 14, 16, 20, 23, 25, 26, 28, 29, 33, 38, 69, 70, 71, 77, 78, 84, 88, 89, 90, 91, 92, 95, 96, 97, 98, 100, 103, 106, 107, 108, 110, 114, 115, 117, 118, 122, 127, 128, 134, 135, 136, 138, 144, 164, 171, 174, 184, 199, 201, 203, 204, 212, 213, 215,217, 221, 232, 240, 251, 253, 261, 264, 273, 275, 278
cotton, 6, 18, 19, 24, 49, 50, 51, 52, 53, 54, 56, 57, 58, 59, 64, 65, 66, 67, 68, 69, 81, 235, 250, 251, 252, 262

counseling, 39, 183, 191
critical infrastructure, 242
crop, viii, 2, 3, 4, 5, 6, 7, 11, 14, 16, 17, 23, 24, 30, 40, 44, 45, 46, 47, 49, 50, 51, 52, 53, 54, 55, 56, 57, 58, 59, 60, 61, 62, 63, 64, 65, 67, 68, 69, 77, 78, 80, 81, 83, 84, 95, 96, 98, 100, 102, 109, 114, 123, 126, 180, 187, 192, 195, 222, 227, 228, 229, 230, 231, 232, 233, 234, 235, 236, 237, 244, 253, 270, 273, 275
crop insurance, viii, 11, 14, 16, 17, 24, 46, 47, 49, 61, 68, 102, 229, 230, 232, 233, 234, 235, 236, 237, 253, 273
crop rotations, 47, 95, 96, 109, 232
crop year, viii, 2, 3, 4, 5, 6, 7, 49, 50, 51, 52, 53, 54, 55, 56, 57, 58, 59, 60, 61, 62, 63, 64, 65, 67, 68, 69, 77, 78, 81, 83, 232, 233, 253, 275
customer service, 263

D

dairies, 70, 72, 74
data collection, 45, 49, 223, 230, 253, 273, 281
data mining, 62, 234
database, 100, 133, 134, 168, 189, 192
deduction, 71, 72, 129, 130
deficiencies, 82, 122
Department of Agriculture, ix, 12, 14, 48, 179, 185, 199, 200, 242, 246, 250, 254, 255, 256, 257, 258, 259, 260, 262, 271
Department of Defense, 256
Department of Energy, 176, 198
Department of Justice, 269
Department of Labor, 256
Department of the Interior, 41, 106, 115, 249
Departments of Agriculture, 196
depository institutions, 35, 154, 155
developing countries, 122, 123, 124, 125, 126, 184
development assistance, 191, 196, 220
diet, 32, 128, 141
Dietary Guidelines for Americans, 140, 141
directives, 127
directors, 35, 153, 154, 155, 160, 161, 229
disaster, ix, 12, 23, 24, 25, 80, 91, 171, 229, 239, 242, 254, 268, 269
disaster assistance, ix, 12, 23, 24, 25, 80, 229
diseases, 32, 180, 187, 192, 227, 238, 240, 243, 244, 273, 274
distribution, 40, 75, 90, 102, 119, 120, 121, 143, 144, 194, 195, 217, 219, 227
District of Columbia, 53, 76, 128, 199
diversification, 237
diversity, 111, 126, 127, 201, 246
dogs, 49, 215, 266
domestic markets, 261, 263
domestic nutrition assistance, vii, 13, 145
domestic violence, 269, 270
donations, 43, 75, 118, 214, 241, 276
drought, 23, 24, 56, 88, 90, 109, 116, 242, 273, 275

E

economic conditions, vii, 13
economic development, 13, 37, 38, 169, 173, 174, 175, 177, 191, 261, 263, 278, 282
economic growth, 272
economic losses, 46, 284
Economic Research Service (ERS), 197
education, x, 6, 13, 32, 38, 44, 47, 48, 76, 99, 100, 110, 125, 132, 142, 146, 156, 169, 174, 177, 179, 181, 183, 184, 185, 186, 187, 188, 190, 191, 195, 196, 197, 200, 203, 218, 221, 222, 225, 234, 237, 238, 240, 244, 245, 246, 247, 249, 277, 278
educational materials, 250
educational opportunities, 272
election, 5, 26, 54, 56, 58, 59, 60, 72, 73, 275
electricity, 217
elementary school, 145
eligibility criteria, 25, 37
eligible countries, 125
emergency, 26, 29, 36, 46, 90, 117, 119, 120, 122, 124, 143, 144, 149, 162, 176, 192, 193, 227, 230, 238, 242, 270, 274, 276, 280, 283
employees, 123, 153, 154, 160, 161, 245, 256, 258, 261, 262, 264
employers, 131
employment, 31, 34, 48, 131, 132, 134, 178, 244
endangered, 46, 88, 205, 209, 225, 226, 267, 268
endangered species, 46, 88, 209, 225, 226
energy, x, 6, 13, 17, 19, 37, 39, 40, 42, 43, 44, 176, 180, 182, 185, 190, 194, 203, 204, 217, 220, 221
enforcement, 16, 32, 74, 89, 107, 130, 131, 153, 154, 160, 161, 223, 234, 267
engineering, 193
enrollment, ix, 12, 27, 28, 32, 86, 87, 88, 89, 91, 93, 94, 95, 103, 107, 109, 133, 134, 201

environment, 14, 39, 136, 146, 171, 190, 226, 235, 271
environmental impact, 42, 205, 209, 220
Environmental Protection Agency (EPA), 42, 46, 101, 114, 225, 226, 227, 228, 263, 269, 279
Environmental Quality Incentives Program (EQIP), ix, 12, 20, 22, 27, 28, 93, 96, 97, 98, 99, 100, 101, 102, 103, 104, 105, 109, 111, 112, 115
environmental services, 107
equipment, 68, 80, 137, 138, 155, 164, 165, 170, 183, 185, 217, 220, 276, 283
erosion, 93, 109, 117, 206, 207
exclusion, 77, 130, 205, 220, 232, 261
execution, 151, 158, 272
expertise, 103, 162, 171, 193, 220, 243, 246, 247, 258

F

farm bills, vii, viii, 1, 2, 3, 4, 5, 6, 7, 11, 13, 23, 29, 30, 31, 34, 37, 41, 43, 44, 248
farm legislation, vii, 13, 14
farmers, vii, 13, 14, 18, 23, 27, 35, 44, 45, 48, 57, 75, 76, 79, 82, 85, 88, 90, 100, 103, 104, 111, 120, 121, 127, 139, 146, 147, 148, 149, 150, 151, 156, 157, 158, 162, 163, 177, 181, 195, 197, 198, 199, 222, 227, 229, 244, 245, 246, 247, 249, 250, 256, 267, 281, 282
farmland, 91, 116, 117, 147, 199, 280, 281, 282
federal agency, 103, 226, 268
federal assistance, 23, 167
federal crop insurance program, 46, 47, 234, 237, 253
federal government, 4, 6, 108, 132, 181, 261, 263
Federal Register, 30, 146, 216, 224, 253, 256, 269, 283
financial, 27, 28, 33, 38, 41, 42, 83, 93, 100, 104, 105, 110, 111, 115, 116, 125, 135, 139, 141, 145, 148, 153, 156, 162, 163, 173, 182, 189, 191, 200, 201, 202, 203, 204, 220, 224, 235, 237, 253, 278
financial incentives, 139, 141
fiscal year, viii, 2, 3, 4, 7, 31, 83, 87, 98, 102, 117, 118, 119, 121, 122, 123, 124, 126, 127, 132, 135, 140, 142, 143, 145, 149, 157, 165, 169, 170, 171, 172, 175, 182, 189, 192, 198, 199, 211, 213, 219, 220, 223, 234, 236, 237, 244, 245, 247, 248, 252, 261, 264, 265, 273, 277, 282, 283
Fish and Wildlife Service, 115, 226, 267, 269
flexibility, 29, 69, 74, 97, 103, 124, 151, 158, 218, 253
food, vii, viii, ix, 1, 2, 4, 6, 11, 13, 14, 18, 19, 29, 30, 33, 39, 40, 44, 45, 70, 75, 93, 118, 119, 120, 121, 122, 123, 124, 125, 126, 128, 135, 136, 137, 138, 140, 141, 142, 143, 144, 145, 146, 172, 177, 179, 180, 181, 182, 183, 186, 188, 190, 191, 192, 193, 195, 196, 200, 222, 223, 224, 239, 246, 248, 249, 262, 263, 276, 277, 279
Food and Drug Administration, 200, 259
food policy, vii, viii, 11, 13, 181
food products, 30, 118, 128, 144, 172
food programs, viii, ix, 11, 177
Food, Conservation, and Energy Act of 2008, 187, 193
force, 36, 88, 179, 189, 256, 272, 273, 278, 279
forest management, 43, 90, 91, 96, 203, 205, 209, 210, 217
forest restoration, 109, 201, 202, 206, 216
forestry, vii, 13, 15, 19, 20, 22, 39, 41, 42, 70, 182, 193, 196, 200, 202, 210, 241, 246, 258, 261, 263, 266
formula, 24, 26, 34, 38, 52, 66, 132, 142, 144, 184, 185, 196, 199, 253
fraud, ix, 12, 32, 84, 136, 137, 229, 234, 265
fruits, 46, 57, 139, 140, 141, 143, 144, 145, 227, 235
funding authorization, 37, 117
fungi, 192

G

governments, 43, 49, 110, 113, 166, 200, 214, 216, 243, 269, 271, 273, 284
grades, 180, 215
grant programs, x, 12, 32, 162, 272
grants, 6, 31, 35, 36, 37, 38, 39, 40, 44, 111, 120, 122, 134, 139, 141, 143, 144, 145, 162, 164, 165, 166, 170, 171, 172, 173, 174, 175, 177, 178, 180, 181, 183, 184, 185, 186, 187, 189, 191, 192, 194, 195, 198, 202, 203, 204, 219, 220, 222, 223, 237, 244, 246,247, 248, 251, 252, 265, 269, 270, 271, 272, 277, 278, 279, 283
grazing, 28, 47, 50, 89, 90, 91, 95, 97, 100, 106, 108, 206, 215, 230, 273
growth, 68, 203, 205, 228, 265, 272
guidance, 35, 97, 110, 111, 112, 118, 119, 137, 138, 144, 154, 191, 223, 240, 248, 256, 258, 276

H

habitat, 28, 42, 88, 90, 91, 92, 93, 97, 104, 108, 109, 111, 115, 185, 201, 205, 206, 207, 208, 209, 225, 226, 268, 275
harvesting, 40, 68, 90, 91, 189, 205
hazardous substance, 108, 213
hazards, 117, 174
health, x, 12, 36, 38, 39, 90, 94, 96, 99, 100, 109, 122, 141, 142, 162, 163, 166, 169, 171, 174, 177, 182, 189, 190, 191, 194, 195, 204, 206, 226, 238, 239, 243, 244, 258, 264, 270
health care, 141, 142, 166, 169, 174, 191, 258
hemp, ix, 12, 39, 44, 45, 185, 194, 197, 225, 231, 232, 235, 274
higher education, 99, 110, 132, 181, 187, 197, 225, 278
homeland security, 242
House of Representatives, 16, 21
household income, 134, 171
housing, 37, 129, 139, 173, 266, 270, 271, 272, 278
Housing and Urban Development, 271, 272
human, 49, 70, 171, 181, 183, 194, 226, 239, 264, 266, 267
human health, 171, 194, 226, 239
hunting, 269
hurricanes, 236

I

identification, 138, 151, 159, 238, 243, 280
import documentation, 223
improvements, 93, 94, 96, 167, 168, 212
income, ix, 12, 14, 24, 25, 29, 32, 37, 48, 71, 72, 75, 77, 80, 92, 98, 100, 105, 109, 111, 122, 123, 125, 129, 130, 132, 133, 134, 139, 142, 145, 166, 171, 177, 178, 184, 203, 228, 231
individuals, 23, 25, 32, 34, 36, 37, 47, 75, 79, 81, 101, 103, 120, 125, 131, 132, 133, 134, 141, 142, 162, 171, 173, 178, 186, 191, 193, 249, 267, 276
inflation, 35, 128, 129, 130, 135, 142, 147, 148, 154, 157, 161
information retrieval, 136
information technology, 120, 234, 261, 264
infrastructure, x, 13, 17, 36, 67, 108, 111, 144, 162, 164, 167, 175, 176, 177, 178, 195, 201, 206, 217, 239, 241, 242, 252, 258, 271
institutions, 35, 38, 39, 142, 144, 148, 153, 154, 155, 160, 161, 164, 180, 181, 182, 183, 184, 185, 187, 188, 191, 195, 196, 199, 270, 282
insurance policy, 230
integrity, 31, 45, 74, 83, 113, 135, 234, 235, 253, 259
intellectual property, 224, 265
intellectual property rights, 224
interagency coordination, 223
Internal Revenue Service, 132, 273
investment, 37, 107, 136, 166, 169, 170, 178, 189, 221, 272, 282
irrigation, 28, 47, 84, 98, 101, 110, 111, 183, 232, 236
issues, vii, 1, 2, 4, 35, 41, 42, 43, 48, 119, 147, 155, 224, 240, 242, 246, 249, 258, 281

L

labeling, 118, 125, 218, 224, 226, 228
lame duck Congress, viii, 2, 5
landscapes, 201, 213
laws, 14, 38, 41, 43, 49, 85, 94, 153, 160, 161, 187, 197, 216, 221, 225, 242, 257, 265, 284
laws and regulations, 49, 153, 160, 161
leadership, 146, 156, 243
legislation, vii, viii, 2, 13, 14, 29, 114
lending, 148, 241
limited liability, 25, 77, 79
livestock, 23, 25, 28, 72, 77, 84, 97, 99, 109, 187, 192, 206, 236, 238, 241, 242, 267, 273, 275, 276
living arrangements, 139
loan guarantees, 36, 37, 147, 165, 167, 168, 170, 179, 219, 220, 281
loans, ix, x, 12, 35, 36, 37, 63, 64, 65, 66, 67, 69, 78, 146, 147, 148, 149, 150, 151, 152, 153, 154, 156, 157, 158, 159, 160, 161, 162, 163, 164, 165, 166, 167, 169, 170, 173, 175, 176, 177, 178, 179, 217, 218, 230, 248, 277, 280, 281
local government, 49, 89, 103, 106, 110, 113, 141, 166, 191, 200, 273, 284
local television stations, 179

M

man-made disasters, 126
manufacturing, 193, 203

marketing, 6, 24, 51, 52, 59, 60, 62, 63, 64, 65, 66, 67, 68, 69, 70, 75, 76, 78, 121, 139, 189, 196, 223, 224, 230, 253, 265, 271
marketplace, 181, 265
materials, 97, 194, 240, 244, 250
Medicaid, 142
medical, 238, 258, 283
medicine, 193, 238, 240
membership, 180, 188, 198, 210, 256
mentoring, 35, 146, 147, 156, 157, 250
military, 35, 37, 129, 146, 156, 173, 203
mission, 45, 186, 198, 218, 222, 249
modernization, 223, 264, 265
modifications, 24, 47, 108
mortality, 77, 78, 204

N

National Academy of Sciences, 198
National Environmental Policy Act (NEPA), 42, 85, 204, 205
National Forest System, 41, 204
National Oceanic and Atmospheric Administration (NOAA), 273
National School Lunch Program, 33, 146, 279
natural disaster, 23, 78, 91, 117, 171, 242
natural resources, 29, 39, 106, 115, 117, 190, 195, 246
Natural Resources Conservation Service (NRCS), 83, 103, 245, 258, 263
nonprofit organizations, 75, 88, 103, 105, 131, 139, 145, 147, 170, 191, 200, 219, 246, 281
nutrition, vii, viii, ix, 1, 2, 3, 7, 11, 12, 13, 14, 15, 16, 17, 18, 19, 20, 22, 29, 31, 32, 33, 39, 46, 70, 75, 76, 118, 119, 122, 124, 125, 126, 128, 136, 137, 139, 141, 142, 143, 144, 145, 146, 181, 190, 195, 224, 241, 246, 258, 261, 263, 266, 279
nutrition assistance, viii, 1, 2, 13, 75

O

Occupational Safety and Health Act, 46, 228
officials, 7, 105, 211
oil, 66, 109, 264, 275
oilseed, 23, 51, 54, 55, 56, 66
operations, 7, 25, 26, 44, 48, 71, 72, 73, 74, 84, 96, 99, 109, 151, 187, 191, 223, 243, 244, 246, 269
opportunities, 31, 34, 131, 172, 177, 178, 191, 221, 222, 230, 244, 245, 247, 255, 272, 278
organic agriculture, vii, 13, 44, 189
Organic Foods Production Act, 96, 223
organic matter, 94
outreach, 18, 19, 100, 101, 110, 112, 191, 196, 197, 218, 238, 240, 244, 245, 246, 247, 250, 258, 262, 281
outreach programs, 19, 246
ownership, ix, 12, 35, 71, 78, 79, 106, 146, 147, 148, 149, 150, 156, 157, 177, 199, 280, 281, 282

P

participants, 28, 77, 96, 98, 114, 126, 131, 132, 133, 134, 137, 139, 141, 142, 144, 149
pathogens, 222
penalties, 64, 136, 226, 227, 266
permit, 36, 37, 125, 164, 168, 175, 189, 196, 212, 226, 227
pesticide, 46, 192, 225, 226, 227
pests, 187, 227, 238, 243, 273, 274
plant disease, 244
plants, 203, 220, 224, 276
policy, vii, viii, 11, 13, 14, 15, 16, 31, 32, 106, 133, 179, 181, 230, 232, 233, 234, 235, 236, 256, 259, 269, 273
population, 37, 88, 123, 131, 141, 142, 166, 170, 172, 173, 174, 178, 197
preparedness, ix, 12, 48, 239, 242
prescribed burning, 207
prevention, x, 13, 36, 38, 58, 109, 117, 134, 162, 177, 239
Price Loss Coverage program (PLC), ix, 12, 23, 24, 50, 51, 52, 53, 54, 55, 56, 57, 58, 59, 60, 63, 64, 66, 78, 80, 82, 83
private enterprises, 172
procurement, 6, 30, 44, 120, 124, 135, 218
producers, ix, 12, 14, 24, 25, 26, 27, 28, 40, 45, 46, 47, 49, 51, 58, 59, 60, 63, 64, 67, 69, 71, 72, 76, 77, 82, 83, 84, 85, 92, 94, 96, 97, 98, 99, 101, 102, 103, 104, 105, 109, 110, 111, 112, 114, 115, 117, 123, 124, 143, 172, 177, 189, 192, 196, 219, 220, 221,222, 223, 225, 228, 229, 230, 231, 232, 233, 234, 236, 237, 240, 241, 245, 250, 251, 253, 254, 262, 267, 271, 275, 284
profit, 71, 72, 113, 139, 141, 146, 166, 170, 176, 180, 198, 276

program administration, 34, 201
program incentives, 139
project, 29, 33, 36, 37, 42, 87, 88, 98, 100, 110, 111, 116, 132, 134, 137, 138, 140, 141, 142, 143, 144, 145, 148, 165, 166, 167, 169, 170, 195, 203, 204, 205, 206, 208, 210, 213, 214, 216, 219, 223, 234, 264
protection, 18, 23, 24, 25, 43, 47, 48, 63, 64, 65, 70, 71, 72, 73, 74, 93, 94, 100, 104, 108, 109, 189, 204, 209, 214, 224, 230, 231, 241, 268, 269, 275, 276
prototype, 40, 195
Public Health Service Act, 283
Puerto Rico, 53, 76, 139, 143, 276

Q

quality assurance, 118
quality improvement, 108, 109
quotas, 69

R

race, 149, 150, 282
ranchers, vii, 13, 20, 48, 57, 82, 88, 90, 100, 103, 104, 111, 146, 147, 148, 149, 150, 151, 156, 157, 158, 162, 163, 181, 195, 197, 198, 229, 244, 245, 246, 247, 249, 250, 281, 282
rangeland, 106, 109, 186, 210, 232
rape, 133
recommendations, 105, 155, 156, 171, 179, 180, 188, 231, 240, 246, 249, 264, 266, 273
reconciliation, 4, 5, 7, 10
recovery, 36, 38, 117, 137, 162, 184, 201, 212, 213, 215, 225, 226, 244
reform, 113, 187, 191, 199, 222, 250
regulations, 33, 49, 71, 74, 80, 83, 85, 94, 112, 117, 119, 124, 131, 135, 136, 137, 140, 146, 153, 160, 161, 209, 215, 228, 253, 256
regulatory requirements, x, 12, 45, 46, 96, 109, 112
regulatory system, 125
rehabilitation, 18, 25, 77, 78, 256
Rehabilitation Act, 255
rehabilitation program, 256
renewable energy, 6, 44, 176, 180, 185, 217, 220
Reorganization Act, 48, 195, 199, 200, 242, 246, 254, 255, 256, 257, 258, 259, 260, 262
requirement, 25, 28, 30, 31, 33, 35, 64, 79, 83, 85, 90, 91, 92, 93, 94, 97, 99, 100, 104, 105, 106, 107, 112, 118, 119, 131, 132, 144, 146, 147, 150, 151, 156, 166, 167, 170, 180, 187, 197, 199, 201, 202, 203, 205, 206, 210, 236, 253, 254, 257, 267
resale, 75, 220, 266
research facilities, 195, 198
resolution, 2, 6, 216, 261
resource management, 187, 207, 208
resources, 29, 39, 92, 96, 98, 105, 106, 115, 117, 118, 141, 156, 173, 179, 188, 190, 195, 217, 229, 241, 246, 262, 264, 265, 279
responsiveness, 240
restoration, 42, 108, 109, 114, 115, 201, 202, 206, 207, 210, 213, 214, 216, 253
restrictions, 28, 30, 89, 90, 271
restructuring, 149, 153, 160, 175
revenue, viii, 1, 14, 17, 24, 43, 47, 50, 53, 60, 61, 62, 63, 71, 72, 79, 206, 216, 230
rights, 35, 108, 153, 154, 155, 160, 211, 212, 214, 215, 224, 256, 257, 280
risk, 40, 42, 47, 52, 62, 70, 71, 72, 73, 74, 86, 113, 114, 124, 136, 138, 149, 186, 204, 206, 210, 227, 229, 230, 231, 232, 236, 237, 238, 244, 265, 270, 271, 274
risk management, 71, 72, 73, 74, 236, 237
rules, 16, 17, 31, 52, 63, 111, 129, 131, 169, 232
rural areas, 36, 37, 163, 164, 165, 167, 169, 170, 171, 172, 173, 174, 176, 178, 179, 192, 261, 263, 277, 282, 283
rural development, vii, x, 13, 14, 17, 19, 36, 37, 109, 147, 162, 177, 218, 271, 281

S

safety, 38, 44, 46, 123, 169, 177, 191, 206, 222, 223, 258, 269, 271, 272
secondary education, 146
Secretary of Agriculture, x, 6, 12, 30, 36, 42, 43, 44, 49, 52, 125, 176, 181, 202, 203, 205, 208, 209, 215, 217, 229, 231, 234, 237, 240, 245, 250, 254, 255, 257, 259, 260, 262, 268, 269, 271
Secretary of Commerce, 218, 279
Secretary of Defense, 203
security, 39, 126, 135, 136, 168, 190, 194, 242, 243, 271
sediment, 87, 93, 109

seed, 50, 51, 52, 53, 54, 56, 57, 58, 59, 65, 66, 69, 90, 91, 126, 224
service organization, 162
service provider, 103, 137, 138, 146
services, 36, 38, 39, 75, 82, 103, 107, 117, 120, 125, 127, 129, 131, 132, 137, 155, 161, 162, 164, 167, 174, 180, 183, 191, 198, 215, 224, 240, 245, 249, 253, 262, 270, 271, 277, 279, 283
shellfish, 267
shelter, 129, 130, 270
skills training, 255
small business, 217, 278
South Dakota, 116, 117, 233
soybeans, 50, 52, 235
specialty crop, 30, 44, 45, 46, 102, 180, 192, 194, 222, 223, 224, 229, 230, 273
species, 39, 46, 51, 88, 188, 189, 192, 201, 202, 205, 206, 208, 209, 215, 225, 226, 235, 240, 267, 268
spending, viii, 11, 13, 16, 27, 31, 33, 34, 38, 40, 47, 82, 127, 143, 174, 177, 190, 197, 198, 222, 244, 247
stakeholders, 8, 179, 198, 201, 218, 223, 228, 243, 258, 272, 273, 277, 279
state laws, 49
state of emergency, 90
statute of limitations, 284
statutes, 29, 40, 45, 127, 153, 160, 250
statutory authority, 109
storage, 6, 65, 66, 67, 120, 121, 126, 137, 217, 220, 221
strategic planning, 258, 259
structure, 38, 72, 77, 116, 153, 160, 215
subsidy, 47, 170, 232, 233
substance abuse, x, 13, 38, 132, 162
Supplemental Nutrition Assistance Program (SNAP), viii, 2, 3, 7, 17, 20, 22, 31, 32, 33, 34, 128, 129, 130, 131, 132, 133, 135, 136, 137, 138, 139, 140, 141, 142, 143, 145
support services, 270, 279
surplus, 144, 194, 215, 220
sustainability, 103, 109, 170

T

target population, 118, 142
teams, 240, 247
technical assistance, 27, 28, 30, 32, 37, 38, 41, 84, 88, 93, 101, 102, 103, 105, 106, 107, 110, 112, 115, 117, 123, 125, 126, 140, 164, 170, 171, 173, 176, 177, 191, 196, 197, 203, 221, 224, 225, 244, 246, 247, 249, 250, 256, 258, 265, 270, 271, 272, 281
techniques, 150, 274, 280
technology, vii, 13, 36, 45, 98, 100, 120, 136, 138, 140, 172, 179, 181, 185, 186, 194, 215, 219, 223, 234, 238, 261, 264, 273, 274
technology transfer, 100, 172, 194
telecommunications, 162, 164, 167
tenure, 116, 152, 159, 199, 281, 282
territory, 53, 165, 171
testing, 40, 101, 136, 218, 225
thinning, 90, 91, 101
time frame, 90, 124, 209
Title I, viii, 2, 3, 5, 7, 20, 22, 23, 29, 30, 43, 44, 81, 84, 119, 120, 121, 122, 124, 168, 210, 217, 253
Title II, 7, 20, 22, 29, 30, 119, 120, 121, 122, 124, 168, 210, 253
Title IV, 20, 22
Title V, 20, 22, 43, 45, 163, 164, 168
tobacco, 139, 231, 235
trade, vii, viii, 2, 3, 6, 7, 13, 14, 17, 18, 29, 30, 49, 81, 125, 127, 128, 181, 223, 237, 259, 284
trade and international food aid, vii, 13
training, 31, 32, 34, 38, 125, 132, 139, 140, 162, 164, 170, 173, 176, 177, 185, 188, 189, 191, 193, 197, 240, 241, 245, 246, 247, 255, 256, 258, 259, 265, 275, 278, 283
training programs, 170, 193
transport, 75, 121, 266, 267
transportation, 67, 120, 121, 132, 189, 221, 266, 270
treatment, 24, 36, 38, 42, 55, 78, 95, 110, 132, 139, 140, 162, 204, 205, 208, 209, 211, 227, 266
tribal colleges, 39, 171, 195, 196
trust fund, 18, 49, 250, 251, 273
Tuskegee University, 181, 182, 196

U

U.S. Department of Agriculture (USDA), 12, 14
U.S. Treasury, 40, 168, 186
unemployment rate, 131, 272
universities, 32, 38, 39, 82, 100, 114, 123, 124, 125, 126, 172, 177, 182, 183, 184, 185, 192, 199, 202, 230, 238, 243, 246, 250
urban, 39, 40, 45, 99, 172, 189, 190, 204, 248

V

vaccine, ix, 12, 48, 239
varieties, 40, 51, 180, 224, 274
vegetables, 46, 57, 139, 140, 141, 143, 144, 145, 227, 230, 235
vegetation, 84, 90, 93, 204, 206, 208, 214
vegetative cover, 84, 89, 90, 91
veteran farmers, vii, 13, 48, 100, 103, 104, 198, 244, 245, 246, 247, 250, 281
vocational education, 146
vouchers, 29, 30, 120

W

waiver, 90, 92, 105, 107, 111, 119, 136, 137, 140
Washington, George, 216
waste, 33, 36, 37, 75, 84, 110, 120, 144, 170, 172, 221, 229, 234, 262, 263
waste disposal, 37, 170
waste management, 172
water, 18, 28, 36, 37, 40, 87, 90, 92, 93, 94, 98, 104, 105, 108, 109, 110, 111, 112, 113, 117, 118, 170, 171, 190, 206, 210, 214, 275
water quality, 28, 87, 90, 92, 94, 104, 108, 109, 112, 113
watershed, 18, 26, 29, 43, 98, 109, 111, 115, 116, 210
weather patterns, 275
wetland mitigation, 85
wetlands, 18, 28, 84, 85, 93, 105, 106, 114, 116, 117
wilderness, 43, 205, 208, 209, 211
wildfire, 90, 204, 206, 209, 217
wildlife, 28, 85, 87, 88, 90, 91, 92, 93, 97, 105, 106, 108, 115, 206, 207, 267, 269
workforce, 131, 132, 185, 190

FARM BILL OF 2008: MAJOR PROVISIONS AND LEGISLATIVE ACTION

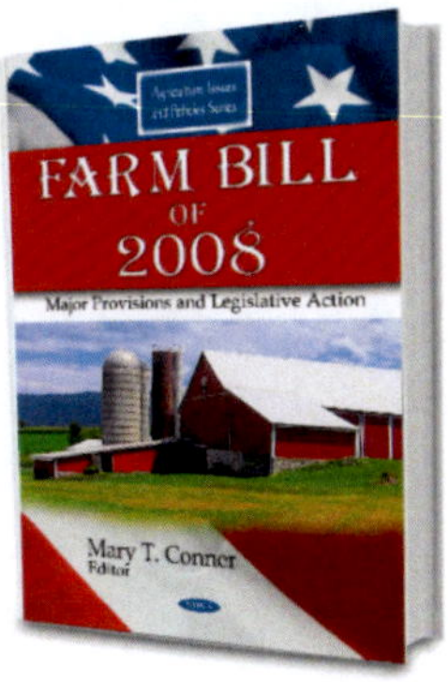

EDITOR: Mary T. Conner

SERIES: Agriculture Issues and Policies

BOOK DESCRIPTION: This book is a study of the new Farm Bill and its costs, provisions by title, programs and related topics.

HARDCOVER ISBN: 978-1-60741-750-7
RETAIL PRICE: $139

THE SUPPLEMENTAL NUTRITION ASSISTANCE PROGRAM (SNAP): BENEFITS, ELIGIBILITY, AND PROVISIONS IN THE 2014 FARM BILL

EDITOR: Samuel C. Ward

SERIES: Hunger and Poverty: Causes, Impacts and Eradication

BOOK DESCRIPTION: This book describes the rules related to eligibility for SNAP benefits as well as the rules for benefits and their redemption. In addition, this book discusses categorical eligibility and some of the issues raised by it.

HARDCOVER ISBN: 978-1-63483-730-9
RETAIL PRICE: $140

Federal Crop Insurance: Farm Bill Provisions, Trends, and Premium Reduction Considerations

Editor: Tristan E. Bonner

Series: Government Procedures and Operations

Book Description: This book provides a primer on the federal crop insurance program and briefly summarizes changes to the program by the 2014 farm bill.

Hardcover ISBN: 978-1-63463-688-9
Retail Price: $140

U.S. Dairy Support Programs: Farm Bill Provisions and Gross Margin-Dairy Insurance

Editor: Carla Edie

Series: Agriculture Issues and Policies

Book Description: This book describes the major dairy provisions contained in the 2014 Farm Bill as well as Congressional Budget Office cost projections of historical program outlays compared with outlays under the new dairy programs. The book also includes a discussion of potential issues related to the new dairy policies.

Softcover ISBN: 978-1-63321-715-7
Retail Price: $69